Lecture Notes in Computer Science   11180

Commenced Publication in 1973
Founding and Former Series Editors:
Gerhard Goos, Juris Hartmanis, and Jan van Leeuwen

Editorial Board

More information about this series at http://www.springer.com/series/7407

Cliff Jones · Ji Wang · Naijun Zhan (Eds.)

Symposium on Real-Time and Hybrid Systems

Essays Dedicated to Professor Chaochen Zhou on the Occasion of His 80th Birthday

Editors
Cliff Jones
Newcastle University
Newcastle
UK

Naijun Zhan
Institute of Software, CAS
Beijing
China

Ji Wang
National University of Defense Technology
Changsha
China

ISSN 0302-9743 ISSN 1611-3349 (electronic)
Lecture Notes in Computer Science
ISBN 978-3-030-01460-5 ISBN 978-3-030-01461-2 (eBook)
https://doi.org/10.1007/978-3-030-01461-2

Library of Congress Control Number: 2018955709

LNCS Sublibrary: SL1 – Theoretical Computer Science and General Issues

Cover illustration: Z. Chaochen and M. R. Hansen (Eds.), Duration Calculus, paragraph of page 156.

This Springer imprint is published by the registered company Springer Nature Switzerland AG
The registered company address is: Gewerbestrasse 11, 6330 Cham, Switzerland

Above: Chaochen Zhou together with his wife Yuping Zhang
Below: Chaochen Zhou and his wife together with Dines Bjørner and Anders Ravn.
The photographs are published with permission.

Preface

In October 2017, friends, colleagues and former students met in honour of Professor Zhou Chaochen's 80th birthday. The conference in Changsha heard papers on a range of topics to which Chaochen had made his own scientific contributions. This volume contains papers from most of the speakers at the memorable event.

Zhou Chaochen has had a distinguished international career that has addressed the foundations of real-time and hybrid systems as well as distributed computing. To single out just one of his many scientific insights, his seminal contribution to the *Duration Calculus* has led to many developments and wide application.

Internationally, he has worked in Oxford with Professor Tony Hoare, in Denmark with Professor Dines Bjørner and at the United Nations University International Institute for Software Technology (UNU/IIST) in Macau. At the latter, of these he was a Principal Research Fellow and then Director of the Institute from 1992–2002.

Recognition for his contributions include being elected a member of the Chinese Academy of Sciences and a winner of the National Award for Natural Sciences.

The warm personal praise and gratitude from his friends and colleagues reflected another dimension of Chaochen's impact on the scientific community: his students recognised the key impact of his teaching and his colleagues such as Anders Ravn spoke warmly of his penetrating and constructive criticism. Everyone at the Changsha event had special stories of friendship and help from both Chaochen and his charming wife, Yuping Zhang.

The editors and all participants at the memorable conference wish Yuping and Chaochen many more years of happiness.

July 2018

Cliff Jones
Ji Wang
Naijun Zhan

Organization

Program Committee

Yunwei Dong	Northwestern Polytechnical University, China
Wenfei Fan	The University of Edinburgh, UK
Martin Fränzle	University of Oldenburg, Germany
Cliff Jones	Newcastle University, UK
Xiaoshan Li	University of Macau, SAR China
Xuandong Li	Nanjing University, China
Xinxin Liu	Institute of Software, Chinese Academy of Sciences, China
Zhiming Liu	Southwest University, China
Ernst-Ruediger Olderog	University of Oldenburg, Germany
Anders Ravn	Aalborg University, Denmark
Ji Wang	National University of Defense Technology, China
Mingsheng Ying	University of Technology Sydney, Australia
Naijun Zhan	Institute of Software, Chinese Academy of Sciences, China

Additional Reviewers

Ahmad, Ehsan	Li, Yangjia
Bu, Lei	Liu, Wanwei
Chen, Mingshuai	Yin, Liangze

Contents

Think Sequential, Run Parallel

Wenfei Fan[1,2(✉)], Muyang Liu[2], Ruiqi Xu[1], Lei Hou[2(✉)], Dongze Li[2(✉)],
and Zizhong Meng[2(✉)]

[1] University of Edinburgh, Edinburgh, UK
wenfei@ed.ac.uk
[2] Beihang University, Beijing, China
{houlei,lidz}@act.buaa.edu.cn, mengzizhong@buaa.edu.cn

Abstract. Parallel computation is often a must when processing large-scale graphs. However, it is nontrivial to write parallel graph algorithms with correctness guarantees. This paper presents the programming model of GRAPE, a parallel <u>GRAP</u>h <u>E</u>ngine [19]. GRAPE allows users to "plug in" sequential (single-machine) graph algorithms as a whole, and it parallelizes the algorithms across a cluster of processors. In other words, it simplifies parallel programming for graph computations, from think parallel to think sequential. Under a monotonic condition, it guarantees to converge at correct answers as long as the sequential algorithms are correct. We present the foundation underlying GRAPE, based on simultaneous fixpoint computation. As examples, we demonstrate how GRAPE parallelizes our familiar sequential graph algorithms. Furthermore, we show that in addition to its programming simplicity, GRAPE achieves performance comparable to the state-of-the-art graph systems.

1 Introduction

There has been increasing demand for graph computations, *e.g.*, graph traversal, connectivity, pattern matching, and collaborative filtering. Indeed, graph computations have found prevalent use in mobile network analysis, pattern recognition, knowledge discovery, transportation networks, social media marketing and fraud detection, among other things. In addition, real-life graphs are typically big, easily having billions of nodes and trillions of edges [24]. With these comes the need for parallel graph computations. In response to the need, several parallel graph systems have been developed, *e.g.*, Pregel [33], GraphLab [22,32], Trinity [42], GRACE [47], Blogel [50], Giraph++ [44], and GraphX [23].

However, users often find it hard to write and debug parallel graph programs using these systems. The most popular programming model for parallel graph algorithms is the vertex-centric model, pioneered by Pregel and GraphLab. For instance, to program with Pregel, one needs to "think like a vertex", by writing a user-defined function *compute(msgs)* to be executed at a vertex v, where v communicates with other vertices by message passing (*msgs*). Although graph computations have been studied for decades and a large number of sequential (single-machine) graph algorithms are already in place, to use Pregel, one has to

© Springer Nature Switzerland AG 2018
C. Jones et al. (Eds.): Zhou-Festschrift, LNCS 11180, pp. 1–25, 2018.
https://doi.org/10.1007/978-3-030-01461-2_1

recast the existing algorithms into vertex-centric programs. Trinity and GRACE also support vertex-centric programming. While Blogel and Giraph++ allow blocks to have their status as a "vertex" and support block-level communication, they still adopt the vertex-centric programming paradigm. GraphX also recasts graph computation into its distributed dataflow framework as a sequence of join and group-by stages punctuated by map operations, on the Spark platform. The recasting is nontrivial for users who are not very familiar with the parallel models. Moreover, none of the systems provides a guarantee on the correctness or even termination of parallel programs developed in their models. These make the existing systems a privilege for experienced users only.

Is it possible to simplify parallel programming for graph computations, from think parallel to think sequential? That is, can we have a system that allows users to plug in existing sequential graph algorithms for a computational problem, and it automatically parallelizes the computation across a cluster of processors? Better yet, is there a general condition under which the parallelization guarantees to converge at correct answers as long as the sequential algorithms plugged in are correct? After all, humans find it far easier to devise sequential processes that cope with the interference and synchronisation required in parallel algorithms.

It was to answer this question that we developed GRAPE [19], a parallel GRAPh Engine for graph computations. The main objective of GRAPE is to make parallel graph computations accessible to a large group of users. It allows users to think sequential and go parallel, by parallelizing sequential graph algorithms as a whole. Moreover, under a monotonic condition, it guarantees to converge at correct answers when provided with correct sequential graph algorithms. As proof of concept, GRAPE has been developed [18] and evaluated in industry. In addition to its programming simplicity, it outperforms the state-of-the-art parallel graph systems in scalability and efficiency.

The remainder of the paper is organized as follows. We present the parallel model underlying GRAPE (Sect. 2), based on simultaneous fixpoint computation with partial evaluation and incremental computation. We then demonstrate how our familiar sequential graph algorithms are parallelized by GRAPE (Sect. 3), including single-source shortest path (SSSP), graph simulation (Sim), connected components (CC) and minimum spanning tree (MST). In addition, we provide an empirical study to demonstrate the scalability and efficiency of GRAPE, compared to the state-of-the-art graph systems (Sect. 4). Finally, we discuss related work and identify topics for future research (Sect. 5).

2   From Think Parallel to Think Sequential

We next present the programming model and parallel model of GRAPE [19].

2.1   Graphs and Graph Partition

We start with basic notations, in particular graph partitions.

Graphs. We consider graphs $G = (V, E, L)$, directed or undirected, where (1) V is a finite set of nodes; (2) $E \subseteq V \times V$ is a set of edges; and (3) each node v in V (resp. edge $e \in E$) carries $L(v)$ (resp. $L(e)$), indicating its content, as found in social networks, knowledge bases and property graphs.

We will use two notions of subgraphs. A graph $G' = (V', E', L')$ is called a *subgraph of G* if $V' \subseteq V$, $E' \subseteq E$, and for each node $v \in V'$ (resp. edge $e \in E'$), $L'(v) = L(v)$ (resp. $L'(e) = L(e)$). Subgraph G' is said to be *induced by V'* if E' consists of all the edges in G whose endpoints are both in V'.

Partition strategy. GRAPE supports data-partitioned parallelism: it partitions a graph G and distributes fragments of G across m processors, such that computations on G can be conducted in parallel on the fragments. More specifically, given a graph G and a number m, a graph partition strategy $\mathcal{P}$ partitions G into *fragments* $(F_1, \ldots, F_m)$ such that each $F_i = (V_i, E_i, L_i)$ is a subgraph of G, $E = \bigcup_{i \in [1,m]} E_i$, $V = \bigcup_{i \in [1,m]} V_i$, and F_i resides at processor P_i for $i \in [1, m]$.

GRAPE allows users to pick a strategy $\mathcal{P}$ to partition G, *e.g.*, vertex-cut [30] or edge-cut [7]. When $\mathcal{P}$ is vertex-cut, denote by

- $F_i.O$ the set of *border nodes* $v \in V_i$ such that there exists a copy of v in another fragment F_j ($i \neq j$); and
- $\mathcal{F}.O = \bigcup_{i \in [1,m]} F_i.O$.

Similarly, border nodes are defined under edge-cut, which have an edge to (or from) nodes in another fragment (see [19] for details).

We adopt vertex-cut in the sequel unless stated otherwise; the results of the paper still hold under other partition strategies.

2.2 Programming Model

Consider a graph computation problem $\mathcal{Q}$. Informally, a parallel program for $\mathcal{Q}$ is a program that operates on a graph G, where G is partitioned and distributed across a cluster of processors. Here we assume that the cluster adopts the shared nothing architecture in which processors do not share memory or disk storage, and the processors exchange information among themselves by message passing, as commonly adopted nowadays. In our familiar terms, we refer to an instance of the problem (excluding graph G) as a query Q of $\mathcal{Q}$. Given a query $Q \in \mathcal{Q}$, the program computes the set $Q(G)$ of answers to Q in graph G by operating on the fragments of G in parallel with the processors.

To develop a parallel algorithm for a class $\mathcal{Q}$ of queries with GRAPE, one only needs to specify the following three functions.

(1) PEval: a sequential (single-machine) algorithm for $\mathcal{Q}$ that given a query $Q \in \mathcal{Q}$ and a graph G, computes the answer $Q(G)$ to Q in G.
(2) IncEval: a sequential incremental algorithm for $\mathcal{Q}$ that given Q, G, $Q(G)$ and updates ΔG to G, computes updates ΔO to the old output $Q(G)$ such that $Q(G \oplus \Delta G) = Q(G) \oplus \Delta O$, where $G \oplus \Delta G$ denotes G updated by ΔG [40].

(3) **Assemble:** a function that collects partial answers computed locally at each processor by PEval and IncEval, and assembles the partial results into complete answer $Q(G)$. This function is often straightforward.

The three functions are referred to as *a* PIE *program for* Q (PEval, IncEval and Assemble). Note that PEval and IncEval can be any *existing sequential* (incremental) algorithms for Q that operate on a fragment F_i of graph G partitioned via a strategy $\mathcal{P}$. Note that fragment F_i is a graph itself.

The only additions are the following declarations in PEval.

(a) Update parameters. PEval declares *status variables* $\bar{x}$ for a set C_i of nodes in a fragment F_i, which store contents of F_i or intermediate results of a computation. Here C_i is a set of nodes and edges within d-hops of the nodes in $F_i.O$, for an integer d that is determined by Q. When $d = 0$, C_i is $F_i.O$.

We denote by $C_i.\bar{x}$ the set of *update parameters* of F_i, including status variables associated with the nodes and edges in C_i. As will be seen shortly, the variables in $C_i.\bar{x}$ are candidates to be updated by incremental steps IncEval.

(b) Aggregate functions. PEval also specifies an aggregate function f_{aggr}, *e.g.*, min and max, for conflict resolution, *i.e.*, to resolve conflicts when multiple processors attempt to assign different values to the same update parameter.

Update parameters and aggregate function are specified in PEval and are shared by IncEval. We will provide examples in Sect. 3.

2.3   Parallel Computation Model

We next show how GRAPE parallelizes a PIE program ρ (PEval, IncEval, Assemble) for Q. Given a partition strategy $\mathcal{P}$ and PIE program ρ, GRAPE first partitions G into $(F_1, \ldots, F_m)$ with $\mathcal{P}$, and distributes the fragments across m shared-nothing *virtual workers* (*i.e.*, processors) $(P_1, \ldots, P_m)$, respectively. It maps m virtual workers to n physical workers. When $n < m$, multiple virtual workers that are mapped to the same worker share memory.

Note that graph G is partitioned *once* for *all queries* $Q \in \mathcal{Q}$ on G.

We start with basic ideas behind GRAPE parallelization.

(1) Given a function $f(s, d)$ and the s part of its input, *partial evaluation* is to specialize $f(s, d)$ *w.r.t.* the known input s [29]. That is, it performs the part of f's computation that depends only on s, and generates a partial answer, *i.e.*, a residual function f' that depends on the as yet unavailable input d. For each worker P_i in GRAPE, its local fragment F_i is its known input s, while the data residing at other workers is the yet unavailable input d. As will be seen shortly, given a query $Q \in \mathcal{Q}$, GRAPE computes $Q(F_i)$ in parallel as partial evaluation.

(2) Workers exchange *changed values* of their local update parameters with each other. Upon receiving message M_i that consists of changes to the update parameters at fragment F_i, worker P_i treats M_i as *updates* to F_i, and *incrementally* computes changes ΔO_i to $Q(F_i)$ such that $Q(F_i \oplus M_i) = Q(F_i) \oplus \Delta O_i$, making maximum reuse of previous results $Q(F_i)$. This is often more efficient than recomputing $Q(F_i \oplus M_i)$ starting from scratch, since in practice M_i is typically

small, and so is O_i. Better still, the incremental computation may be *bounded*: its cost can be expressed as a function in $|M_i| + |\Delta O_i|$, *i.e.*, the size of changes in the input and output, instead of $|F_i|$, no matter how big F_i is [16, 40].

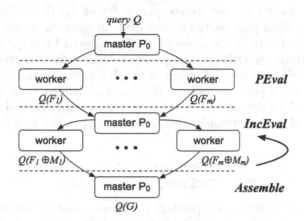

Fig. 1. Workflow of GRAPE

Model. Given a query $Q \in \mathcal{Q}$ at the master (processor) P_0, GRAPE answers Q in the partitioned graph G following BSP [45]. It posts the same query Q to all the workers, and computes $Q(G)$ in three phases as follows, as shown in Fig. 1.
(1) *Partial evaluation* (**PEval**). In the first superstep, upon receiving Q, each worker P_i applies function PEval to its local fragment F_i, to compute partial results $Q(F_i)$, in parallel ($i \in [1, m]$). After $Q(F_i)$ is computed, PEval generates a message at each worker P_i and sends it to master P_0. The message is simply the set $C_i.\bar{x}$ of update parameters at fragment F_i.

For each $i \in [1, m]$, master P_0 maintains update parameters $C_i.\bar{x}$. It deduces a message M_i to worker P_i based on the following *message grouping policy*. (a) For each status variable $x \in C_i.\bar{x}$, it collects the set S_x of values from messages of all workers, and computes $x_{\mathsf{aggr}} = f_{\mathsf{aggr}}(S_x)$ by applying the aggregate function f_{aggr} declared in PEval. (b) Message M_i includes only those $f_{\mathsf{aggr}}(S_x)$'s such that $f_{\mathsf{aggr}}(S_x) \neq x$, *i.e.*, only the *changed* values of the update parameters of F_i.
(2) *Incremental computation* (**IncEval**). GRAPE iterates the following supersteps until it terminates. Following BSP, each superstep starts after the master P_0 receives messages (possibly empty) from *all workers* P_i for $i \in [1, m]$. A superstep has two steps itself, one at P_0 and the other at the workers.

(a) Master P_0 routes (nonempty) messages from the last superstep to workers, if there exist any.
(b) Upon receiving message M_i, worker P_i *incrementally* computes $Q(F_i \oplus M_i)$ by applying IncEval, and by *treating M_i as updates*, in parallel for $i \in [1, m]$.

At the end of IncEval process, P_i sends a message to P_0 that encodes *updated values* of $C_i.\bar{x}$, if any. Upon receiving messages from all workers, master P_0

deduces a message M_i to each worker P_i following the message grouping policy given above; it sends message M_i to worker P_i in the next superstep.

(3) Termination (**Assemble**). At each superstep, master P_0 checks whether for all $i \in [1, m]$, P_i is inactive, *i.e.*, P_i is done with its local computation, and there exist no more changes to any update parameter of F_i. If so, GRAPE invokes Assemble at P_0, which pulls partial results from all workers, groups together the partial results and gets the final result at P_0, denoted by $\rho(Q, G)$. It returns $\rho(Q, G)$ and terminates. Otherwise, it proceeds to the next superstep (step (2)).

Fixpoint. The GRAPE parallelization of the PIE program can be modeled as a simultaneous fixed point operator $\phi(R_1, \ldots, R_m)$ defined on m fragments. It starts with PEval for partial evaluation, and conducts incremental computation by taking IncEval as the intermediate consequence operator, as follows:

$$R_i^0 = \mathsf{PEval}(Q, F_i^0[\bar{x}_i]), \tag{1}$$

$$R_i^{r+1} = \mathsf{IncEval}(Q, R_i^r, F_i^r[\bar{x}_i], M_i), \tag{2}$$

where $i \in [1, m]$, r indicates a superstep, R_i^r denotes partial results in step r at worker P_i, fragment $F_i^0 = F_i$, $F_i^r[\bar{x}_i]$ is fragment F_i at the end of superstep r carrying update parameters $\bar{x}_i$, and M_i is a message indicating changes to $\bar{x}_i$. More specifically, (1) in the first superstep, PEval computes partial answers R_i^0 ($i \in [1, m]$). (2) At step $r+1$, the partial answers R_i^{r+1} are incrementally updated by IncEval, taking Q, R_i^r and message M_i as input. (3) The computation proceeds until $R_i^{r_0+1} = R_i^{r_0}$ at a fixed point r_0 for all $i \in [1, m]$. Function Assemble is then invoked to combine all partial answers $R_i^{r_0}$ and get the final answer $\rho(Q, G)$.

2.4   Features of GRAPE

As outlined above, GRAPE has the following unique features.

(1) Parallel programming simplicity. GRAPE allows users to plug in sequential graph algorithms as a whole (subject to declarations of update parameters and aggregate function in PEval), and executes these algorithms on fragmented and distributed graphs. That is, users can "think sequential" when programming with GRAPE, instead of think parallel. Moreover, a large number of sequential graph algorithms are already in place after decades of study, and are well optimized. Moreover, there have been methods for incrementalizing graph algorithms, to get incremental algorithms from their batch counterparts [6,14]. Furthermore, as will be shown in Sects. 3.2 and 3.4, it is quite straightforward to develop IncEval by revising a batch sequential algorithm. These make parallel graph computations accessible to college students who know conventional graph algorithms covered in undergraduate textbooks.

This said, GRAPE cannot be used without some insight by simply plugging in sequential algorithms without making any change. Programming with GRAPE still requires to declare update parameters and an aggregate function.

(2) Correctness guarantees. Under a general condition, GRAPE parallelization is guaranteed to converge at correct answers. To see this, we use the following notations. (a) A sequential algorithm PEval for $\mathcal{Q}$ is *correct* if given all

$Q \in \mathcal{Q}$ and graphs G, it terminates and returns $Q(G)$. (b) A sequential incremental algorithm IncEval for $\mathcal{Q}$ is *correct* if given all $Q \in \mathcal{Q}$, graphs G, old output $Q(G)$ and updates ΔG to G, it computes changes ΔO to $Q(G)$ such that $Q(G \oplus \Delta G) = Q(G) \oplus \Delta O$. (c) We say that Assemble is *correct for $\mathcal{Q}$ w.r.t.* $\mathcal{P}$ if when GRAPE with PEval, IncEval and $\mathcal{P}$ terminates at superstep r_0, $\text{Assemble}(Q(F_1[\bar{x}_1^{r_0}]), \ldots, Q(F_m[\bar{x}_m^{r_0}])) = Q(G)$, where $\bar{x}_i^{r_0}$ denotes the values of parameters $C_i.\bar{x}_i$ at round r_0. (d) We say that GRAPE *correctly parallelizes* a PIE program ρ with a partition strategy $\mathcal{P}$ if for all queries $Q \in \mathcal{Q}$ and graphs G, GRAPE guarantees to reach a fixed point such that $\rho(Q, G) = Q(G)$.

As shown in [19], GRAPE correctly parallelizes a PIE program ρ for a graph computation problem $\mathcal{Q}$ if (a) its PEval and IncEval are correct sequential algorithms for $\mathcal{Q}$, and (b) Assemble correctly combines partial results, and (c) PEval and IncEval satisfy the following monotone condition: for all variables $x \in C_i.\bar{x}$, $i \in [1, m]$, (a) the values of x are computed from the active domain of G, and (b) there exists a partial order p_x on the values of x such that IncEval updates x in the order of p_x. That is, x draws values from a finite domain (condition (a) above), and x is updated "monotonically" following p_x (condition (b)).

It should be remarked that the monotonicity above is just a sufficient condition for GRAPE computations to converge, but it is not a necessary condition. Indeed, a variety of contracting conditions have been developed for fixpoint computation, *e.g.*, [10–12]. These conditions can be adapted to GRAPE convergence as well, in addition to the monotonic condition given above.

Moreover, it does not mean that only algorithms satisfying the monotonic condition can be parallelized in GRAPE. As will be seen shortly, any MapReduce algorithm can be migrated to GRAPE without extra complexity. Obviously not all MapReduce algorithms have the monotonicity. In other words, the monotonicity is just a condition under which one does not have to worry about convergence.

(3) Expressive power. The programming simplicity does not imply degradation in functionality of the existing systems. Following [46], we say that a parallel model $\mathcal{M}_1$ can *optimally simulate* model $\mathcal{M}_2$ if there exists a compilation algorithm that transforms any program with cost C on $\mathcal{M}_2$ to a program with cost $O(C)$ on $\mathcal{M}_1$. The cost includes computational cost and communication cost.

As shown in [19], GRAPE can optimally simulate MapReduce [13], BSP [45] and PRAM (Parallel Random Access Machine) [46]. That is, all algorithms in MapRedue, BSP or PRAM with n workers can be simulated by GRAPE using n workers with the same number of supersteps and memory cost. As a consequence, these algorithms can be migrated to GRAPE without increasing the complexity.

The result above aims to show the expressive power of GRAPE. In particular, graph computations that have effective (*e.g.*, bounded) incremental algorithms may be substantially accelerated by GRAPE. Nonetheless, for algorithms that make only one fragment active at a time, we do not expect that GRAPE speeds up their parallel computations. A particular example is Depth First Search (DFS), which is known to be hard to parallelize. While DFS can be parallelized by GRAPE, GRAPE may not make it more efficient than other platforms.

(4) Graph-level optimization. GRAPE naturally inherits all optimization strategies available for sequential graph algorithms, *e.g.*, indexing, compression and partitioning. Indeed, PEval and IncEval work on fragments, which are graphs themselves. Hence prior optimization strategies developed for sequential graph algorithms remain effective for PEval and IncEval. In contrast, these strategies are hard to implement for, *e.g.*, vertex-centric programs.

(5) Reducing redundant computations. GRAPE reduces the costs of iterative graph computations by using IncEval, to minimize unnecessary recomputations. We should remark that IncEval speeds up iterative computations by making use of prior partial results $Q(F_i)$ at each worker P_i, *no matter whether IncEval is bounded or not*. Indeed, boundedness is not the only criterion for the effectiveness of incremental algorithms. Alternative performance guarantees for incremental graph algorithms have been developed, such as semi-boundedness [16], localizable incremental algorithms and relative boundedness [14].

(6) Compatibility. To simplify the discussion, we have focused on synchronous model BSP, when iterative computation is separated into supersteps, and messages from one superstep are only accessible in the next one. Our recent results have shown that the programming model of GRAPE remains intact under asynchronous parallel model (AP), when a worker has immediate access to incoming messages, and when fast workers can move ahead, without waiting for stragglers. Moreover, the convergence condition given above can be adapted to the asynchronous model. In other words, with GRAPE, it is no longer hard to write, debug and analyze parallel algorithms, no matter whether under BSP or AP.

3   Programming with GRAPE

We next show how GRAPE parallelizes familiar graph algorithms, by taking single-source shortest distance (SSSP), graph simulation (Sim), connected components (CC) and minimum spanning tree (MST) as examples. We parallelize these algorithms in Sects. 3.1–3.4 under a vertex-cut partition. Taken together with the parallelization of [19] under edge-cut, these show that GRAPE programming works equally well under vertex-cut and edge-cut partition.

3.1   Graph Traversal

Consider $\mathcal{Q}$ denoting *the single source shortest path problem* (SSSP). It targets a directed graph $G = (V, E, L)$ in which for each edge e, $L(e)$ is a positive number. The length of a path $(v_0, \ldots, v_k)$ in G is the sum of $L(v_{i-1}, v_i)$ for $i \in [1, k]$. For a pair (s, v) of nodes, denote by $\mathsf{dist}(s, v)$ the *shortest distance* from s to v. *i.e.*, the length of a shortest path from s to v. SSSP is stated as follows.

- Input: A directed graph G as above, and a node s in G.
- Output: Distance $\mathsf{dist}(s, v)$ for all nodes v in G.

It is known that SSSP is in $O(|E| + |V|\log|V|)$ time [20].

Input: Fragment $F_i(V_i, E_i, L_i)$, source vertex s.
Output: A set $Q(F_i)$ consisting of current dist(s, v) for all $v \in V_i$.
Message preamble: /* candidate set C_i is $F_i.O$*/
       for each node $v \in V_i$, an integer variable dist(s, v);
1.   initialize priority queue Que;   dist$(s, s) := 0$;
2.   **for each** v in V_i **do**
3.   **if** $v! = s$ **then** dist$(s, v) := \infty$;
4.   Que.addOrAdjust$(s,$ dist$(s, s))$;
5.   **while** Que is not empty **do**
6. $u := $ Que.pop() /* pop vertex with minimal distance */
7.   **for each** child v of u **do** /* only if v has not been visited */
8. $alt := $ dist$(s, u) + L_i(u, v)$;
9.   **if** $alt < $ dist(s, v) **then**
10.   dist$(s, v) := alt$;
11.   Que.addOrAdjust$(v,$ dist$(s, v))$;
12. $Q(F_i) := \{(v, \text{dist}(s, v)) \mid v \in V_i\}$;
Message segment: $M_i := \{(v, \text{dist}(s, v)) \mid v \in F_i.O\}$;
         $f_{\text{aggr}} = \min(\{\text{dist}(s, v)\})$;

Fig. 2. PEval for SSSP

For SSSP under vertex cut, GRAPE takes existing sequential (incremental) algorithms for SSSP as PEval and IncEval, just like GRAPE under edge-cut [19]. *(1)* PEval. As shown in Fig. 2, PEval (lines 1–11 of Fig. 2) is verbally identical to Dijsktra's algorithm [20], except that it declares the following (underlined):

(a) for each node $v \in V_i$, an integer variable dist(s, v), initially ∞ (except dist(s, s) $= 0$); the candidate set C_i is the set $F_i.O$ of border nodes and the set of updated parameters is $C_i.\bar{x} = \{\text{dist}(s, v) \mid v \in F_i.O\}$; and
(b) an aggregate function f_{aggr} defined as min to resolve the conflicts: if multiple values are assigned to the same dist(s, v) by different workers, the smallest value is taken by the linear order on integers.

At the end of its process, PEval sends $C_i.\bar{x}$ to master P_0. At P_0, GRAPE maintains dist(s, v) for all nodes $v \in F_i.O$ ($i \in [1, m]$). Upon receiving messages from all workers, it takes the smallest value for dist(s, v) of each border node $v \in C_i.\bar{x}$. For each $i \in [1, m]$, it finds those variables with smaller dist(s, v) for $v \in F_i.O$, groups them into message M_i, and sends M_i to P_i.
(2) IncEval. As shown in Fig. 3, IncEval is the sequential incremental algorithm for SSSP developed in [39], in response to changed dist(s, v) for v in $F_i.O$ (here M_i includes changes to dist(s, v) for $v \in F_i.O$). Using a queue Que, it starts with M_i, propagates the changes to affected area, and updates the distances (see [40]). The partial result is now the set of revised distances (line 11). At the end of the process, the updated values of $C_i.\bar{x}$ are sent to the master as messages, where the aggregate function min is applied to resolve conflicts as in PEval.

Input: Fragment $F_i(V_i, E_i, L_i)$, partial result $Q(F_i)$, message M_i.
Output: New output $Q(F_i \oplus M_i)$.
1.   initialize priority queue Que;
2.   **for each** dist(s, v) in M_i **do**
3.   Que.addOrAdjust$(v, \text{dist}(s, v))$;
4.   **while** Que is not empty **do**
5. $u :=$ Que.pop() /* pop vertex with minimum distance*/
6.   **for each** children v of u **do** /* only if v has not been visited*/
7. $alt :=$ dist$(s, u) + L_i(u, v)$;
8.   **if** $alt <$ dist(s, v) **then**
9.   dist$(s, v) := alt$;
10.   Que.addOrAdjust$(v, \text{dist}(s, v))$;
11. $Q(F_i) := \{(v, \text{dist}(s, v)) \mid v \in V_i\}$;
Message segment: $M_i := \{(v, \text{dist}(s, v)) \mid v \in F_i.O, \text{dist}(s, v) \text{ decreased}\}$;

Fig. 3. IncEval for SSSP

Here IncEval is bounded. Following [39], it can be verified that its cost is determined by the size of "updates" $|M_i|$ and the changes to the output. This reduces the cost of iterative computation of SSSP (the While and For loops).

<u>*(3)* Assemble</u> simply takes $Q(G) = \bigcup_{i \in [1,n]} Q(F_i)$, the union of the shortest distance for each node in V.

<u>*(4)* Correctness.</u> Termination is guaranteed since the values of update parameters are from a finite domain and are monotonically decreasing in the process. The correctness is assured since (a) the algorithms for PEval [20] and IncEval [40] are correct and (b) IncEval are monotonic by taking min as f_{aggr}.

3.2   Graph Simulation

We next study graph simulation, which is commonly used in social media marketing [17] and social network analysis [15], among other things.

A *graph pattern* is a graph $Q = (V_Q, E_Q, L_Q)$, where (a) V_Q is a set of *query nodes*, (b) E_Q is a set of *query edges*, and (c) each u in V_Q carries a label $L_Q(u)$.

A graph $G = (V, E, L)$ *matches* a pattern $Q = (V_Q, E_Q, L_Q)$ via *graph simulation* if there exists a binary relation $R \subseteq V_Q \times V$ such that

(a) for each query node $u \in V_Q$, there is a node $v \in V$ such that $(u, v) \in R$, and
(b) for each pair $(u, v) \in R$, (i) $L_Q(u) = L(v)$, and (ii) for each (u, u') in E_Q, there exists (v, v') in graph G such that $(u', v') \in R$.

For $(u, v) \in R$, we refer to v as a *match* of u. It is known that if G matches Q, then there exists a *unique maximum* relation [27], referred to as $Q(G)$. If G does not match Q, $Q(G)$ is the empty set. Moreover, it is known that $Q(G)$ can be computed in $O((|V_Q| + |E_Q|)(|V| + |E|))$ time [15,27].

Graph pattern matching via graph simulation is stated as follows.

- Input: A directed graph G and a graph pattern Q.
- Output: The unique maximum relation $Q(G)$.

Input: $Q = (V_Q, E_Q, L_Q)$, and $F_i = (V_i, E_i, L_i)$.
Output: Maximum match relation sim for $Q(F_i)$.

Message preamble: /* candidate set C_i is $F_i.O$ */
    for each node u in V_Q and v in V_i, an integer variable $\mathsf{cnt}_{(v,u)} := 0$;

/* Initialize variable $\gamma(v) = \mathsf{true}$ if v has a successor in G, at loading time */
1.   **for each** $u \in V_Q$ **do**
2.   **if** $\mathsf{post}(u) = \emptyset$ **then**
3. $\mathsf{sim}(u) := \{v \in V_i \mid L_Q(u) = L_i(v)\}$;
4.   **else** $\mathsf{sim}(u) := \{v \in V_i \mid L_Q(u) = L_i(v) \wedge \gamma(v) = \mathit{true}\}$;
5.   **for each** $v \in V_i$ **do**
6. $\mathsf{cnt}_{(v,u)} = |\{w \in V_i \mid w \in \mathsf{post}'(v) \wedge w \in \mathsf{sim}(u)\}|$;
7. $Q(F_i) := \mathsf{sim}$;
Message segment: $M_i := \{\Delta\mathsf{cnt}_{(v,u)} \mid u \in V_Q \wedge v \in F_i.O\}$;
        $f_{\mathsf{aggr}} = \mathsf{sum}\ (\Delta\mathsf{cnt}_{(v,u)})$;

Fig. 4. PEval for graph simulation

GRAPE parallelizes Sim by adopting the sequential algorithm gsim for Sim developed in [27]. It uses the initialization of gsim as PEval to generate candidate matches $\mathsf{sim}(u)$ for each query node $u \in V_Q$; it then uses the main loop of gsim as IncEval, to refine $\mathsf{sim}(u)$ by recursively filtering out false positives in $\mathsf{sim}(u)$.
(1) PEval. As shown in Fig. 4, PEval adopts the initialization step of gsim. It sets C_i to $F_i.O$ and declares, for each query node $u \in V_q$ and data node v in fragment F_i, a status variable $\mathsf{cnt}_{(v,u)}$. Here $\mathsf{cnt}_{(v,u)}$ denotes the number of successors of v that are candidate matches of u in G, defined as $|\{w \mid w \in \mathsf{post}(v) \wedge w \in \mathsf{sim}(u)\}|$, where $\mathsf{post}(v)$ denotes the set of successors of v in G. It will be used by IncEval to filter out invalid candidate matches of u from $\mathsf{sim}(u)$. PEval initializes $\mathsf{sim}(u)$ in the same way as sequential algorithm gsim (lines 1–4), except that it uses a Boolean variable $\gamma(v)$ to check candidate matches in C_i for $\mathsf{sim}(u)$, where $\gamma(v)$ is set to *true* if v has any successor in G and is initialized when loading the data graph G. It also initializes $\mathsf{cnt}_{(v,u)}$ as the number of "local" successors of v that are in fragment F_i and are candidate matches of u in F_i (lines 5–6). As will be seen shortly, we use counters $\mathsf{cnt}_{(v,u)}$ to determine invalid match candidates.

We take $F_i.O$ as C_i, and treat $C_i.\mathsf{cnt}$ as update parameters. After $\mathsf{cnt}_{(v,u)}$ is locally initialized in PEval, the set $C_i.\mathsf{cnt}$ is sent to master P_0. At P_0, upon receiving messages from all workers, the changes to $\mathsf{cnt}_{(v,u)}$ are aggregated using $f_{\mathsf{aggr}} = \mathsf{sum}$ to generate the global value of $\mathsf{cnt}_{(v,u)}$. GRAPE then groups these variables into message M_i and sends M_i to P_i.
(2) IncEval. As shown in Fig. 5, IncEval is a minor revision of IncGSim; it refines candidate matches (lines 1–14). In particular, it uses $\mathsf{cnt}_{(v,u)}$ to speedup the

---

Input: pattern Q, fragment F_i, partial result sim and message M_i.
Output: maximum match relation sim for Q and $F_i \oplus M_i$.

1.   queue remove $:= \emptyset$;
2.   **for each** Δcnt$_{(v,u)}$ in M_i **do**
3.   cnt$_{(v,u)}$ $:=$ cnt$_{(v,u)}$ $+ \Delta$cnt$_{(v,u)}$;
4.   **for each** cnt$_{(v,u)}$ that is updated to 0 **do**
5.   remove(u) $:=$ remove$(u) \cup \{v\}$;
6.   **while** there exists $u \in V_Q$ such that remove$(u) \neq \emptyset$ **do**
7.   **for each** $u' \in$ pre(u) **do**
8.   **for each** $w \in$ remove(u) **do**
9.   **if** $w \in$ sim(u') **then**
10.   sim(u') $:=$ sim$(u') \setminus \{w\}$;
11.   **for each** $w' \in$ pre$'(w)$ **do**
12.   decrease cnt$_{(w',u')}$ by 1;
13.   **if** cnt$_{(w',u')} = 0$ **then** remove(u') $:=$ remove$(u') \cup \{w'\}$;
14.   remove(u) $:= \emptyset$;
15. $Q(F_i)$ $:=$ sim;
Message segment:
      $M_i := \{\Delta$cnt$_{(v,u)} \mid u \in V_Q, v \in F_i.O,$ cnt$_{(v,u)}$changed$\}$;

Fig. 5. IncEval for graph simulation

refinement: if cnt$_{(v,u)} = 0$, then no children of v can match u, and hence v cannot match any query node u' that is a parent of u in Q. The counter cnt on v's parents is then updated, which is used to identify more false matches. More specifically, IncEval first updates cnt$_{(v,u)}$ on border nodes, by applying changes to cnt$_{(v,u)}$ in the message. For each (u,v), if cnt$_{(v,u)} = 0$, then there is no match of u in post(v). Hence v cannot match any vertex in pre(u) in V_Q. After false match (u',v) is spotted, cnt$_{(w,u')}$ is reduced by 1 for all w in pre(v). This is propagated through incoming edges iteratively, to identify more false matches.

Similar to the edge-cut version of IncEval in [16], one can verify that IncEval is *semi-bounded*: its cost is decided by the size of updates M_i and changes to the affected area necessarily checked by all incremental algorithms for Sim, rather than by F_i. This guarantees the efficiency of IncEval for graph simulation.
(3) Assemble takes $Q(G) = \bigcup_{i \in [1,n]} Q(F_i)$, the union of all partial matches, *i.e.*, the sim relation computed at each fragment F_i at the end of the process.
(4) Correctness of the GRAPE parallelization above is warranted by monotonic updates to C_i.cnt and by the correctness of sequential algorithm gsim [27]. More specifically, cnt$_{(v,u)}$ is initially the maximum count of possible matches in post(v) with u after the process of PEval; it is monotonically reduced in the IncEval process, until it reaches the number of true matches in post(v) with u.

3.3   Graph Connectivity

We next study graph connectivity, for computing connected components (CC).

Consider an undirected graph G. A subgraph G_s of G is a *connected component* of G if (a) it is connected, *i.e.*, for any pair (v, v') of nodes in G_s, there exists a path between v to v', and (b) it is maximum, *i.e.*, adding any node to G_s makes the induced subgraph no longer connected. The CC problem is as follows.

- Input: An undirected graph $G = (V, E, L)$.
- Output: All connected components of G.

The problem is known to be in $O(|G|)$ time [9].

GRAPE parallelizes CC as follows. It picks a sequential CC algorithm as PEval. At each fragment F_i, PEval computes its local connected components and creates their ids. The component ids of the border nodes are exchanged with neighboring fragments. The (changed) ids are then used to incrementally update local components in each fragment by IncEval, which simulates a "merging" of two components whenever possible, until no more changes can be made.

Input: $F_i = (V_i, E_i, L_i)$.
Output: $Q(F_i)$ consisting of $v.cid$ for each $v \in V_i$.
Message preamble: /* candidate set C_i is $F_i.I$ */
      for each $v \in V_i$, an integer variable $v.cid$ initialized as v's id;
1. $CC := DFS(F_i)$; /* use DFS to find the set of local CCs */
2.   **for each** local component $C \in CC$ **do**
3.   add a new single root node v_r;
4. $v_r.cid := \min\{v.cid \mid v \in C\}$;
5.   **for each** node $v \in C$ **do**
6.   link v to v_r; $v.root := v_r$; $v.cid := v_r.cid$;
7. $Q(F_i) := \{v.cid \mid v \in V_i\}$;
Message segment: $M_i := \{v.cid \mid v \in F_i.O\}$;
        $f_{aggr} = \min(v.cid)$;

Fig. 6. PEval for CC

(1) PEval declares an integer status variable $v.cid$ for each node v in fragment F_i, initialized as its node id. As shown in Fig. 6, PEval first uses a standard sequential traversal DFS (Depth-First Search) to compute the local connected components of F_i. For each local component C, (a) PEval creates a "root" node v_r carrying the minimum node id in C as $v_r.cid$, and (b) links all the nodes in C to v_r, and sets their cid as $v_r.cid$. These can be completed in one pass of the edges of F_i via DFS. At the end of process, PEval sends $\{v.cid \mid v \in F_i.O\}$ to master P_0. The set consists of the update parameters at fragment F_i.

At master P_0, GRAPE maintains $v.cid$ for each all $v \in F_i.O$ ($i \in [1, m]$). It updates $v.cid$ by taking the smallest cid if multiple cids are received, by taking min as f_{aggr} in the message segment of PEval. It groups the nodes with updated cids into messages M_i, and sends M_i to worker P_i.

(2) IncEval incrementally updates the cids of the nodes in each fragment F_i upon receiving M_i, in parallel, as shown in Fig. 7. Observe that message M_i sent to P_i consists of v.cid with updated (smaller) values. For each v.cid in M_i, IncEval finds the root v_r of v (line 3), and updates v_r.cid to the smaller v.cid. IncEval then propagates the changes from every updated root node v_r to all nodes linked to v_r by changing their cids to v_r.cid. At the end of the process, IncEval sends to master P_0 the updated cids of nodes in $F_i.O$ just like in PEval.

One can verify that the incremental algorithm IncEval is *bounded*: it takes $O(|M_i|)$ time to identify the root nodes, and $O(|\text{AFF}|)$ time to update cids by following the direct links from the roots, where AFF consists of only those nodes with their cid *changed*. Hence, it avoids redundant local traversal.

Input: $F_i = (V_i, E_i, L_i)$, partial result $Q(F_i)$, message M_i (grouped cid).
Output: $Q(F_i \oplus M_i)$.
/* incremental connected component (pseudo-code) */
1. $\Delta := \emptyset$;
2.   **for each** v.cid $\in M_i$ **do**   /* $v \in F_i.O$ */
3. $v_r := v$.root;
4.   **if** v.cid $< v_r$.cid **then**
5. v_r.cid := v.cid; $\Delta := \Delta \cup \{v_r\}$;
6.   **for each** $v_r \in \Delta$ **do**   /* propagate the change*/
7.   **for each** $v' \in V_i$ linked to v_r **do**
8. v'.cid := v_r.cid;
9. $Q(F_i) := \{v.\text{cid} \mid v \in V_i\}$;
Message segment: $M_i := \{v.\text{cid} \mid v \in F_i.O, v.\text{cid decreased}\}$;

Fig. 7. IncEval for CC

(3) Assemble merges all the nodes that have the same cid in the same connected component, and returns all the connected components.

(4) Correctness. The process terminates as the cids of the nodes are monotonically decreasing by f_{aggr} until no changes can be made. Moreover, it correctly merges two local connected components by propagating the smaller cid.

3.4   Minimum Spanning Tree

Consider a connected undirected graph $G = (V, E, W)$, where for each edge $e = (v, v')$, $W(e)$ is a number specifying the cost to connect v and v'. A *spanning tree* T of G is a subgraph of G that is a tree (*i.e.*, an undirected graph in which any two nodes are connected by exactly one path), and includes all the vertices of V. A *minimum weighted spanning tree* T of G is a spanning tree of G such that the total weight $w(T) = \Sigma_{e \in T} W(e)$ is minimized. To simplify the discussion, we assume that each edge e in G has a distinct cost $W(e)$. It is known that a unique MST exists in such a graph G [21]. The MST problem is stated as follows.

- Input: A graph $G = (V, E, W)$ as described above.
- Output: The minimum spanning tree MST of G.

It is known that MST is in $O(|E| + |V| \log |V|)$ time.

GRAPE parallelizes MST as follows. It combines Prim's sequential MST algorithm [37] and Borůvka's sequential algorithm [35] as PEval: it adopts Prim's algorithm to generate initial partial MSTs (*i.e.*, sub-trees of the final MST), and uses Borůvka's algorithm to generate messages. For IncEval, it employs Borůvka's algorithm alone to iteratively connect those partial MSTs, forming the final MST. It should be remarked that marrying Prim's and Borůvka's MST algorithms is a common practice for efficiently computing MST in parallel (see *e.g.*, [8]).

(1) PEval. As shown in Fig. 8, PEval takes $F_i.O$ as C_i and declares, for each node u in C_i, a triple $u.\mathsf{m}(u, \mathsf{tid}, \mathsf{e})$ initialized as $(u, u.\mathsf{id}, nil)$, where $u.\mathsf{id}$ is the node id of u. It generates a set $\mathcal{T}$ of partial MSTs of F_i *excluding* border nodes in $F_i.O$, using Prim$'$, a minor revision of Prim's algorithm to ensure such partial MSTs are guaranteed to be sub-trees of the global MST of G (line 1). It then treats each border node in $F_i.O$ as a partial MST and includes them in $\mathcal{T}$ as well (line 2). For each partial MST T in $\mathcal{T}$, it maintains an index for T, denoted by $T.\mathsf{tid}$, using the minimum node id of nodes in T (line 3). Such tids will be used to combine partial MSTs by IncEval. For convenience, we also write T_u as the unique partial MST that contains u and $u.\mathsf{tid}$ as $T_u.\mathsf{tid}$.

Input: Fragment $F_i = (V_i, E_i, W_i)$.
Output: $Q(F_i)$ consisting of all edges in partial MSTs.
Message preamble: /* Candidate set C_i is $F_i.O$ */
    for each node $u \in C_i$, a triple $u.\mathsf{m}(u, \mathsf{tid}, \mathsf{e})$ is initialized as $(u, u.\mathsf{id}, nil)$.

1. $\mathcal{T} := \mathsf{Prim}'(F_i')$;   /* F_i' denotes F_i excluding border nodes */
2.   **for each** $v \in F_i.O$ **do** add $T_v := (\{v\}, \emptyset)$ as a partial MST to $\mathcal{T}$;
3.   **for each** partial MST $T \in \mathcal{T}$ **do** $T.\mathsf{tid} := \min_{v \in T} v.\mathsf{id}$;
4.   **for each** $T \in \mathcal{T}$ **do**
5. $e := \arg\min_{(u,v) \in E_i, u \in T, v \notin T, u.\mathsf{tid} \neq v.\mathsf{tid}} W(u, v)$; /* assume $e = (u, v)$ */
6.   **if** $u \notin F_i.O$ **then** add (u, v) to T_u; update $T_u.\mathsf{tid}$ to $\min(T_u.\mathsf{tid}, v.\mathsf{tid})$;
7.   **else** $u.\mathsf{m} := (u, u.\mathsf{tid}, (u, v))$;   /* generate message for u */
8.   **for each** u in $F_i.O$ whose message has not been generated **do**
9. $u.\mathsf{m} := (u, u.\mathsf{tid}, nil)$;   /* generate message for u */
10. $Q(F_i) := \mathcal{T}$;

Message segment: $M_i := \{u.\mathsf{m} \mid u \in C_i\}$;
          $f_{\mathsf{aggr}} = (u, \min_{u.\mathsf{m}[\mathsf{tid}]} u.\mathsf{m}[\mathsf{tid}], \arg\min_{u.\mathsf{m}[\mathsf{e}]} W(u.\mathsf{m}[\mathsf{e}]))$

Fig. 8. PEval for MST

It then generates messages for border nodes by using Borůvka's algorithm (lines 4–7). Following Borůvka's algorithm, it treats each MST in $\mathcal{T}$ as a "virtual" node and expands each "virtual" node, say, MST $T \in \mathcal{T}$, with the edge e adjacent to T that has the minimum weight among all edges connecting T and some other MSTs in $\mathcal{T}$ (line 5). It merges the new edge $e = (u, v)$ into T and updates the MST index of T accordingly if $u \in T$ and u is not a border node (line 6). When u is a border node, PEval cannot decide whether the local minimum weighted adjacent edge e is the global minimum edge in G for u, and hence PEval encodes it together with u.tid in the message for u (line 7). For those border nodes whose messages have not been generated in this way, a default message without the adjacent edge (*i.e.*, *nil*) is generated (lines 8–9).

The message for each border node u on all fragments will be gathered at master P_0. The minimum tid and the global minimum adjacent edge for u will be deduced by f_{aggr} specified in the message segment of PEval.

Input: a set of partial MST $\mathcal{T}$, message M_i.
Output: $Q(F_i \oplus M_i)$.

1.   **for each** $m = (u_0, \mathrm{tid}_0, e_0) \in M_i$ **do**   /* update tid's */
2. $T_{u_0}.\mathrm{tid} := \min(T_{u_0}.\mathrm{tid}, \mathrm{tid}_0)$;
3.   **for each** $m = (u_0, \mathrm{tid}_0, e_0 = (u, v)) \in M_i$ **do**   /* merge local MSTs */
4.   **if** e_0 is in F_i and $T_u.\mathrm{tid} \neq T_v.\mathrm{tid}$ **then**
5.   merge T_u and T_v in $\mathcal{T}$ (denoted by T'); $T'.\mathrm{tid} := \min(T_u.\mathrm{tid}, T_v.\mathrm{tid})$;
6.   **for each** $T \in \mathcal{T}$ **do**   /* generate messages */
7.   **if** there exists $u \in T$ such that $v \notin T$, $u.\mathrm{tid} \neq v.\mathrm{tid}$ and $(u, v) \in E_i$ **then**
8. $e := \arg\min_{(u,v)\in E_i, u\in T, v\notin T, u.\mathrm{tid}\neq v.\mathrm{tid}} W(u, v)$; /* assume $e = (u, v)$ */
9.   **for each** border node u in T **do** $u.m := (u, u.\mathrm{tid}, (u, v))$;
10.   **for each** u in $F_i.O$ whose message has not been generated **do**
11.   **if** $u.\mathrm{tid}$ has been changed **then** $u.m := (u, u.\mathrm{tid}, \mathit{nil})$;
12. $Q(F_i \oplus M_i) := \mathcal{T}$;

Message segment: $M_i := \{u.m \mid u \in C_i\}$;

Fig. 9. IncEval for MST

(2) IncEval. Following Borůvka's algorithm, IncEval iteratively merges partial MSTs in $\mathcal{T}$. Since each message $(u_0, \mathrm{tid}_0, e_0)$ for border node u_0 tells us that (a) the minimum tid for partial MSTs containing u_0 on all fragments is tid_0, and (b) the global minimum weighted adjacent edge for expanding u_0 is e_0, IncEval connects the partial MSTs upon receiving messages in two steps. It first updates tids of all local MSTs with tid_0 so that all MSTs containing u_0 on all fragments are assigned with the same tid (lines 1–2). It further merges partial MSTs on each fragment via the aggregated global minimum weighted adjacent edge e_0 in the message, and updates the tid accordingly (lines 3–5). It then expands each updated MST in $\mathcal{T}$ and generates messages for border nodes in the same way as PEval (lines 6–11). Note that by only connecting MSTs with distinct tids (line 4) and using tids to choose minimum weighted adjacent edges (line 8), IncEval ensures that no cycle is produced in the entire process of IncEval iterations.

One can verify that the incremental IncEval is *bounded*: it takes $O(|M_i|)$ time to update the tids and merge partial MSTs, and $O(|\mathsf{AFF}|)$ time to generate messages, where AFF consists of border nodes in $F_i.O$ with changed tids, and hence, $|\mathsf{AFF}|$ is bounded by the changes of the output of IncEval.

(3) Assemble simply merges edges in the partial MSTs from all fragments and returns all the edges, as the final MST.

(4) Correctness. The process terminates as the tid's and the weights of selected adjacent edges of border nodes for connecting MSTs are monotonically decreasing by f_{aggr} until no changes can be made. Its correctness follows from the following: (a) by Prim's algorithm, PEval correctly computes MSTs of the subgraph consisting of inner edges in each fragment; and (b) by Borůvka's algorithm, IncEval correctly merges the MSTs computed by PEval into the final MST of G.

4   Experimental Study

Using real-life and synthetic graphs, we next evaluate the performance of GRAPE for its (1) efficiency, (2) communication cost, and (3) scale-up. We compared the performance of GRAPE with that of three state-of-the-art graph systems: (a) Giraph [3] and synchronized GraphLab$_{\mathsf{sync}}$ (PowerGraph [22]) under the bulk synchronous parallel model (BSP), and (b) asynchronized GraphLab$_{\mathsf{async}}$ under asynchronous model (AP) without global synchronization, when a worker has immediate access to messages, allowing fast workers to move ahead [1].

Table 1. Real-life graph information

	Graph Type	$|V|$	$|E|$	Algorithm
DBpedia	Knowledge graph	28 million	33.4 million	For Sim, MST
traffic	Road network	23 million	58 million	For SSSP, CC, MST
Friendster	Social network	65 million	1.8 billion	For SSSP, CC, Sim
UKWeb	Web graph	133 million	5 billion	For SSSP, CC, Sim

Experimental setting. We start with our settings.

Graphs. We used four real-life graphs of different types, including DBpedia [1], traffic [4], Friendster [2] and UKWeb [5], as shown in Table 1, such that each algorithm was evaluated with at least two real-life graphs. We randomly assigned weights to traffic, Friendster and UKWeb for testing SSSP and MST, and assigned up to 50 node labels to unlabeled Friendster for testing Sim.

To test the scalability of GRAPE, we developed a generator to produce graphs $G = (V, E, L)$ controlled by the number $|V|$ of nodes (up to 0.4 billion) and edges $|E|$ (up to 20 billion), with L drawn from an alphabet of 100 labels.

---

[1] GraphLab$_{\mathsf{sync}}$ and GraphLab$_{\mathsf{async}}$ run different modes of GraphLab (PowerGraph).

Queries. We randomly generated queries for SSSP and Sim. (a) For SSSP, we sampled 10 source nodes from each graph G used, such that each source node can reach 90% nodes in G. We constructed an SSSP query for each node. (b) We generated 20 pattern queries Q for Sim, controlled by $|Q| = (|V_Q|, |E_Q|, L_Q)$, where $|V_Q|$ and $|E_Q|$ denote the number of nodes and edges, respectively, using labels L_Q drawn from the graphs experimented with.

It should be remarked that GRAPE is able to load a graph G once and process query workload (*i.e.*, a set of queries) posed on G, without reloading G. In contrast, Giraph and GraphLab require the graph to be reloaded each time a single query is issued, and loading is costly over large graphs. In favor of these systems, we exclude the loading cost when reporting the experimental results.

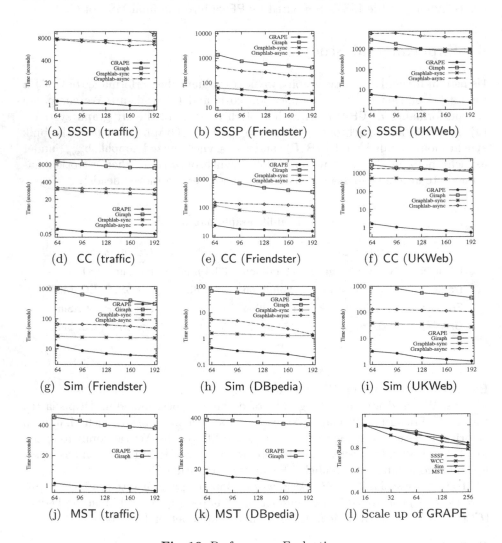

Fig. 10. Performance Evaluation

Algorithms. We evaluated the PIE programs developed in Sect. 3 for SSSP, CC, Sim and MST on GRAPE. We used "default" code provided by Giraph and GraphLab when it was available. Otherwise, we made our best efforts to develop and optimize the algorithms on the competitor systems if possible (see below).

We used the degree-based hashing (DBH) [48] algorithm to partition graphs as the default graph partition strategy. It was a state-of-the-art vertex-cut graph partition strategy. To improve the locality of partition, we first applied Xtra-PuLP [43] to graphs, and then took its output as the input of DBH.

We deployed these systems on an HPC cluster, and used servers with 16 cores of 2.40GHz, 128GB memory. Each core is treated as a worker. We ran each experiment 5 times, and the average of results is reported here.

Experimental results. We next report our findings.

Exp-1: Efficiency. We first evaluated the efficiency of GRAPE by varying the number n of workers used, from 64 to 192, compared with Giraph, GraphLab$_{sync}$ and GraphLab$_{async}$ when possible. For SSSP and CC, we experimented with real-life graphs traffic, Friendster and UKWeb; for Sim, we used Friendster, DBpedia and UKWeb; and for MST, we used traffic and DBpedia, based on applications of these algorithms in transportation networks, knowledge bases, Web and social graph analysis. We do not report times that exceeded 20000 s.

(1) SSSP. We compared the efficiency of GRAPE for SSSP with that of Giraph, GraphLab$_{sync}$ and GraphLab$_{async}$ by using "default" code provided by these systems. The results are reported in Figs. 10(a)–(c), which tell us the following.

(a) GRAPE consistently outperforms these systems. Over traffic (resp. Friendster and UKWeb), it is on average 15449 (resp. 21.5 and 310.8), 6261 (resp. 2.0 and 438.5) and 4026.7 (resp. 10.0 and 1749) times faster than Giraph, GraphLab$_{sync}$ and GraphLab$_{async}$, respectively. Note that the improvement of GRAPE on traffic is far more significant than on Friendster and UKWeb. This is because Giraph, GraphLab$_{sync}$ and GraphLab$_{async}$ adopt vertex-centric programming, which takes more "rounds" to converge on graphs with larger diameters. For instance, on Friendster, Giraph takes 36 rounds to converge, similarly for GraphLab$_{sync}$, compared with 21 rounds by GRAPE. In contrast, on traffic, a graph with larger diameter, Giraph and GraphLab$_{sync}$ take 10789 and 10778 rounds, respectively, while GRAPE takes 31 rounds. These verify the efficiency of GRAPE as a parallel engine for graph traversal algorithms such as SSSP.

(b) GRAPE is on average 2.0, 2.2 and 2.6 times faster on traffic, Friendster and UKWeb, respectively, when the number n of workers varies from 64 to 192. That is, the more workers are used, the faster SSSP runs on GRAPE.

(2) CC. We evaluated GRAPE versus Giraph, GraphLab$_{sync}$ and GraphLab$_{async}$ using their "default" code for CC. As shown in Figs. 10(d)–(f) over traffic, Friendster and UKWeb, respectively, (a) GRAPE substantially outperforms these systems. When $n = 192$, GRAPE is on average 28787, 10960 and 3957 times faster than Giraph, GraphLab$_{sync}$ and GraphLab$_{async}$ over these real-life graphs, respectively. (b) GRAPE scales well with the number of workers used: it is on average 2.3 times faster when n varies from 64 to 192.

(3) Sim. Fixing $|Q| = (6, 10)$, *i.e.*, patterns Q with 6 nodes and 10 edges, we evaluated GRAPE versus Giraph, GraphLab$_{sync}$ and GraphLab$_{async}$ for Sim. We developed Sim algorithms for the other platforms with our best efforts since neither Giraph nor GraphLab provides code for Sim. As shown in Figs. 10(g), (h) over Friendster, DBpedia and UKWeb, respectively, (a) GRAPE outperforms other systems. When $n = 192$, GRAPE is on average 195, 10.5 and 36.0 times faster than Giraph, GraphLab$_{sync}$ and GraphLab$_{async}$ over the three graphs, respectively. (b) On average GRAPE is 2.4 times faster when n varies from 64 to 192.

(4) MST. We evaluated the efficiency of GRAPE for MST versus Giraph, with code for MST from [25]. We did not compare with GraphLab$_{sync}$ and GraphLab$_{async}$ since as observed in [26], MST "cannot be implemented efficiently on GraphLab because GraphLab does not fully support graph mutations", *e.g.*, deletions of edges and vertices; such mutations are needed for an efficient implementation of MST. As shown in Figs. 10(j), (k) over traffic and DBpedia, respectively, (a) GRAPE is on average 502.7 (resp. 35.75) times faster than Giraph on traffic (resp. DBpedia), when $n = 192$. (b) GRAPE is on average 2.1 times faster when n is increased from 64 to 192, *i.e.*, GRAPE makes good use of parallelism.

Table 2. Communication cost (MB)

	Giraph	GraphLab$_{sync}$	GraphLab$_{async}$	GRAPE
SSSP				
traffic	1426920	4016909	4548842	1.2
Friendster	101758	112673	377529	11840
UKWeb	89015	297179	1514413	152.6
CC				
traffic	61419	266594	579265	1.66
Friendster	74864	100087	227475	11000
UKWeb	227754	202706	810039	112.9
Sim				
Friendster	15901	114311	10149	1182
DBpedia	871	7213	12990	7.8
UKWeb	24158	222290	310658	4.3
MST				
traffic	9300	/	/	29.6
DBpedia	2701	/	/	1119

Exp-2: Communication. We next report the communication costs of the systems. Different systems measure communication costs in different ways because each system makes use of its own implementation of message blocks and protocols [26]. For a fair comparison, we monitored the system file /proc/net/dev to report total bytes of message sent by each machine, following the practice of [26]. This metric reveals consistent results with better insights.

The communication costs over real-life graphs are reported in Table 2, when 192 workers were used. These results tell us the following. For all these algorithms, GRAPE incurs less communication costs than the other systems. On average GRAPE ships 3.9%, 3.5%, and 1.0% of data shipped by Giraph, GraphLab$_{sync}$ and GraphLab$_{async}$ for SSSP, 4.9%, 3.6% and 2.4% for CC, and 2.8%, 0.38% and 0.41% for Sim, respectively. For MST, the communication cost of GRAPE accounts for 20.5% of Giraph. In particular, GRAPE ships only 0.2%, 0.0003% and 0.00016% of data shipped by Giraph, GraphLab$_{sync}$ and GraphLab$_{async}$ on traffic. This is because GRAPE converge in far less rounds than vertex-centric systems. Among other things, GRAPE reduces communication costs by employing incremental IncEval, which ships only changed values of update parameters.

Exp-3 Scale-up of GRAPE. As observed in [34], the speed-up of a distributed system may degrade when using more workers. Thus we evaluated the scale-up of GRAPE, which measures the degradation of speed-up when both the size of graph $G = (|V|, |E|)$ and the number n of workers increase proportionally. We varied n from 16 to 256, and for each n, deployed GRAPE over a synthetic graph of size varied from $(25M, 1.25B)$ to $(0.4B, 20B)$, proportional to n.

As reported in Fig. 10(l) for SSSP, CC, Sim and MST, respectively, GRAPE preserves a reasonable scale-up, all above 0.8. We did not test with single-thread since many of the graphs are too large to fit in a single machine.

Summary. From the experimental study we find the following. (1) GRAPE consistently outperforms the state-of-the-art systems. Over real-life graphs and with 192 workers, compared to Giraph, GraphLab$_{sync}$ and GraphLab$_{async}$, GRAPE is on average (a) 5260, 2233 and 1940 times faster for SSSP, (b) 28787, 10960 and 3957 times faster for CC, and (c) 195, 10.5 and 36.0 times faster for Sim, respectively. It is 7187 times faster than Giraph for MST (as remarked earlier, GraphLab does not efficiently support MST). (2) GRAPE speeds up SSSP, CC, Sim and MST on average 2.3, 2.3, 2.4 and 2.1 times, respectively, when the number of workers n varies from 64 to 192. (3) On average, its communication costs account for 2.8%, 3.7%, 1.2% and 20.5% of the other systems for SSSP, CC, Sim and MST, respectively. (4) GRAPE has a reasonable scale-up.

These results are consistent with their counterparts reported in [19] under edge-cut partition. Compared to GRAPE under edge-cut partition, GRAPE under vertex-cut is on average 0.91 times slower for SSSP but is 1.21 times faster for CC. It incurs 79% and 56% of the communication cost under edge-cut for SSSP and CC, respectively. That is, GRAPE has comparable performance under vertex-cut and edge-cut for SSSP and CC. The PIE program for Sim under vertex-cut (Sect. 3.2) is slightly different from its counterpart under edge-cut [19]. It employs a different version of IncEval, which has to synchronize the status of border nodes. As a result, the PIE program for SIM under vertex-cut is 0.75 times slower and incurs on average 4 times more communications cost than its edge-cut counterpart. As remarked earlier, MST was not studied in [19].

5   Concluding Remarks

The main objective of GRAPE is to simplify parallel programming for graph computations, from think parallel to think sequential. It allows users to devise existing sequential graph algorithms (with declarations of update parameters and an aggregate function; see Sect. 2.2), and parallelizes the computation across a cluster of machines. It reduces the total cost of ownership and makes parallel graph computations accessible to companies that cannot afford experienced developers who are able to write, debug and analyze parallel graph algorithms. Moreover, GRAPE guarantees to converge at correct answers under a general condition as long as it is provided with correct single-machine graph algorithms, and it inherits optimization strategies developed for sequential graph algorithms.

As proof of concept (PoC), we have deployed and evaluated GRAPE at three companies. In a large online payment company, GRAPE serves as the graph computing infrastructure supporting its financial risk control system. The company employs graphs in which vertices denote customers, and edges represent transactions and associations with other customers; it needs to evaluate the customers and assign a credit. The company used to deploy its system on Neo4j + Hive + Spark. However, none of the systems can process the tasks alone; the workflow spans three systems and takes 15 minutes on average for a single query. In contrast, GRAPE provides a unified solution for this scenario. It supports real-time ad-hoc queries and offline complex score computation, without the need to couple with other systems. Moreover, GRAPE improves the performance of financial risk analyses: it is 9.0 times faster in graph batch ingesting and streaming, 128.8 times faster in association analysis, and is faster by up to 5 orders of magnitude in batch processing of real-life business applications.

GRAPE also works well for other applications. We have also carried out PoC at a company that provides big data services, and at one of the largest telecommunication equipment and service companies in the world. The results are consistent and very promising: GRAPE is able to perform a number of tasks that are not supported by the state-of-the-art graph systems, and for jobs that can also be run at other systems, it substantially outperforms the existing systems.

To the best of our knowledge, GRAPE is the first system that is able to parallelize existing sequential graph algorithms as a whole, without recasting the algorithms into a new model. Prior work on automated parallelization has focused on the instruction or operator level [36,41] by breaking dependencies via symbolic and automate analyses. There has also been work at a data partition level [51], to perform multi-level partition ("parallel abstraction") and adapt locality-optimized access to different parallel abstraction. In contrast, GRAPE does not require users to revise the logic of the existing algorithms. It makes parallel computation accessible to end users, while [36,41,51] target experienced developers of parallel algorithms. There have also been tools for translating imperative code to MapReduce, e.g., word count [38]. GRAPE advocates a different approach, by parallelizing the runs of sequential graph algorithms to benefit from data-partitioned parallelism, without translating the algorithms.

This paper extends [19] in the following. (a) We develop PIE algorithms for SSSP, CC and Sim under vertex-cut, demonstrating the adaptability of GRAPE to vertex-cut from edge-cut [19]. (b) We provide a new PIE algorithm for MST. (c) We conduct experiments using larger graphs, and demonstrate the performance of GRAPE under vertex-cut compared to its counterpart under edge-cut [19].

As a topic for future work, we are developing a new parallel model that subsumes BSP, AP and SSP (Stale Synchronous Parallel model [28] for machine learning with parameter servers [31,49]) as special cases. We are currently extending GRAPE to support the new model such that it is able to automatically switch among these models at different stages in a single execution, to optimize performance. Another topic is to support streaming updates when answering continuous queries for, *e.g.*, fraud detection, beyond static graphs assumed by existing graph systems. GRAPE is well positioned to accomplish this given that incremental computation is built in its parallel computation model.

Acknowledgments. The paper is a tribute to Professor Chaochen Zhou, who took Fan as an MSc student 30 years ago, despite pressure from a powerful person, whom Fan confronted to get justice done for his late former MSc adviser. The authors are supported in part by 973 Program 2014CB340302, ERC 652976, EPSRC EP/M025268/1, NSFC 61421003, Beijing Advanced Innovation Center for Big Data and Brain Computing, Shenzhen Peacock Program 1105100030834361, and Joint Research Lab between Edinburgh and Huawei.

References

1. DBpedia. http://wiki.dbpedia.org/Datasets
2. Friendster. https://snap.stanford.edu/data/com-Friendster.html
3. Giraph. http://giraph.apache.org/
4. Traffic. http://www.dis.uniroma1.it/challenge9/download.shtml
5. UKWeb. http://law.di.unimi.it/webdata/uk-union-2006-06-2007-05/, 2006
6. Acar, U.A.: Self-adjusting computation. Ph.D thesis, CMU (2005)
7. Andreev, K., Racke, H.: Balanced graph partitioning. Theory Comput. Syst. **39**(6), 929–939 (2006)
8. Bader, D.A., Cong, G.: Fast shared-memory algorithms for computing the minimum spanning forest of sparse graphs. J. Parallel Distrib. Comput. **66**(11), 1366–1378 (2006)
9. Bang-Jensen, J., Gutin, G.Z.: Digraphs: Theory, Algorithms and Applications. Springer, Berlin (2008)
10. Baudet, G.M.: Asynchronous iterative methods for multiprocessors. J. ACM **25**(2), 226–244 (1978)
11. Bertsekas, D.P.: Distributed asynchronous computation of fixed points. Math. Program. **27**(1), 107–120 (1983)
12. Chazan, D., Miranker, W.: Chaotic relaxation. Linear Algebr. Appl. **2**(2), 199–222 (1969)
13. Dean, J., Ghemawat, S.: MapReduce: Simplified data processing on large clusters. Commun. ACM **51**(1) (2008)
14. Fan, W., Hu, C., Tian, C.: Incremental graph computations: doable and undoable. In: SIGMOD (2017)

15. Fan, W., Li, J., Ma, S., Tang, N., Wu, Y., Wu, Y.: Graph pattern matching: from intractability to polynomial time. In: PVLDB (2010)
16. Fan, W., Wang, X., Wu, Y.: Incremental graph pattern matching. TODS **38**(3) (2013)
17. Fan, W., Wang, X., Wu, Y., Xu, J.: Association rules with graph patterns. PVLDB **8**(12), 1502–1513 (2015)
18. Fan, W., Xu, J., Wu, Y., Yu, W., Jiang, J.: GRAPE: parallelizing sequential graph computations. PVLDB **10**(12), 1889–1892 (2017)
19. Fan, W., et al.: Parallelizing sequential graph computations. In: SIGMOD (2017)
20. Fredman, M.L., Tarjan, R.E.: Fibonacci heaps and their uses in improved network optimization algorithms. JACM **34**(3), 596–615 (1987)
21. Gallager, R.G., Humblet, P.A., Spira, P.M.: A distributed algorithm for minimum-weight spanning trees. TOPLAS **5**(1), 66–77 (1983)
22. Gonzalez, J.E., Low, Y., Gu, H., Bickson, D., Guestrin, C.: PowerGraph: distributed graph-parallel computation on natural graphs. In: USENIX (2012)
23. Gonzalez, J.E., Xin, R.S., Dave, A., Crankshaw, D., Franklin, M.J., Stoica, I.: GraphX: graph processing in a distributed dataflow framework. In: OSDI (2014)
24. Grujic, I., Bogdanovic-Dinic, S., Stoimenov, L.: Collecting and analyzing data from E-Government Facebook pages. In: ICT Innovations (2014)
25. Han, M., Daudjee, K.: Giraph unchained: barrierless asynchronous parallel execution in pregel-like graph processing systems. PVLDB **8**(9), 950–961 (2015)
26. Han, M., Daudjee, K., Ammar, K., Ozsu, M.T., Wang, X., Jin, T.: An experimental comparison of Pregel-like graph processing systems. VLDB **7**(12) (2014)
27. Henzinger, M.R., Henzinger, T., Kopke, P.: Computing simulations on finite and infinite graphs. In: FOCS (1995)
28. Ho, Q., et al.: More effective distributed ML via a stale synchronous parallel parameter server. In: NIPS, pp. 1223–1231 (2013)
29. Jones, N.D.: An introduction to partial evaluation. ACM Comput. Surv. **28**(3) (1996)
30. Kim, M., Candan, K.S.: SBV-Cut: vertex-cut based graph partitioning using structural balance vertices. Data Knowl. Eng. **72**, 285–303 (2012)
31. Li, M., et al.: Parameter server for distributed machine learning. In: NIPS Workshop on Big Learning (2013)
32. Low, Y., Gonzalez, J., Kyrola, A., Bickson, D., Guestrin, C., Hellerstein, J.M.: Distributed graphlab: a framework for machine learning in the cloud. PVLDB **5**(8) (2012)
33. Malewicz, G., et al.: Pregel: a system for large-scale graph processing. In: SIGMOD (2010)
34. McSherry, F., Isard, M., Murray, D.G.: Scalability! but at what cost? In: HotOS (2015)
35. Nesetril, J., Milková, E., Nesetrilová, H.: Otakar boruvka on minimum spanning tree problem. Discret. Math. **233**(1–3), 3–36 (2001)
36. Pingali, K., et al.: The tao of parallelism in algorithms. In: PLDI (2011)
37. Prim, R.C.: Shortest connection networks and some generalizations. Bell Syst. Tech. J. **36**(6) (1957)
38. Radoi, C., Fink, S.J., Rabbah, R.M., Sridharan, M.: Translating imperative code to mapreduce. In: OOPSLA (2014)
39. Ramalingam, G., Reps, T.: An incremental algorithm for a generalization of the shortest-path problem. J. Algorithms **21**(2), 267–305 (1996)
40. Ramalingam, G., Reps, T.: On the computational complexity of dynamic graph problems. TCS **158**(1–2) (1996)

41. Raychev, V., Musuvathi, M., Mytkowicz, T.: Parallelizing user-defined aggregations using symbolic execution. In: SOSP (2015)
42. Shao, B., Wang, H., Li, Y.: Trinity: a distributed graph engine on a memory cloud. In: SIGMOD (2013)
43. Slota, G.M., Rajamanickam, S., Devine, K., Madduri, K.: Partitioning trillion-edge graphs in minutes. In: IPDPS (2017)
44. Tian, Y., Balmin, A., Corsten, S.A., Shirish Tatikonda, J.M.: From "think like a vertex" to "think like a graph". PVLDB **7**(7), 193–204 (2013)
45. Valiant, L.G.: A bridging model for parallel computation. Commun. ACM **33**(8), 103–111 (1990)
46. Valiant, L.G.: General purpose parallel architectures. Handbook of Theoretical Computer Science, vol. A (1990)
47. Wang, G., Xie, W., Demers, A.J., Gehrke, J.: Asynchronous large-scale graph processing made easy. In: CIDR (2013)
48. Xie, C., Yan, L., Li, W.-J., Zhang, Z.: Distributed power-law graph computing: theoretical and empirical analysis. In: NIPS (2014)
49. Xing, E.P., Ho, Q., Dai, W., Kim, J.K., Wei, J., Lee, S., Zheng, X., Xie, P., Kumar, A., Petuum, YYu.: A new platform for distributed machine learning on big data. IEEE Trans. Big Data **1**(2), 49–67 (2015)
50. Yan, D., Cheng, J., Lu, Y., Ng, W.: Blogel: a block-centric framework for distributed computation on real-world graphs. PVLDB **7**(14), 1981–1992 (2014)
51. Zhou, Y., Liu, L., Lee, K., Pu, C., Zhang, Q.: Fast iterative graph computation with resource aware graph parallel abstractions. In: HPDC (2015)

Concurrency: Handling Interference Formally

Cliff B. Jones[✉]

School of Computing, Newcastle University, Newcastle upon Tyne, UK
cliff.jones@ncl.ac.uk

Abstract. Interference between threads makes it difficult to design concurrent programs. Faced with such a difficulty, it is reasonable to seek clarification and leverage from formality. Whereas powerful abstractions have been found for sequential programming languages, the inherent operational nature of interference infects attempts to describe it formally. Model-oriented (i.e. operational and denotational) and property-oriented (mainly axiomatic) descriptions of the semantics of programming languages that support shared-variable concurrency look totally different. This paper identifies the source of the challenge as accommodating interference and highlights some important connections between the approaches.

1 Introduction

Frighteningly many *high level* programming languages have been invented over the relatively short history of computer science. Some of the thousands of languages genuinely offer new concepts (e.g. *objects* in Simula [DMN68]); all too often new languages are marred by failure on the parts of their designers to learn from previous successes and failures; almost invariably new features interact in unpredictable and confusing ways with previously understood concepts. In only a handful of cases has an explicit use of formalism informed the design of a language. More often, the formalist is faced with the unenviable task of *post facto* formalisation and finding abstractions that model undesirable feature interactions.

The focus of this paper is on those languages that allow concurrent threads to access and change shared variables. Here again, there is a significant diversity of ways in which concurrency is initiated and controlled. A central challenge is the *interference* that is the inevitable result of shared-variable concurrency. The interest in this paper is on approaches to the formal description of programming languages that admit interference. The description task is to characterise exactly the range of possible outcomes of executing a program. It proves difficult to achieve this without becoming concrete about low-level details of the language in question.

The near-standard taxonomy of formal semantic methods distinguishes operational, denotational and axiomatic approaches (with the more recent addition

© Springer Nature Switzerland AG 2018
C. Jones et al. (Eds.): Zhou-Festschrift, LNCS 11180, pp. 26–43, 2018.
https://doi.org/10.1007/978-3-030-01461-2_2

of algebraic semantics). It is sometimes useful to think of operational and denotational approaches as *model-oriented* and to group axiomatic and algebraic approaches as *property-oriented*.[1] This grouping reflects the fact that the former pair use an explicit notion of *state* (albeit abstract) in their descriptions whereas property-oriented descriptions attempt to eschew explicit states.

Rather than contribute yet another formal semantic approach, the objective here is to discuss in detail how the various approaches record the meaning of interfering threads. By considering the underlying concepts of an approach (and getting behind their syntactic details), it is possible to observe deep connections and throw the actual differences into sharper relief.

As an indication of the challenge of interference, consider the possible executions of Program 1 that has two threads each of which consist of a sequence of assignment statements:

$$(x \leftarrow 1; \ x \leftarrow x + 3) \ || \ (x \leftarrow 2; \ x \leftarrow x * 2) \tag{1}$$

For now, it is assumed that assignments are executed as atomic statements—finer granularity of merges is addressed in Sect. 2.2 below. There are six different ways in which the threads can merge in Program 1; depending on which happens, the final value of x' can be any value in the set $\{4, 5, 7, 8, 10\}$

Program 1 is not likely to be useful but the interference can actually be at least as complicated in realistic examples. The following code is an implementation of an example taken from [Owi75]—the task is to find the lowest index (t) to a vector of values (v, indexed from $1..N$) such that $p(v(t))$ holds—executing two[2] parallel threads has the potential to reduce the execution time:

```
var ot, et ← N + 1, N + 1;
/  var oc ← 1;                        var ec ← 2;                \
|  while oc < min(ot, et) do          while ec < min(et, ot) do   |
|     if p(v(oc)) then ot ← oc           if p(v(ec)) then et ← ec  | ;
\     else oc ← oc + 2                    else ec ← ec + 2        /
t ← min(ot, et)
```

(A version of the above in which both threads can assign to t has a write/write data race on t which would require messy locking. Reifying t to $min(ot, et)$ removes the need for locking but leaves interference between –say– writing ot in one thread and it being read in the while test of the other thread. The proof in [HJ18] does not make unrealistic atomicity assumptions.)

---

[1] A wider review of the challenges that arise in writing formal semantic descriptions is given in [JA17]; more historical context is given in [JA16] (which will appear in the proceedings of HaPoP-16 as [AJ18]).

[2] Any partition of $\{1..N\}$ will serve—choosing to split odd/even indexes is notationally convenient and abbreviates the presentation.

2   Model-Oriented Formal Semantics

Underlying a model-oriented semantics is the choice of the semantic objects in terms of which the effect of a computation is expressed. For a basic language, the states might be simple associations of values with the names of identifiers:[3]

$$\Sigma = Id \xrightarrow{m} \mathbb{N}$$

and the denotations of statements would be functions from states to states:

$$\Sigma \to \Sigma$$

For a sequential language without concurrency, the meaning function (M) would map assignments (or sequences thereof) to such denotations:

$$M: Assn^* \to (\Sigma \to \Sigma)$$

A commonly used argument for denotational semantics is that it is compositional in the sense that the meaning of a composite construct C in the language is given (by a homomorphic function) in terms of the meanings of the constituents of C.

$$M[\![([s] \curvearrowright rl)]\!] \triangleq M[\![s]\!] \circ M[\![rl]\!]$$

The majority of the discussion of model-oriented semantics below is based on the operational approach; Sect. 2.4 briefly reviews the additional issues seen in denotational semantics.

For most sequential language constructs, the differences between a denotational and a *Structural Operational Semantics* (SOS) [Plo81] are small: one could say they differ only by a Lambda abstraction (on Σ). Compare:

$$M[\![mk\text{-}Assn(lhs, rhs)]\!] \triangleq \lambda\sigma \cdot \sigma \dagger \{lhs \mapsto eval(rhs, \sigma)\}$$

with:

$$exec : Assn \times \Sigma \to \Sigma$$

$$exec(mk\text{-}Assn(lhs, rhs), \sigma) \triangleq \sigma \dagger \{lhs \mapsto eval(rhs, \sigma)\}$$

Gordon Plotkin had made fundamental contributions to domain theory [Plo76] before he went on sabbatical to Aarhus in 1981 (see Sect. 2.4). It is therefore interesting that he took the decision to base his lectures on operational semantics. His 1981 Aarhus notes [Plo81] were republished as [Plo04b] and he wrote an accompanying reflection [Plo04a].[4]

---

[3] The use of VDM notation will hopefully present no difficulty: it has been widely used for decades and is the subject of an ISO standard; one useful reference is [Jon90].

[4] At the time Plotkin's useful commentary was being written, the current author was writing [Jon03b] and drafts were exchanged between Plotkin and Jones that enriched the cross references.

A *big step* (or *natural*) SOS rule for sequences of assignments can still be viewed as *compositional* in some sense:

$execl : Assn^* \times \Sigma \to \Sigma$

$execl([s] \frown rl, \sigma) \triangleq execl(rl, exec(s, \sigma))$

The crucial difference between the two model-oriented approaches is that proofs about operational semantics nearly always revolve around induction over the computation whereas reasoning about denotational descriptions of semantics can be conducted at a higher level of abstraction. The material in the remainder of this section casts doubt on whether this advantage for denotational semantics survives the challenge of concurrency.

2.1   SOS of Concurrency

The operational semantics in the preceding section is presented as functions; the crucial step made in [Plo81] was to simplify the move to a relational view of semantics by writing SOS descriptions as rules of inference.

For a language whose programs contain two threads of assignments:

$Program :: sl1 : Assn^*$
$\qquad\qquad\ \ sl2 : Assn^*$

Using the relations:

$$\xrightarrow{stl}: \mathscr{P}((Stmt^* \times \Sigma) \times \Sigma)$$

$$\xrightarrow{nd}: \mathscr{P}((Program \times \Sigma) \times \Sigma)$$

the following two SOS rules:

$$\frac{(sl1, \sigma) \xrightarrow{stl} \sigma'}{(sl2, \sigma') \xrightarrow{stl} \sigma''}$$
$$\frac{}{(sl1 \parallel sl2, \sigma) \xrightarrow{nd} \sigma''}$$

$$\frac{(sl2, \sigma) \xrightarrow{stl} \sigma'}{(sl1, \sigma') \xrightarrow{stl} \sigma''}$$
$$\frac{}{(sl1 \parallel sl2, \sigma) \xrightarrow{nd} \sigma''}$$

introduce non-determinacy but admit only two of the possible outcomes of Program 1. In order to express all of the results identified in Sect. 1, it is necessary to have a relation over *configurations* that pair the text remaining to be executed with a state:

$$\xrightarrow{par}: \mathscr{P}((Program \times \Sigma) \times (Program \times \Sigma))$$

the SOS rules then become:

$$\frac{(s1, \sigma) \xrightarrow{st} \sigma'}{([s1] \curvearrowright rl1 \parallel sl2, \sigma) \xrightarrow{par} ((rl1 \parallel sl2), \sigma')}$$

$$\frac{(s2, \sigma) \xrightarrow{st} \sigma'}{(sl1 \parallel [s2] \curvearrowright rl2, \sigma) \xrightarrow{par} ((sl1 \parallel rl2), \sigma')}$$

these form a *small step* semantics. It is important to look carefully at what is going on in such a semantic description: not only is it the case that either rule matches a program in which both threads are non-empty (as is the case initially in Program 1); it is also true that the pattern matching with the program part of the configuration reconsiders the whole program at each step of the computation.

Section 2.3 contains some comments about the evolution of research into operational semantics but it is worth noting here that Plotkin's SOS rules:

- make it explicit that the semantics for non-determinacy must be a relation; and
- neatly factor out the non-determinism to the selection of which semantic rule is chosen.

The second point leads to a much more readable description than would attempts to use:

$$exec: Stmt^* \times \Sigma \rightarrow \Sigma\text{-set}$$

2.2   Granularity

The task of the person describing semantics of a language is to delimit exactly the set of permissible outcomes of executing a text in that language. Investigating a finer level of atomicity (than assignments) makes it possible to reinforce and perhaps clarify some points about model-oriented semantics and interference.

The assumption that assignment statements can be executed atomically (e.g. in Program 1) is unrealistic. Any compiler will map each assignment statement to a series of load and store instructions and the most likely unit of atomicity at the machine level would be access and change of a machine word. A compiler could in theory generate something like semaphores that achieved atomicity at the assignment level but the code would be inefficient.[5]

At the finer level of granularity, Program 1 could deliver a state where $x' = 2$ because execution of $x \leftarrow x * 2$ could effectively be interrupted between the right hand access to x and the left hand change—making this explicit with a temporary variable t the computation could be:

$$x \leftarrow 2; \; x \leftarrow 1; \; t \leftarrow x; \; x \leftarrow x + 3; \; x \leftarrow t * 2 \qquad (2)$$

---

[5] The rule that is erroneously referred to as *Reynold's rule* states that there should be only one shared variable in any assignment—this does not provide a general semantics.

Leaving aside the possibility of side effects caused by function calls, the semantics of expression evaluation would need to contain rules such as:

$$\frac{e \in Id}{(e,\sigma) \xrightarrow{ex} (\sigma(e),\sigma)}$$

$$\frac{v1, v2 \in \mathbb{Z}}{(mk\text{-}Addition(v1, v2),\sigma) \xrightarrow{ex} (v1 + v2,\sigma)}$$

It is important to realise that, after any variable de-reference to obtain its value, the tree of the remaining text is updated by replacing the identifier with the value; then the whole text in the configuration is available for the next match.

This semantics is now very much *small step*. But that is precisely what is required to explain realistic interference.

There is also an interesting contrast that can be made: there is a distinction between the non-determinism that results from (assignment) statement execution and expression evaluation:

- at the statement level, the state can be changed and it is necessary to carry forward both the remaining text and the current state (in the configuration);
- at the expression level, the effect of accessing a variable is represented by substituting the value in place of the identifier which caused its access.

2.3   Operational Semantics: A Little Context

As indicated in Sect. 1, the main purpose of the current paper is to investigate technical issues around concurrency; although historical material has been reviewed at some length elsewhere [JA16, JA17], a brief review of some earlier attempts to provide operational semantic descriptions helps clarify technical issues.

A key contributor to formal semantics was John McCarthy. The paper [McC66] that he presented at the 1964 IFIP Working Conference in Baden-bei-Wien on *Formal Language Description Languages*[6] is a useful checkpoint:

- it argues that an *abstract* syntax is a better basis for recording semantics than the more widely known concrete syntax (e.g. as given by BNF);
- it provides an operational semantics for "micro-ALGOL".

McCarthy's choice of features for inclusion in his subset of ALGOL is interesting. He could have chosen assignment, sequential composition, conditional and while loops; this would have illustrated most of what he wanted to show and would have had a more elegant and tractable semantics. In fact, he included labels and jumps. This choice necessitates keeping the whole program text plus a form of program counter in the state.

---

[6] The proceedings [Ste66] took two years to appear but are invaluable partly because they include transcripts of the recorded discussions.

The group at the IBM Vienna Laboratory always acknowledged (e.g. in [LW69])[7] McCarthy as providing a key influence on their efforts to formalise the semantics of the PL/I language using their VDL (operational) approach. PL/I was, of course, a vastly more challenging object of study:

- PL/I is a huge language!
- it certainly includes non-determinacy on the order of expression evaluation (complicated by the fact that side-effects can be caused by invoking functions)
- there is even deliberate under specification of how composite values are mapped onto machine storage—this led Hans Bekič and Kurt Walk to devise a form of axiomatic storage model [BW71]
- concurrency comes about from an involved *Tasking* feature
- PL/I also provides a complex exception mechanism

Although PL/I is entirely different in scale from Micro-ALGOL, one can see the complex *control tree* of VDL descriptions as an extension of McCarthy's way of handling jumps: control trees in VDL models retain the entire active text of a program being executed. In the case of concurrent execution, the single program counter is replaced by the rule that any leaf of the tree is available as the next step of a computation.

An even more interesting comparison is between VDL and SOS. Superficially, definitions in these two styles look totally different: VDL descriptions are written as though the semantics was a (non-deterministic) function; as seen in Sect. 2.1, the inference rules of SOS descriptions succeed in allowing non-determinism whilst retaining a natural reading. But underneath this notational difference, both styles are representing the text that still has to be executed. There is the oft-repeated argument that it was unfortunate that VDL descriptions used a *grand state* approach[8] but this does not really set SOS apart from VDL because configurations in SOS descriptions actually pair the text with the state and appear on both sides of the semantic relation. Even the worry that the control tree could be changed in arbitrary ways can be reproduced with configurations (in neither case would it be wise to do this without good reason).

2.4   Denotational Semantics and Interference

The powerful abstraction of using functions from states to states (see [Sto77]) as denotations of sequential programs does not cope with *interference*. The clearest connection with operational semantics is the use of *resumptions* that embody a step-by-step behaviour.

An additional issue that becomes more delicate with concurrency is the denotation of program constructs that fail to terminate.

---

[7] They also always mentioned Cal Elgot and Peter Landin.
[8] The adverse effects on proofs of putting unnecessary things in the state are examined in [JA16, §3].

Denotations that are sets of traces are used for process algebras. It is, however, worth emphasising that process algebras do not avoid the problem of *interference* as can be seen by the ease with which analogues of shared variables can be programmed in, for example, the π-calculus [MPW92,SW01].

3 Axiomatic View

Axiomatic semantics are tuned to reasoning about programs in a language (as opposed to reasoning about processors of the language—or the language *per se*). There is a deliberate attempt to minimise any underlying (state) model in axiomatic descriptions. The question here, however, is the impact of *interference* on the axiomatic approach to semantics.

For sequential programs, Tony Hoare's seminal paper [Hoa69] on the axiomatic method[9] offers rules of inference about judgements represented as triples that relate pre and post conditions to program constructs — for example:

$$; \text{-}intro \frac{\{P\}\ S1\ \{Q\}\quad \{Q\}\ S2\ \{R\}}{\{P\}\ S1; S2\ \{R\}}$$

for sequential composition.[10] There is, again, a sense in which this rule is *compositional*: the task of satisfying some overall specification (P/R), can be decomposed into two sub-tasks whose specifications are independent of that of their sibling and of the overall specification.

A relational view of specifications copes well with non-determinism and this has the pleasing payoff that non-deterministic specifications can be used to delay design decisions in formal developments. Unfortunately, even the powerful idea of non-deterministic post conditions does not itself overcome the challenge of interference. The difficulty is precisely that a post condition is inadequate to describe semantics in the presence of *interference*.

In [Hoa72], various degrees of interaction between parallel processes are considered. For the simplest case, the following rule holds:

$$\| \text{-}intro \frac{\{P1\}\ S1\ \{Q1\}\quad \{P2\}\ S2\ \{Q2\}}{\{P1 \wedge P2\}\ S1 \parallel S2\ \{Q1 \wedge Q2\}}$$

---

[9] Hoare's path from a comment made at the 1964 *Formal Language Description Languages* Working Conference in Baden-bei-Wien to his *Axiomatic Basis* paper [Hoa69] is outlined in [JA16]. The relation to (but lack of influence of) earlier work by Turing and von Neumann is discussed in [Jon03a].

[10] The decision to employ predicates of a single state even for post conditions looks convenient especially in this rule but the choice results in messy tricks to circumvent the fact that a specification should obviously relate the initial and final states—VDM [Jon80], Z [Hay86] and B [Abr96] all use relations.

But this "axiom" holds only if there is no interference between $S1$ ans $S2$.. This points to a discussion of Separation Logic (Sect. 3.1).

Susan Owicki's thesis [Owi75] (see also [OG76]) addresses reasoning about programs that admit interference. Essentially, the *Owicki/Gries* approach requires that normal Hoare-style proofs are first conducted for each thread; this is then followed by a global *Einmischungsfrei* proof that establishes that the proofs of the threads do not interfere with each other. Apart from requiring a lot of work, there is one obvious major reservation about this approach: it is non-compositional in the sense that final code must be available for all threads before the *interference freedom* proof obligation can be discharged. Thus it is completely possible that a designer could decompose an overall task into –say– two threads, record their pre/post conditions and have programmers develop verified code that satisfies the specifications of each thread but then discover that their proofs interfere facing the programmers with no choice but to start over!

There is also a less obvious danger in the *Owicki-Gries* method and that is the assumption about granularity. The interference freedom step (as well as the proof outlines of the threads) is conducted under the assumption that assignment statements are executed atomically. As is made clear in Sect. 2.2, this is not a realistic assumption.

3.1   Separation Logic

At a conference in Cambridge (UK) in April 2009, Peter O'Hearn acknowledged that the $\parallel$ *-intro* rule in the preceding section can be seen as a pre-echo of the ideas behind *Concurrent Separation Logic* (CSL).

John Reynolds introduced *Separation Logic* in [Rey02] as a way of reasoning about sequential programs that manipulate heap variables. After some strong interaction with colleagues at CMU (recalled in [BO16]), O'Hearn's key publication on CSL [O'H07] was presented at a session of MFPS in honour of John Reynolds.

The key rule in CSL for introducing parallelism uses *separating conjunction* ($*$):

$$\boxed{\parallel \text{-}intro\text{-}SL}\ \frac{\{P1\}\ S1\ \{Q1\}\quad \{P2\}\ S2\ \{Q2\}}{\{P1 * P2\}\ S1 \parallel S2\ \{Q1 * Q2\}}$$

In contrast to the standard form, separating conjunction is only applicable where the variables affecting the two conjuncts are disjoint. This is also another significant step beyond Hoare's rule above: Hoare was considering *stack variables* where disjointness was a simple check of identifiers; CSL treats *heap variables* that are identified by their addresses. In fact, it might have been useful to use the adjective *ownership* for such logics.

An interesting observation is that an operational semantics rule along the lines of:

$$\frac{(S1, \sigma) \xrightarrow{st} \sigma' \quad (S2, \tau) \xrightarrow{st} \tau'}{(S1 \parallel S2, \sigma \cup \tau) \xrightarrow{par} \sigma' \cup \tau'}$$

$$\sigma, \sigma', \tau, \tau' \in (Address \xrightarrow{m} Value)$$

actually gives precisely the separation (or ownership) condition of Separation Logic because VDM's map union operator is undefined if the domains of its operands are not disjoint.

Another interesting perspective on Separation Logic is given in [JY15] where it is argued that separation can be viewed as an abstraction that has to be realised in any reification to heap data structures. The examples tackled in [JY15] are:

- Reynolds' in-place list reversal where it is straightforward to see how an abstraction which separates the initial and final sequences can be represented in a single heap. It then becomes a proof obligation to establish that the chosen heap representation preserves the assumption of separation. Since this first example has no concurrency, neither Separation Logic nor Rely/Guarantee reasoning (see Sect. 3.2) are required.
- The second example is taken from O'Hearn's treatment in CSL of parallel merge sort [O'H07]. In [JY15], the use of the abstraction of separation serves to give an initial algorithm whose correctness is obvious. Because sub-lists are sorted in parallel, a single simple use of a Rely/Guarantee law is needed to complete the development—the development without Separation Logic makes an interesting comparison with [O'H07].

It is perhaps worth summarising some other observations about SL that have been made elsewhere (e.g. [JA17]):

- although SL handles ownership reasoning in some cases, it appears to be challenged by the ownership of 'slots' in Simpson's '4-slot' implementation of *Asynchronous Communication Mecanisms* (ACMs): Richard Bornat who is a contributor to (and fan of) SL uses both SL and R/G in [BA10] and R/G and *Linearisability* in [BA11]; Wang&Wang do use SL to argue about slot ownership in [WW10] but fail to prove the crucial 'freshness' property of ACMs;
- there is somewhat of a 'growth industry' in that new Separation Logics are perhaps too frequently introduced; Matt Parkinson who is a key contributor warned of this tendency in his paper [Par10] on *The next 700 SLs*; it remains to be seen if *Views* [DYBG+13] stem the flow..

As its adjective implies, Separation Logic is not an approach that helps with interference.

3.2 Rely/Guarantee

The motivation for the research on *Rely/Guarantee* (R/G) methods was to find a compositional development method for concurrent programs. To achieve this, it was realised that interference must be tackled head on in both specifications and proof obligations.

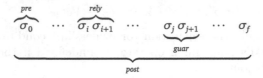

Fig. 1. A trace of states made by execution of a component and its environment

Basic R/G Concept. The core of the idea is simple: details of actual interference can be abstracted by recording relations about environmental state changes. See Fig. 1 which shows a component step constrained by *guar* and an environment step similarly constrained by *rely* (as well as the conventional *pre* limiting initial states and *post* defining the valid relation between initial and final states).

More references both to R/G research and related approaches can be found in [HJ18][11]—here the following summary should suffice:

- the first book on the program development aspects of VDM was [Jon80] but it only coped with sequential programs (the approach did however embody a meaningful notion of compositionality in both operation decomposition and data refinement);
- R/G was an attempt to provide a related compositional development method for concurrent programs;
- as indicated at the beginning of Sect. 3, the Owicki/Gries method was not compositional (for more detail on this, see [dR01]);
- Jones' Oxford thesis [Jon81] provides proof obligations (POs) for rely and guarantee conditions—the key PO is shown to be sound with respect to a (rather heavy) VDL semantics;
- early publications [Jon83a, Jon83b] used keywords to identify rely and guarantee conditions (in addition to defining the *frame* of each operation together with its pre and post conditions);
- specifications could also be presented as five-tuples $\{P, R\} \ S \ \{G, Q\}$;
- more recently, in collaboration with Ian Hayes [HJC14, JHC15], R/G has been completely recast in a *refinement calculus* style [Mor90, BvW98];
- the R/G idea has been shown to be rather general and has been applied to the development of fault-tolerant control systems that link to components which change continuously [HJJ03, JHJ07, Jon10].

---

[11] Particularly interesting Chinese references include [Fen09, LFF12, Lia14].

Pulling R/G Apart. The details of one or other presentation of the R/G concept are actually less important than the overall picture shown in Fig. 1 but to give a flavour of how [HJC14, JHC15] has "pulled apart" the five-tuple form of R/G:

- the *Refinement Calculus* presents specifications as $x \colon [P, Q]$ (with the option of omitting pre conditions that are **true**);
- the ordering $S \sqsubseteq C$ asserts that S refines to C in the sense that C meets all of the requirements of S;
- $S1 = S2$ means that both $S1 \sqsubseteq S2$ and $S2 \sqsubseteq S1$ hold;
- it is allowed to wrap **rely** $R \cdot C$ or **guar** $G \cdot C$ around any construct C.

Some R/G Laws. A crucial advantage of this refinement calculus presentation is that algebraic properties of R/G are apparent as is illustrated by the following four laws:

- nested guarantee conditions correspond to the conjunction of the guarantee relations
  $$(\mathbf{guar}\ g_1 \cdot (\mathbf{guar}\ g_2 \cdot c)) = (\mathbf{guar}\ g_1 \wedge g_2 \cdot c)$$
- introducing a guarantee condition only makes implementation more challenging
  $$c \sqsubseteq (\mathbf{guar}\ g \cdot c)$$
- because a guarantee condition has to apply to every step of a computation, its transitive closure can be removed from a post condition
  $$(\mathbf{guar}\ g \cdot [g^* \wedge q]) = (\mathbf{guar}\ g \cdot [q])$$
- a symmetric version[12] of the basic R/G concurrency law is
  $$[\wedge_i q_i] \sqsubseteq \ \|_i\ (\mathbf{guar}\ gr \cdot (\mathbf{rely}\ gr \cdot [q_i]))$$

The above four laws can be used to justify the abstract level of a *parallel sieve of Eratosthenes* that computes the prime numbers up to some given maximum; [HJ18] takes this development through to running code using a *compare and swap* instruction at the level of setting bits within a word.

The R/G approach is to cope with interference by *abstraction*: a rely condition r indicates that its specified component must tolerate steps of interference but that the state changes that occur will not violate the rely relation r.

An important aspect of R/G development is that the approach does not commit to a level of granularity; this is a subtle point that is easier to comprehend in actual complete developments but it can be seen as deriving from the algebraic property that guarantee conditions distribute over both semicolon and parallel decomposition.

Semantic Model(s). Any set of R/G laws needs to be shown to be consistent with an underlying model of the language: a *Structural Operational Semantics* is used in [Col08, CJ07]; more recent papers (e.g. [CHM16]) use *Aczel traces*

---

[12] The asymmetric version needed in examples such as *concurrent garbage collection* [JVY17] or *Asynchronous Communication Mechanisms* [JH16] is actually more interesting.

[Acz83] as denotations. In [Hay16], proofs are simplified by using properties such as *interchange laws*.

Expressiveness. The description in this section on R/G is not aimed at selling the approach as a way of developing concurrent, shared-variable, programs. In fact, the limitation of using only relations as a way of abstracting interference is discussed in [JVY17]. The point of the description of R/G is to make clear that it is quite difficult to step away from the operational nature of such interference.

An alternative is to use a more expressive logic like that from the Augsburg group: RGITL [STE+14] marries *Interval Temporal Logic* [Mos86] with R/G. This combination is powerful enough to express details of the interference but as argued in [HJ18] might be too expressive in the sense that ITL can be used to encode every environment step.

Further insight into interference can be obtained by looking at a notation that arose as an extension of R/G. Interference has the effect that a variable might have many values during the execution of an operation. Suppose an operation has read access to a variable y, writing:

$$x \colon [x' = y \vee x' = y']$$

expresses only that the final value of x has either the value of y at the beginning of the operation or the value of y at the end of the execution. Such a specification fails, for example, to be satisfied by:

$$x \leftarrow y$$

in a context where the interfering environment could change the value of y several times. This realisation led to the introduction of a notation for *possible values* where $\widehat{y}$ denotes the set of values that can arise during execution of the operation in whose post condition this is written. Thus:

$$x \colon [x' \in \widehat{y}] \sqsubseteq (x \leftarrow y)$$

The need for a concept such as *possible values* is a direct consequence of interference. The need was realised and introduced in [JP11], is related to *non-deterministic expression evaluation* in [HBDJ13] and studied further in [JH16].

4   Conclusions

Even for a non-concurrent language, it is essential that the semantics fixes the order of execution of statements. This normally left-to-right order is easy to see in an operational or denotational semantics. Interference in programming languages is a very operational concept and pushes language descriptions into allowing and constraining the ways that processes can merge. One strength of SOS descriptions is that they somewhat mitigate this complication. But at their core, they have to fix the granularity and control the merging just as much as was required in VDL control trees: interference from other threads must be allowed to occur between each step.

Axiomatic semantics either attempt to ban interference (data races) or abstract from the details of interference. It is clearly worth considering ways in which programming language design can constrain interference and there is a long history of proposals such as monitors [Bri73, Hoa74]. The fact that object-oriented languages such as Pierre America's POOL [Ame89] limit access to variables to their defining object makes them particularly promising. But, whatever constraints are adopted, the fact that some applications require shared resources must be accommodated. The descriptions of SL (Sect. 3.1) and R/G (Sect. 3.2) are unlikely to be seen as impartial but the presentation is not intended in a competitive way. The topic of the paper is interference and it should be clear that R/G thinking does take this aspect of concurrency seriously. If there is one idea that is argued to be universally important it is the use of abstraction (in various contexts) — hopefully few would argue with this claim.

A final word is in order about algebraic approaches to semantics. These are attractive in the sense that they can elevate the level of reasoning about languages but more research is required to see how properties that do not even determine the order of execution to be left-to-right can fix the level of granularity of interference.

These difficulties could be met with a reaction that designers should make interference impossible in the programming language that they propose. This is one of the motivations behind the development of process algebras such as CSP [Hoa85], CCS [Mil89] and π-calculus [SW01] but, since it is possible to emulate shared variables as processes, this can at most shift the argument to the question of whether reasoning about interference in terms of trace assertions is really easier than assertions about the values of shared variables themselves.

Dedication

It is an enormous pleasure to dedicate this paper to my friend and colleague Zhou Chaochen. From our first time together in Oxford around 1980, I have followed his work with interest and admiration. The wonderful visit that he arranged for Tony Hoare, me and both of our families cemented the contact between our families and so it was a special privilege to join in the 2017 celebration in his honour. I humbly offer this paper with best wishes to Chaochen.

References

[Abr96] Abrial, J.-R.: The B-Book: Assigning Programs to Meanings. Cambridge University Press, Cambridge (1996)

[Acz83] Aczel, P.H.G.: On an inference rule for parallel composition. (private communication) Manuscript, Manchester (1983)

[AJ18]   Astarte, T.K., Jones, C.B.: Formal semantics of ALGOL 60: four descriptions in their historical context. In: De Mol, L., Primiero, G. (eds.) Reflections on Programming Systems - Historical and Philosophical Aspects. Springer Philosophical Studies Series, pp. 71–141. In press (2018)

[Ame89]   America, P.: Issues in the design of a parallel object-oriented language. Form. Asp. Comput. **1**, 366–411 (1989)

[BA10]   Bornat, R., Amjad, H.: Inter-process buffers in separation logic with rely-guarantee. Form. Asp. Comput. **22**(6), 735–772 (2010)

[BA11]   Bornat, R., Amjad, H.: Explanation of two non-blocking shared-variable communication algorithms. Form. Asp. Comput. 1–39 (2011)

[BO16]   Brookes, S., W O'Hearn, P.: Concurrent separation logic. ACM SIGLOG News 3(3), 47–65 (2016)

[Bri73]   Brinch Hansen, P.: Concurrent programming concepts. ACM Comput. Surv. **5**, 223–245 (1973)

[BvW98]   Back, R.-J.R., von Wright, J.: Refinement Calculus: A Systematic Introduction. Springer, New York (1998)

[BW71]   Bekič, H., Walk, K.: Formalization of storage properties. In: Engeler, E. (ed.) Eng71, pp. 28–61. Springer, Berlin (1971)

[CHM16]   Colvin, R.J., Hayes, I.J., Meinicke, L.A.: Designing a semantic model for a wide-spectrum language with concurrency. Form. Asp. Comput. 1–22 (2016)

[CJ07]   Coleman, J.W., Jones, C.B.: A structural proof of the soundness of rely/guarantee rules. J. Logic Comput. **17**(4), 807–841 (2007)

[Col08]   Coleman, J.W.: Constructing a Tractable Reasoning Framework upon a Fine-Grained Structural Operational Semantics. Ph.D. thesis, Newcastle University School of Computer Science (2008)

[DMN68]   Dahl, O.-J., Myhrhaug, B., Nygaard, K.: SIMULA 67 common base language. Technical Report S-2, Norwegian Computing Center, Oslo (1968)

[dR01]   de Roever, W.-P.: Concurrency Verification: Introduction to Compositional and Noncompositional Methods. Cambridge University Press, Cambridge (2001)

[DYBG+13] Dinsdale-Young, T., Birkedal, L., Gardner, P., Parkinson, M., Yang, H.: Views: compositional reasoning for concurrent programs. In: Proceedings of the 40th Annual ACM SIGPLAN-SIGACT Symposium on Principles of Programming Languages, pp. 287–300. ACM (2013)

[Eng71]   Engeler, E. (ed.): Symposium on Semantics of Algorithmic Languages. LNM, vol. 188. Springer, Heidelberg (1971). https://doi.org/10.1007/BFb0059689

[Fen09]   Feng, X.: Local rely-guarantee reasoning. In: Proceedings of the 36th Annual ACM SIGPLAN-SIGACT Symposium on Principles of Programming Languages, POPL 2009, pp. 315–327. ACM, New York, NY, USA (2009)

[Hay86]   Hayes, I. (ed.): Specification Case Studies. Prentice-Hall International, Upper Saddle River (1986)

[Hay16]   Hayes, I.J.: Generalised rely-guarantee concurrency: an algebraic foundation. Form. Asp. Comput. **28**(6), 1057–1078 (2016)

[HBDJ13]   Hayes, I.J., Burns, A., Dongol, B., Jones, C.B.: Comparing degrees of non-deterministic in expression evaluation. Comput. J. **56**(6), 741–755 (2013)

[HJ18]   Hayes, I.J., Jones, C.B.: A guide to rely/guarantee thinking. In: Bowen, J., Liu, Z., Zhan, Z. (eds.), Engineering Trustworthy Software Systems - Second International School, SETSS 2017, LNCS. Springer (2018)

[HJC14] Hayes, I.J., Jones, C.B., Colvin, R.J.: Laws and semantics for rely-guarantee refinement. Technical Report CS-TR-1425, Newcastle University (2014)

[HJJ03] Hayes, I.J., Jackson, M.A., Jones, C.B.: Determining the Specification of a Control System from That of Its Environment. In: Araki, K., Gnesi, S., Mandrioli, D. (eds.) FME 2003. LNCS, vol. 2805, pp. 154–169. Springer, Heidelberg (2003). https://doi.org/10.1007/978-3-540-45236-2_10

[Hoa69] Hoare, Charles Antony, Richard, : An axiomatic basis for computer programming. Commun. ACM **12**(10), 576–580 (1969)

[Hoa72] Hoare, C.A.R.: Towards a theory of parallel programming. In: Hoare, C.A.R., Perrot, R. (eds.) Operating System Techniques, pp. 61–71. Academic Press (1972)

[Hoa74] Hoare, C.A.R.: Monitors: an operating system structuring concept. Commun. ACM **17**, 549–557 (1974)

[Hoa85] Hoare, C.A.R.: Communicating Sequential Processes. Prentice-Hall, Upper Saddle River (1985)

[JA16]   Jones, C.B., Astarte, T.K.: An Exegesis of Four Formal Descriptions of ALGOL 60. Technical Report CS-TR-1498, Newcastle University School of Computer Science (2016). Forthcoming as a paper in the HaPoP 2016 proceedings

[JA17]   Jones, C.B., Astarte, T.K.: Challenges for semantic description: comparing responses from the main approaches. Technical Report CS-TR-1516, Newcastle University School of Computer Science (2017)

[JH16]   Jones, C.B., Hayes, I.J.: Possible values: exploring a concept for concurrency. J. Log. Algebr. Methods Program. (2016)

[JHC15] Jones, C.B., Hayes, I.J., Colvin, R.J.: Balancing expressiveness in formal approaches to concurrency. Form. Asp. Comput. **27**(3), 465–497 (2015)

[JHJ07] Jones, C.B., Hayes, I.J., Jackson, M.A.: Deriving specifications for systems that are connected to the physical world. In: Jones, C.B., Liu, Z., Woodcock, J. (eds.) Formal Methods and Hybrid Real-Time Systems. LNCS, vol. 4700, pp. 364–390. Springer, Heidelberg (2007). https://doi.org/10.1007/978-3-540-75221-9_16

[Jon80] Jones, C.B.: Software Development: A Rigorous Approach. Prentice Hall International, Englewood Cliffs (1980)

[Jon81] Joncs, C.B.: Development Methods for Computer Programs including a Notion of Interference. Ph.D. thesis, Oxford University (1981). Printed as: Programming Research Group, Technical Monograph 25

[Jon83a] Jones, C.B.: Specification and design of (parallel) programs. In: Proceedings of IFIP 1983, pp. 321–332. North-Holland (1983)

[Jon83b] Jones, C.B.: Tentative steps toward a development method for interfering programs. Trans. Program. Lang. Syst. **5**(4), 596–619 (1983)

[Jon90] Jones, C.B.: Systematic Software Development using VDM, 2nd edn. Prentice Hall International, Upper Saddle River (1990)

[Jon03a] Jones, C.B.: The early search for tractable ways of reasoning about programs. IEEE, Ann. Hist. Comput. **25**(2), 26–49 (2003)

[Jon03b] Jones, C.B.: Operational semantics: concepts and their expression. Inf. Process. Lett. **88**(1–2), 27–32 (2003)

[Jon10]   Jones, C.B.: From problem frames to HJJ (and its known unknowns). In: Nuseibeh, B., Zave, P. (eds.), Software Requirements and Design: The Work of Michael Jackson, chapter 16, pp. 357–372. Good Friends Publishing Company (2010)

[JP11]   Jones, C.B., Pierce, K.G.: Elucidating concurrent algorithms via layers of abstraction and reification. Form. Asp. Comput. **23**(3), 289–306 (2011)

[JVY17]   Jones, C.B., Velykis, A., Yatapanage, N.: General lessons from a rely/guarantee development. In: Larsen, K.G., Sokolsky, O., Wang, J. (eds.) SETTA 2017. LNCS, vol. 10606, pp. 3–24. Springer, Cham (2017). https://doi.org/10.1007/978-3-319-69483-2_1

[JY15]   Jones, C.B., Yatapanage, N.: Reasoning about separation using abstraction and reification. In: Calinescu, R., Rumpe, B. (eds.) SEFM 2015. LNCS, vol. 9276, pp. 3–19. Springer, Cham (2015). https://doi.org/10.1007/978-3-319-22969-0_1

[LFF12]   Liang, H., Feng, X., Fu, M.: A rely-guarantee-based simulation for verifying concurrent program transformations. In: Proceedings of the 39th Annual ACM SIGPLAN-SIGACT Symposium on Principles of Programming Languages, POPL 2012, pp. 455–468. ACM, New York, NY, USA (2012)

[Lia14]   Liang, H.: Refinement Verification of Concurrent Programs and Its Applications. Ph.D. thesis, USTC, China (2014)

[LW69]   Lucas, P.: Walk, Kurt: on the formal description of PL/I. Ann. Rev. Autom. Program. **6**, 105–182 (1969)

[McC66]   McCarthy, J.: A formal description of a subset of ALGOL. In: Formal Language Description Languages for Computer Programming, pp. 1–12. North-Holland (1966)

[Mil89]   Milner, R.: Communication and Concurrency. Prentice Hall, Upper Saddle River (1989)

[Mor90]   Morgan, C.: Programming from Specifications. Prentice-Hall, Upper Saddle River (1990)

[Mos86]   Moszkowski, B.: Executing Temporal Logic Programs. Cambridge University Press, Cambridge (1986)

[MPW92]   Milner, R., Parrow, J., Walker, D.: A calculus of mobile processes. Inf. Comput. **100**, 1–77 (1992)

[OG76]   Owicki, S.S., Gries, D.: An axiomatic proof technique for parallel programs I. Acta Inf. **6**, 319–340 (1976)

[O'H07]   O'Hearn, P.W.: Resources, concurrency and local reasoning. Theor. Comput. Sci. **375**(1–3), 271–307 (2007)

[Owi75]   Owicki, S.S.: Axiomatic Proof Techniques for Parallel Programs. Ph.D. thesis, Department of Computer Science, Cornell University (1975). Hard copy - Published as technical report 75-251

[Par10]   Parkinson, M.: The next 700 separation logics. In: Leavens, G., O'Hearn, P., Rajamani, S. (eds.) Verified Software: Theories. Tools, Experiments, volume 6217 of LNCS, pp. 169–182. Springer, Berlin/Heidelberg (2010)

[Plo76]   Plotkin, G.D.: A powerdomain construction. SIAM J. Comput. **5**, 452–487 (1976)

[Plo81]   Plotkin, G.D.: A structural approach to operational semantics. Technical Report DAIMI FN-19, Aarhus University (1981)

[Plo04a]   Plotkin, G.D.: The origins of structural operational semantics. J. Logic Algebr. Program. **60–61**, 3–15 (2004)

[Plo04b] Plotkin, G.D.: A structural approach to operational semantics. J. Logic Algebr. Program. **60–61**, 17–139 (2004)

[Rey02] Reynolds, J.: A logic for shared mutable data structures. In: Plotkin, G. (ed.) LICS 2002. IEEE Computer Society Press (2002)

[Ste66] Steel, T.B.: Formal Language Description Languages for Computer Programming. North-Holland (1966)

[STE+14] Schellhorn, G., Tofan, B., Ernst, G., Pf'ahler, J., Reif, W.: Rgitl: a temporal logic framework for compositional reasoning about interleaved programs. Ann. Math.Artif. Intell. **71**(1–3), 131–174 (2014)

[Sto77] Stoy, J.E.: Denotational Semantics: The Scott-Strachey Approach to Programming Language Theory. MIT Press, Cambridge (1977)

[SW01] Sangiorgi, D., Walker, D.: The π-calculus: A Theory of Mobile Processes. Cambridge University Press, Cambridge (2001)

[WW10] Wang, S., Wang, X.: Proving simpson's four-slot algorithm using ownership transfer. In: VERIFY Workshop, Edinburgh (2010)

Decidability of the Initial-State Opacity of Real-Time Automata

Lingtai Wang[1,2] and Naijun Zhan[1,2(✉)]

[1] State Key Lab. of Comp. Sci., Institute of Software, Chinese Academy of Sciences,
Beijing, China
znj@ios.ac.cn
[2] University of Chinese Academy of Sciences, Beijing, China

Abstract. In this paper, we investigate the initial-state opacity of real-time automata. A system is called *initial-state opaque* if an intruder with partial observability is unable to determine whether or not the execution starts from a secret state. In order to prove that the initial-state opacity problem is decidable, we first calculate the lapse of time between each pair of observable events. Two real-time automata are constructed which accept the projection of languages from secret initial states and non-secret ones, respectively. Then, the two real-time automata are further transformed into trace-equivalent finite-state automata. Subsequently, we adapt complement and product on the finite-state automata, and check accepting language of the finally-obtained automaton. The system is initial-state opaque if it accepts nothing or only empty trace, and not initial-state opaque otherwise.

Keywords: Real-time automata · Initial-state opacity · Decidability
Trace-equivalence

1 Introduction

In the wake of development of network communications and online services, security and privacy have become more significant and thus received more and more attention. Opacity is an information flow property aiming at keeping the "secret" of a system opaque to its outsider (called the intruder). There are two types of "secrets": subsets of traces and subsets of states. This divides opacity properties into language-based opacity and state-based opacity. The intruder is believed to know the structure of the system, but only has partial observability over it. Once the intruder has observed the execution, he can get an estimation whether the execution belongs to the secret. This paper focuses on initial-state opacity, which is state-based, that is, the secret S is a set of states. The system is initial-state opaque if the intruder can never determine whether it starts from a

This work is funded partly by NSFC under grant No. 61625206 and 61732001, by "973 Program" under grant No. 2014CB340701, and by the CAS/SAFEA International Partnership Program for Creative Research Teams.

secret state or a non-secret one no matter what he has observed. Examples from tracking problems in sensor networks have been used to motivate initial-state opacity in [1], where the sensor network only has partial observation.

Systems being investigated are often modelled as discrete event systems (DES), for example, Petri nets [2,3], labeled transition systems (LTS) [4] and finite-state automata (FSA) [1,5–7]. Probabilistic models are also taken into consideration, such as [8–11]. However, in [12], the notion of opacity was extended to dense-time systems, with the result that the (language-based) opacity problem is already undecidable for a very restrictive class of event-recording automata (ERA).

As time is an important attack vector against secure systems, we extend the notion of initial-state opacity to real-time automata [13]. Real-time automata is a class of timed automata with a single clock which is reset at each transition, also regarded as finite automata with time information for each transition. Classical results for finite automata can thus be extended to real-time automata such as Kleene's theorem, Pumping Lemma and the closure under complementation [13]. Besides, as pointed out in [13], RTA is not comparable with ERA.

Our analysis mainly focuses on calculating time taken by unobservable transitions and then constructing two real-time automata accepting the projection of languages from secret initial states and non-secret ones respectively. A relationship between languages of real-time automata and their corresponding finite-state automata, called trace-equivalence, is introduced, so that the initial-opacity problem is transformed into the problem of language inclusion of finite-state automata. Thus, the initial-state opacity problem is proved to be *decidable*.

The remainder of this paper is organized as follows. In Sect. 2, we recall preliminaries for finite-state automata, regular expressions, real-time automata, and the initial-state opacity problem of real-time automata. The correspondence of real-time automata and finite-state automata is introduced in Sect. 3. Section 4 provides a procedure to determine whether a real-time automaton is initial-state opaque w.r.t. a given set of secret states and an observable alphabet, and Sect. 5 concludes this paper.

2   Preliminaries

We use $\mathbb{R}_{\geq 0}$, $\mathbb{Q}_{\geq 0}$, and $\mathbb{N}$ to denote the set of nonnegative real numbers, non-negative rational numbers, and natural numbers, respectively.

Let E, a set of events, be the *alphabet*. A *word* or *string* over E is a finite sequence $w = a_1 a_2 \ldots a_n$, where $a_i \in E$ for $i = 1, 2, \ldots, n$. $|w| = n$ is the length of w. ε is the empty word, whose length $|\varepsilon| = 0$. E^* is the set of all the finite words over E including ε. L is a *language* over E if $L \subseteq E^*$.

Commonly used operations on languages include union, intersection, and difference as in set theory, as well as concatenation, Kleene closure and projection which are defined below:

Concatenation: Let $L_1, L_2 \subseteq E^*$, the concatenation $L_1 L_2 = \{s_1 s_2 \mid s_1 \in L_1 \wedge s_2 \in L_2\}$.

Kleene closure: Let $L \subseteq E^*$, and $L^0 = \{\varepsilon\}$, $L^1 = L$, $L^k = (L^{k-1})L$ for $k > 1$, then the Kleene closure of L is $L^* = \bigcup_{k \in \mathbb{N}} L^k = \{\varepsilon\} \cup L \cup LL \cup \cdots$.

Projection: Given E and a subset $E_o \subseteq E$, we can define a projection $P_{E_o} : E^* \to E_o^*$, where

$$P_{E_o}(\varepsilon) = \varepsilon$$

$$P_{E_o}(as) = \begin{cases} aP_{E_o}(s), & \text{if } a \in E_o \\ P_{E_o}(s), & \text{otherwise} \end{cases}, \text{ for } a \in E \text{ and } s \in E^*.$$

Given any $B \subseteq E^*$ and $C \subseteq E_o^*$, the image of B under P_{E_o} is $P_{E_o}(B) = \{P_{E_o}(s) \mid s \in B\} \subseteq E_o^*$ and the inverse image of C under P_{E_o} is $P_{E_o}^{-1}(C) = \{s \in E^* \mid P_{E_o}(s) \in C\} \subseteq E^*$.

Consider the alphabet $\Sigma \times \mathbb{R}_{\geq 0}$. A *timed word* over Σ is a finite word over the alphabet $\Sigma \times \mathbb{R}_{\geq 0}$ with the form of $w_t = (a_1, t_1)(a_2, t_2) \ldots (a_n, t_n)$, where $0 \leq t_1 \leq t_2 \leq \cdots \leq t_n$, meaning that a_i occurs at t_i successively for $1 \leq i \leq n$. $TW^*(\Sigma)$ denotes the set of all timed words over Σ. A subset of $TW^*(\Sigma)$ is a *timed language*. If $\Sigma_o \subseteq \Sigma$ is the observable alphabet, $P_{\Sigma_o, t}$ denotes the projection from $TW^*(\Sigma)$ into $TW^*(\Sigma_o)$. For example, if $w_t = (a, 2)(b, 3)(a, 5)(b, 8)$, $P_{\{b\}, t}(w_t) = (b, 3)(b, 8)$ and $P_{\{a\}, t}(w_t) = (a, 2)(a, 5)$.

2.1   Finite-State Automata and Regular Expressions

Automata are a kind of well-known model to study discrete transition systems and their behaviours. Finite-state automata (FAs) are automata with finitely many states. They can be deterministic or non-deterministic.

Definition 1.   – *A deterministic finite-state automaton (DFA) is a 5-tuple $A_d = (S, \Sigma, \delta, s_0, F)$, where*
- *S is a finite set of states;*
- *Σ is a finite alphabet;*
- *$\delta : S \times \Sigma \to S$ is the transition relation, a partial function on $S \times \Sigma$;*
- *$s_0 \in S$ is the initial state; and*
- *$F \subseteq S$ is the set of accepting states.*

– *A non-deterministic finite-state automaton (NFA) is a 5-tuple $\mathcal{A}_n = (S, \Sigma \cup \{\varepsilon\}, \delta, Init, F)$, where*
- *S is a finite set of states;*
- *Σ is a finite alphabet;*
- *$\delta : S \times (\Sigma \cup \{\varepsilon\}) \to 2^S$ is the transition function;*
- *$Init \subseteq S$ is the set of initial states; and*
- *$F \subseteq S$ is the set of accepting states.*

Obviously, a DFA can be viewed as a special kind of NFA, where there is only one initial state, one or zero state in each $\delta(s, a)$, and no ε-transition.

For an NFA $\mathcal{A}$, if $s_2 \in \delta(s_1, \sigma)$, (s_1, σ, s_2) is called a σ-transition, written as $s_1 \xrightarrow{\sigma} s_2$. A *run* of $\mathcal{A}$ is either a single state s_0, where $s_0 \in Init$, or a sequence $s_0 \xrightarrow{\sigma_1} s_1 \xrightarrow{\sigma_2} \cdots s_{n-1} \xrightarrow{\sigma_n} s_n$, where $n > 0$, $s_0 \in Init$, $\sigma_i \in \Sigma \cup \{\varepsilon\}$ and

$s_i \in \delta(s_{i-1}, \sigma_{i-1})$ for $1 \le i \le n$. The *trace* of the run s_0 is ε, and the *trace* of the sequence from s_0 to s_n is the finite word obtained by projecting $\sigma_1\sigma_2\ldots\sigma_n$ onto Σ^*, that is, the string $a_1a_2\ldots a_m$ obtained by removing each ε from $\sigma_1\sigma_2\ldots\sigma_n$; hence the length of the trace is m, less than or equal to n. An *accepting run* is a run ending in a state $s_n \in F$. The language generated by $\mathcal{A}$, denoted by $L(\mathcal{A})$ is the set of traces of runs of $\mathcal{A}$; the language accepted by $\mathcal{A}$, denoted by $L_f(\mathcal{A})$ is the set of traces of accepting runs. A language is said to be *regular* if it can be accepted by a finite-state automaton.

Two automata are called *language-equivalent*, or *equivalent* for short, if they generate and accept the same languages. An NFA $\mathcal{A}_n = (S, \Sigma, \delta, Init, F)$ can be transformed into an equivalent DFA $\mathcal{A}_d = (S', \Sigma, \delta', Init', F')$ defined below. Let $\varepsilon R(s, \varepsilon)$ denote the set of states which are reachable from state s via no transitions or only ε-transitions, and $\varepsilon R(s, a)$ the set of states which are reachable from state s via one a-transition together with ε-transitions before and after it. Then in $\mathcal{A}_d$, $S' = 2^S$; $\delta'(S_1, a) = \bigcup_{s_1 \in S_1} \varepsilon R(s_1, a)$; $Init' = \varepsilon R(s_0, \varepsilon)$; $F' = \{S_1 \mid S_1 \cap F \ne \emptyset\}$.

Regular expressions are another way to describe regular languages.

Definition 2. *Regular expressions over alphabet Σ can be defined recursively as follows:*

1. *(Base Clause): $\emptyset$, ε, $a \in \Sigma$ are regular expressions, where $\emptyset$ denotes the empty set, ε denotes the set $\{\varepsilon\}$, and a denotes the set $\{a\}$ for $a \in E$.*
2. *(Inductive Clause): If r, r_1, r_2 are regular expressions, then $r_1 \cdot r_2$, $r_1 + r_2$, r^* are regular expressions. $r_1 \cdot r_2$ denotes the concatenation of language denoted by r_1 and r_2, $r_1 + r_2$ denotes the union of the two languages, and r^* denotes the Kleene closure of the language denotes by r.*
3. *(External Clause): Regular expressions can only be constructed by applying 1 and 2.*

Theorem 1 (Kleene's Theorem). *Any regular language is accepted by a finite automaton; any language accepted by a finite automaton is regular.*

Complement and product operations on DFAs. Consider a DFA $\mathcal{A} = (S, \Sigma, \delta, s_0, F)$. The complement automaton $\mathcal{A}^{comp}$ which accepts $L_f(\mathcal{A})^c = \Sigma^* \setminus L_f(\mathcal{A})$ can be constructed as follows:

1. Augment S with a new state $s_{new} \notin S$;
2. Augment δ such that it becomes a total function, denoted as δ^{comp}. For all $(s, a) \in S \times \Sigma$, if $\delta(s, a)$ is defined, let $\delta^{comp}(s, a) = \delta(s, a)$; if $\delta(s, a)$ is not defined, let $\delta^{comp}(s, a) = s_{new}$. Also $\delta(s_{new}, a) = s_{new}$ for each $a \in \Sigma$. After that Σ^* becomes the language generated, while the language accepted keeps unchanged;
3. Let the accepting set of states be $(S \setminus F) \cup \{s_{new}\}$.

To sum up, $\mathcal{A}^{comp} = (S \cup \{s_{new}\}, \Sigma, \delta^{comp}, s_0, S \setminus F \cup \{s_{new}\})$.

Given two DFAs $\mathcal{A}_1 = (S_1, \Sigma_1, \delta_1, s_{0,1}, F_1)$ and $\mathcal{A}_2 = (S_2, \Sigma_2, \delta_2, s_{0,2}, F_2)$ with $S_1 \cap S_2 = \emptyset$, the product of $\mathcal{A}_1$ and $\mathcal{A}_2$ is $\mathcal{A}^p = \mathcal{A}_1 \times \mathcal{A}_2 = $

$(S^p, \Sigma^p, \delta^p, s_0^p, F^p)$, defined as follows: $S^p = S_1 \times S_2$; $\Sigma^p = \Sigma_1 \cap \Sigma_2$; $\delta^p((s_1, s_2), a) = (s_1', s_2')$ if $\delta(s_1, a) = s_1'$ and $\delta(s_2, a) = s_2'$, and is not defined otherwise; $s_0^p = (s_{0,1}, s_{0,2})$; $F^p = F_1 \times F_2$.

Then $L_f(\mathcal{A}_1 \times \mathcal{A}_2) = L_f(\mathcal{A}_1) \cap L_f(\mathcal{A}_2)$.

2.2 Real-Time Automata

Real-time automata are very similar to classical automata despite their taking time into account as well. We can easily get a real-time automaton by attaching time information to each transition of a given automaton.

Definition 3. *A real-time automaton is a 6-tuple* $\mathcal{A} = (S, \Sigma, \Delta, Init, F, \mu)$, *where*

- *S is a finite set of states;*
- *Σ is a finite alphabet;*
- *$\Delta \subseteq S \times \Sigma \times S$ is the transition relation;*
- *$Init \subseteq S$ is the set of initial states;*
- *$F \subseteq S$ is the set of accepting states; and*
- *$\mu : \Delta \to 2^{\mathbb{R}_{\geq 0}} \setminus \{\emptyset\}$ is the time labelling function, whose range, $\mu(\Delta)$, is usually a set of intervals whose endpoints are in $\mathbb{N} \cup \{+\infty\}$ or $\mathbb{Q}_{\geq 0} \cup \{+\infty\}$.*

A *transition* $(s_1, a, s_2) \in \Delta$ starts in s_1, ends in s_2 and is labelled by a. Transitions of the form (s_1, a, s_2) are called a-transitions. Δ_a denotes the set of all a-transitions. Pre_a and $Post_a$ denotes the set of states from which and to which are a-transitions respectively, i.e., $Pre_a = \{s_1 \mid \exists (s_1, a, s_2) \in \Delta\}$ and $Post_a = \{s_2 \mid \exists (s_1, a, s_2) \in \Delta\}$. A *run* of $\mathcal{A}$ is either a single initial state s_0 from $Init$ or a finite sequence $\rho = s_0 \xrightarrow[\lambda_1]{a_1} s_1 \xrightarrow[\lambda_2]{a_2} \cdots s_{n-1} \xrightarrow[\lambda_n]{a_n} s_n$, where $n > 0$, $s_0 \in Init$, $(s_{i-1}, a_i, s_i) \in \Delta$, and $\lambda_i \in \mu(s_{i-1}, a_i, s_i)$ for $i \geq 1$. The *trace* of a run ρ, denoted by $trace(\rho)$, is defined as follows: if $\rho = s_0$, $trace(\rho) = \varepsilon_t$, where subscript "$t$" is used to emphasize the time factor; if ρ is of the form $s_0 \xrightarrow[\lambda_1]{a_1} s_1 \xrightarrow[\lambda_2]{a_2} \cdots s_{n-1} \xrightarrow[\lambda_n]{a_n} s_n$, $trace(\rho)$ is the timed word $(a_1, t_1)(a_2, t_2) \ldots (a_n, t_n)$ where $t_i = \sum_{j=1}^{i} \lambda_j$, for $i = 1, \ldots, n$. Let $Tr(s_0)$ be the set of traces of runs from state s_0, and $Tr(S_0)$ be the set of traces of runs from any state $s_0 \in S_0$, i.e., $Tr(S_0) = \bigcup_{s_0 \in S_0} Tr(s_0)$. $L(\mathcal{A}) = Tr(Init) = \bigcup_{s_0 \in Init} Tr(s_0)$, is called the timed language generated by $\mathcal{A}$, and $L_f(\mathcal{A}) = \{trace(\rho) \mid \rho$ starts from $s_0 \in S_0$ and ends in $s_n \in F\}$ is the set of traces accepted by $\mathcal{A}$.

Example 1. In Fig. 1, transitions are depicted as arrows, with their labels from the alphabet $\{a, b\}$ above and time-labels below. For the real-time automaton $\mathcal{A}_1$, $Tr(s_0) = \{\varepsilon_t\} \cup \{(a, t_a) \mid t_a \in [1, 2]\} \cup \{(a, t_a)(b, t_b) \mid t_a \in [1, 2], t_b \in [2, 3]\}$, and $Tr(s_3) = \{\varepsilon_t\} \cup \{(b, t_b) \mid t_b \in [3, 4]\}$.

$\mathcal{A}_1$ generates $L(\mathcal{A}_1) = \{\varepsilon_t\} \cup \{(a, t_a) \mid t_a \in [1, 2]\} \cup \{(a, t_a)(b, t_b) \mid t_a \in [1, 2], t_b \in [2, 3]\} \cup \{(b, t_b) \mid t_b \in [3, 4]\}$ and accepts $L_f(\mathcal{A}_1) = \{(a, t_a)(b, t_b) \mid t_a \in [1, 2], t_b \in [2, 3]\} \cup \{(b, t_b) \mid t_b \in [3, 4]\}$. □

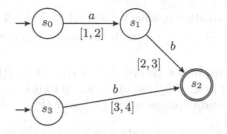

Fig. 1. A real-time automaton $\mathcal{A}_1$

2.3 Initial-State Opacity of Real-Time Automata

Given a real-time automaton $\mathcal{A}$ with an alphabet Σ and an observable alphabet $\Sigma_o \subseteq \Sigma$, intruders can only observe timed words in $P_{\Sigma_o,t}(L(\mathcal{A}))$. Suppose we have a set of secret states S_{secret}. In this case, can intruders detect whether the current run of the system starts from the secret set S_{secret} according to what they have observed? This is considered in the initial-state opacity problem. Formally,

Definition 4. *Given a real-time automaton $\mathcal{A} = (S, \Sigma, \Delta, Init, F, \mu)$, an observable alphabet $\Sigma_o \subseteq \Sigma$ and a secret set of states $S_{secret} \subseteq S$, $\mathcal{A}$ is* initial-state opaque *w.r.t. S_{secret} and Σ_o iff for all $s_0 \in Init \cap S_{secret}$ and all $w \in Tr(s_0)$, $\exists s_0' \in Init \setminus S_{secret}$, $\exists w' \in Tr(s_0')$ s.t.*

$$P_{\Sigma_o,t}(w) = P_{\Sigma_o,t}(w'),$$

or equivalently,

$$P_{\Sigma_o,t}(Tr(Init \cap S_{secret}))) \subseteq P_{\Sigma_o,t}(Tr(Init \setminus S_{secret})).$$

The *initial-state opacity problem* of real-time automata is thus expressed as follows: Is a real-time automaton $\mathcal{A} = (S, \Sigma, \Delta, Init, F, \mu)$ initial-state opaque w.r.t. some given secret set $S_{secret} \subseteq S$ and $\Sigma_o \subseteq \Sigma$?

In the following, we would like to use L_s and L_{ns} instead of $P_{\Sigma_o,t}(Tr(Init \cap S_{secret})))$ and $P_{\Sigma_o,t}(Tr(Init \setminus S_{secret}))$ respectively for sake of convenience.

Note that in the initial-state opacity problem, the set of accepting states of the real-time automaton $\mathcal{A}$ does not play any role. Therefore, without loss of generality, each state of the real-time automaton under study can be regarded as an accepting state such that $L_f(\mathcal{A}) = L(\mathcal{A})$.

Example 2. (Ctd.) We still consider the automata $\mathcal{A}_1$ shown in Fig. 1. Let $\Sigma_o = \{b\}$ and $S_{secret} = \{s_0\}$. If $P_{\Sigma_o,t}(w_t) = (b, 3.5)$, possible runs include $\rho_1 = s_0 \xrightarrow[1]{a} s_1 \xrightarrow[2.5]{b} s_2$ and $\rho_2 = s_3 \xrightarrow[3.5]{b} s_2$. In this case the intruders are incapable of ascertaining the secret. If $P_{\Sigma_o,t}(w_t) = (b, 5)$, we can easily know that $w_t = (a, 2)(b, 5)$ and the unique run is $\rho = s_0 \xrightarrow[2]{a} s_1 \xrightarrow[3]{b} s_2$. Thus, the secret is exposed in this case. From the above, $\mathcal{A}_1$ is not initial-state opaque w.r.t. $\{s_0\}$ and $\{b\}$.

However, $\mathcal{A}_1$ is initial-state opaque w.r.t. $\{s_3\}$ and $\{b\}$. This is because there always exists a run $s_0 \xrightarrow[1]{a} s_1 \xrightarrow[t-1]{b} s_2$ with the same projection as $s_3 \xrightarrow[t]{b} s_2$ with $3 \leq t \leq 4$.

From the perspective of set theory, $P_{\{b\},t}(Tr(s_3)) = \{(b,t) \mid t \in [3,4]\} \subsetneq P_{\{b\},t}(Tr(s_0)) = \{(b,t) \mid t \in [3,5]\}$, so $\mathcal{A}_1$ is not initial-state opaque w.r.t. $\{s_0\}$ and $\{b\}$, and is initial-state opaque w.r.t. $\{s_3\}$ and $\{b\}$.   □

If there exist two real-time automata which accept the two languages L_s and L_{ns}, respectively, then we can solve the initial-state opacity problem by checking whether the accepting language of the former is included in that of the latter. This checking can be achieved by utilizing trace-equivalence relation given in the next section. The basic idea is to translate the two real-time automata into their trace-equivalent finite-state automata, and construct another finite-state automaton $\mathcal{A}_{dfa}^p$ according to the two resulting finite-state automata. The fact that $\mathcal{A}_{dfa}^p$ accepts nothing or ε implies that $L_s \subseteq L_{ns}$, i.e., the original real-time automaton is initial-state opaque.

3   Correspondence Between NFAs and Real-Time Automata

As real-time automata and non-deterministic automata have very similar structures, a real-time automaton with alphabet Σ can be translated into an NFA with alphabet $\Sigma \times (2^{\mathbb{R}_{\geq 0}} \setminus \{\emptyset\})$.

Given a real-time automaton $\mathcal{A} = (S, \Sigma, \Delta, Init, F, \mu)$, let μ_a denote the set of time information of all a-transitions, that is, $\mu_a = \{\mu(s_1, a, s_2) \mid (s_1, a, s_2) \in \Delta\}$, which is finite since Δ is finite. Each element of μ_a is a non-empty subset Λ_a of $\mathbb{R}_{\geq 0}$, such as a point, an interval, or a more complicated set. For each μ_a, a partition of $\mathbb{R}_{\geq 0}$ (i.e., a set of $\mathbb{R}_{\geq 0}$'s non-empty subsets satisfying each real number $x \geq 0$ is in one and only one of those subsets) should be constructed such that any $\Lambda_a \in \mu_a$ is the union of some elements from the partition. Here we define a function I to compute a partition of $\mathbb{R}_{\geq 0}$ based on a finite $C \in 2^{\mathbb{R}_{\geq 0}} \setminus \{\emptyset\}$. I is defined by induction: if $|C| = 1$, say $\mu_a = \{\Lambda\}$, the partition is $\mathcal{I}(C) = \{\Lambda, \mathbb{R}_{\geq 0} \setminus \Lambda\} \setminus \{\emptyset\}$; if $|C| = k$ with $\mathcal{I}(C) = \{I_1, \ldots, I_{m_C}\}$ and $\Lambda \notin C$, $\mathcal{I}(C \cup \{\Lambda\}) = \{I_1 \cap \Lambda, I_1 \setminus \Lambda, \ldots, I_{m_C} \cap \Lambda, I_{m_C} \setminus \Lambda, \} \setminus \{\emptyset\}$. Additionally, it can be easily proved from the definition that $|\mathcal{I}(C)|$ is no more than $2^{|C|}$. So we can obtain the partition $\mathcal{I}(\mu_a)$ satisfying the aforementioned constraint. For instance, if $\mu_a = \{[2,5], [3,6]\}$, we can construct $\{[3,5], [2,3), (5,6], [0,2) \cup [6,+\infty)\}$ as one partition based on Λ_a. Then a non-deterministic finite-state automaton $\mathcal{A}_{nfa} = (S_{nfa}, \Sigma_{nfa}, \delta_{nfa}, Init_{nfa}, F_{nfa})$ can be constructed.

Definition 5. *Given* $\mathcal{A} = (S, \Sigma, \Delta, Init, F, \mu)$, *the corresponding NFA* $\mathcal{A}_{nfa} = (S_{nfa}, \Sigma_{nfa}, \delta_{nfa}, Init_{nfa}, F_{nfa})$ *can be constructed as follows.*

- $S_{nfa} = S$;
- $\Sigma_{nfa} = \bigcup_{a \in \Sigma} (\{a\} \times \mathcal{I}(\mu_a))$;

- $\delta_{nfa}(s_1, (a, I)) = \{s_2 \mid (s_1, a, s_2) \in \Delta \wedge I \subseteq I', \text{ for some } I' \in \mu(s_1, a, s_2)\};$
- $Init_{nfa} = Init;$
- $F_{nfa} = F.$

Example 3. The real-time automaton in Fig. 1 can be translated into the finite-state automaton in Fig. 2. Note that $\mathcal{I}(\mu_a) = \{[1,2], [0,1) \cup (2,+\infty)\}$ and $\mathcal{I}(\mu_b) = \{[3,3], [2,3), (3,4], [0,2) \cup (4,+\infty)\}$ and that the alphabet of the finite-state automaton is $\{a\} \times I(\mu_a) \cup \{b\} \times I(\mu_b)$. □

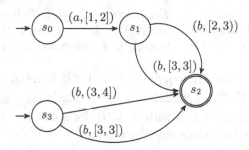

Fig. 2. $\mathcal{A}_2$, the corresponding FA of $\mathcal{A}_1$

Nevertheless, what needs special attention is that languages generated from the two kinds of automata are different. Obviously, the language generated by a real-time automaton $\mathcal{A}$ is a subset of $TW^*(\Sigma)$. By contrast, the language generated by the corresponding finite-state automaton $\mathcal{A}_{nfa}$ is a subset of $(\Sigma \times (2^{\mathbb{R}_{\geq 0}} \setminus \{\emptyset\}))^*$. The relationship between $L(\mathcal{A})$ and $L(\mathcal{A}_{nfa})$ can be described using the trace-equivalence relation defined below.

Definition 6. *Given L_1 a timed language over Σ and L_2 a language over $\Sigma \times (2^{\mathbb{R}_{\geq 0}} \setminus \{\emptyset\})$, L_2 is said to be trace-equivalent to L_1, denoted by $L_2 \approx_{tr} L_1$, if*

0. $\varepsilon_t \in L_1$ iff $\varepsilon \in L_2$;
1. If any timed word $w_t = (a_1, t_1)(a_2, t_2) \ldots (a_n, t_n) \in L_1$, then there exists some $w = (a_1, \Lambda_1)(a_2, \Lambda_2) \ldots (a_n, \Lambda_n) \in L_2$ such that $t_1 \in \Lambda_1$ and $(t_i - t_{i-1}) \in \Lambda_i$ for $1 < i \leq n$;
2. If $w = (a_1, \Lambda_1)(a_2, \Lambda_2) \ldots (a_n, \Lambda_n) \in L_2$, then all timed words of the form $w_t = (a_1, t_1)(a_2, t_2) \ldots (a_n, t_n)$ with $t_1 \in \Lambda_1$ and $(t_i - t_{i-1}) \in \Lambda_i$ for $1 < i \leq n$ are in L_1.

Lemma 1. *For a given real-time automaton $\mathcal{A} = (S, \Sigma, \Delta, Init, F, \mu)$ and its corresponding NFA $\mathcal{A}_{nfa} = (S_{nfa}, \Sigma_{nfa}, \delta_{nfa}, Init_{nfa}, F_{nfa})$ as defined in Definition 5, $L_f(\mathcal{A}_{nfa}) \approx_{tr} L_f(\mathcal{A})$.*

Proof. $L_f(\mathcal{A}) = \emptyset$ iff $L_f(\mathcal{A}_{nfa}) = \emptyset$. This is because $L_f(\mathcal{A}) = \emptyset$ iff no accepting states are reachable in $\mathcal{A}$, iff no accepting states are reachable in $\mathcal{A}_{nfa}$, iff $L_f(\mathcal{A}_{nfa}) = \emptyset$. So, in this case, trivially $L_f(\mathcal{A}_{nfa}) \approx_{tr} L_f(\mathcal{A})$.

If $\varepsilon_t \in L_f(\mathcal{A})$, a possible run is s_0, where $s_0 \in Init \cap F$. Thus, $s_0 \in Init_{nfa} \cap F_{nfa}$ according to Definition 5. Hence, $\mathcal{A}_{nfa}$ has a run s_0 whose trace is ε, i.e., $\varepsilon \in L_f(\mathcal{A}_{nfa})$. On the contrary, suppose $\varepsilon \in L_f(\mathcal{A}_{nfa})$, which implies there exists an initial state $s_0 \in Init_{nfa} \cap F_{nfa}$. It follows that $s_0 \in Init \cap F$ according to Definition 5. Hence, $\varepsilon_t \in L_f(\mathcal{A})$.

Suppose $w_t = (a_1, t_1) \ldots (a_n, t_n) \in L_f(\mathcal{A})$, where $n \geq 1$, then there exists a run of $\mathcal{A}$, say $\rho = s_0 \xrightarrow[\lambda_1]{a_1} s_1 \xrightarrow[\lambda_2]{a_2} \cdots s_{n-1} \xrightarrow[\lambda_n]{a_n} s_n$ such that $s_0 \in Init$, $s_n \in F$, $(s_{i-1}, a_i, s_i) \in \Delta$, and $\lambda_i \in \mu(s_{i-1}, a_i, s_i)$ for $i \geq 1$. So there exists a run of $\mathcal{A}_{nfa}$, that is, $\rho' = s_0 \xrightarrow{(a_1, \Lambda_1)} s_1 \xrightarrow{(a_2, \Lambda_2)} \cdots s_{n-1} \xrightarrow{(a_n, \Lambda_n)} s_n$, where $s_0 \in Init_{nfa}$ and $s_n \in F_{nfa}$, according to Definition 5. Thus, there exists a $w = (a_1, \Lambda_1)(a_2, \Lambda_2) \ldots (a_n, \Lambda_n) \in L_f(\mathcal{A}_{nfa})$ such that $t_1 \in \Lambda_1$ and $(t_i - t_{i-1}) \in \Lambda_i$ for $1 < i \leq n$, where $\Lambda_i \subseteq I_i$, for some $I_i \in \mu(s_{i-1}, a_i, s_i)$ and $1 \leq i \leq n$.

Given a word $w = (a_1, \Lambda_1)(a_2, \Lambda_2) \ldots (a_n, \Lambda_n) \in L_f(\mathcal{A}_{nfa})$, there must be a run of the form $s_0 \xrightarrow{(a_1, \Lambda_1)} s_1 \xrightarrow{(a_2, \Lambda_2)} \cdots s_{n-1} \xrightarrow{(a_n, \Lambda_n)} s_n$, according to Definition 5. Hence $(s_{i-1}, a_i, s_i) \in \Delta$ with $\Lambda_i \subseteq I_i$, for some $I_i \in \mu(s_{i-1}, a_i, s_i)$ and $1 \leq i \leq n$. It follows that there exists a run $s_0 \xrightarrow[\lambda_1]{a_1} s_1 \xrightarrow[\lambda_2]{a_2} \cdots s_{n-1} \xrightarrow[\lambda_n]{a_n} s_n$ and a timed word $w_t = (a_1, t_1)(a_2, t_2) \ldots (a_n, t_n) \in L_f(\mathcal{A})$ such that $t_1 \in I_1$ and $(t_i - t_{i-1}) \in I_i$ for $1 < i \leq n$. $\square$

In order to consider complement and intersection over trace-equivalent languages, we should put some restrictions over these languages over $\Sigma \times (2^{\mathbb{R}_{\geq 0}} \setminus \{\emptyset\})$, for example, the *partitioned* language defined below.

Definition 7. *A language L over an alphabet $E \subseteq \Sigma \times (2^{\mathbb{R}_{\geq 0}} \setminus \{\emptyset\})$, where Σ is finite, is called to be partitioned, if for any $a \in \Sigma$, $\mathfrak{P}_a = \{I_a : (a, I_a) \in E\}$ is a partition of $\mathbb{R}_{\geq 0}$.*

The accepting language of the NFA defined in Definition 5 is partitioned, since $I(\mu_a)$ is a partition of $\mathbb{R}_{\geq 0}$ for each $a \in \Sigma$.

Lemma 2. *If L_1 is a timed language over Σ, L_2 is a partitioned language over $E = \bigcup_{a \in \Sigma}(\{a\} \times \mathfrak{P}_a)$ where each $\mathfrak{P}_a$ is a partition of $\mathbb{R}_{\geq 0}$, and $L_2 \approx_{tr} L_1$ as defined in Definition 6, then it also holds that $(E^* \setminus L_2) \approx_{tr} (TW^*(\Sigma) \setminus L_1)$.*

Proof. $\varepsilon_t \in \Sigma \setminus L_1 \Leftrightarrow \varepsilon_t \notin L_1 \Leftrightarrow \varepsilon \notin L_2 \Leftrightarrow \varepsilon \in E^* \setminus L_2$.

Suppose $w_t = (a_1, t_1)(a_2, t_2) \ldots (a_n, t_n) \in TW^*(\Sigma) \setminus L_1$, then there must be $I_{a_i} \ni t_i - t_{i-1}$ for each i (t_0 is set to 0 here). Thus, it follows $(a_1, I_{a_1})(a_2, I_{a_2}) \ldots (a_n, I_{a_n}) \in E^*$. $(a_1, I_{a_1})(a_2, I_{a_2}) \ldots (a_n, I_{a_n})$ is not in L_2, otherwise w_t would be in L_1. So $(a_1, I_{a_1})(a_2, I_{a_2}) \ldots (a_n, I_{a_n})$ is in $E^* \setminus L_2$.

Suppose $w = (a_1, \Lambda_1)(a_2, \Lambda_2) \ldots (a_n, \Lambda_n) \in E^* \setminus L_2$, let $w_t = (a_1, t_1)(a_2, t_2) \ldots (a_n, t_n)$ be any timed word with $t_1 \in \Lambda_1$ and $t_i - t_{i-1} \in \Lambda_i$ for $i = 2, \ldots, n$. It holds that $w_t \notin L_1$, otherwise there would exist some $w' = (a_1, \Lambda'_1)(a_2, \Lambda'_2) \ldots (a_n, \Lambda'_n)$ such that $t_1 \in \Lambda'_1$ and $t_i - t_{i-1} \in \Lambda'_i$ for $1 < i \leq n$, and therefore $\Lambda_i = \Lambda'_i$ and $w = w'$, which is a contradiction. So w_t is in $TW^*(\Sigma) \setminus L_1$. $\square$

Lemma 3. *If L_1, L_3 are timed languages over Σ, L_2, L_4 are partitioned languages over the same alphabet $E = \bigcup_{a \in \Sigma}(\{a\} \times \mathfrak{P}_a)$ where $\mathfrak{P}_a$ is a partition of $\mathbb{R}_{\geq 0}$, and $L_2 \approx_{tr} L_1$ and $L_4 \approx_{tr} L_3$ as defined in Definition 6, it also holds that $(L_2 \cap L_4) \approx_{tr} (L_1 \cap L_3)$.*

Proof. $\varepsilon_t \in L_1 \cap L_3 \Leftrightarrow \varepsilon_t \in L_1 \wedge \varepsilon_t \in L_3 \Leftrightarrow \varepsilon \in L_2 \wedge \varepsilon \in L_4 \Leftrightarrow \varepsilon \in L_2 \cap L_4$.

If $w_t = (a_1, t_1)(a_2, t_2) \ldots (a_n, t_n) \in L_1 \cap L_3$, then $w_t \in L_1 \wedge w_t \in L_3$. There exists a $w^2 = (a_1, \Lambda_1^2)(a_2, \Lambda_2^2) \ldots (a_n, \Lambda_n^2) \in L_2$ such that $t_i - t_{i-1} \in \Lambda_i^2$ for each i (here $t_0 = 0$), and there exists a $w^4 = (a_1, \Lambda_1^4)(a_2, \Lambda_2^4) \ldots (a_n, \Lambda_n^4) \in L_4$ such that $t_i - t_{i-1} \in \Lambda_i^4$ for each i (also $t_0 = 0$). Since L_2 and L_4 are partitioned language over a common alphabet E, Λ_i^2 and Λ_i^4 are both in the partition $\mathfrak{P}_{a_i}$. $\Lambda_i^2 \cap \Lambda_i^4 \neq \emptyset$ means that $\Lambda_i^2 = \Lambda_i^4$ for $i = 1, \ldots, n$ and $w^2 = w^4$. So $w^2 \in L_2 \wedge w^2 \in L_4$. Then $w^2 \in L_2 \cap L_4$.

If $w = (a_1, \Lambda_1)(a_2, \Lambda_2) \ldots (a_n, \Lambda_n) \in L_2 \cap L_4$, $w \in L_2$ and $w \in L_4$. For any $w_t = (a_1, t_1)(a_2, t_2) \ldots (a_n, t_n)$ where $t_i - t_{i-1} \in \Lambda_i$ ($t_0 = 0$), $w_t \in L_1$ and $w_t \in L_3$, so $w_t \in L_1 \cap L_3$. □

4 Decidability

Time plays an important role in real-time automata, since all transitions take some time to execute no matter whether their labels are observable. When unobservable labels are deleted from a trace, their elapsed time cannot vanish. In an observed timed word $v_t = (a_1, t_1)(a_2, t_2) \ldots (a_n, t_n)$, each a_i-transition takes some time less or equal to $t_i - t_{i-1}$ ($t_0 = 0$) due to possible unobservable transitions. For example, in Fig. 1, if $P_{\{b\}, t}(w_t) = (b, 4.5)$, there must be an a occurring before b in w_t, that is, $w_t = (a, t_a)(b, 4.5)$ with $1.5 \leq t_a \leq 2$.

If there exists a real-time automaton accepting the observable language generated by the original one, then we can translate this real-time automaton into its trace-equivalent finite-state automata and then into an equivalent deterministic automaton. Thus, two DFAs can be constructed $\mathcal{A}_{dfa}^s$ and $\mathcal{A}_{dfa}^{ns}$, which accept languages that are trace-equivalent to L_s and L_{ns} respectively as defined in Sect. 2.3.

We will describe the constructions in details in the following, with $\mathcal{A} = (S, \Sigma, \Delta, Init, F, \mu)$ being the original real-time automaton, $S_{secret} \subseteq S$ being the secret, and $\Sigma_o \subseteq \Sigma$ being the observable alphabet. τ is used to denote all the unobservable events in the set $\Sigma \setminus \Sigma_o$.

4.1 Calculating Time Between Observable Events

Unobservable transitions are similar to ε-transitions of non-deterministic automata. The only difference is that unobservable transitions still take some time.

Consider a run of $\mathcal{A}$: $s_0 \xrightarrow[\lambda_1]{\tau} s_1 \xrightarrow[\lambda_2]{\tau} \cdots \xrightarrow[\lambda_{n-1}]{\tau} s_{n-1} \xrightarrow[\lambda_n]{a_n} s_n$, which consists of $n - 1$ unobservable transitions and one observable transition in sequence. Then a_n occurs at $\sum_{i=1}^n \lambda_i$. Similarly, if we consider a segment of a run: $s_0' \cdots \xrightarrow[\lambda_0]{a_0}$

$s_0 \xrightarrow[\lambda_1]{\tau} s_1 \xrightarrow[\lambda_2]{\tau} \cdots \xrightarrow[\lambda_{n-1}]{\tau} s_{n-1} \xrightarrow[\lambda_n]{a_n} s_n$, the time difference between a_n and a_0 is also $\sum_{i=1}^{n} \lambda_i$. It includes two parts: the sum of time taken by unobservable ones, and the time taken by the final observable one.

Based on the analysis above, there are two things to be done for each pair of states (s, s'), where s is an initial state or the post-state of an observable transition, and s' is the pre-state of an observable one. The first is to calculate how much time it can probably take to transit from s to s' via unobservable transitions, and the result is denoted by $\Lambda_{uo}(s, s')$, which is a subset of $\mathbb{R}_{\geq 0}$. The second is to sum up $\Lambda_{uo}(s, s')$ with the time taken by each observable transition from s', say (s', a, s''), thus we can obtain new transitions of the form (s, a, s'') whose corresponding time is the sum of $\Lambda_{uo}(s, s')$ and $\mu(s', a, s'')$. And therefore we can build a new real-time automaton whose alphabet is Σ_o alone.

In order to calculate $\Lambda_{uo}(s, s')$ for each pair (s, s'), we construct the *timing automaton* $\mathcal{A}_t$, a finite-state automaton with the alphabet $\bigcup_{\tau \in \Sigma \setminus \Sigma_o} \mu_\tau$, where $\mu_\tau = \{\mu(s_1, \tau, s_2) \mid (s_1, \tau, s_2) \in \Delta\}$. Only unobservable transitions of $\mathcal{A}$ and time taken by them are considered in $\mathcal{A}_t$. Each event in the alphabet of $\mathcal{A}_t$ is actually a non-empty subset of $\mathbb{R}_{\geq 0}$. Formally,

Definition 8. *The timing automaton of a real-time automaton $\mathcal{A}$ is a finite-state automaton $\mathcal{A}_t = (S_t, \Sigma_t, \delta_t, Init_t, F_t)$, where*

- $S_t = \mathcal{A}.S$;
- Σ_t is $\bigcup_{\tau \in \Sigma \setminus \Sigma_o} \mu_\tau = \bigcup_{\tau \in \Sigma \setminus \Sigma_o} \{\mu(s_1, \tau, s_2) \mid (s_1, \tau, s_2) \in \Delta\}$;
- $\delta_t(s_1, \Lambda) = \{s_2 \mid \exists \tau \in \Sigma_{uo}((s_1, \tau, s_2) \in \mathcal{A}.\Delta \wedge \mathcal{A}.\mu(s_1, \tau, s_2) = \Lambda)\}$;
- $Init_t = \mathcal{A}.Init \cup \bigcup_{a \in \Sigma_o} Post_a$, *and*
- $F_t = \bigcup_{a \in \Sigma_o} Pre_a$.

Based on $\mathcal{A}_t$, we can calculate $\Lambda_{uo}(s, s')$ using regular expressions by following the proof methods for Kleene's theorem.

Suppose the set of states is $\{s_i\}_{i \in \{1, \dots, n\}}$. Let $R(s_{i_1}, s_{i_2}, k)$ be the regular expression denoting all the traces of runs from s_{i_1} to s_{i_2} where there are no states in between for $k = 0$, and no states with subscripts larger than k in between, for $1 \leq k \leq n$.

For any (s_{i_1}, s_{i_2}), the set $\{\Lambda \mid s_{i_2} \in \delta_t(s_{i_1}, \Lambda)\}$ is the events of all transitions from s_{i_1} to s_{i_2}. Let $R_0(s_{i_1}, s_{i_2})$ be the regular expression which is the sum of all events in $\{\Lambda \mid s_{i_2} \in \delta_t(s_{i_1}, \Lambda)\}$. If there is no such Λ, $R_0(s_{i_1}, s_{i_2})$ is set to $\emptyset$.

Then $R(s_{i_1}, s_{i_2}, k)$ is computed inductively: $R(s_{i_1}, s_{i_1}, 0) = \varepsilon + R_0(s_{i_1}, s_{i_1})$, and $R(s_{i_1}, s_{i_2}, 0) = R_0(s_{i_1}, s_{i_2})$ if $i_1 \neq i_2$. And $R(s_{i_1}, s_{i_2}, k+1) = R(s_{i_1}, s_{i_2}, k) + R(s_{i_1}, s_{k+1}, k) \cdot R(s_{k+1}, s_{k+1}, k)^* \cdot R(s_{k+1}, s_{i_2}, k)$.

So we can finally obtain $R(s_{i_1}, s_{i_2}, n)$ for each pair of states $(s_{i_1}, s_{i_2}) \in Init_t \times F_t$, which denotes the traces of runs from s_{i_1} to s_{i_2}.

After regular expressions have been obtained, the next step is to translate them into subsets of $\mathbb{R}_{\geq 0}$. Here $\emptyset$ means an empty set, ε means the set $\{0\}$, and Λ means the set Λ. And if r, r_1, r_2 are regular expressions and Λ, Λ_1, Λ_2 are their corresponding sets, we can translate $r_1 \cdot r_2$ into $\Lambda_1 + \Lambda_2 := \{\lambda_1 + \lambda_2 \mid \lambda_1 \in \Lambda_1, \lambda_2 \in \Lambda_2\}$, $r_1 + r_2$ into $\Lambda_1 \cup \Lambda_2 := \{\lambda \mid \lambda \in \Lambda_1 \vee \lambda \in \Lambda_2\}$, and r^* into $\Lambda^* := \bigcup_{k \in \mathbb{N}} k\Lambda$, where $0\Lambda = \{0\}$ and $(k+1)\Lambda = k\Lambda + \Lambda$ for $k \geq 0$.

Following these steps, we can obtain $\Lambda_{uo}(s_{i_1}, s_{i_2})$ from $R(s_{i_1}, s_{i_2}, n)$ for each pair of states $(s_{i_1}, s_{i_2}) \in Init_t \times F_t$.

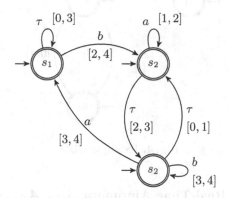

Fig. 3. Example: $\mathcal{A}$, the original real-time automaton under study

Example 4. In the real-time automaton $\mathcal{A}$ in Fig. 3, Σ is divided into two sets, the observable $\{a, b\}$ and the unobservable $\{\tau\}$. The states s_1, s_2, s_3 are all initial and accepting. Transitions are arrows from one state to another with a label a, b, or τ, and timing information of each transition is the interval written near its label.

Its timing automaton, denoted as $\mathcal{A}_t$, is depicted in Fig. 4.

$R(s_{i_1}, s_{i_2}, k)$ not equal to $\emptyset$ are listed below:

$k = 0$: $R(s_1, s_1, 0) = \varepsilon + [0, 3]$, $R(s_2, s_2, 0) = \varepsilon$, $R(s_2, s_3, 0) = [2, 3]$, $R(s_3, s_2, 0) = [0, 1]$, $R(s_3, s_3, 0) = \varepsilon$;

$k = 1$: $R(s_1, s_1, 1) = (\varepsilon + [0, 3]) + (\varepsilon + [0, 3])(\varepsilon + [0, 3])^*(\varepsilon + [0, 3]) = [0, 3]^*$, $R(s_2, s_2, 1) = \varepsilon$, $R(s_2, s_3, 1) = [2, 3]$, $R(s_3, s_2, 1) = [0, 1]$, $R(s_3, s_3, 1) = \varepsilon$;

$k = 2$: $R(s_1, s_1, 2) = [0, 3]^*$, $R(s_2, s_2, 2) = \varepsilon$, $R(s_2, s_3, 2) = [2, 3] + \varepsilon \varepsilon^*[2, 3] = [2, 3]$, $R(s_3, s_2, 2) = [0, 1] + [0, 1]\varepsilon^*\varepsilon = [0, 1]$, $R(s_3, s_3, 2) = \varepsilon + [0, 1]\varepsilon^*[2, 3] = \varepsilon + [0, 1] \cdot [2, 3]$;

$k = 3$: $R(s_1, s_1, 3) = [0, 3]^*$, $R(s_2, s_2, 3) = \varepsilon + [2, 3](\varepsilon + [0, 1] \cdot [2, 3])^*[0, 1] = ([2, 3] \cdot [0, 1])^*$, $R(s_2, s_3, 3) = [2, 3] + [2, 3](\varepsilon + [0, 1] \cdot [2, 3])^*(\varepsilon + [0, 1] \cdot [2, 3]) = [2, 3]([0, 1] \cdot [2, 3]))^*$, $R(s_3, s_2, 3) = [0, 1] + (\varepsilon + [0, 1] \cdot [2, 3])(\varepsilon + [0, 1] \cdot [2, 3])^*[0, 1] = [0, 1]([2, 3] \cdot [0, 1])^*$, $R(s_3, s_3, 3) = (\varepsilon + [0, 1] \cdot [2, 3]) + (\varepsilon + [0, 1] \cdot [2, 3])(\varepsilon + [0, 1] \cdot [2, 3])^*(\varepsilon + [0, 1] \cdot [2, 3]) = ([0, 1] \cdot [2, 3])^*$.

Finally, $\Lambda_{uo}(s_{i_1}, s_{i_2})$ can be obtained from $R(s_{i_1}, s_{i_2}, 3)$: $\Lambda_{uo}(s_1, s_1) = [0, +\infty)$, $\Lambda_{uo}(s_2, s_2) = \Lambda_{uo}(s_3, s_3) = \{0\} \cup [2, +\infty)$, $\Lambda_{uo}(s_3, s_2) = [0, 1] \cup [2, +\infty)$, $\Lambda_{uo}(s_2, s_3) = [2, +\infty)$, and $\Lambda_{uo}(s_1, s_2) = \Lambda_{uo}(s_1, s_3) = \Lambda_{uo}(s_2, s_1) = \Lambda_{uo}(s_3, s_1) = \emptyset$. □

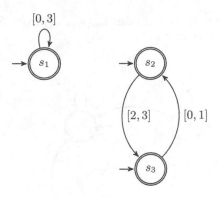

Fig. 4. Example: $\mathcal{A}_t$

4.2   Constructing Real-Time Automata $\mathcal{A}_{obs}$, $\mathcal{A}_{obs,s}$ and $\mathcal{A}_{obs,ns}$

After that, we can define a real-time automaton $\mathcal{A}_{obs}$. Its alphabet is Σ_o, and each of its transition starts from an initial state or a post-state of an observable transition and ends in a post-state of an observable transition of $\mathcal{A}$. Formally,

Definition 9. $\mathcal{A}_{obs} = (S_{obs}, \Sigma_{obs}, \Delta_{obs}, Init_{obs}, F_{obs}, \mu_{obs})$ *can be constructed as follows:*

- $S_{obs} = \mathcal{A}.Init \cup \bigcup_{a \in \Sigma_o} Post_a$,
- $\Sigma_{obs} = \Sigma_o$,
- $\Delta_{obs} = \{(s_1, a, s_2) \mid \exists s_3 \in \mathcal{A}.S(\Lambda_{uo}(s_1, s_3) \neq \emptyset \wedge (s_3, a, s_2) \in \mathcal{A}.\Delta)\}$,
- $Init_{obs} = \mathcal{A}.Init$,
- $F_{obs} = \bigcup_{a \in \Sigma_o} Post_a$, *and*
- $\mu_{obs}(s_1, a, s_2) = \bigcup\{\Lambda_{uo}(s_1, s_3) + \mathcal{A}.\mu(s_3, a, s_2) \mid \exists s_3 \in \mathcal{A}.S(\Lambda_{uo}(s_1, s_3) \neq \emptyset \wedge (s_3, a, s_2) \in \mathcal{A}.\Delta)\}$.

Example 5 (Ctd.). Now we build $\mathcal{A}_{obs} = (S_{obs}, \Sigma_{obs}, \Delta_{obs}, Init_{obs}, F_{obs}, \mu_{obs})$ shown in Fig. 5. $S_{obs} = Init_{obs} = F_{obs} = \{s_1, s_2, s_3\}$. $\Sigma_{obs} = \{a, b\}$. Transitions and their corresponding time labels are listed below:
(s_1, b, s_2): $\mu(s_1, b, s_2) = [2, +\infty)$;
(s_2, a, s_2): $\mu(s_2, a, s_2) = [1, 2] \cup [3, +\infty)$;
(s_3, a, s_2): $\mu(s_3, a, s_2) = [1, +\infty)$;
(s_2, b, s_3): $\mu(s_2, b, s_3) = [5, +\infty]$;
(s_3, b, s_3): $\mu(s_3, b, s_3) = [3, 4] \cup [5, +\infty)$;
(s_2, a, s_1): $\mu(s_2, a, s_1) = [5, +\infty)$;
(s_3, a, s_1): $\mu(s_3, a, s_1) = [3, 4] \cup [5, +\infty)$.
The time information is neglected in the figure for the sake of simplicity.   □

Lemma 4. *Given* w_t *in* $Tr(s_0)$ *of* $\mathcal{A}$, $P_{\Sigma,t}(w_t)$ *is in* $Tr(s_0)$ *of* $\mathcal{A}_{obs}$ *if* $P_{\Sigma,t}(w_t) \neq \varepsilon_t$.

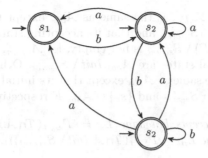

Fig. 5. Example: $\mathcal{A}_{obs}$

Proof. $P_{\Sigma,t}(w_t) \neq \varepsilon_t$ means that there is at least one observable label in w_t. Suppose observable labels occurring in w_t are a_1, a_2, ..., and a_n at t_1, t_2, ..., and t_n respectively, then $P_{\Sigma,t}(w_t) = (a_1, t_1)(a_2, t_2)\ldots(a_n, t_n)$. Let ρ be a run of $\mathcal{A}$ from s_0 whose trace is w_t. There must be transitions (s_1, a_1, s_1'), (s_2, a_2, s_2'), ..., and (s_n, a_n, s_n') in ρ, and s_{i+1} is reachable from s_i' for $0 \leq i < n$. (Let $s_0' = s_0$ and $t_0 = 0$ here.) Each $t_k - t_{k-1}$ is the sum of two parts: one is time taken by unobservable transition(s) from s_{k-1}' to s_k, and the other is time taken by transition (s_k, a_k, s_k'). In other words, there exists some $\lambda_{uo,k} \in \Lambda_{uo}(s_{k-1}', s_k)$ and $\lambda_{o,k} \in \mathcal{A}.\mu(s_k, a_k, s_k')$ such that $t_k - t_{k-1} = \lambda_{uo,k} + \lambda_{o,k}$. Based on the constructing steps of $\mathcal{A}_{obs}$, there exists transitions (s_{k-1}', a_k, s_k') in $\mathcal{A}_{obs}$ whose time labels include $t_k - t_{k-1}$ respectively, so that there exists a run $\rho_{obs} = s_0 \xrightarrow[t_1]{a_1}$ $s_1' \xrightarrow[t_2 - t_1]{a_2} s_2' \cdots s_{n-1}' \xrightarrow[t_n - t_{n-1}]{a_n} s_n'$, whose trace is $P_{\Sigma,t}(w_t)$. $\square$

Lemma 5. *Given $v_t \neq \varepsilon_t$ in $Tr(s_0)$ of $\mathcal{A}_{obs}$, there exists some w_t in $Tr(s_0)$ of $\mathcal{A}$ such that $P_{\Sigma,t}(w_t) = v_t$.*

Proof. Suppose there exists a run of $\mathcal{A}_{obs}$, say $\rho_{obs} = s_0 \xrightarrow[t_1]{a_1} s_1' \xrightarrow[t_2 - t_1]{a_2} s_2' \cdots$ $s_{n-1}' \xrightarrow[t_n - t_{n-1}]{a_n} s_n'$, whose trace is $v_t = (a_1, t_1)(a_2, t_2)\ldots(a_n, t_n)$. There must be transitions (s_1, a_1, s_1'), (s_2, a_2, s_2'), ..., and (s_n, a_n, s_n') in $\mathcal{A}$, and s_{i+1} is reachable from s_i' via only unobservable transitions for $0 \leq i < n$ ($s_0' = s_0$ here). Each $t_k - t_{k-1}$ is the sum of some $\lambda_{uo,k} \in \Lambda_{uo}(s_{k-1}', s_k)$ and $\lambda_{o,k} \in \mathcal{A}.\mu(s_k, a_k, s_k')$ ($t_0 = 0$ here). Hence, there is a run of $\mathcal{A}$, $\rho = s_0 \cdots s_1 \xrightarrow[\lambda_{o,1}]{a_1} s_1' \cdots s_2 \xrightarrow[\lambda_{o,2}]{a_2}$ $s_2' \cdots s_n \xrightarrow[\lambda_{o,n}]{a_n} s_n'$ with $P_{\Sigma_o,t}(trace(\rho)) = (a_1, t_1)(a_2, t_2)\ldots(a_n, t_n) = v_t$. $\square$

Based on the above discussion, two real-time automata, $\mathcal{A}_{obs,s}$ and $\mathcal{A}_{obs,ns}$, can be constructed according to the given S_{secret} as follows:

– If $(\mathcal{A}_{obs}.Init \cap \mathcal{A}_{obs}.F) \cap S_{secret}$ is not empty, let $\mathcal{A}_{obs,s}$ be the same as $\mathcal{A}_{obs}$ except that its initial states are $\mathcal{A}_{obs}.Init \cap S_{secret}$. Otherwise, we introduce a new state s_ε, having no transition starts from or ends in it, to ensure ε_t is also accepted. Here $\mathcal{A}_{obs,s}$ is the same as $\mathcal{A}_{obs}$ except that its initial states are $\{s_\varepsilon\} \cup \mathcal{A}_{obs}.Init \cap S_{secret}$, and that its accepting states are $\{s_\varepsilon\} \cup \mathcal{A}_{obs}.F$.

– If $(\mathcal{A}_{obs}.Init \cap \mathcal{A}_{obs}.F) \setminus S_{secret}$ is not empty, let $\mathcal{A}_{obs,ns}$ be the same as $\mathcal{A}_{obs}$ except that its initial states are $\mathcal{A}_{obs}.Init \setminus S_{secret}$. Otherwise, we introduce s_ε, then $\mathcal{A}_{obs,s}$ is the same as $\mathcal{A}_{obs}$ except that its initial and accepting states are $\{s_\varepsilon\} \cup \mathcal{A}_{obs}.Init \setminus S_{secret}$ and $\{s_\varepsilon\} \cup \mathcal{A}_{obs}.F$ respectively.

Theorem 2. $\mathcal{A}_{obs,s}$ *accepts language* $L_s = P_{\Sigma_o,t}(Tr(\mathcal{A}.Init \cap S_{secret})))$, *and* $\mathcal{A}_{obs,ns}$ *accepts language* $L_{ns} = P_{\Sigma_o,t}(Tr(\mathcal{A}.Init \setminus S_{secret})))$.

Proof. This is straightforward from Lemmas 4 and 5 and the constructions of $\mathcal{A}_{obs,s}$ and $\mathcal{A}_{obs,ns}$. □

Example 6 (Ctd.). Let $S_{secret} = \{s_1\}$. Then $\mathcal{A}_{obs,s}$ and $\mathcal{A}_{obs,ns}$ are depicted in Fig. 6. Their time information is also neglected in this figure, the same as the previous example's. □

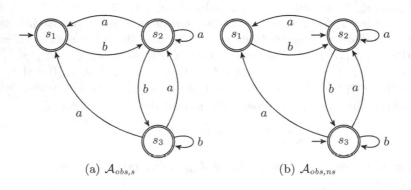

(a) $\mathcal{A}_{obs,s}$ (b) $\mathcal{A}_{obs,ns}$

Fig. 6. Example: $\mathcal{A}_{obs,s}$ and $\mathcal{A}_{obs,ns}$

4.3   Building Trace-Equivalent NFAs

Since $\mathcal{A}_{obs,s}$ and $\mathcal{A}_{obs,ns}$ are built, they can be transformed into their corresponding NFAs $\mathcal{A}_{nfa,s}$ and $\mathcal{A}_{nfa,ns}$, which are trace-equivalent to them respectively. Thus can be built DFAs $\mathcal{A}_{dfa,s}$ and $\mathcal{A}_{dfa,ns}$ further, which are equivalent to $\mathcal{A}_{nfa,s}$ and $\mathcal{A}_{nfa,ns}$ respectively. By exploiting complement and product operations over DFAs, $\mathcal{A}_{dfa}^p = \mathcal{A}_{dfa,ns}^{comp} \times \mathcal{A}_{dfa,s}$ can be obtained. $\mathcal{A}_{dfa}^p$ accepts the language trace-equivalent to the intersection of $L_s = L_f(\mathcal{A}_{obs,s})$ and complement of $L_{ns} = L_f(\mathcal{A}_{obs,ns})$, based on Sect. 3.

Theorem 3. *The initial-state opacity problem of real-time automata is decidable.*

Proof. Given a real-time automaton $\mathcal{A}$, Σ_o and S_{secret}, an automaton $\mathcal{A}_{dfa}^p$ can be constructed by following the steps discussed above. $\mathcal{A}_{dfa}^p$ accepts the language $L_f(\mathcal{A}_{dfa,ns})^c \cap L_f(\mathcal{A}_{dfa,s})$, which is trace-equivalent to the timed language $L_{ns}^c \cap L_s$.

The problem is to check whether $\mathcal{A}_{dfa}^p$ accepts any word $w \neq \varepsilon$. A word $w = (a_1, \Lambda_1)\ldots(a_n, \Lambda_n)$ being accepted means that any timed word $w_t = (a_1, t_1)\ldots(a_n, t_n)$ with $t_i - t_{i-1} \in \Lambda_i$ ($t_0 = 0$) is in the set $L_{ns}^c \cap L_s$, that is, $\mathcal{A}$ is not initial-state opaque w.r.t S_{secret} and Σ_o. Otherwise, $\mathcal{A}$ is opaque w.r.t S_{secret} and Σ_o. $\qquad\square$

5   Conclusion

In this paper, we investigated the initial-state opacity problem of real-time automata. The original real-time automaton is first translated into a new one whose alphabet is the observable alphabet, and then into two real-time automata accepting the projection of secret and non-secret languages respectively. We introduce a relation between timed words over Σ and untimed words over $\Sigma \times (2^{\mathbb{R}_{\geq 0}} \setminus \{\emptyset\})$ called trace-equivalence, and transform real-time automata into finite-state automata. We also introduce the notion of partitioned languages, to guarantee the closure under complementation and product. Therefore results of finite-state automata can be applied. Finally, we come up with the conclusion that the initial-state opacity problem of real-time automata is decidable.

A system is called *language-opaque* if an intruder with partial observability can never determine whether a trace of the system is secret no matter what he has observed. As an on-going and future work, it deserves to investigate the language opacity problem of RTA, which will be reported in another paper. In addition, it is quite interesting how to apply RTA to model security properties of communication protocols with time in the real-world.

References

1. Saboori, A., Hadjicostis, C.N.: Verification of initial-state opacity in security applications of discrete event systems. Inf. Sci. **246**, 115–132 (2013)
2. Bryans, J.W., Kounty, M., Ryan, P.Y.: Modelling opacity using petri nets. Electron. Notes Theor. Comput. Sci. **121**, 101–115 (2005). Proceedings of the 2nd International Workshop on Security Issues with Petri Nets and other Computational Models (WISP 2004)
3. Tong, Y., Li, Z., Seatzu, C., Giua, A.: Verification of state-based opacity using Petri nets. IEEE Trans. Autom. Control. **62**(6), 2823–2837 (2017)
4. Bryans, J.W., Kounty, M., Mazaré, L., Ryan, P.Y.A.: Opacity generalised to transition systems. Int. J. Inf. Secur. **7**(6), 421–435 (2008)
5. Saboori, A., Hadjicostis, C.N.: Verification of k-step opacity and analysis of its complexity. In: Proceedings of the 48th IEEE Conference on Decision and Control (CDC) held jointly with 2009 28th Chinese Control Conference, pp. 205–210 (2009)
6. Saboori, A., Hadjicostis, C.N.: Opacity-enforcing supervisory strategies via state estimator constructions. IEEE Trans. Autom. Control. **57**(5), 1155–1165 (2012)

7. Saboori, A., Hadjicostis, C.N.: Verification of infinite-step opacity and complexity considerations. IEEE Trans. Autom. Control. **57**(5), 1265–1269 (2012)
8. Keroglou, C., Hadjicostis, C.N.: Initial state opacity in stochastic des. In: 2013 IEEE 18th Conference on Emerging Technologies & Factory Automation (ETFA), pp. 1–8 (2013)
9. Bérard, B., Chatterjee, K., Sznajder, N.: Probabilistic opacity for Markov decision processes. Inf. Process. Lett. **115**(1), 52–59 (2015)
10. Bérard, B., Mullins, J., Sassolas, M.: Quantifying opacity. In: 2010 Seventh International Conference on the Quantitative Evaluation of Systems, pp. 263–272 (2010)
11. Ibrahim, M., Chen, J., Kumar, R.: Secrecy in stochastic discrete event systems. In: Proceedings of the 11th IEEE International Conference on Networking, Sensing and Control, pp. 48–53 (2014)
12. Cassez, F.: The dark side of timed opacity. In: Park, J.H., Chen, H.-H., Atiquzzaman, M., Lee, C., Kim, T., Yeo, S.-S. (eds.) ISA 2009. LNCS, vol. 5576, pp. 21–30. Springer, Heidelberg (2009). https://doi.org/10.1007/978-3-642-02617-1_3
13. Dima, C.: Real-time automata. J. Autom. Lang. Comb. **6**(1), 3–24 (2001)

Domain Science and Engineering
A Review of 10 Years Work and a Laudatio
The ZCC Fest, 20 October 2017, Changsha, China

Dines Bjørner[1,2(✉)]

[1] Technical University of Denmark, 2800 Kongens Lyngby, Denmark
[2] Fredsvej 11, 2840 Holte, Danmark
bjorner@gmail.com
http://www.imm.dtu.dk/~db

Abstract. A personal account is given of my scientific work since I retired 10 years ago. This work centers around a new dimension to computing science: that of domain science & engineering. By a *domain* we shall understand a *rationally describable* segment of a *human assisted* reality, i.e., of the world, its *physical parts*, and *living species*. These are *endurants* ("still"), existing in space, as well as *perdurants* ("alive"), existing also in time. Emphasis is placed on *"human-assistedness"*, that is, that there is *at least one (man-made) artifact* and that *humans* are a primary cause for change of endurant *states* as well as perdurant *behaviours*. Section 7 brings my laudatio.

1 Introduction

I survey recent work in the area of *domain science & engineering*[1].

A strict interpretation of the *triptych* of software engineering dogma suggests that software development "ideally" proceeds in three phases:

- First a phase of *domain engineering* in which an analysis of the application domain leads to a description of that domain.
- Then a phase of *requirements engineering* in which an analysis of the domain description leads to a prescription of requirements to software for that domain.
- And, finally, a phase of *software design* in which an analysis of the requirements prescription leads to software for that domain.

We see *domain science & engineering* as a discipline that *need not be justified as a precursor to requirements engineering. Just as physicists study nature, irrespective of engineering, so we can study manifest domains irrespective of computing.*

---

[1] It is appropriate, at this point, to state that my use of the term 'domain' is not related to that of *Domains and Processes* such as in the *Proceedings of 1st International Symposium on Domain Theory, Shanghai, China, October 1999*, eds.: Klaus Keimel, Zhang Guo-Qiang, Liu Ying-Ming and Chen Yi-Chang. Springer Science + Business Media, New York, 2001.

© Springer Nature Switzerland AG 2018
C. Jones et al. (Eds.): Zhou-Festschrift, LNCS 11180, pp. 61–84, 2018.
https://doi.org/10.1007/978-3-030-01461-2_4

1.1   Recent Papers and Reports

Over the last decade I have iterated a number of investigations of aspects of this *triptych* dogma. This has resulted in a number of papers (and revised reports):

- Manifest Domains: Analysis & Description (2018, 2014)   [29,35]
- Domain Facets: Analysis & Description (2018. 2008)   [12,31]
- From Domains to Requirements (2018, 2008)   [8,25]
- Formal Models of Processes and Prompts (2014,2017)   [20,23]
- To Every Domain Mereology a CSP Expression (2017, 2009)   [10,33]
- Domains: Their Simulation, Monitoring and Control (2008)   [16,24]
- A Philosophy of Domain Science & Engineering (2018)   [30]

[30], a report, is the most recent.

1.2   Recent Experiments

Applications of the domain science and engineering outlined in [8–29] are exemplified in reports and papers on experimental domain analysis & description. Examples are:

- *Urban Planning* [41],   - *Road Transportation* [19],
- *Documents* [28]   - *Web/Transaction-based Software* [14],
- *Credit Cards* [22],   - *"The Market"* [4],
- *Weather Information Systems* [26], - *Container [Shipping]Lines*[7],
- *The Tokyo Stock Exchange* [34],   - *Railway Systems* [3,5,37,51,56].
- *Pipelines* [18],

1.3   My Emphasis on Software Systems

An emphasis in my work has been on research into and experiments with application areas that required seemingly large scale software. Not on tiny, beautiful, essential data structures and algorithms.

I first worked on the proper application of formal methods in software engineering at the *IBM Vienna Laboratory* in the early 1970s. That was to the formalisation of the semantics of IBMs leading programming language then, *PL/I*, and to a systematic development of a compiler for that language. The latter never transpired.

Instead I got the chance to formulate the stages of development of a compiler from a denotational semantics description to so-called "running code" [2, 1977]. That led, from 1978 onward, to two MSc students and a colleague and I working on a formal description of the *CCITT Communications High Level Language, CHILL* and its compiler [1,46]. And that led, in 1980, to five MSc students of ours producing a formal description of a semantics for the *US DoD Ada programming language, Ada* [40]. And that led to the formation of *Dansk Datamatik Center* [38] which embarked on the CHILL and Ada compiler developments [42,50]. *To my knowledge that project which was on time, at budget, and with a history of less that 3% cost of original budget for subsequent error correction over the first 20 years of use of that compiler was a first, large, successful example of the systematic use of formal methods in large scale (42 man years) software development.*

1.4 How Did We Get to Domain Science and Engineering?

So that is how we came from the semantics of programming languages to the semantics of human-centered, manifest application domain software development. Programming language semantics has to do with the meaning of abstract concepts such as programs, procedures, expressions, statements, GOTOs, labels, etc. Domain semantics, for manifest domains, in so far as we can narrate and formalize it, or them, must capture some "meanings" of the manifest objects that we can touch and see, of the actions we perform on them, and of the sentences by means of which we talk about those phenomena in the domain.

1.5 Preliminaries

We need formulate a few characterisations.

Method & Methodology: By a *method* I understand a set of principles for selecting and applying techniques and tools for constructing a manifest or an abstract artifact.

By *methodology* I understand the study and knowledge of methods.

My contributions over the years have contributed to methods for software design and, now, for the last many years, methods for domain analysis & description.

In my many experiments with domain analysis & description, cf. Sect. 5, I have found that I often let a so-called "streak of creativity" enter my analysis & description – and, as a result I get stuck in my work. Then I recall, ah!, but there are these principles, techniques and tools for analysis & description, and once I apply them, "strictly", i.e., methodically, I am back on the track, and, in my view, a more beautiful description emerges!

Computer & Computing Sciences: By *computer science* I understand the study and knowledge about the things that can exist inside computing devices.

By *computing science* I understand the study and knowledge about how to construct the things that can exist inside computing devices. Computing science is also often referred to as *programming methodology. My work is almost exclusively in the area of computing science.*

A Triptych of Informatics: Before software can be designed we must have a firm grasp on its/their requirements. Before requirements can be prescribed we must have a firm grasp on their basis: the domain. We therefore see informatics as consisting of

- *domain science & engineering*,
- *requirements science & engineering*, and
- *programming methodology*.

This paper contributes to the establishment of *domain science & engineering*, while hinting that *requirements science & engineering* can benefit from the relation between the two [8,25]. *How much of a domain must we analyse & describe* before we attempt the second and third phases of the triptych?. When this question is raised, after a talk of mine over the subject, and by a colleague researcher & scientist I usually reply: *As large a domain as possible!* This reply is often met by this *comment* (from the audience) *Oh ! No, that is not reasonable!* To me that comment shows either or both of: the questioner was not asking as a researcher/scientist, but as an engineer. Yes, an engineer needs only analyse & describe up to and slightly beyond the "border" of the domain-of-interest for a current software development – but a researcher cum scientist is, of course, interested not only in a possible requirements engineering phase beyond domain engineering, but is also curious about the larger context of the domain, in possibly establishing a proper domain theory, etc.

1.6   The Papers

IM^{2}HO I consider the first of the papers reviewed, [29], *my most important paper.* It was conceived of last[2], after publication of three of the other papers [8,12, 16]. Experimental evidence then necessitated extensive revisions to these other papers, resulting in [24,25,31].

1.7   Structure of This Paper

Section 2 reviews [29, *Analysis & Description Prompts*], and Sect. 3 reviews related science and methodology papers. [31, *Domain Facets*] (Sect. 3.1), [25, *From Domains to Requirements*] (Sect. 3.2), [23, *An Analysis & Description Process Model*] (Sect. 3.3), and [33, *From Mereologies to Lambda-Expressions*] (Sect. 3.4), Finally, Sect. 4 briefly reviews [30, *A Philosophy Basis*] *work-in-progress.*

2   Manifest Domains: Analysis & Description [29]

This work grew out of many years of search for principles, techniques and tools for systematically analyzing and describing manifest domains. By a manifest domain we shall understand a domain whose entities we can observe and whose endurants we can touch!

---

[2] Publication [13,15] is a predecessor of [35] which is then a predecessor of [29].

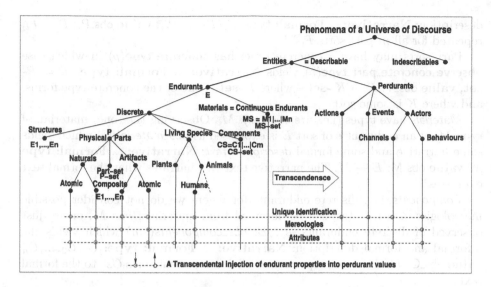

Fig. 1. Domain Ontology

2.1 A Domain Ontology

Parts, Components and Materials: The result became a calculus of analysis and description prompts[3]. These prompts are tools that the domain analyser & describer uses. The domain analyser & describer is in the domain, sees it, can touch it, and then applies the prompts, in some orderly fashion, to what is being observed. So, on one hand, there is the necessarily informal domain, and, on the other hand, there are the seemingly formal prompts and the *"suggestions for something to be said"*, i.e., written down: narrated and formalised. Fig. 1 suggests a number of *analysis* and *description* prompts. The domain analyser & describer is "positioned" at the top, the "root". If what is observed can be conceived and described then it *is an entity*. If it can be described as a "complete thing" at no matter which given snapshot of time then it *is an endurant*. If it is an entity but for which only a fragment exists if we look at or touch them at any given snapshot in time, then it *is a perdurant*. Endurants are either *discrete* or *continuous*. With discrete endurants we can choose to associate, or to not associate *mereologies*[4]. If we do we shall refer to them as *parts*, else we shall call them *components*. The continuous endurants we shall also refer to as *(gaseous or liquid) materials*. *Parts* are either *atomic* or *composite* and all parts have *unique identifiers*, *mereology* and *attributes*. Atomic parts *may have* one or more *components* and/or one or more *materials*

If the observed part, $p:P$, is composite then we can observe the part sorts, $P_1, P_2, ..., P_m$ of p: *observe_part_sorts(p)* which yields the informal and formal

---

[3] Prompt, as a verb: to move or induce to action; to occasion or incite; inspire; to assist (a person speaking) by. *"suggesting something to be said"*.

[4] — 'mereology' will be explained next.

description: **Narrative:** ... **Formal: type** $P_1, P_2, ..., P_m$, **value** obs_P_i: $P \rightarrow P_i$, repeated for all m part sorts P_is" !

Part sorts may have a concrete type: **has_concrete_type**(p) in which case **observe_concrete_part_type**(p) yields **Narrative:** ... **Formal: type:** $T = P$-set, **value** obs_T: $P \rightarrow K$ **-set** – where K-**set** is one of the concrete type forms, and where K is some sort.

Materials have types (i.e., are of sorts): M_i. Observing the (one) material, of type M, of an endurant e of sort E is expressed as *obs_materials*(e) which yields some narrative and some formal *description text:* **Narrative:** ... **Formal: type** M **value** obs_M: $E \rightarrow M$. The narrative text (...) narrates what the formal text expresses[5].

Components, i.e., discrete endurants for whom we do not consider possible mereologies or attributes, can be observed from materials, $m : M$, or are just observed of discrete endurants, $e : E$: *obs_components*(em) which yields the informal and formal description: **Narrative:** ... **Formal: type:** $C_1, C_2, ..., C_n$ **value** obs_C_i: $(E|M) \rightarrow C_i$ repeated for all n component sorts Cs" to the formal text !

• • •

The above is a pedagogic simplification. As shown in Fig. 1 there are not only parts. There are also *living species: plants* and *animals*, including *humans*. And, because there are humans in the domains, parts and materials are either *natural* or *artifacts* (man-made). Humans create artifacts, usually with an *intent*. Humans have *intents*, and artifacts "possess" *intents*. Intents are like *attributes*, see below.

• • •

We have just summarised the analysis and description aspects of endurants in *extension* (their "form"). We now summarise the analysis and description aspects of endurants in *intension* (their "contents"). There are three kinds of intensional *qualities* associated with parts, two with components, and one with materials. Parts and components, by definition, have *unique identifiers*; parts have *mereologies*, and all endurants have *attributes*.

Unique identifiers: Unique identifiers are further undefined tokens that uniquely identify parts and components. The description language observer *uid_P*, when applied to parts $p:P$ yields the unique identifier, $\pi:\Pi$, of p. The *observe_part_sorts(p)* invocation yields the description text: ... [added to the narrative and] **type** $\Pi_1, \Pi_2, ..., \Pi_m$; **value** uid_Π_i : $P_i \rightarrow \Pi_i$, repeated for all m part sorts P_is and added to the formalisation.

Mereology: *Mereology is the study and knowledge of parts and part relations.* The mereology of a part is an expression over the unique identifiers of the (other) parts with which it is related, hence *mereo_P*: $P \rightarrow \mathcal{E}(\Pi_j, ..., \Pi_k)$, $\mathcal{E}(\Pi_j, ..., \Pi_k)$ is a type expression. The *observe_part_sorts*(p) invocation yields the description text: ... [added to the narrative and] **value** mereo_P_i : $P_i \rightarrow \mathcal{E}_i(\Pi_{i_j}, ..., \Pi_{i_k})$ [added to the formalisation]

---

[5] – not how it expresses it, as, here, in the RAISE [44] Specification Language, RSL [43].

Example: The mereologies, (i, o), of pipe units in a pipeline system thus express, for each kind of pipe unit,whether it is a well, a linear pipe, a fork, a join, a pump, a valve, or a sink, the identities of the zero, one or two pipe units that it is "connected" to on the input, i, respectively the output, o, side: for well $(0, 1)$, for pipe $(1, 1)$, for fork $(1, 2)$, for join $(2, 1)$, for valve $(1, 1)$, for pump $(1, 1)$, for sink $(1, 0)$ units

Attributes: Attributes are the remaining qualities of endurants. The analysis prompt **obs_attributes** applied to an endurant yields a set of type names, $A_1, A_2, ..., A_t$, of attributes. They imply the additional description text: **Narrative:** ... **Formal: type** $A_1, A_2, ..., A_t$ **value** attr_A_i: $E \rightarrow A_i$ repeated for all t attribute sorts A_is! **Examples:** Typical attributes of a person are Gender, Weight, Height, Birth date, etcetera. Dynamic and static attributes of a pipe unit include current flow into the unit, per input, if any, current flow out of the unit, per output, if any current leak from the unit, guaranteed maximum flow into the unit, guaranteed maximum flow out of the unit, guaranteed maximum leak from the unit, etcetera. Michael A. Jackson [49] categorizes attributes as either *static* or *dynamic*, with dynamic attributes being either *inert*, *reactive* or *active*. The latter are then either *autonomous*, *biddable* or *programmable*. This categorization has a strong bearing on how these (f.ex., part) attributes are dealt with when now interpreting parts as behaviours.

2.2 From Manifest Parts to Domain Behaviours

[35] then presents an interpretation, τ, which to manifest *parts* associate *behaviours*. These are then specified as CSP [48] *processes*. This interpretation amounts to a *transcendental deduction*!

The Transcendental Deduction Idea — by means of an example: The term *train* can have the following "meanings": The *train*, as an *endurant*, parked at the railway station platform, i.e., as a *composite part*. The *train*, as a *perdurant*, as it "speeds" down the railway track, i.e., as a *behaviour*. The *train*, as an *attribute*,

Atomic Parts: Atomic parts translate into their core behaviours: $b_{core}^{P_{atom}}$. The *core* behaviours are tail recursively defined, that is, are cyclic. $b_{core}^{P_{atom}}(...) \equiv (.... ;$ $b_{core}^{P_{atom}}(...))$ where $(...)$ indicate behaviour (i.e., function) arguments.

Composite Parts: A composite part, p, "translates", τ, into the parallel composition of a core behaviour: $b_{core}^{P_{comp}}(...)$, for part p, with the parallel composition of the translations, τ, for each of the parts, $p_1, p_2, ..., p_m$, of p, $(\tau(p_1)||\tau(p_2)||...||\tau(p_m))$ that is: $\tau(p) \equiv b_{core}^{P_{comp}}(...) \ || \ (\tau(p_1)||\tau(p_2)||...||\tau(p_m))$

Concrete Parts: The translation of concrete part set, t, types, $t : T = K-\textbf{set}$, is $\tau(t) \equiv ||\{\tau(k_i)|k_i : K \bullet k_i \in t\}$.

Translation of Part Qualities (...): Part qualities, that is: *unique identifiers*, *mereologies* and *attributes*, are translated into behaviour arguments – of one kind or another, i.e., (...). Typically we can choose to *index* behaviour names, b by the *unique identifier*, id, of the part based on which they were translated, i.e., b_{id}. *Mereology values* are usually static, and can, as thus, be treated like we treat static attributes (see next), or can be set by their behaviour, and are then treated like we treat programmable attributes (see next), i.e., (...). *Static attributes* become behaviour definition (body) constant values. *Inert, reactive* and *autonomous attributes* become references to channels, say *ch_dyn*, such that when an inert, reactive and autonomous attribute value is required it is expressed as *ch_dyn ?*. *Programmable* and *biddable attributes* become arguments which are passed on to the tail-recursive invocations of the behaviour, and possibly updated as specified [with]in the body of the definition of the behaviour, i.e., (...).

2.3   Contributions of [29] – and Open Problems

For the first time we have, now, the beginnings of a calculus for developing domain descriptions. In [13,15] we speculate on laws that these analysis & description prompts (i.e., their "meanings") must satisfy. With this calculus we can now systematically develop domain descriptions [41–56]. I am right now working on understanding issues of *implicit/explicit* semantics[6] Since December 2017 I have revised [35] extensively: simplified it, extended it, clarified some issues, provided analysis & description techniques for channels and arguments, et cetera. The revised paper is [29][7].

3   Related Papers

3.1   Domain Facets: Analysis & Description [12,31]

Overview. By a domain facet we shall understand one amongst a finite set of generic ways of analyzing a domain: a view of the domain, such that the different facets cover conceptually different views, and such that these views together cover the domain.

[31] is an extensive revision of [12]. Both papers identify the following facets: *intrinsics, support technologies, rules & regulations, scripts, license languages, management & organisation,* and *human behaviour.* Recently I have "discovered" what might be classified as a domain facet: classes of *attribute semantics:* the diversity of attribute semantics resolving the issue of so-called implicit and explicit semantics. I shall not cover this issue in this talk.

Intrinsics: *By domain intrinsics we shall understand those phenomena and concepts of a domain which are basic to any of the other facets, with such domain intrinsics initially covering at least one specific, hence named, stakeholder view.*

Support Technology: *By a domain support technology we shall understand ways and means of implementing certain observed phenomena or certain conceived concepts.*

---

[6] Cf. http://impex2017.loria.fr/.

[7] You can find it on the Internet: http://www.imm.dtu.dk/~dibj/2018/tosem/Bjorner-TOSEM.pdf.

Rules and Regulations: *By a domain* rule *we shall understand some text (in the domain) which prescribes how people or equipment are expected to behave when dispatching their duties, respectively when performing their functions.*

By a domain regulation *we shall understand some text (in the domain) which prescribes what remedial actions are to be taken when it is decided that a rule has not been followed according to its intention.*

Scripts: *By a domain* script *we shall understand the structured, almost, if not outright, formally expressed, wording of a procedure on how to proceed, one that possibly has legally binding power, that is, which may be contested in a court of law.*

Management & Organisation: *By domain* management *we shall understand such people (such decisions) (i) who (which) determine, formulate and thus set standards (cf. rules and regulations) concerning strategic, tactical and operational decisions; (ii) who ensure that these decisions are passed on to (lower) levels of management and to floor staff; (iii) who make sure that such orders, as they were, are indeed carried out; (iv) who handle undesirable deviations in the carrying out of these orders cum decisions; and (v) who "backstops" complaints from lower management levels and from "floor" staff.*

By domain organisation *we shall understand (vi) the structuring of management and non-management staff "overseeable" into clusters with "tight" and "meaningful" relations; (vii) the allocation of strategic, tactical and operational concerns to within management and non-management staff clusters; and hence (viii) the "lines of command": who does what, and who reports to whom, administratively and functionally.*

Human Behaviour: *By domain* human behaviour *we shall understand any of a quality spectrum of carrying out assigned work: (i) from careful, diligent and accurate, via (ii) sloppy dispatch, and (iii) delinquent work, (iv) to outright criminal pursuit.*

Contributions of [12,31] **– and Open Problems:** [31] now covers techniques and tools for analyzing domains into these facets and for their modeling. The issue of *license languages* are particularly intriguing. The delineations between the listed[8] facets is necessarily not as precise as one would wish: we are dealing with an imprecise world, that of (manifest) domains. License languages are treated in [31].

3.2   From Domains to Requirements [8, 25]

Overview: [25] outlines a calculus of refinements and extensions which applied to domain descriptions yield requirements prescriptions. As for [35] the calculus is to be deployed by human users, i.e., requirements engineers. Requirements are for a *machine*, that is, the hardware and software to be developed from

---

[8] We have omitted a facet: *license languages*.

the requirements. A distinction is made between *domain, interface* and *machine requirements.* I shall briefly cover these in another order.

Machine requirements: Machine requirements are such which can be expressed using only technical terms of the machine: performance and dependability accessibility, availability, integrity, reliability, safety, security and robustness). and development requirements development process, maintenance, platform, management and documentation). Within *maintenance requirements* there are adaptive, corrective, perfective, preventive, and extensional requirements. Within *platform requirements* there are development, execution, maintenance, and demonstration requirements. Etcetera. [25] does not cover these. See instead [6, Sect. 19.6].

Domain Requirements: Domain requirements are such which can be expressed using only technical terms of the domain. The are the following domain-to-requirements specification transformations: *projection, instantiation, determination, extension* and *fitting. I consider my work on these domain requirements issues the most interesting.*

1. Projection: By a *domain projection* we mean *a subset of the domain description, one which projects out all those endurants: parts, materials and components, as well as perdurants: actions, events and behaviours that the stake-holders do not wish represented or relied upon by the machine.*

2. Instantiation: By *domain instantiation* we mean a *refinement of the partial domain requirements prescription (resulting from the projection step) in which the refinements aim at rendering the endurants: parts, materials and components, as well as the perdurants: actions, events and behaviours of the domain requirements prescription more concrete, more specific.*

3. Determination: By *domain determination* we mean a *refinement of the partial domain requirements prescription, resulting from the instantiation step, in which the refinements aim at rendering the endurants: parts, materials and components, as well as the perdurants: functions, events and behaviours of the partial domain requirements prescription less non-determinate, more determinate.*

4. Extension: By *domain extension* we understand the *introduction of endurants and perdurants that were not feasible in the original domain,* but for which, with *computing and communication, and with new, emerging technologies, for example, sensors, actuators and satellites, there is the possibility of feasible implementations, hence the requirements, that what is introduced becomes part of the unfolding requirements prescription.*

5. Fitting: Often a domain being described "fits" onto, is "adjacent" to, "interacts" in some areas with, another domain: *transportation* with *logistics, health-care* with *insurance, banking* with *securities trading* and/or *insurance,* and so on. The issue of requirements fitting arises when two or more software development projects are based on what appears to be the same domain. The problem then is to harmonize the two or more software development projects by harmonizing, if not too late, their requirements developments.

Interface Requirements: Interface requirements are such which can be expressed only by using technical terms of both the domain and the machine. Thus interface requirements are about that which is *shared* between the domain and the machine: *endurants* that are represented in machine storage as well as co-existing in the domain; *actions* and *behaviours* that are performed while interacting with phenomena in the domain; etc.

Contributions of [8, 25]: [25] does not follow the "standard division" of requirements engineering into systems and user requirements etcetera. Instead [25] builds on domain descriptions and eventually gives a rather different "division of requirements engineering labour" – manifested in the domain, the interface and the machine requirements paradigms, and these further into sub-paradigms, to wit: projection, instantiation, determination, extension and fitting. Some readers have objected to my use of the term *refinement* for the domain-to-requirements transformations.

3.3 Formal Models of Processes and Prompts [20, 23]

Overview: [35] outlines a calculus of prompts, to be deployed by human users, i.e., the domain analyzers & describers. That calculus builds on the *assumption* that the domain engineers build, *in their mind*, i.e., *conceptually*, a *syntactical* structure of the domain description, although, what the domain engineers can "see & touch" are *semantic* objects. A formal model of the analysis and description prompt process and of the meanings of the prompts therefore is split into a model for the process and a model of the syntactic and semantics structures.

A Summary of Analysis and Description Prompts
The Analysis Prompts:

[a] is_entity	[f] is_part	[k] has_concrete_type
[b] is_endurant	[g] is_component	[l] has_mereology
[c] is_perdurant	[h] is_material	[m] has_components
[d] is_discrete	[i] is_atomic	[n] has_material
[e] is_continuous	[j] is_composite	[o] has_parts

The Description Prompts:

[1] observe_part_sorts	[5] observe_attributes
[2] observe_concrete_type	[6] observe_component_sorts
[3] observe_unique_identifier	[7] observe_part_material_sort
[4] observe_mereology	[8] observe_material_part_sorts

A Glimpse of the Process Model

Process "Management": Domain description involves the "generation" and use of an indefinite number of type (sort) names, Nm. The global, assignable variables αps and νps serve to hold the names of the sorts to be analysed, respectively the names of the sorts for which unique identifiers, mereologies and attributes have to be analysed and described.

type

Nm = PNm | MNm | KNm

variable

αps := [Δnm] **type** Nm-set

νps := [Δnm] **type** Nm-set

value

sel_and_remove_Nm: **Unit** → Nm

sel_and_remove_Nm() ≡

let nm:Nm • nm ∈ νps in

νps := νps \ {nm} ; nm end; **pre**: νps ≠ {}

Some Process Functions: The analyse_and_describe_endurants function is the major function. It invokes a number of other analysis & description functions. We illustrate two:

value

analyse_and_describe_endurants: **Unit** → **Unit**

analyse_and_describe_endurants() ≡

while ∼is_empty(νps) **do**

let nm = sel_and_remove_Nm() in

analyse_and_describe_endurant_sort(nm,ι:nm) **end end** ;

for all nm:PNm • nm ∈ αps **do if** *has_mereology*(nm,ι:snm)

then *observe_mereology*(nm,ι:nm) **end end**

for all nm:Nm • nm ∈ αps **do** *observe_attributes*(nm,ι:nm) **end**

analyse_and_describe_endurant_sort: NmVAL → **Unit**

analyse_and_describe_endurant_sort(nm,val) ≡

is_part(nm,val) → *analyse_and_describe_part_sorts*(nm,val),

is_material(nm,val) → *observe_material_part_sort*(nm,val),

is_component(nm,val) → *observe_component_sort*(nm,val)

A Glimpse of the Syntax and Semantics Models

We suggest a syntax and a semantics of domain descriptions.

The Syntactical Structure of Domains: First the syntax of domains – divided into the syntax of endurants parts, materials and components.

TypDef = PTypes ∪ MTypes ∪ KTypes

PTypes = PNm $\overrightarrow{m}$ PaTyp

MTypes = MNm $\overrightarrow{m}$ MaTyp

KTypes = KNm $\overrightarrow{m}$ KoTyp

ENDType = PaTyp | MaTyp | KoTyp

PaTyp == AtPaTyp | AbsCoPaTyp | ConCoPaTyp

AtPaTyp :: mkAtPaTyp(s_qs:PQ,s_omkn:({|" nil"|}|MNn|KNm))

AbsCoPaTyp :: mkAbsCoPaTyp(s_qs:PQ,s_pns:PNm-set)

axiom ∀ mkAbsCoPaTyp(pq,pns):AbsCoPaTyp • pns ≠ {}

ConCoPaTyp :: mkConCoPaTyp(s_qs:PQ,s_p:PNm)

MaTyp :: mkMaTyp(s_qs:MQ,s_opn:({|" nil"|}|PNm))

KoTyp :: mkKoTyp(s_qs:KQ)

Then the syntax of the internal qualities of endurants:

$$PQ = s\_ui:UI \times s\_me:ME \times s\_atrs:ATRS\}$$
$$UI$$
$$ME == "nil" | mkUI(s\_ui:UI) | mkUIset(s\_uil:UI) | ...$$
$$ATRS = ANm \xrightarrow{\overrightarrow{m}} ATyp$$
$$ANm, ATyp$$
$$MQ = s\_atrs:ATRS$$
$$KQ = s\_uid:UI \times s\_atrs:ATRS$$

The Semantical Values of Domains: Corresponding, homomorphically, to these syntaxes are their semantics types:

$$ENDVAL = PVAL | MVAL | KVAL$$
$$PVAL == AtPaVAL | AbsCoPVAL | ConCoPVAL$$
$$AtPaVAL :: mkAtPaVAL(s\_qval:PQVAL,$$
$$s\_omkvals:(\{| "nil" |\} | MVAL | KVAL\text{-set}))$$
$$AbsCoPVAL :: mkAbsCoPaVAL(s\_qval:PQVAL, s\_pvals:(PNm \xrightarrow{\overrightarrow{m}} PVAL))$$
$$\textbf{axiom} \; \forall \; mkAbsCoPaVAL(pqs,ppm):AbsCoPVAL \bullet ppm \neq []$$
$$ConCoPVAL :: mkConCoPaVAL(s\_qval:PQVAL, s\_pvals:PVAL\text{-set})$$
$$MVAL :: mkMaVAL(s\_qval:MQVAL, s\_pvals:PVAL\text{-set})$$
$$KVAL :: mkKoVAL(s\_qval:KQVAL)$$

Qualities: Semantic Types

$$PQVAL = UIVAL \times MEVAL \times ATTRVALS$$
$$UIVAL$$
$$MEVAL == mkUIVAL(s\_ui:UIVAL) | mkUIVALset(s\_uis:UIVAL\text{-set}) | ...$$
$$ATTRVALS = ANm \xrightarrow{\overrightarrow{m}} AVAL$$
$$ANm, AVAL$$
$$MQVAL = ATTRVALS$$
$$KQVAL = UIVAL \times ATTRVALS$$

From Syntax to Semantics and "Back Again!" We define mappings from sort names to the possibly infinite set of values of the named type, and from endurant values to the names of their sort.

type
    Nm_to_ENDVALS =
        $(PNm \xrightarrow{\overrightarrow{m}} PVAL\text{-set}) \cup (MNm \xrightarrow{\overrightarrow{m}} MVAL\text{-set}) \cup (KNm \xrightarrow{\overrightarrow{m}} KVAL\text{-set})$
    ENDVAL_to_Nm =
        $(PVAL \xrightarrow{\overrightarrow{m}} PNm) \cup (MVAL \xrightarrow{\overrightarrow{m}} MNm) \cup (KVAL \xrightarrow{\overrightarrow{m}} KNm)$
value
    typval: TypDef $\xrightarrow{\sim}$ Nm_to_ENDVALS
    typval(td) $\equiv$ **let** $\rho =$
        $[n \mapsto M(td(n))(\rho) | n:(PNm|MNm|KNm) \bullet n \in \textbf{dom} \; td]$ **in** ρ **end**

    valtyp: Nm_to_ENDVALS $\xrightarrow{\sim}$ ENDVAL_to_Nm
    valtyp(ρ) $\equiv$
        $[v \mapsto n | n:(PNm|MNm|CNm), v:(PVAL|MVAL|KVAL) \bullet$
           $n \in \textbf{dom} \; \rho \wedge v \in \rho(n)]$

M: (PaTyp → ENV$\overset{\sim}{\to}$PVAL-set)|
  (MaTyp→ENV$\overset{\sim}{\to}$MVAL-set)|
  (KoTyp→ENV$\overset{\sim}{\to}$KVAL-set)

The environment, ρ, of typval is the least fix point of the recursive equation. The crucial function is M, in the definition of typval. Examples of its definition, by part category, is given below.

value
  ι nm:Nm $\equiv$ iota(nm)
  iota: Nm → TypDef → VAL
  iota(nm)(td) $\equiv$
    let val:(PVAL|MVAL|KVAL)•val$\in$(typval(td))(nm)
    in val **end**

Analysis Functions: We exemplify the semantics functions for three analysis prompts.

value
  is_endurant: Nm×VAL → TypDef $\overset{\sim}{\to}$ **Bool**
  is_endurant(_,val)(td) $\equiv$ val $\in$ **dom** valtyp(typval(td));
        pre: VAL is any value type

  is_discrete: NmVAL → TypDef $\overset{\sim}{\to}$ **Bool**
  is_discrete(_,val)(td) $\equiv$ (is_PaTyp|is_CoTyp)(td((valtyp(typval(td)))(val)))

  is_part: NmVAL → TypDef $\overset{\sim}{\to}$ **Bool**
  is_part(_,val)(td) $\equiv$ is_PaTyp(td((valtyp(typval(td)))(val)))

Description Functions: We exemplify the semantics of one of the description prompts. The generated description **RSL-text** is enclosed within [” ... ”].

variable
    $\tau :=$ [ ] **Text-set**
value
    observe_part_sorts: Nm×VAL → TypDef → **Unit**
    observe_part_sorts(nm,val)(td) $\equiv$
        let mkAbsCoPaTyp(_,{$P_1,P_2,...,P_n$})
          = td((valtyp(typval(td)))(val)) **in**
      $\tau := \tau \oplus$ [” **type** $P_1,P_2,...,P_n$;
                value
                        obs_part_P_1: nm →P_1
                        obs_part_P_2: nm →P_2
                        ...,
                        obs_part_P_n: nm →P_n;
                proof obligation
                        $\mathcal{D}$; ”]
    || νps := νps $\oplus$ ([” $P_1,P_2,...,P_n$ ”] \ αps)

$\|\ \alpha\mathsf{ps} := \alpha\mathsf{ps} \oplus [\text{"}\ \mathsf{P}_1,\mathsf{P}_2,...,\mathsf{P}_n\ \text{"}]$
    end
  pre: is_AbsCoPaTyp(td((valtyp(typpval(td)))(val)))

The M Function

1 The meaning of an atomic part type expression,
- mkAtPaTyp((ui,me,attrs),omkn) in
- mkAtPaTyp(s_qs:PQ,s_omkn:({ |"nil" | }|MNn|KNm)),
- is the set of all atomic part values,
  mkAtPaVAL((uiv,mev,attrvals),omkval) in
- mkAtPaVAL(s_qval:(UIVAL×MEVAL×(ANm $\overrightarrow{m}$ AVAL)),
            s_omkvals:({ |"nil" | }|MVAL|KVAL-set)).

a uiv is a value in UIVAL of type ui,
b mev is a value in MEVAL of type me,
c attrvals is a value in (ANm $\overrightarrow{m}$ AVAL) of type (ANm $\overrightarrow{m}$ ATyp), and
d omkvals is a value in ({ |"nil" | }|MVAL|KVAL-set):
    i either ''nil'',
   ii or one material value of type MNm,
  iii or a possibly empty set of component values, each of type KNm.

1. M: mkAtPaTyp((UI×ME×(ANm $\overrightarrow{m}$ ATyp))×({|"nil"|}|MVAL|KVAL-set))
1.   →ENV$\overset{\sim}{\to}$PVAL-set
1. M(mkAtPaTyp((ui,me,attrs),omkn))(ρ) $\equiv$
1.   { mkATPaVAL((uiv,mev,attrval),omkvals) |
1a.   uiv:UIVAL•type_of(uiv)=ui,
1b.   mev:MEVAL•type_of(mev)=me,
1c.   attrval:(ANm $\overrightarrow{m}$ AVAL)•type_of(attrval)=attrs,
1d.   omkvals: **case** omkn **of**
1(d)i.   "nil" → "nil",
1(d)ii.   mkMNn(_) → mval:MVAL•type_of(mval)=omkn,
1(d)iii.   mkKNm(_) →
1(d)iii.   kvals:KVAL-set•kvals⊆{kv|kv:KVAL•type_of(kval)=omkn}
1d.   **end** }

Formula terms 1a–1(d)iii express that any applicable uiv is combined with any applicable mev is combined with any applicable attrval is combined with any applicable omkvals.

2 The meaning of an abstract composite part type expression,
- mkAbsCoPaTyp((ui,me,attrs),pns) in
- mkAbsCoPaTyp(s_qs:PQ,s_pns:PNm-set), is the set of all abstract, composite part values,
- mkAbsCoPaVAL((uiv,mev,attrvals),pvals) in
- mkAbsCoPaVAL(s_qval:(UIVAL×MEVAL×(ANm $\overrightarrow{m}$ AVAL)),
    s_pvals:(PNm $\overrightarrow{m}$ PVAL)).

a uiv is a value in UIVAL of type ui: UI,
b mev is a value in MEVAL of type me: ME,
c attrvals is a value in (ANm $\overrightarrow{m}$ AVAL) of type (ANm $\overrightarrow{m}$ ATyp), and
d pvals is a map of part values in (PNm $\overrightarrow{m}$ PVAL), one for each name, pn:PNm, in pns such that these part values are of the type defined for pn.

2. M: mkAbsCoPaTyp((UI×ME×(ANm $\overrightarrow{m}$ ATyp)),PNm-set)
2.   → ENV $\overset{\sim}{\to}$ PVAL-set
2. M(mkAbsCoPaTyp((ui,me,attrs),pns))(ρ) ≡
2.   { mkAbsCoPaVAL((uiv,mev,attrvals),pvals) |
2a.   uiv:UIVAL•type_of(uiv)=ui
2b.   mev:MEVAL•type_of(mev)=me,
2c.   attrvals:(ANm $\overrightarrow{m}$ ATyp)•type_of(attrsval)=attrs,
2d.   pvals:(PNm $\overrightarrow{m}$ PVAL) •
2d.   pvals∈{[pn↦pval|pn:PNm,pval:PVAL•pn∈ pns∧pval∈ρ(pn)]} }

Contributions of [23]. The contributions of [23] are to suggest and carry through a "formalisation" of the *conceptual, syntactical* and *semantical* structures *perceived* by the domain engineer, to formalise the *meaning of the informal* analysis & description prompts, and to formalise the possible sets of sequences of valid prompts.

3.4   To Every Manifest Domain Mereology a CSP Expression [33]

Overview. In [35] we have shown how parts can be endowed with mereologies. Mereology, as was mentioned earlier, is the study and knowledge of *"part-hood"*: of how parts are related parts to parts, and parts to *"a whole"*. Mereology, as treated by us, originated with the Polish mathematician/logician/philosopher Stanislaw Lešhniewski.

An Axiom System for Mereology:

$$
\begin{aligned}
\text{part\_of}: \quad & \mathbb{P}: \mathcal{P} \times \mathcal{P} \to \textbf{Bool} \\
\text{proper\_part\_of}: \quad & \mathbb{PP}: \mathcal{P} \times \mathcal{P} \to \textbf{Bool} \\
\text{overlap}: \quad & \mathbb{O}: \mathcal{P} \times \mathcal{P} \to \textbf{Bool} \\
\text{underlap}: \quad & \mathbb{U}: \mathcal{P} \times \mathcal{P} \to \textbf{Bool} \\
\text{over\_crossing}: \quad & \mathbb{OX}: \mathcal{P} \times \mathcal{P} \to \textbf{Bool} \\
\text{under\_crossing}: \quad & \mathbb{UX}: \mathcal{P} \times \mathcal{P} \to \textbf{Bool} \\
\text{proper\_overlap}: \quad & \mathbb{PO}: \mathcal{P} \times \mathcal{P} \to \textbf{Bool} \\
\text{proper\_underlap}: \quad & \mathbb{PU}: \mathcal{P} \times \mathcal{P} \to \textbf{Bool}
\end{aligned}
$$

Let $\mathbb{P}$ denote *part-hood*; p_x is part of p_y, is then expressed as $\mathbb{P}(p_x, p_y)$.[9] (1) Part p_x is part of itself (reflexivity). (2) If a part p_x is part of p_y and, vice versa, part

---

[9] Our notation now is not RSL but a conventional first-order predicate logic notation.

p_y is part of p_x, then $p_x = p_y$ (anti-symmetry). (3) If a part p_x is part of p_y and part p_y is part of p_z, then p_x is part of p_z (transitivity).

$$\forall p_x : \mathcal{P} \bullet \mathbb{P}(p_x, p_x) \tag{1}$$

$$\forall p_x, p_y : \mathcal{P} \bullet (\mathbb{P}(p_x, p_y) \wedge \mathbb{P}(p_y, p_x)) \rightarrow p_x = p_y \tag{2}$$

$$\forall p_x, p_y, p_z : \mathcal{P} \bullet (\mathbb{P}(p_x, p_y) \wedge \mathbb{P}(p_y, p_z)) \rightarrow \mathbb{P}(p_z, p_z) \tag{3}$$

We exemplify one of the mereology propositions: *proper underlap*, $\mathbb{P}\mathbb{U}$: p_x and p_y are said to properly underlap if p_x and p_y under-cross and p_y and p_x under-cross.

$$\mathbb{P}\mathbb{U}(p_x, p_y) \triangleq \mathbb{U}\mathbb{X}(p_x, p_y) \wedge \mathbb{U}\mathbb{X}(p_y, p_x) \tag{4}$$

A Model for the Axioms [33] now gives a model for parts: atomic and composite, commensurate with [23,35], and their unique identifiers, mereology and attributes and show that the model satisfies the axioms.

Contributions of [33]. [33] thus contributes to a domain science, helping to secure a firm foundation for domain engineering.

4   Domain Science & Engineering: A Philosophy Basis [30]

My most recent work is documented in [30]. It examines the question:

– *What must inescapably be in any domain description?*

Another formulation is:

– *Which are the necessary characteristics of each and every possible world and our situation in it.*

Recent works by the Danish philosopher Kai Sørlander [52–55] appears to direct us towards an answer.

Here is how it is done, in brief. On the basis of *possibility of truth*[10] Sørlander establishes the logical connectors and from them the existence of a world with symmetry, asymmetry and transitivity. By a transcendental deduction Sørlander then reasons that *space* and *time*, inescapably, are "in the world"[11]. Further logical reasoning and transcendental deductions establishes the inescapability of *Newton's 1st, 2nd and 3rd Laws*. And from that *kinematics*, *dynamics*, and *gravitational pull*. And so forth. Thus the worlds that can possibly be described must all satisfy the *laws of physics*.

This line of reasoning and deduction thus justifies the focus, in our calculi, on natural parts, components and materials.

---

[10] Sørlander makes his *logical reasoning* and *transcendental deductions* on the basis of the *possibility of truth* – where Immanuel Kant [45], according to Sørlander, builds on the *possibility of self-awareness*, which is shown to lead to contradictions.

[11] Kant assumes space and time.

But Sørlander goes on and reasons and transcendentally deduce the inescapable existence of *living species: plants* and *animals*, and, among the latter, *humans*. Because of reasoned characteristics of humans we inescapably have *artifacts: man-made parts components* and *materials*. Humans construct artifacts with an *intent*, an attribute of both humans and artifacts. These *shared intents* lead to a notion of *intentional "pull"*[12] and so forth.

This line of reasoning and deduction thus justifies the inclusion, in our calculi, of living species and artifacts.

[30] is presently an approximately 90 page report. As such it is presently a repository for a number of "texts" related to the issue of *"what must inescapably be in any domain description?"* It may be expected that a far shorter paper may emerge.

5   The Experiments [41–56]

In order to test and tune the domain analysis & description method a great number of experiments were carried out. In our opinion, when applied to manifest domains, they justify the calculi reported in [23,35].

- *Urban Planning*   [41],
- *A Space of Swarms of Drones* [27],
- *Documents*   [28],
- *Credit Cards*   [22],
- *Weather Information Systems* [26],
- *The Tokyo Stock Exchange*   [34],
- *Pipelines*   [18],
- *Road Transportation*   [19],
- *Web/Transaction*-based   Software [14],
- *"The Market"*   [4],
- *Container [Shipping] Lines*   [7],
- *Railway Systems*   [3,5,37,51,56].

6   Summary

We have identified a discipline of domain science and engineering. Its first "rendition" was applied to the semantics of programming languages and the development of their compilers [46, CHILL] and [42, Ada]. Domain science and engineering, as outlined here, is directed at a wider spectrum of "languages": the "meaning" of computer application domains and software for these applications. Where physicists model facets of the world emphasizing physical, dynamic phenomena in nature, primarily using differential calculi, domain scientists cum engineers emphasize logical and both discrete phenomena of man and human institutions primarily using discrete mathematics.

---

[12] We shall here give an example of *intentional "pull"*: humans create *automobiles* and *roads*. An intention of automobiles is to drive on roads, and an intention of roads is to have automobiles move along roads. We can thus speak of the *traffic history of an automobile* as the time-stamped sequence of vehicle positions along roads, and of the *traffic history of a road* as the time-stamped sequence of vehicle positions along that road. Now, for the sum total of all automobiles and all roads the two consolidate histories must be identical. *It cannot be otherwise.*

7 Laudatio

At the Zhou ChaoChen Fest dinner I gave a dinner speech. It is not about
Zhou Chaochen's scientific life. But it is a laudatio expressed in admiration for
a wonderful man and our lives together.

– It was in 1981, in Beijing, 36 years ago.
  At the Institute of Computing Technology.
  On my first day of a three week visit. 30 lectures, 30 degrees Celsius. I liked it.
  I was being received. All sat in soft cushioned armchairs along the walls.
  I sat to the right of this wonderful man, Xu KongShi.
  During our conversation I queried about a young researcher, Zhou ChaoChen.
  Tony Hoare had told me to watch out for him.
  So I did, with an invitation letter, right in my pocket, for him to visit my dept.
  Asked Xu KongShi as to the whereabouts of Zhou?
  And he smiled: right next to the right of you !

– That became the first day of a 36 year acquaintance.
  Almost half of our life-times !
  Zhou came to visit us, 3 months every other winter. It was during the 1980s.
  What a wonderful time, for me, for my colleagues and for our students.
  One time I asked him to tutor a young MSc student. She performed brilliantly.
  It was something about "the meeting calendar problem".
  Even Zhou was impressed.
  Perhaps he has forgotten it now.
  When I took him to the airport, some weeks later.
  I told him that Ulla, that was her name, was a great granddaughter of Niels Bohr.
  Zhou appreciated then that I only told him then.

– For the 1989 visit I had "stipulated" that Zhou bring his family.
  Three months to Lyngby, three months to Oxford.
  And Zhou kindly agreed. All was set to go.
  But a certain incident early that June caused us all concern.
  Yet, on July 1st that year the whole family arrived.

– Zhou wasn't keen to return to China.
  I speed-dialled Tony's Oxford number.
  "Tony on the line" was the reply
  "Tony: Zhou is with me here, in my office in Lyngby."
  "Hello Zhou"
  "Hello Tony".
  "Tony, I have just offered Zhou a three year appointment."
  Well I hadn't, but there it was, and Zhou got listening.
  "8 months a year here at Lyngby. 4 with you at Oxford."
  Tony's reply: "Well, I had got it wrong, the other way around".
  "Let Zhou decide", I replied, and Zhou said:

"It is as Dines proposes."

- Those became three great years, at Lyngby and at Oxford.
  Zhang Yi Ping and children lodged in Oxford - Zhou commuting.
  Science progressing.
  It was at a ProCoS meeting in Viborg.
  E.V.Sørensen had given a talk on signal transitions of electric circuits.
  The concept of 'duration' was mentioned.
  Afterwards I saw Zhou, A.P. and Tony, in an adjacent room.
  Discussing, standing at the white board, scribbling.
  And "The Duration Calculus" was born.

- The following year I was asked to become Director of UNU-IIST.
  On the flight home, in May 1991, from Japan, via a visit to Macau
  I decided to ask Zhou to join me in Macau.
  And a year later, things take time in international affairs, we began.
  With Zhou in charge of theory and I of engineering, an institute was built.
  After my five years followed Zhou's five years.
  Some of you, in this room, can look back at defining years at UNU-IIST.
  I returned to Lyngby and eventually Zhou to Beijing.

- The Duration Calculus took root.
  Painstakingly a theory was cemented and applications realized.
  The ProCoS project and UNU-IIST played an important rôle in this.
  But at the core of all this was Zhou ChaoChen.

- Dear Zhou:
  Thank you for your tremendous contributions to science.
  Thank you for inspiring generations of scientists.
  Thank you for hosting our daughter, Charlotte, the fall of 1986–31 years ago!
  Thank you for putting our son, Nikolaj, on the road to science
  – also 31 years ago!

8   Bibliography

8.1   Bibliographical Notes

In the last ten years I have also worked on related topics:

- Domains: Their Simulation, Monitoring and Control, see [16],   [24] 2008,
- Compositionality: Ontology and Mereology of Domains[13],   [36] 2008,
- Domain Science & Engineering,   [13,15] 2010,
- Computation for Humanity: Domain Science and Engineering,   [17] 2012,

---

[13] With Asger Eir.

- 40 Years of Formal Methods — Obstacles and Possibilities[14],   [39] 2014,
- Domain Engineering – A Basis for Safety Critical Software,   [21] 2014,
- Implicit and Explicit Semantics and the Domain Calculi,   [32] 2017.

Work on these papers and on the many, extensive experiments has helped solidify the basic domain analysis & description method.

Acknowledgments. I am grateful to Prof. Zhan NaiJun for inviting me to the Zhou ChaoChen Fest and for inviting me to submit my talk as a paper for this Festschrift. I am grateful to my "old student", now Prof. Ji Wang for his arranging a wonderful stay in Changsha, my fourth visit to that great city, and for his fantastic cheerful welcome.

References

1. Anon: C.C.I.T.T. High Level Language (CHILL), Recommendation Z.200, Red Book Fascicle VI.12. See [47], ITU (Intl. Telecmm. Union), Geneva, Switzerland (1980–1985)
2. Bjørner, D.: Programming languages: formal development of interpreters and compilers. In: Morlet, E., Ribbens, D. (eds.) International Computing Symposium, vol. 77, pp. 1–21. European ACM, North-Holland Publ. Co., Amsterdam (1977)
3. Bjørner, D.: Formal software techniques in railway systems. In: Schnieder, E. (ed.) 9th IFAC Symposium on Control in Transportation Systems, pp. 1–12. VDI/VDEGesellschaft Mess- und Automatisieringstechnik, VDIGesellschaft für Fahrzeug- und Verkehrstechnik, Technical University, Braunschweig, Germany (13–15 June 2000), invited talk
4. Bjørner, D.: Domain models of "the market" – in preparation for e-transaction systems. In: Kilov, H., Baclawski, K. (eds.) Practical Foundations of Business and System Specifications. Kluwer Academic Press, The Netherlands (December 2002), Final draft version. http://www2.imm.dtu.dk/~db/themarket.pdf
5. Bjørner, D.: Dynamics of railway nets: on an interface between automatic control and software engineering. In: Tsugawa, S., Aoki, M. (eds.) CTS2003: 10th IFAC Symposium on Control in Transportation Systems. Elsevier Science Ltd., Oxford, UK (August 4–6 2003). https://doi.org/10.1016/S1474-6670(17)32424-2, Symposium Held at Tokyo, Japan. Final version. http://www2.imm.dtu.dk/~db/ifac-dynamics.pdf
6. Bjørner, D.: Software Engineering, Volume 3: Domains, Requirements and Software Design. Texts in Theoretical Computer Science, the EATCS Series. Springer, Berlin (2006), See [9,11]
7. Bjørner, D.: A container line industry domain. Technical Report, Fredsvej 11, DK-2840 Holte, Denmark (June 2007), Extensive Draft. http://www2.imm.dtu.dk/~db/container-paper.pdf
8. Bjørner, Dines: From domain to requirements. In: Degano, P., De Nicola, R., Meseguer, J. (eds.) Concurrency, Graphs and Models. LNCS, vol. 5065, pp. 278–300. Springer, Heidelberg (May 2008). https://doi.org/10.1007/978-3-540-68679-8_18
9. Bjørner, D.: Software Engineering, Volume 3: Domains, Requirements and Software Design (Qinghua University Press). Springer, Berlin (2008)

---

[14] With Klaus Havelund.

10. Polkowski, Lech: Mereology in engineering and computer science. In: Calosi, Claudio, Graziani, Pierluigi (eds.) Mereology and the Sciences. SL, vol. 371, pp. 47–70. Springer, Cham (2014). https://doi.org/10.1007/978-3-319-05356-1_10
11. Bjørner, D.: Chinese: Software Engineering, Volume 3: Domains, Requirements and Software Design (Qinghua University Press). Springer, Berlin (2010) (Translated by Dr Liu Bo Chao et al.)
12. Bjørner, D.: Domain engineering. In: Boca, P., Bowen, J. (eds.) Formal Methods: State of the Art and New Directions, pp. 1–42. Springer, London (2010). https://doi.org/10.1007/978-1-84882-736-3_1
13. Bjørner, D.: Domain Science & Engineering - From Computer Science to The Sciences of Informatics, Part I of II: The Engineering Part. Kibernetika i sistemny analiz, vol. 4, pp. 100–116 (2010)
14. Bjørner, D.: On Development of Web-based Software: A Divertimento of Ideas and Suggestions. Technical, Technical University of Vienna (August–October 2010). http://www.imm.dtu.dk/~dibj/wfdftp.pdf
15. Bjørner, D.: Domain Science & Engineering - From Computer Science to The Sciences of Informatics Part II of II: The Science Part. Kibernetika i sistemny analiz, vol. 2, pp. 100–120 (2011)
16. Bjørner, Dines: Domains: their simulation, monitoring and control—a divertimento of ideas and suggestions. In: Calude, Cristian S., Rozenberg, Grzegorz, Salomaa, Arto (eds.) Rainbow of Computer Science. LNCS, vol. 6570, pp. 167–183. Springer, Heidelberg (2011). https://doi.org/10.1007/978-3-642-19391-0_13
17. Bjørner, D.: Domain science and engineering as a foundation for computation for humanity. In: Zander, J., Mosterman, P.J. (eds.) Computational Analysis, Synthesis, and Design of Dynamic Systems, pp. 159–177. CRC [Francis & Taylor] (2013)
18. Bjørner, D.: Pipelines - a Domain Description. http://www.imm.dtu.dk/~dibj/pipe-p.pdf. Experimental Research Report 2013–2, DTU Compute and Fredsvej 11, DK-2840 Holte, Denmark (Spring 2013)
19. Bjørner, D.: Road Transportation - a Domain Description. http://www.imm.dtu.dk/~dibj/road-p.pdf. Experimental Research Report 2013–4, DTU Compute and Fredsvej 11, DK-2840 Holte, Denmark (Spring 2013)
20. Bjørner, D.: Domain Analysis: Endurants - An Analysis & Description Process Model. In: Iida, S., Meseguer, J., Ogata, K. (eds.) Specification, Algebra, and Software: A Festschrift Symposium in Honor of Kokichi Futatsugi. Springer, Berlin (May 2014)
21. Bjørner, D.: Domain Engineering - A Basis for Safety Critical Software. Invited Keynote, ASSC2014: Australian System Safety Conference, Melbourne, 26–28 May (December 2014)
22. Bjørner, D.: A Credit Card System: Uppsala Draft. Technical Report: Experimental Research, Fredsvej 11, DK-2840 Holte, Denmark (November 2016). http://www.imm.dtu.dk/~dibj/2016/credit/accs.pdf
23. Bjørner, D.: Domain Analysis and Description - Formal Models of Processes and Prompts (2016), extensive revision of [20]. http://www.imm.dtu.dk/~dibj/2016/process/process-p.pdf
24. Bjørner, D.: Domains: Their Simulation, Monitoring and Control - A Divertimento of Ideas and Suggestions. Technical report Fredsvej 11, DK-2840 Holte, Denmark (2016), extensive revision of [16]. http://www.imm.dtu.dk/~dibj/2016/demo/faoc-demo.pdf
25. Bjørner, D.: From Domain Descriptions to Requirements Prescriptions - A Different Approach to Requirements Engineering (2016), Extensive revision of [8]

26. Bjørner, D.: Weather Information Systems: Towards a Domain Description. Technical Report: Experimental Research, Fredsvej 11, DK-2840 Holte, Denmark (November 2016), http://www.imm.dtu.dk/~dibj/2016/wis/wis-p.pdf

27. Bjørner, D.: A Space of Swarms of Drones. Research Note (November–December 2017). http://www.imm.dtu.dk/~dibj/2017/swarms/swarm-paper.pdf

28. Bjørner, D.: What are Documents? Research Note (2017). http://www.imm.dtu.dk/~dibj/2017/docs/docs.pdf

29. Bjørner, D.: A Domain Analysis & Description Method - Principles, Techniques and Modeling Languages. Research Note based on [35] (February 20 2018). http://www.imm.dtu.dk/~dibj/2018/tosem/Bjorner-TOSEM.pdf

30. Bjørner, D.: A Philosophy of Domain Science & Engineering - An Interpretation of Kai Sørlander's Philosophy. Research Note (Spring 2018). http://www.imm.dtu.dk/~dibj/2018/philosophy/filo.pdf

31. Bjørner, D.: Domain Facets: Analysis & Description (May 2018), extensive revision of [12]. http://www.imm.dtu.dk/~dibj/2016/facets/faoc-facets.pdf

32. Bjørner, D.: The Manifest Domain Analysis & Description Approach to Implicit and Explicit Semantics. EPTCS: Electronic Proceedings in Theoretical Computer Science, Yasmine Ait-Majeur, Paul J. Gibson and Dominique Méry: First International Workshop on Handling IMPlicit and EXplicit Knowledge in Formal Fystem Development, 17 November 2017. Xi'an, China (2018)

33. Bjørner, D.: To every manifest domain a CSP expression – a rôle for mereology in computer science. J. Log. Algebr. Methods Program. **94**, 91–108 (2018). https://doi.org/10.1016/j.jlamp.2017.09.005. January

34. Bjørner, D.: The Tokyo Stock Exchange Trading Rules. R&D Experiment, Fredsvej 11, DK-2840 Holte, Denmark (January and February, 2010), Version 1.http://www2.imm.dtu.dk/~db/todai/tse-1.pdf, Version 2.http://www2.imm.dtu.dk/~db/todai/tse-2.pdf

35. Bjørner, D.: Manifest domains: analysis & description. Form. Asp. Comput. **29**(2), 175–225 (2016). https://doi.org/10.1007/s00165-016-0385-z

36. Bjørner, Dines, Eir, Asger: Compositionality: ontology and mereology of domains. In: Dams, Dennis, Hannemann, Ulrich, Steffen, Martin (eds.) Concurrency, Compositionality, and Correctness. LNCS, vol. 5930, pp. 22–59. Springer, Heidelberg (2010). https://doi.org/10.1007/978-3-642-11512-7_3

37. Bjørner, D., George, C.W., Prehn, S.: Computing Systems for Railways – A Rôle for Domain Engineering. Relations to Requirements Engineering and Software for Control Applications. In: Integrated Design and Process Technology. Editors: Bernd Kraemer and John C. Petterson. Society for Design and Process Science, P.O. Box 1299, Grand View, Texas 76050–1299, USA (24–28 June 2002), Extended version.http://www2.imm.dtu.dk/~db/pasadena-25.pdf

38. Bjørner, D., Gram, C., Oest, O.N., Rystrømb, L.: Dansk Datamatik Center. In: Wangler, B., Lundin, P. (eds.) History of Nordic Computing. Springer, Stockholm, Sweden (18–20 October 2010)

39. Bjørner, Dines, Havelund, Klaus: 40 years of formal methods — 10 obstacles and 3 possibilities. In: Jones, Cliff, Pihlajasaari, Pekka, Sun, Jun (eds.) FM 2014. LNCS, vol. 8442, pp. 42–61. Springer, Cham (2014). https://doi.org/10.1007/978-3-319-06410-9_4

40. Bjørner, D., Nest, O.N. (eds.): Towards a Formal Description of Ada. LNCS, vol. 98. Springer, Heidelberg (1980). https://doi.org/10.1007/3-540-10283-3

41. Bjørner, D.: Urban Planning Processes. Research Note (July 2017). http://www.imm.dtu.dk/~dibj/2017/up/urban-planning.pdf

42. Clemmensen, G., Oest, O.: Formal specification and development of an Ada compiler - a VDM case study. In: Proceedings of the 7th International Conference on Software Engineering, 26–29. March 1984, Orlando, Florida, pp. 430–440. IEEE (1984)

43. George, C.W., et al.: The RAISE Specification Language. The BCS Practitioner Series. Hemel Hampstead, Prentice-Hall, England (1992)

44. George, C.W., Haxthausen, A.E., Hughes, S., Milne, R., Prehn, S., Pedersen, J.S.: The RAISE Development Method. The BCS Practitioner Series. Prentice-Hall, Hemel Hampstead, England (1995)

45. Guyer, P. (ed.): The Cambridge Companion to Kant. Cambridge University Press, England (1992)

46. Haff, Peter, Olsen, Anders: Use of VDM within CCITT. In: Bjørner, Dines, Jones, Cliff B., Mac an Airchinnigh, Mícheál, Neuhold, Erich J. (eds.) VDM 1987. LNCS, vol. 252, pp. 324–330. Springer, Heidelberg (1987). https://doi.org/10.1007/3-540-17654-3_18

47. Haff, P. (ed.): The Formal Definition of CHILL. ITU (Intl. Telecmm. Union), Geneva, Switzerland (1981)

48. Hoare, C.: Communicating Sequential Processes. C.A.R. Hoare Series in Computer Science. Prentice-Hall International (1985), published electronically: http://www.usingcsp.com/cspbook.pdf (2004)

49. Jackson, M.A.: Software Requirements & Specifications: A Lexicon of Practice, Principles and Prejudices. ACM Press, Addison-Wesley, Reading, England (1995)

50. Oest, O.N.: VDM from research to practice (invited paper). In: IFIP Congress, pp. 527–534 (1986)

51. Pěnička, M., Strupchanska, A.K., Bjørner, D.: Train maintenance routing. In: Tarnai, G., Schnieder, E. (eds.) FORMS'2003: Symposium on Formal Methods for Railway Operation and Control Systems. L'Harmattan Hongrie (15–16 May 2003), conf. held at Technical University of Budapest, Hungary, Germany. Final version. http://www2.imm.dtu.dk/~db/martin.pdf

52. Sørlander, K.: Det Uomgængelige - Filosofiske Deduktioner [The Inevitable - Philosophical Deductions, with a foreword by Georg Henrik von Wright]. Munksgaard · Rosinante, 168 p. (1994)

53. Sørlander, K.: Under Evighedens Synsvinkel [Under the viewpoint of eternity]. Munksgaard · Rosinante, 200 p. (1997)

54. Sørlander, K.: Den Endegyldige Sandhed [The Final Truth]. Rosinante, 187 p. (2002)

55. Sørlander, K.: Indføring i Filosofien [Introduction to The Philosophy]. Informations Forlag, 233 p. (2016)

56. Strupchanska, A.K., Pěnička, M., Bjørner, D.: Railway staff rostering. In: Tarnai, G., Schnieder, E. (eds.) FORMS2003: Symposium on Formal Methods for Railway Operation and Control Systems. L'Harmattan Hongrie (15–16 May 2003), conf. held at Techn. Univ. of Budapest, Hungary, Germany. Final version. http://www2.imm.dtu.dk/~db/albena.pdf

HAT: Analyzing Linear Hybrid Automata as Labelled Transition System

Lei Bu$^{(\boxtimes)}$, Hui Jiang, Xin Chen, Enyi Tang, and Xuandong Li

State Key Laboratory for Novel Software Technology, Department of Computer Science and Technology, Nanjing University, Nanjing, Jiangsu 210093, People's Republic of China
bulei@nju.edu.cn

Abstract. Linear Hybrid Automata (LHA) is a natural modeling language for real-time embedded systems. However, due to the existences of both discrete and continuous behaviors, formal analysis of LHA is recognized as a very challenging task. Despite decades of active research, the kinds of LHA problems that can be efficiently analyzed is rather limited. On the other hand, Labelled Linear Transition System (LTS) is a widely used modeling language to describe the state changes of the system before and after certain transitions. Lots of research efforts have been devoted into the verification of LTS models. Many off-the-shelf formal techniques and tools are available for analyzing different kinds of problems for LTS systems. In this paper, we propose to express an LHA as an equivalent LTS model explicitly. Then, we can take advantage of all the off-the-shelf formal checkers of LTS to answer different problems of the LHA model. A prototype tool HAT is implemented under this idea. By integrating typical LTS checkers like ARMC and Interproc, we conduct considerably difficult checking problems like reachability verification, termination analysis, and invariant generation of LHA successfully and efficiently. It shows the open possibility of analyzing more kinds of difficult problems of LHA by LTS checkers easily in the future.

Keywords: Linear hybrid automata · Transition system
Reachability checking · Termination analysis · Invariant generation

1 Introduction

Real-time embedded systems are widely used in the safety-critical area. Therefore, formal verification of these systems is crucial. Linear Hybrid Automata (LHA) [16] is a mainstream modeling language for such system. However, due to the existences of both discrete and continuous state changes in the system, the infinite state space of LHA is extremely difficult to verify. Currently, the verification of LHA is still mainly focusing on the basic reachability/safety problem, which has been proved to be undecidable [1,16]. Other typical classes of problems, e.g. invariant generation (for stability) [26,27], termination analysis (for

© Springer Nature Switzerland AG 2018
C. Jones et al. (Eds.): Zhou-Festschrift, LNCS 11180, pp. 85–104, 2018.
https://doi.org/10.1007/978-3-030-01461-2_5

liveness) [22,23] and so on, which are widely discussed in areas like hardware and software are rarely studied in the area of LHA.

Labelled Linear Transition System (LTS) [22,23] is a basic formal modeling language which describes the changes of the system variables' valuations between states. Different from LHA whose variables' valuations can be changed along with time continuously when staying in certain locations, the valuations of the system variables in the LTS can only be changed by discrete transitions. This gives a nice support of modeling the behavior of general systems. Taking an assignment expression in a software code for example, $x := x - 2$ can be modeled by a discrete transition labelled with linear constraint $x' = x - 2$, where x' stands for the valuation of x after the transition is fired.

Compared with LHA, LTS can be applied more widely in the modeling and analysis of different kinds of system. Therefore, decades of efforts have been devoted into formal analysis of LTS. Numerous technologies and tools have been proposed/implemented for the analysis of different kinds of problems of LTS, not only reachability. For example, as mentioned before, ranking function based termination analysis [22,23], abstract interpretation based invariant generation [9,17] and of course counterexample-guided-abstraction-refinement (CEGAR) [8] based reachability verification.

In general, the behavior of any system is a sequence of transitions from one state to another. Therefore, LTS is widely used to describe the semantics of many formal languages, including LHA. This brings the motivation of this paper: transform an LHA into an equivalent LTS model; then solve the generated LTS model by existing off-the-shelf LTS checkers to answer questions that can not be (efficiently) answered so far about the behavioral state space of the LHA model.

However, due to the existences of both discrete and continuous behaviors, LHA is an infinite state system. Therefore, if we want to describe an LHA as an LTS in the typical way by enumerating all the possible states and connecting them by transitions, standing for the discrete jumps and/or continuous flows, the resulting LTS will have infinite number of nodes and transitions, which will be impossible to be passed to any checker to solve. Furthermore, the continuous part also makes the presentation of the LHA's semantic in the form of LTS with existential and universal quantifiers included [16]. For example, when an LHA model stays in location v, $\forall$ continuous states in v must satisfy the invariants and flow conditions of v. Clearly, this is not the class of LTS that can be solved by existing LTS checkers.

As a result, in order to take advantage of the existing techniques and tools on LTS models to analyze the state space of LHA model, we have to transform the LHA model into an equivalent LTS model with finite structure and no quantifier, which is solvable by the existing tools. Luckily, for the class of LHA, this problem is solvable. By extending the idea from path-oriented linear programming encoding [20] and SMT-based BMC encoding of LHA [3], we present a method to transform an LHA into an equivalent LTS without quantifiers explicitly. We introduce a self loop on each control node to represent the continuous flow step. We also introduce a variable t to stand for the numeric value of the time spent during the past continuous step. As the value of t is reset to a nondeterministic positive value after the transition is fired, we can represent all the possible behavior of the LHA model in the LTS model by assigning random values to t in each loop.

Although the generated LTS is still an infinite state system, it gives us an opportunity to take full advantage of the numerous achievements on all the aspects of verification of LTS to analyze different properties, far more than reachability analysis, of the original LHA model. Based on the above idea, we present a prototype tool HAT in this paper. First, HAT transforms an LHA into an equivalent LTS. Then, HAT can feed the generated LTS into different LTS checkers to conduct different analysis. So far, HAT supports the interaction with three mature LTS checkers which are, ARMC [24] for both reachability analysis and termination analysis, Invgen [14] and Interproc [19] for invariant generation. We conduct sets of case studies on a series of well-known benchmarks. The experiment results show that, by using the method and tool presented in this paper, we can answer many considerably difficult questions on LHA easily and also efficiently.

Structure of the Paper. This paper is organized as follows. In the next section, we give the formal definitions of the LHA and LTS model used in this paper. We present the construction of the equivalent LTS model from the LHA model in Sect. 3. The equivalence proof is given in the same section. The implementation and case studies are given in Sect. 4. We discuss the related works in Sect. 5. Finally, the conclusion is stated in Sect. 6.

2 Notations

In this section, we give the formal definitions of the class of LHA and LTS used in our paper.

2.1 Linear Hybrid Automata

The linear hybrid automata (LHA) considered in this paper is a variation of the definition given in [16]. The flow conditions of variables in an LHA considered here can be given as ranges of values for their derivatives.

Definition 1. An LHA is a tuple $H = (X, V, V^0, E, \alpha, \beta, \gamma)$, where

- X is a finite set of real-valued variables; V is a finite set of *locations*; $V^0 \subseteq V$ is a set of *initial locations*.
- E is a *transition relation* set whose elements are of the form (v, ϕ, ψ, v'), where v, v' are in V, ϕ is a set of *transition guards* of the form $\sum_{i=0}^{m} b_i x_i \sim a$, and ψ is a set of *reset actions* of the form $x := c$ where $x_i \in X$, $x \in X$, $a, b_i, c \in \mathcal{R}$, $\sim \in \{<, \leq, >, \geq, =\}$.
- α is a labeling function which maps each location in V to a *location invariant* which is a set of *variable constraints* of the form $\sum_{i=0}^{m} b_i x_i \sim a$ where $x_i \in X$, $a, b_i \in \mathcal{R}$, $\sim \in \{<, \leq, >, \geq, =\}$.

- β is a labeling function which maps each location in V to a set of *flow conditions* which are of the form of ordinary differential inclusion $\dot{x} \in [a, b]$ where $x \in X$, and $a, b \in \mathcal{R}$ and $(a \leq b)$. For any $v \in V$, for any $x \in X$, there is one and only one flow condition $\dot{x} \in [a, b] \in \beta(v)$.
- γ is a labeling function which maps each location in V^0 to a set of *initial conditions* which are of the form $x \in [a, b]$. For any $v \in V^0$, for any $x \in X$, there is at most one initial condition definition $x \in [a, b] \in \gamma(v)$, where $x \in X$, $a, b \in \mathcal{R}$.

Definition 2. Given an LHA $H = (X, V, V^0, E, \alpha, \beta, \gamma)$, a *state* s of H is a pair (v, q) where

- $v \in V$
- $q = (x_{1_q}, x_{2_q} \ldots x_{m_q})$ is a valuation of all the continuous variables in X, such that q satisfies the location invariant $\alpha(v)$ of v.

2.2   Labelled Linear Transition System

Definition 3. A *Labelled Linear Transition System* (LTS) is a tuple $T = (X_T, V_T, V_T^O, E_T, I)$, where

- X_T is a finite set of variables;
- V_T is a finite set of locations;
- V_T^O is a set of initial locations, such that $V_T^O \subseteq V_T$;
- E_T is a *transition relation* whose elements are of the form (v, ϕ_T, v'), where v, v' are in V_T, ϕ_T is a set of *linear constraints* of the form $\sum_{i=0}^{m} b_i x_i + c_i x_i' \sim a$, where $x_i, x_i' \in X_T$, a, b_i and $c_i \in \mathcal{R}$, $\sim \in \{<, \leq, >, \geq, =\}$. The constraint ϕ_T gives the relations between the valuations of system variables before and after certain transitions, which are represented as x and x' respectively.
- I is a labeling function which maps each location in V_T^O to a set of *initial conditions* in the form of $\sum_{i=0}^{m} b_i x_i + c_i x_i' \sim a$, where $x_i, x_i' \in X_T$, a, b_i and $c_i \in \mathcal{R}$, $\sim \in \{<, \leq, >, \geq, =\}$.

Definition 4. Given an LTS $T = (V_T, V_T^O, X_T, E_T, I)$, a *state* s of T is a pair (v, q) such that

- $v \in V_T$
- $q = (x_{1_q}, x_{2_q} \ldots x_{m_q})$ is a valuation of all the continuous variables in X_T.

Definition 5. The behavior of a LTS T is a run σ which is a sequence of states $s_0, s_1, \ldots, s_n$, such that:

- $s_0 = (v_0, q_0)$ where $v_0 \in V_T^O$ and q_0 satisfy $I(v_0)$.
- for each $i \geq 0$ there exists a transition $e \in E_T$ such that $s_i = (v_i, q_i)$ goes to $s_{i+1} = (v_{i+1}, q_{i+1})$ under e, formally $e = (v_i, \phi_e, v_{i+1})$, and (q_i, q_{i+1}) satisfies ϕ_e.

If a state s is in a behavior of T, we say s is *reachable*.

2.3 LTS Semantic for LHA

Definition 6. The behavior of a LHA H is a sequence of states $s_0, s_1, \ldots, s_n$, such that:

- Each state s_i is a pair (v_i, q_i) where $v_i \in V$ and $q_i = (x_{1_{q_i}}, x_{2_{q_i}} \ldots x_{m_{q_i}})$ is a valuation of all the continuous variables in X, such that q satisfies the location invariant $\alpha(v)$ of v $(0 \le i \le n)$.
- $s_0 = (v_0, q_0)$ where $v_0 \in V^0$ and q_0 satisfies the initial conditions in $\gamma(v_0)$.
- For each state $s_i = (v_i, q_i)$ and $s_j = (v_j, q_j)$, either
  - $v_i \ne v_j$ (discrete jump): there is transition $(v_i, \phi_i, \psi_i, v_j) \in E$, q_i and q_j satisfy ϕ_i and ψ_i.
  - $v_i = v_j$ (continuous jump): there exists ($\exists$) a positive real $\delta_i \in \mathbb{R}$ and a differentiable function $W_k : [0, \delta_i] \to \mathbb{R}$ for each variable $x_k \in X (1 \le i \le n, 1 \le k \le m)$, with the first derivative $w_k : [0, \delta_i] \to \mathbb{R}$, such that
    1. $W_k(0) = x_{k_{q_i}}$ and $W_k(\delta_i) = x_{k_{q_j}}$
    2. For all ($\forall$) reals $\varepsilon \in [0, \delta_i]$
       - (a) $W_k(\varepsilon)$ satisfies all the invariants in $\alpha(v_i)$
       - (b) $w_k(\varepsilon) \in [a_j, b_j] \subseteq \beta_{v_i}$

Definition 7. For an LHA $H = (X, V, V^0, E, \alpha, \beta, \gamma)$, if a sequence of states $s_0, s_1, \ldots, s_n$ is a behavior of H, we say s_n is *reachable*.

Definition 8. For an LHA $H = (X, V, V^0, E, \alpha, \beta, \gamma)$, if an infinite sequence of states $s_0, s_1, \ldots, s_n, \ldots$ is a behavior of H and visits a discrete transition $e_i \in E$ infinitely many times, we say H is not *terminating*[1].

In general, the behavior of any model/language can be represented as transitions from state to state. Therefore, LTS has been used to represent the semantics for lots of formal languages, including LHA.

Of course, we can connect all the states of an LHA by either discrete jump or continuous jump, then the state space of the LHA is an LTS. However, due to the existence of continuous flow conditions, the state space of LHA is infinite. Furthermore, the LTS presentation of such infinite state space is an LTS with infinite structure and quantifiers, including both $\exists$ and $\forall$, as we can see from Definition 6 in this paper and also the Definition 1.3 in [16], which is the first introduction of hybrid automata. Clearly, this class of LTS is not the typical LTS that can be processed efficiently by existing techniques.

3 Quantifier-Free LTS Construction for LHA

As shown in the previous section, if we want to use any mature off-the-shelf LTS checker to analyze LHA, it is necessary to present a method to transfer the LHA model into an equivalent LTS model with finite structure and no quantifiers at first. Luckily, researchers have started to encode the transition relations

---

[1] Please refer to [23] for the detail definition of termination for LTS.

between states of LHA symbolically in many studies, e.g. path-oriented reachability encoding in [20] and SMT-based BMC encoding in [3]. By extending such methods, we present a method to transform an LHA H to a quantifier-free LTS T explicitly, which preserves the same behavior of H.

Given an LHA $H = (X, V, V^0, E, \alpha, \beta, \gamma)$, the LTS $T = (V_T, V_T^O, X_T, E_T, I)$ corresponding to H can be constructed in the following way:

- Model Structure:
  - For each location $v_i \in V$, generate a location: v_{i_T} in V_T. If $v_i \in V^O$, $v_{i_T} \in V_T^O$.
  - For each location $v_i \in V$, generate a self-loop transition $e_{v_i} : v_{i_T} \to v_{i_T}$ in E_T. The self-loop transition stands for the continuous jump of H in location v_i.
  - For each transition $e_i \in E$, which is in the form of $v_i \to v_j$, generate transition $e_{i_T} : v_{i_T} \to v_{j_T}$ in E_T.
- Variable:
  - Generate a new specific variable t in X_T to stand for the time spent in each continuous flow.
  - For each variable $x \in X$, generate a variable with the same name x in X_T.
- Constraint Label:
  - Constraints on Continuous Flow Self Loop Transition $e_{v_i} : (v_{i_T}, \phi_{C_T}, v_{i_T})$:
    * For each invariant $inv = \sum_{i=0}^{l} b_i x_i \sim a$ in $\alpha(v_i)$ of location $v_i \in V$, generate a constraint $inv' = \sum_{i=0}^{m} b_i x_i' \sim a$ based on variable x', add inv and inv' to the constraint set ϕ_{C_T}. These two constraints ask that the valuations of all the variables must satisfy the invariants of location v_i before and after the system takes a continuous flow.
    * For each flow condition $flow$ in β_{v_i} of location $v_i \in V$, e.g., $\dot{x} \in [a, b]$, generate two new constraints: $flow' : x' - at - x \geq 0$ and $flow'' : x' - bt - x \leq 0$, add $flow'$ and $flow''$ to the constraint set ϕ_{C_T}. These two constraints ask that before and after the system takes a continuous flow in location v_i, the relation of the valuations of certain variable must obey the flow conditions.
    * For each location $v_i \in V$, generate constraints $t > 0$ and $t' > 0$, and add them to ϕ_{C_T}. By $t > 0$, we mean, if the self loop transition is fired, then the time spent in this continuous flow is t which is a positive real value. Furthermore, $t' > 0$ is a reset of the timer indicate that the time spent in next continuous flow behavior would be a random positive value. It is worth to note that we use $t > 0$ rather than $t \geq 0$ because $t == 0$ means the system takes a continuous jump in the location without spending any time. In that case, everything keeps the same. It's not necessary to distinguish the states before and after this "0" time continuous flow in the system behavior.
  - Constraints on Discrete Switch Transition $e_{i_T} : (v_{i_T}, \phi_{D_T}, v_{j_T})$
    * For each constraint $guard = \sum_{i=0}^{m} b_i x_i \sim a$ in guard ϕ of transition $e_i = (v_i, \phi, \psi, v_j)$, add $guard$ to ϕ_{D_T}.

  * For each reset $reset : x = a$ in ψ of transition $e_i = (v_i, \phi, \psi, v_j)$, generate constraint $reset' : x' = a$, add $reset'$ to ϕ_{D_T}. For any variable x which is not reset in the transition, add $x' = x$ to ϕ_{D_T}.
  * For each invariant $inv = \sum_{i=0}^{m} b_i x_i \sim a$ in $\alpha(v_j)$ of location v_j, generate a constraint $inv' = \sum_{i=0}^{m} b_i x_i' \sim a$ based on variable x', add inv and inv' to ϕ_{D_T}. These two constraints ask that before and after the system takes the discrete jump, the valuations of all the variables must satisfy the invariants of the source and target location respectively.
  * If $v_i \in V^0$, for each $x \in [a, b]$ in γ_{v_i}, add $x' \in [a, b]$ to $I(v_{i_T})$

Now, we use a simple LHA model to help to illustrate our transformation from the LHA model to the LTS system. The automaton in Fig. 1 describes a model of water level monitor cited from [1]. The LTS we get after the transformation is shown below in Fig. 2[2]. We will mainly use the location v_1 and transition e_1 to illustrate the transformation as follows.

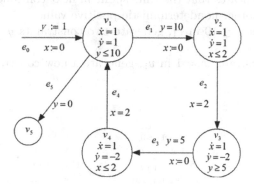

Fig. 1. The LHA model of water-level monitor

- For the graph structure and discrete behavior in the LHA:
  - Two system variables are generated in the LTS: x, y corresponding to x, y in the LHA respectively.
  - For location v_1, generate the corresponding location v_{1_T} in the LTS.
  - For transition $e_1 : v_1 \rightarrow v_2$ in the LHA, generate the corresponding new transition $e_{1_T} : v_{1_T} \rightarrow v_{2_T}$ in the LTS.
  - For guard $y = 10$ on transition e_1 in the LHA, generate new constraint $y = 10$ and add it into e_{1_T} in the LTS.

---

[2] For any variable z which is not reset in the transition, the corresponding constraint $z' = z$ is omitted in the picture to keep the figure neat. Meanwhile, the initial conditions in this model are in the format of $x := a$, which can be considered as a special case of the general form $x \in [a, b]$.

- For reset $x := 0$ on transition e_1, generate new constraint $x' = 0$ and add it into e_{1_T} in the LTS, where x' stands for the valuation of x after the transition is fired. As y is not reset on e_1, generate constraint $y' = y$ to indicate the value of y keeps the same after the transition. $y' = y$ is omitted in the graph as explained in the footnote below.
- For invariant $y \leq 10$ in v_1, generate constraint $y \leq 10$ in e_{1_T}.
- For invariant $x \leq 2$ in v_2, generate constraint $x' \leq 2$ in e_{1_T}.
- For the continuous behavior in the LHA:
  - One additional system variables t is generated in the LTS as a timer which stands for the time spent in each continuous flow.
  - For location v_1, generate one new transition e_{v_1} from $v_{1_T} \rightarrow v_{1_T}$. The self-loop transition stands for the continuous jump of H in location v_1
  - For location v_1, generate two new constraints $t > 0$ and $t' > 0$, in transition e_{v_1}. $t > 0$ means if the self-loop transition is fired, the time spent in this continuous flow is positive real value t. While, $t' > 0$ is a reset of the timer indicates that the time spent in next continuous flow behavior would be another nondeterministic positive value.
  - For invariant $y \leq 10$ in v_1, generate two constraints $y \leq 10$ and $y' \leq 10$ in e_{v_1}.
  - For flow constraint $\dot{x} = 1$ in v_1, generate a new constraint $x' = x + t$ in e_{v_1}.

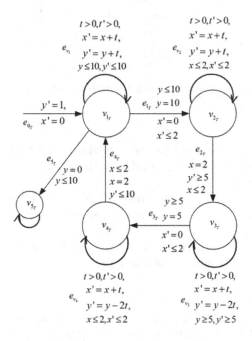

Fig. 2. The Generated LTS model of water-level monitor

Theorem 1. Given an LHA H, and an LTS T, which is generated from H according to the above transformation rules, a sequence of states in H is a behavior of H **if and only if** there is a corresponding sequence of states in T, which consists a run of T.

Here, we give the proof sketch of the equivalence between the LHA and the generated LTS.

   Proof:

1. If a sequence of states $s_1, s_2, \ldots, s_m$, where $s_i = (v_i, q_i), 1 \le i \le m$, is a behavior of H. Clearly, there is a corresponding sequence of states in the LTS T.
   - If $v_i == v_{i+1}$, the transition between s_i and s_{i+1} is a continuous jump. We can have two corresponding states (v_{i_T}, q_{i_T}) and (v_{i_T}, q_{i+1_T}) in the LTS, where q_{i_T} and q_{i+1_T} satisfy the constraints on the self loop of location v_{i_T} in T.
   - If $v_i \ne v_{i+1}$, the transition between s_i and s_{i+1} is a discrete jump. We can have two corresponding states (v_{i_T}, q_{i_T}) and (v_{i+1_T}, q_{i+1_T}) in the LTS, where q_{i_T} and q_{i+1_T} satisfy the constraints on the jump between location v_{i_T} and v_{i+1_T} in T.
2. On the other direction, if there is a run, sequence states, of the LTS, there is a corresponding behavior of the LHA.
   - Similar with the above proof, for any pair of states which composes a discrete jump in the LTS, there is a corresponding discrete jump in the LHA for sure.
   - What we need to prove is for any pair of states which composes a continuous self-loop jump in the LTS, there is a legal continuous behavior in the LHA. Since all the constraints, e.g. invariants and flow conditions, in the LHA model are linear, the corresponding potential state space in one location of the LHA is a convex set. According to the convex theory, given any two points in a convex set, if we connect these two points by a straight line π, all the points on π are in the convex set. In another word, given two legal states (v_i, x_{t_1}) and (v_i, x_{t_2}) on the same location v_i, there must have a differentiable function which can connect these two states and satisfies all the constraints. For example, connect these two states by a straight line, where the flow condition $w(t)$, the slope of the line: $(x_{t_2} - x_{t_1})/(t_2 - t_1)$, satisfies β_{v_1}, and every states on this line must satisfy all the invariants in $\alpha(v_i)$.

   Take the water-level LHA for example, the state sequence $(v_1, (x == 0, y == 1))$, $(v_1, (x == 5.5, y == 6.5))$, $(v_1, (x == 9, y == 10))$, $(v_2, (x == 0, y == 10))$, $(v_2, (x == 0.9, y == 10.9))$, $(v_2, (x == 2, y == 12))$, $(v_3, (x == 2, y == 12))$, $(v_3, (x == 3, y == 10))$, $(v_3, (x == 5.5, y == 5))$, $(v_4, (x == 0, y = 5))$, $(v_4, (x == 1.5, y = 2))$ is a valid behavior of the automaton, Fig. 1.

   This behavior spends 5.5 time units then 3.5 time units in v_1, then $y == 10$ so it jumps to v_2. It spends 0.9 time unit at first, then 1.1 time units in v_2 before it jumps to v_3. In v_3, it spends 1 time unit and then 2.5 time units, then goes to v_4, where it spends 1.5 time units and stops finally.

We have an equivalent run of the corresponding LTS, Fig. 2, as follows: $(v_{1_T}, (x == 0, y == 1, t == 5.5))$, $(v_{1_T}, (x == 5.5, y == 6.5, t == 3.5))$, $(v_{1_T}, (x == 9, y == 10, t == 0.9))$, $(v_{2_T}, (x == 0, y == 10, t == 0.9))$, $(v_{2_T}, (x == 0.9, y == 10.9, t == 1.1))$, $(v_{2_T}, (x == 2, y == 12, t == 1))$, $(v_{3_T}, (x == 2, y == 12, t == 1))$, $(v_{3_T}, (x == 3, y == 10, t == 2.5))$, $(v_{3_T}, (x == 5.5, y == 5, t == 1.5))$, $(v_{4_T}, (x == 0, y == 5, t == 1.5))$, $(v_{4_T}, (x == 1.5, y == 2, t == 0.2))$. Note that, according to our transformation rule the timer t is reassigned to a random value in each continuous step. Therefore, even the system ends in the final state, we still assign a random value 0.2 to t.

Based on Theorem 1, we can have the following corollaries straightforwardly.

Corollary 1. A state (v_i, q_i) in LHA H is reachable *iff* the corresponding state (v_{i_T}, q_{i_T}) is reachable in the generated LTS T.

Corollary 2. An invariant $\sum_{i=0}^{m} b_i x_i \sim a$ of location v_{i_T} in the generated LTS T is an invariant for location v_i in the original LHA H as well.

Corollary 3. An infinite sequence of states $\delta_T = s_{0_T}, s_{1_T}, s_{2_T}, \ldots$, where $s_{i_T} = (v_{i_T}, q_{i_T})$, is a behavior of the generated LTS T and visits a transition e_{i_T} infinite times, *iff* the corresponding infinite sequence of states $\delta = s_0, s_1, s_2, \ldots$, where $s_i = (v_i, q_i)$, is a behavior of the original LHA H and visits e_i infinitely times as well.

Now, we have an approach to construct an equivalent LTS T of a given LHA H. We can analyze the state space of the generated LTS system by taking advantage of the off-the-shelf LTS checkers. According to Corollary 1–3, such verification results are also valid for the state space of the original LHA. For example, now we can conduct ranking function based termination analysis, abstract interpretation based invariant generation and CEGAR based reachability verification on the state space of the LHA.

4   Implementation and Experiment

4.1   Tool Implementation

A prototype tool HAT, *H*ybrid *A*utomata Checker Based on Labelled *T*ransition System Construction and Analysis, is implemented to demonstrate the feasibility of our method. HAT automates the LTS construction and the subsequent interactions with the LTS checkers. Currently, HAT supports the interaction with three LTS checkers, including ARMC [24] which performs both CEGAR based reachability checking and ranking function detection based termination analysis of LTS system; Interproc [19] which is a typical abstract interpretation based invariant generator built upon APRON library [17]; and InvGen [14] which is another invariant generator of LTS system based on constraint solving technique. Due to the space limitation, we focus on the introduction of the integration and experience of ARMC and Interproc in the following paragraph, as InvGen targets a similar problem with Interproc, by different techniques though.

First of all, the structure and workflow of HAT is shown below in Fig. 3. After a LHA model is generated using the graphical LHA editor in HAT[3], HAT transforms the LHA H into an internal LTS data structure automatically. Then, according to the problem/tool user chose, HAT generates the input file for the specific tool, feeds the input file to the tool and translates the analysis result back to the state space of the LHA H. The functionalities of HAT include:

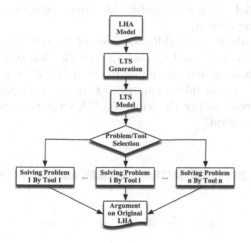

Fig. 3. Workflow of HAT

– Invariant generation by Interproc[4]: As Interproc is abstract interpretation based, it asks the user to select the abstract domain first. In HAT, the domains can be selected including: box, octagon, polyhedral and so on. According to Corollary 2, the invariant for each node v_{i_T} in the LTS model is also the invariant for the node v_i in the original LHA model. Therefore, after the invariants are generated on the LTS, HAT adds the generated invariants into the original LHA model, resulting a refined LHA model. For example, the model shown in the left part of Fig. 4 is the water level monitor model from Fig. 1. The right part of Fig. 4 is the refined model based on the generated invariants. Take location v_4 for example, compared with Fig. 1, we can find new invariants like $2x + y = 5$ and $x \geq 0$ which are marked by red. These invariants are generated by Interproc and added into the model by HAT.

---

[3] The editor is integrated from LHA BMC checker BACH [6].
[4] In order to make Interproc handle LTS much easier, we modify the input language syntax of Interproc slightly. The modified version of Interproc is available upon request.

Furthermore, location v_5 disappears in the refined model as the invariant generated by Interproc for v_5 is $\perp$, which means v_5 is not reachable at all.

- Termination Analysis by ARMC: ARMC conducts the termination analysis of LTS by looking for well-founded ranking functions [22] in the system. An informal definition of well-founded ranking function is an expression like $f(x) \leq a$, while the valuation of $f(x)$ is keeping increasing with the executing of the system. If such function exists for the transition relation of a system, the system terminates [22]. According to Corollary 3, if ARMC claims such ranking function doesn't exist and presents a witness infinite loop in the system, such infinite state loop can be mapped back to a infinite state sequence in the LHA model straightforwardly, this implies the execution of the LHA is not terminating as well.

- Reachability Analysis by ARMC: Besides of termination analysis, ARMC also supports CEGAR based reachability verification of LTS. According to Corollary 1, a node is not reachable in the LHA iff it is reachable in the LTS. Therefore, we can take advantage of the powerful CEGAR techniques to perform the reachability checking of LHA without performing expensive geometric computation.

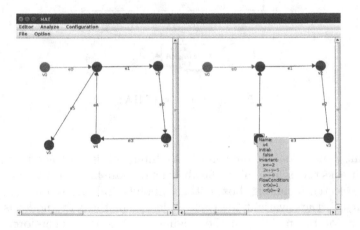

Fig. 4. GUI of interproc based invariant generation in HAT

4.2   Case Studies

In order to evaluate the performance of HAT, we conduct a series of case studies on a set of widely-used LHA benchmarks. The first LHA is the water-level monitor system (WLM) used through this paper in Fig. 1. The second one is the temperature control rod system (TCS) in Fig. 5.

Besides of the above small scale models, we also conduct the case studies on the scalable automated highway system from [18] in Fig. 6. It is worth noting that the size of the highway system model can be easily expanded by introducing more cars into the system, which will increase new locations and variables in the model. For example, Figs. 7 and 8 are the models for the automated highway system with three cars and four cars respectively.

The experiments are conducted on a normal desktop PC (Intel Core2 Quad 2.66GHz, 4GB RAM, UBUNTU12.04). The tool HAT, all the sample models and the output results are all available from http://seg.nju.edu.cn/HAT/. For the following experiment data, the time usage is recorded by tool runlim [5]. If any tool fails to give the result in the time limit, one hour, the corresponding blank is marked by "N/A".

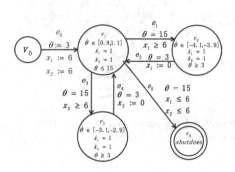

Fig. 5. Temperature control system   **Fig. 6.** Automated highway system

Invariant Generation. The performance data of invariant generation in HAT, by Interproc, are given in Table 1. In this table, we record the size of the model, number of variables and locations, and the time spend for invariant generation on different domain as well. Due to the space limitation, the detail information about the invariants generated are refer to http://seg.nju.edu.cn/HAT/.

From this table and the generated invariants on the website we can see that, consistent with the common sense, by choosing abstract domain like box or octagon, HAT/ Interproc can solve the system very efficiently and the scalability is very nice. For example, for a system with 100 variables and 101 locations, we can get the invariants for all the nodes in 26.17 s.

However, if the user chooses complex domain like polyhedral (PPL), the size of the system that can be solved is much smaller. Nevertheless, the invariants generated in PPL domain are much more accurate. For example, by PPL, HAT can annotate the invariants of certain locations of WLM and Motor series models as ⊥. While the results on domains like box and octagon are much more abstract.

The above experiments show the process capability and scalability of our method about invariant generation for LHA. Furthermore, we can get deeper information of the system under investigation from the generated invariants. Such information can benefits the future analysis for sure. For example, when the invariant on certain location is marked as ⊥, the location is definitely not reachable. The model that need to verify shall be much easier to handle. The topic of how to use the invariants generated for the future analysis, like model checking, theorem proving or stability analysis, has been widely discussed in numerous studies. Therefore, we will not discuss it in detail in this paper.

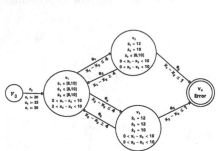 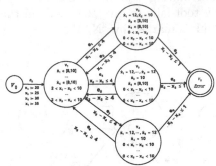

Fig. 7. Automated highway system with three cars

Fig. 8. Automated highway system with four cars

Table 1. Invariant generation performance data

System	Variable	Location	Box	Octagon	PPL
WLM	2	5	0.4s	0.31s	0.97s
TCS	3	4	0.4s	0.94s	0.82s
$Motor_5$	5	6	0.44s	0.64s	3.21s
$Motor_{10}$	10	11	0.76s	3.15s	N/A
$Motor_{30}$	30	31	1.22s	180.29s	N/A
$Motor_{60}$	60	61	6.16s	N/A	N/A
$Motor_{100}$	100	101	26.17s	N/A	N/A

Termination Analysis. It is really rare to see works perform termination analysis on the infinite state space of real time systems. By taking advantage of ARMC, it is possible to conduct such analysis of LHA by looking for ranking functions in the corresponding LTS system. We slightly modify some constraints in each model to generate two versions of each model, one is able to terminating, one is not. Then, both of the versions are feed to HAT for analysis. The

Table 2. Termination analysis performance data

Name	Variable	Location	Model type	Time	Result
WLM	2	5	NonTermi.	4.74s	ARMC: cannot find rank
			Termi.	1.6s	ARMC: program is correct
TCS	3	4	NonTermi.	0.69s	ARMC: feasible counterexample
			Termi.	0.76s	ARMC: program is correct
$Motor_5$	5	6	NonTermi.	1.45s	ARMC: feasible counterexample
			Termi.	0.58s	ARMC: program is correct
$Motor_{20}$	20	21	NonTermi.	1455.65s	ARMC: feasible counterexample
			Termi.	2.0s	ARMC: program is correct
$Motor_{30}$	30	31	NonTermi.	N/A	N/A
			Termi.	3.78s	ARMC: program is correct
$Motor_{50}$	50	51	NonTermi.	N/A	N/A
			Termi.	14.84s	ARMC: program is correct
$Motor_{100}$	100	101	NonTermi.	N/A	N/A
			Termi	142.52s	ARMC: program is correct

performance data for the corresponding models are given in Table 2. The detail information is available on the website as well.

From the data we can see that, by using ARMC, HAT successfully reports "program is correct" for all the models which are able to terminating. For those which cannot terminate, ARMC either reports a feasible counterexample which is a infinite loop or reports it cannot find a ranking function. In one hour time limit, the largest nonterminating model solved is $Motor_{20}$, which has 20 variables and 21 locations. For terminating ones, even for a large model like $Motor_{100}$, 100 variables and 101 locations, HAT/ARMC finishes the computing in 142.5 s.

Reachability Verification. We also use ARMC in HAT to conduct the reachability verification of all the benchmarks as well. Furthermore, different from the above two problems which are difficult to find related tools to compare, there are many mature works about reachability verification of LHA. Therefore, we compare the performance of HAT with the state-of-the-art LHA model checker SpaceEx [12], which is the upgraded version of PHAVer [11], with both of its underlying algorithms. The first one is the algorithm in PHAVer, marked as $SpaceEx_{phav}$. The second one is the lately introduced "support function" algorithm [12], marked as $SpaceEx_{supp}$[5].

The experiment data for the time spent in each benchmark is shown in Table 3. From Table 3, we can see that HAT outperforms both configurations

---

[5] The comparison between HAT and the PHAVer algorithm $SpaceEx_{phav}$ is fair as they are addressing the same class of HA. On the other hand, support function algorithm ($SpaceEx_{supp}$) is more suitable to handle HA with piecewise affine dynamics which is different from the class of HA considered in this paper. We just list the data here for reference.

of SpaceEx significantly on most of the cases, especially on large scale models, like the series of *Motor* problems. For example, the largest problem SpaceEx solved in the time limit is $Motor_5$ which has only 5 variables, while the largest problem HAT solved in the one hour time limit has 70 variables and 71 locations included.

Table 3. Reachability Verification Performance Data

Name	Variable	Location	HAT$_{ARMC}$	SpaceEx$_{phav.}$	SpaceEx$_{supp.}$
WLM	2	5	0.63s	0.27s	0.16s
TCS	3	4	0.84s	N/A	1.10s
$Motor_5$	5	6	0.42s	3.99s	N/A
$Motor_{20}$	20	21	16.41s	N/A	N/A
$Motor_{30}$	30	31	77.53s	N/A	N/A
$Motor_{50}$	50	51	628.74s	N/A	N/A
$Motor_{70}$	70	71	3087.63s	N/A	N/A

5   Related Works

5.1   Reachability Analysis

Formal analysis of LHA is considerably difficult. Most of the research efforts are devoted to the reachability verification problem, which is recognized as a basic problem in the context of formal analysis of LHA [11,12]. However, it has been proved that the reachability problem for LHA is undecidable [16]. The typical procedures of reachability verification is to compute the closure of the system's state space by geometric computation, which is very expensive. As we shown in the last paragraph, the capability of the-state-of-the-art checker is limited. They do not scale well to the high dimension system.

In recent years, *Bounded Model Checking* [4] has been presented. The basic idea is to encode the next-state relation of a system as a propositional formula, unroll this formula to some integer k, and search for a counterexample in the model executions whose length is bounded by k. There are several related works [3,10] to check LHA by the BMC idea. Several tools were developed, such as MathSAT [3] and HySAT [10]. These tools are based on a SAT-solver that calls the solver on demand for conjunctions of the domain-specific constraints. Nevertheless, it is difficult to apply those tools to analyze problems with large bound.

To control the complexity of BMC, a new method path-oriented reachability is proposed in [20]. The basic idea is to check the reachability of one path at a time. As the number of potential paths in the given bound is finite, the BMC can be performed efficiently [6,29]. The construction of LTS from the LHA is inspired by the encoding technique used in these set of BMC works.

ARMC is a CEGAR based checker. The CEGAR [8] technique has also been applied onto reachability verification of hybrid automata directly in studies like [2,7]. These works proposed to apply predicates on the states of HA to abstract the model. However, they have to split the locations of the model during refinement which may cause huge system to analyze. Study [18] proposed a method to drop variables from the original LHA in each iteration, and ask PHAVer to solve the simplified model. As this technique still relies on PHAVer, in another word geometric computation, as the underlying checker for the abstracted model, its scalability is also limited. As the implementations of this work are not available, we can only compare with [18] numerically as it also reported its performance on the *Motor* series problem. According to [18], the largest *Motor* model it solved has 19 variables included. It took [18] 652.51 s to solve such a problem, while for a larger problem, $Motor_{20}$, HAT solved it in only 16.41 s and HAT solved a much larger system $Motor_{70}$ in the one hour time limit successfully.

5.2 Invariant Generation

Invariant generation of hybrid system has been studied widely. In [27], Sankaranarayanan propose to use templates to generate invariants of a specific form for hybrid system by constraint solving. Study [26] present a method to compute the most precise polynomial equational invariant for linear hybrid system based on Gröbner basis computation. However, these techniques cannot handle hybrid systems with inequalities in initial sets or switching surfaces, which is very common in real cases [21].

Study [13] also uses a template with unknown coefficient as the guide of invariant of the LHA system, which will generate a formula with quantifiers like ∃∀. Then, quantifier elimination techniques based on Farkas Lemma are deployed to translate the formula into a ∃ formula, which can be solved by SMT decision procedures. It is well known that quantifier elimination technique has high complexity, which may restrict the size of the system that can be handled.

Region stability of hybrid automata is analyzed in [25] to check whether the behavior of the system will drop into certain region, which is similar with invariant analysis. [25] derives binary reachability relations over hybrid system behavior, then call model checker PHAVer [11] to generate the relations between the valuation of a variable in certain modes. Then, it will try to find the ranking function of the relation. Once a ranking function is found, then the relation can be terminated, which means the variable can fall into certain ranges. However, this technique will double the size of system variables in the system. As it relies on safety verification techniques like polyhedral computation which is very complex, the size of the system can be solved is limited. Furthermore, the stability invariant that can be solved by this technique is only a region box of a given variable, which is rather abstract.

Recently, differential logic is proposed in [21] to generate differential invariant for nonlinear hybrid system. In study [21] the differential invariants are computed as fixed points using theorem proving by differential logic for hybrid systems. This work is interesting and can handle nonlinear systems, while our work is focusing on linear hybrid automata, which is much simpler. Thus, we can generate invariants of LHA efficiently by techniques like abstract interpretation [9].

5.3   Termination Analysis

Termination analysis of hybrid automata has not been studied intensively. Nevertheless, work [28] proved that the liveness problem of infinite state system can be transformed to the fairness termination problem. Therefore, this is an important problem that has been widely discussed in the context of liveness of transition system.

Researchers has achieved significant progress in areas like termination analysis of software code [22–24]. The tool ARMC used in HAT is a typical success product of such research. However, to the best of our knowledge, we have not find any discussion about this topic in the area of LHA yet.

5.4   TS Construction for HA

Most of the works about transforming HA model into transition system are discussed in the invariant generation subsection. Besides that, study [15,30] try to introduce a timer to present the continuous behavior. However, they use a constant time-step dt as a clock, even if the constant is a infinitesimal number, we still cannot describe the behavior of the system in any given time instance, say, in the middle of dt. In this paper, by focusing on LHA and set the timer as a free variable, we are able to present all the possible states in the behavior.

6   Conclusion

In this paper, we propose that by generating the equivalent LTS model of an LHA, we can take advantage of the powerful off-the-shelf LTS checkers to answer many different problems, not only reachability, on the state space of LHA easily.

A prototype tool HAT is implemented. By interacting with ARMC and Interproc in HAT, we show that considerably difficult problems, including invariant generation, termination analysis and reachability verification of high dimension system, are solved efficiently.

Last but not least, HAT is an open framework. In the future HAT can be extended easily by integrating different LTS checkers to answer different kinds of questions about the state space of LHA model seamlessly.

Acknowledgment. The authors want to thank Prof. Edmund Clarke, Dr. Sumit Jha, Dr. Silke Wagner, and Dr. Axel Legay for their constructive discussions on the topic of presenting an LHA as an LTS for fair termination analysis. The authors also want to thank Prof. Andrey Rybalchenko for his help with ARMC. The valuable comments given by all the anonymous reviewers are also appreciated! This paper is supported in part by the National Natural Science Foundation of China (No.61561146394 and No.61572249), in which No.61561146394 is a Joint NSFC-ISF Research Program, jointly funded by the National Natural Science Foundation of China and the Israel Science Foundation.

References

1. Alur, R., Courcoubetis, C., Halbwachs, N., Henzinger, T.A., Ho, P., Nicollin, X., Olivero, A., Sifakis, J., Yovine, S.: The algorithmic analysis of hybrid systems. Theor. Comput. Sci. **138**(1), 3–34 (1995)
2. Alur, R., Dang, T., Ivancic, F.: Counterexample-guided predicate abstraction of hybrid systems. Theor. Comput. Sci. **354**(2), 250–271 (2006)
3. Audemard, G., Bozzano, M., Cimatti, A., Sebastiani, R.: Verifying industrial hybrid systems with mathsat. Electr. Notes Theor. Comput. Sci. **119**(2), 17–32 (2005)
4. Biere, A., Cimatti, A., Clarke, E.M., Strichman, O., Zhu, Y.: Bounded model checking. Adv. Comput. **58**, 117–148 (2003)
5. Biere, A., Jussila, T.: runlim (2000). http://fmv.jku.at/runlim/
6. Bu, L., Li, Y., Wang, L., Li, X.: BACH: bounded reachability checker for linear hybrid automata. In: Formal Methods in Computer-Aided Design, FMCAD 2008, Portland, Oregon, USA, 17–20 November 2008, pp. 1–4 (2008)
7. Clarke, E., Fehnker, A., Han, Z., Krogh, B., Stursberg, O., Theobald, M.: Verification of hybrid systems based on counterexample-guided abstraction refinement. In: Garavel, H., Hatcliff, J. (eds.) TACAS 2003. LNCS, vol. 2619, pp. 192–207. Springer, Heidelberg (2003). https://doi.org/10.1007/3-540-36577-X_14
8. Clarke, E.M., Grumberg, O., Jha, S., Lu, Y., Veith, H.: Counterexample-guided abstraction refinement. In: Computer Aided Verification, 12th International Conference, CAV 2000, Chicago, IL, USA, July 15–19, 2000, Proceedings, pp. 154–169 (2000)
9. Cousot, P., Cousot, R.: Abstract interpretation: a unified lattice model for static analysis of programs by construction or approximation of fixpoints. In: Conference Record of the Fourth ACM Symposium on Principles of Programming Languages, Los Angeles, California, USA, January 1977, pp. 238–252 (1977)
10. Fränzle, M., Herde, C.: Hysat: an efficient proof engine for bounded model checking of hybrid systems. Form. Methods Syst. Des. **30**(3), 179–198 (2007)
11. Frehse, G.: PHAVer: algorithmic verification of hybrid systems past HyTech. In: Morari, M., Thiele, L. (eds.) HSCC 2005. LNCS, vol. 3414, pp. 258–273. Springer, Heidelberg (2005). https://doi.org/10.1007/978-3-540-31954-2_17
12. Gopalakrishnan, G., Qadeer, S. (eds.): CAV 2011. LNCS, vol. 6806. Springer, Heidelberg (2011). https://doi.org/10.1007/978-3-642-22110-1
13. Gupta, A., Malik, S. (eds.): CAV 2008. LNCS, vol. 5123. Springer, Heidelberg (2008). https://doi.org/10.1007/978-3-540-70545-1
14. Gupta, A., Rybalchenko, A.: InvGen: an efficient invariant generator. In: Bouajjani, A., Maler, O. (eds.) CAV 2009. LNCS, vol. 5643, pp. 634–640. Springer, Heidelberg (2009). https://doi.org/10.1007/978-3-642-02658-4_48
15. Hasuo, I., Suenaga, K.: Exercises in *nonstandard static analysis* of hybrid systems. In: Madhusudan, P., Seshia, S.A. (eds.) CAV 2012. LNCS, vol. 7358, pp. 462–478. Springer, Heidelberg (2012). https://doi.org/10.1007/978-3-642-31424-7_34

16. Henzinger, T.A.: The theory of hybrid automata. In: Proceedings, 11th Annual IEEE Symposium on Logic in Computer Science, New Brunswick, New Jersey, USA, July 27–30, 1996, pp. 278–292 (1996)

17. Jeannet, B., Miné, A.: APRON: a library of numerical abstract domains for static analysis. In: Bouajjani, A., Maler, O. (eds.) CAV 2009. LNCS, vol. 5643, pp. 661–667. Springer, Heidelberg (2009). https://doi.org/10.1007/978-3-642-02658-4_52

18. Jha, S.K., Krogh, B.H., Weimer, J.E., Clarke, E.M.: Reachability for linear hybrid automata using iterative relaxation abstraction. In: Bemporad, A., Bicchi, A., Buttazzo, G. (eds.) HSCC 2007. LNCS, vol. 4416, pp. 287–300. Springer, Heidelberg (2007). https://doi.org/10.1007/978-3-540-71493-4_24

19. Lalire, G., Argoud, M., Jeannet, B.: The interproc analyzer (2009). http://popart.inrialpes.fr/people/bjeannet/bjeannet-forge/interproc/

20. Li, X., Aanand, S.J., Bu, L.: Towards an efficient path-oriented tool for bounded reachability analysis of linear hybrid systems using linear programming. Electr. Notes Theor. Comput. Sci. **174**(3), 57–70 (2007)

21. Platzer, A., Clarke, E.M.: Computing differential invariants of hybrid systems as fixedpoints. In: Gupta, A., Malik, S. (eds.) CAV 2008. LNCS, vol. 5123, pp. 176–189. Springer, Heidelberg (2008). https://doi.org/10.1007/978-3-540-70545-1_17

22. Podelski, A., Rybalchenko, A.: A complete method for the synthesis of linear ranking functions. In: Steffen, B., Levi, G. (eds.) VMCAI 2004. LNCS, vol. 2937, pp. 239–251. Springer, Heidelberg (2004). https://doi.org/10.1007/978-3-540-24622-0_20

23. Podelski, A., Rybalchenko, A.: Transition predicate abstraction and fair termination. In: Proceedings of the 32nd ACM SIGPLAN-SIGACT Symposium on Principles of Programming Languages, POPL 2005, Long Beach, California, USA, January 12–14, 2005, pp. 132–144 (2005)

24. Podelski, A., Rybalchenko, A.: ARMC: the logical choice for software model checking with abstraction refinement. In: Hanus, M. (ed.) PADL 2007. LNCS, vol. 4354, pp. 245–259. Springer, Heidelberg (2006). https://doi.org/10.1007/978-3-540-69611-7_16

25. Podelski, A., Wagner, S.: Model checking of hybrid systems: from reachability towards stability. In: Hespanha, J.P., Tiwari, A. (eds.) HSCC 2006. LNCS, vol. 3927, pp. 507–521. Springer, Heidelberg (2006). https://doi.org/10.1007/11730637_38

26. Rodríguez-Carbonell, E., Tiwari, A.: Generating polynomial invariants for hybrid systems. In: Morari, M., Thiele, L. (eds.) HSCC 2005. LNCS, vol. 3414, pp. 590–605. Springer, Heidelberg (2005). https://doi.org/10.1007/978-3-540-31954-2_38

27. Sankaranarayanan, S., Sipma, H.B., Manna, Z.: Constructing invariants for hybrid systems. Form. Methods Syst. Des. **32**(1), 25–55 (2008)

28. Vardi, M.Y.: Verification of concurrent programs: the automata-theoretic framework. Ann. Pure Appl. Log. **51**(1–2), 79–98 (1991)

29. Xie, D., Bu, L., Zhao, J., Li, X.: SAT-LP-IIS joint-directed path-oriented bounded reachability analysis of linear hybrid automata. Form. Methods Syst. Des. **45**(1), 42–62 (2014)

30. Zutshi, A., Sankaranarayanan, S., Tiwari, A.: Timed relational abstractions for sampled data control systems. In: Madhusudan, P., Seshia, S.A. (eds.) CAV 2012. LNCS, vol. 7358, pp. 343–361. Springer, Heidelberg (2012). https://doi.org/10.1007/978-3-642-31424-7_27

Overview: System Architecture Virtual Integration based on an AADL Model

Yunwei Dong, Xiaomin Wei[✉], and Mingrui Xiao

School of Computer Science and Engineering, Northwestern Polytechnical University,
Xi'an 710072, PR China
yunweidong@nwpu.edu.cn, {xmwei,xiaomingrui}@mail.nwpu.edu.cn

Abstract. Many large scale embedded systems are safety-critical systems and are becoming increasingly complex. They are designed and developed by a worldwide network of enterprises and companies and often use multiple distributed models with little or late integration. System Architecture Virtual Integration (SAVI) is an effective way to improve system quality and reduce cost. It enables the model-driven virtual integration of complex systems across multiple development environments. It aims to find defects earlier in the development process, thus saving time. Architecture Analysis and Design Language (AADL), as a standard architecture modelling language, supports SAVI virtual integration process and can be a central and integrated model of integration. This paper gives an overview of SAVI virtual integration based on an AADL model. The integration can be performed using model transformation that transforms heterogeneous models into an AADL model, or using the model bus through which various annotated architecture models can interoperate. The focus of SAVI is to integrate and analyze systems, and then build. So, AADL-based non-functional properties analysis approaches are presented. The tool for these methods has been implemented to demonstrate feasibility and applicability.

Keywords: AADL · SAVI · Model transformation · Model bus
Non-functional properties analysis

1 Introduction

Safety-critical embedded systems in avionics, aerospace, medical, robotics, and industrial process controllers are becoming increasingly complex and contain more and more functions. For example, the F-35 Lightning II [1] is a fifth generation fighter and its software has more than 8 million lines of code. Such large scale systems often use multiple distributed models with little or late integration. Additionally, several studies of safety-critical systems have found that 70% of errors are introduced during the requirement and architecture design phases [2]. This results in 300 to 1,000 times the cost of in-phase correction for correcting requirement and design problems in later phases. What is worse is the fact that

© Springer Nature Switzerland AG 2018
C. Jones et al. (Eds.): Zhou-Festschrift, LNCS 11180, pp. 105–115, 2018.
https://doi.org/10.1007/978-3-030-01461-2_6

undiscovered errors exist in the final system. To improve system quality and reduce cost, SAVI is a good choice. SAVI is a model-based virtual integration approach. It uses models as central and indispensable artifacts throughout a product's life cycle.

SAVI aims to provide a new way of performing system integration: a virtual integration process (VIP) based on heterogeneous cross-domain models. It enables the model-driven virtual integration of complex systems across multiple development environments. The purpose is to lower development costs and find defects earlier in the development process, and save time. Return-on-investment (ROI) analysis of the SAVI initiative shows that $2.391 billion can be saved for a system that contains 27 million lines of source code [3]. It is a 26.1% cost saving (of an estimated $9.176 billion). Integration can begin at conceptualization. To get it right sooner, SAVI moves the integration forward and then keeps the integration right when changes occur.

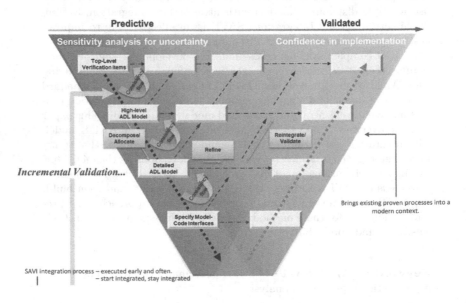

Fig. 1. SAVI virtual integration approach (referenced from AVSI)

The SAVI approach begins during early requirements definition and continuously monitors system evolution for inter-model consistency, as shown in Fig. 1 (referenced from Aerospace Vehicle Systems Institute (AVSI) [4]). It uses new tools, standards, and processes to detect and correct errors and defects much earlier in the development cycle than is possible with a traditional integration approach. Model-driven virtual integration is used to support predictive modelling and analysis across a distributed heterogeneous set of development domains and environments.

AADL [5] was designed to provide a modelling and analysis capability for engineering software systems. It can be a technical foundation for Model-Based

Engineering (MBE) and supports the SAVI virtual integration process [3]. An AADL model is a hierarchical model, which contains software components (such as the thread, process, and data components), execution platform components (such as the processor, memory, bus, and device components), composite and generic components (i.e., system and abstract components) and component interactions (such as port connections and the data access). Three port types are supported, i.e., data, event and event data. AADL allows definition of properties for components to provide information about model elements. Each property has a value or list of values, which is associated with the named property in a given specification. AADL has powerful extendability. Specifically, the Error Model Annex, version 2 (EMV2) [6] and Behavior Annex [7] are the sublanguage extension of AADL. Thus, AADL can not only build architecture models for safety-critical systems, but support safety, reliability and schedulability analysis.

In this paper, an overview of AADL-based SAVI is presented. SAVI integrates and analyzes models early and throughout the life cycle at different levels of fidelity, so that system-level faults can be found earlier in the life cycle. Multiple architecture modelling languages are provided for SAVI. The model repository and model bus are introduced to integrate multiple models. Model transformation techniques are also presented for virtual integration. Moreover, both model bus and model transformation techniques support the transformation to analyzable/computable models acceptable to different analysis tools. To analyze and discover faults, approaches for dynamic reconfiguration and AADL-based non-functional properties analysis (safety, reliability and schedulability) are explained. The tool, which supports our analysis approaches, is also described.

The rest of this paper is organized as follows. Section 2 introduces the SAVI virtual integration for safety-critical systems, including modelling complex safety-critical systems and integrating multiple heterogeneous models through the model bus or model transformation. Section 3 provides our non-functional properties analysis and dynamic reconfiguration approaches for the integrated model. Section 4 presents the structure of our tool that has extended EMV2, created the Hazard Model Annex and implemented analysis approaches. Section 5 highlights challenges for SAVI based on an AADL model. Finally, Sect. 6 concludes this paper.

2   SAVI Virtual Integration for Safety-Critical Systems

Many large scale safety-critical systems are designed and developed by a worldwide network of enterprises and companies. They have a variety of expertise, tools and approaches to the development process. This section will introduce architecture modelling languages for SAVI, and the way to integrate heterogeneous models into a model.

2.1   Modelling Complex Safety-Critical Systems

Multiple Architecture Modelling Languages. Multiple architecture modelling languages have been used in SAVI virtual integration. Because different companies/organizations might describe systems with different architecture languages. SAVI virtual integration can exploit the strengths of these languages. Safety-critical systems can be described by the Systems Modelling Language (SysML), AADL, Simulink, Modelica, etc. The SysML is a general-purpose modelling language for systems engineering applications. AADL is the SAE Standard AS 5506 for modelling safety-critical systems. Simulink is a graphical programming environment for modelling, simulating and analyzing multi-domain dynamic systems. Modelica is an object-oriented, equation based language to conveniently describe complex physical systems. To verify this method, Redman [8] created four models of the same simple system, the sliding mass example system, using different languages: SysML, AADL, Simulink and Modelica.

Extending AADL for Modelling Hybrid Systems. It has been shown [9] that AADL device components cannot describe continuous properties of the data sample and control process therefore AADL is extended for description of properties for continuous process and interaction behavior. Finally, an AADL Hybrid Annex is built. As observed in papers [10,11], Hybrid Communicating Sequential Processes (HCSP) is applied to build the formal semantics for the synchronous subset of AADL models annotated with Hybrid Annex specifications. The correctness of an AADL model with Hybrid Annex is verified with a theorem prover, Hybrid Hoare Logic (HHL) prover.

2.2   Model Transformation-Based Integration

Model transformation techniques are vitally important. They are often used in MBE. The model transformation can be used for virtual integration by transforming heterogeneous models into an AADL model.

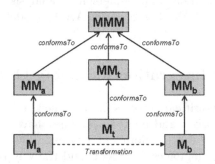

Fig. 2. An overview of ATL model transformation (referenced from [12])

ATLAS Transformation Language (ATL) [12] is a widely used model transformation language. It provides ways to produce a set of target models from a set of source models. For example, Fig. 2 shows the ATL model transformation from a SysML model M_a to an AADL model M_b. Meta models MM_a and MM_b are built for M_a and M_b, respectively. M_a and M_b must conform to MM_a and MM_b, respectively. Transformation rules are defined by the transformation model M_t, which must conform to a transformation meta model MM_t. MM_a, MM_b and MM_t have to conform to a meta-meta model MMM such as Meta Object Facilities (MOF) or Ecore. We are currently doing work on the transformation from SysML models to AADL models and from Simulink models to AADL models. This work can be used to virtually integrate various architecture models into a complete system.

2.3 Model Bus-Based Integration

The model repository and model bus are one key concept of SAVI [13]. The model repository contains two kinds of models. They are the annotated architecture reference model, and detailed models that are refinements of architecture components. For instance, Modelica can describe details for physical system components, and Simulink for control system components.

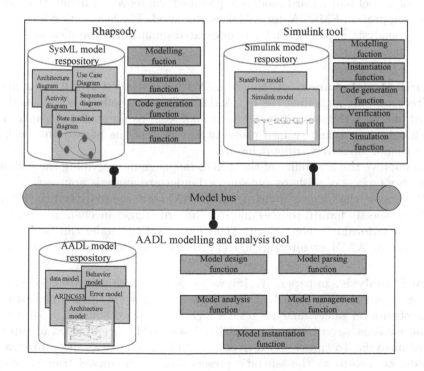

Fig. 3. An example of model bus-based integration

The model bus is a data interchange mechanism, operating with a standardized model representation [13]. It is used for the interchange between model repositories. A standardized XML format can be used to interchange between annotated heterogeneous architecture models. For instance, as shown in Fig. 3, there are several heterogeneous models including the AADL model, SysML model and Simulink model. They are virtually integrated and can communicate with each other through the model bus.

3   Non-functional Properties Analysis for SAVI

"Integrate, analyze ... then build" is the mantra for SAVI. Since an AADL model can be the integrated model after the SAVI virtual integration process, in this section, approaches for safety analysis, dynamic reconfiguration, reliability analysis, and schedulability analysis are presented to analyze an AADL model.

3.1   Safety Analysis

AADL describes safety-critical systems in the early development phase. To reduce errors and mitigate the effect of mishaps as early as possible, we compensate for the weaknesses of EMV2 for AADL-based safety analysis and propose the HMA. Then, an architecture-level hazard analysis for an AADL model (including error model and hazard model) is provided. Moreover, a qualitative safety analysis approach, FMECA, for AADL is presented. The last section introduces a safety analysis approach that has integrated quantitative verification for an AADL model.

Hazard Model Annex. Although EMV2 has extended AADL to support architecture fault modelling [14,15], AADL still cannot effectively be used for hazard analysis [16], since it has some weaknesses, as presented in paper [17]. EMV2 only uses a multi-valued property to represent the hazard and mishap, and it cannot effectively support hazard.

To improve the capability of the AADL language in describing the complex occurrence process of mishaps and supporting hazard analysis approach, papers [17,18] propose the Hazard Model Annex (HMA) language to extend the EMV2. HMA can specify hazard sources, hazards, hazard trigger mechanisms, mishaps and the relationship among them. Therefore, a safety model can be built by annotating an AADL architecture model with the error model and hazard model.

Hazard Analysis. In papers [17,18], we propose an architecture-based hazard analysis approach using AADL. This approach can provide the component-level and system-level safety analysis results including hazard sources, hazard trigger mechanisms, severities and probability levels. HMA is employed to support hazard analysis. To ensure the correctness of the probabilities of occurrence of hazards, we also prove the semantic preservation of the model transformation between an AADL model and a Deterministic Stochastic Petri Net (DSPN) model that is used for quantitative computation.

FMECA. Failure Modes, Effects and Criticality Analysis (FMECA) is a traditional and typical safety analysis method for safety-critical systems and has been used in real systems. In paper [19], EMV2 is extended and AADL-based FMECA is proposed to perform the qualitative safety analysis for safety-critical embedded systems. As quantitative safety analysis using FMECA requires the computation of the occurrence probabilities of errors, hazards and mishaps, we are currently taking full advantage of the computability of the DSPN model by applying the previous model transformation [17,18] from an AADL model to a DSPN model to compute occurrence probabilities for the quantitative FMECA. This work is about to be finished.

QaSten. Quantitative verification is an effective technique for analyzing quantitative aspects of a safety critical system's design. Paper [20] proposes a new methodology, QaSten, which fastens quantitative verification to safety analysis for an AADL model (including error model). QaSten can transform an AADL model to a PRISM model and generate two safety property formulas automatically to check against the PRISM model for each hazardous state. It also can determine the hazard risk acceptance level.

3.2   Dynamic Reconfiguration

Many embedded systems are safety-critical systems and reconfigurable, such as Integrated Modular Avionics (IMA) systems that are required to reconfigure at runtime if components fail. An embedded software reconfiguration technique based on the model is proposed in paper [21,22]. The system model is an hierarchical AADL architecture model. It is divided into four levels, which are the system level, mission level, function level and component level. The reconfiguration is described using modes and mode transitions. Furthermore, paper [23] proposes a safety-based software reconfiguration method for IMA systems at the architecture level. The software reconfiguration method integrates error events and hazard triggers into the reconfiguration process. AADL is extended so that the runtime architecture is described using AADL and EMV2. To simulate the IMA system with the proposed reconfiguration method, mapping rules from an AADL model to DSPNs are formulated.

3.3   Reliability Analysis

System reliability and component reliability may vary with the occurrence probabilities of error events. To compute the reliability, papers [24,25] build a system reliability model for embedded systems using AADL and error models. Transformation rules are made to perform the transformation from an AADL reliability model to a General Stochastic Petri-net (GSPN) model. Paper [24] assesses the reliability of an embedded system based on a GSPN analysis tool, Platform Independent Petri-net Editor 2 (PIPE2) [26]. Moreover, paper [27] takes the system behavior into account for the variation of the system reliability. AADL and Behavior Annex are used to build an embedded system model, which is also transformed to a GSPN model so that we can evaluate and predict the system reliability.

3.4   Schedulability Analysis

To predicate the schedulability of real-time embedded systems in the model design stage, an AADL-based schedulability analysis method is presented in [28]. A Resource Competition Model (RCM) is built according to the AADL system architecture, timing properties and connections between components. By analyzing the RCM, the response time of thread components is calculated for the schedulability analysis. In addition, like some other research, Cheddar is also used to evaluate system schedulability. An AADL model is transformed to an analyzable model for the Cheddar [29] tool, a real-time scheduling simulator. Then, Cheddar will be used to compute the scheduling of a task set for the AADL model. From such scheduling, it can compute various performance criteria, such as worst/best case response time, missed deadlines, deadlocks, etc.

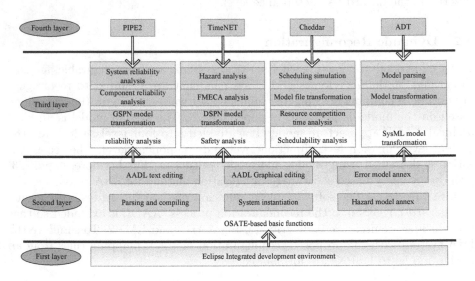

Fig. 4. The architecture of SAVI tool Prototype: ESMEAT

4   A Tool for Non-functional Properties Analysis

The AADL extension and non-functional properties analysis approaches are implemented as the Embedded Software Modelling, Evaluation and Analysis Tool (ESMEAT). The architecture of the tool is provided in Fig. 4. The first layer is the Eclipse Integrated Development Environment, as the basic support framework of the tool. The second layer contains basic functions supporting the system modelling, instantiation and analysis. This layer is based on Open Source AADL Tool Environment (OSATE), version 2.0.2. HMA is designed and implemented to specify hazard behavior. The modelling of EMV2 in OSATE is also extended. The third layer is the implementation of the SysML model transformation and non-functional properties analysis methods including the safety analysis, reliability analysis and schedulability analysis. The fourth layer contains existing tools, such as TimeNET [30], PIPE2, Cheddar and ADT (ATL Development Tool) [12]. They are used to support the third layer.

5 Challenges

There has been much progress towards AADL-based SAVI virtual integration for safety-critical systems. However, some significant challenges have yet to be overcome, as below:

- Security has attracted more and more attention. We will extend modelling capability of AADL for security analysis and perform AADL-based vulnerability analysis for safety-critical systems.
- Resource is limited in safety-critical systems, for example, the memory and I/O in avionics systems. To sufficiently use the resource, resource effectiveness analysis is necessary for the improvement of system performance.
- Model transformation is a significant technique for SAVI. To make it possible to integrate more heterogeneous models into an AADL model, we will do more work to design rules and implement the model transformation from various models, such as Simulink, Modelica, etc.
- The model repository and model bus are good ideas for SAVI, but it is still challenging to implement a model bus that is compatible with various model repositories.

6 Conclusions

This paper presents an overview of SAVI virtual integration based on an AADL model. There are various kinds of architecture modelling languages supporting system specifications. SAVI virtual integration can be implemented through the model bus or model transformation, which also support the transformation from system models to analyzable/computable models acceptable to different analysis tools. An AADL model can be an integrated model of various heterogeneous models. To analyze and improve the integrated model, AADL-based non-functional properties analysis approaches are also provided, including safety analysis, dynamic reconfiguration, reliability analysis and schedulability analysis. The tool named ESMEAT which is designed by Northwestern Polytechnical University, as the implementation of these methods, is introduced.

Acknowledgments. This work was supported by the National Science Foundation of China under Grant No. 61772423, and the Aviation Science Foundation of China under Grant No. 2016ZC31003 and No. 20161953020.

References

1. A digital jet for the modern battlespace, June 2018. https://www.f35.com/about/life-cycle/software
2. Ellison, R.J.: Assuring software reliability. Technical report, Carnegie Mellon University, Aug. 2014
3. Hansson, J., Helton, S., Feiler, P.: ROI analysis of the system architecture virtual integration initiative. Technical report, Carnegie-Mellon Univerity Software Engineering Institute Pittsburgh United States (2018)
4. SAVI virtual integration overview, June 2018. http://savi.avsi.aero/about-savi/virtual-integration/
5. SAE International. AS5506C - (R) Architecture Analysis and Design Language (AADL). SAE International, January 2017
6. SAE International. (R) SAE Architecture Analysis and Design Language (AADL) Annex Volume 1: Annex A: ARINC653 Annex, Annex C: Code Generation Annex, Annex E: Error Model Annex. SAE International, September 2015
7. SAE International. AS5506/2 - SAE Architecture Analysis and Design Language (AADL) Annex Volume 2: Annex D: Behavior Model Annex. SAE International, January 2011
8. Redman, D.: SAVI behavior model integration virtual integration process. Global Product Data Interoperability Summit (2015)
9. Ahmad, E., Larson, B.R., Barrett, S.C., Zhan, N., Dong, Y.: Hybrid annex: an AADL extension for continuous behavior and cyber-physical interaction modeling. In: ACM SIGAda Ada Letters, vol. 34, pp. 29–38. ACM (2014)
10. Ahmad, E., Dong, Y.W., Larson, B., Lü, J.D., Tang, T., Zhan, N.J.: Behavior modeling and verification of movement authority scenario of Chinese train control system using AADL. Sci. China Inf. Sci. **58**(11), 1–20 (2015). Nov
11. Ahmad, E., Dong, Y., Wang, S., Zhan, N., Zou, L.: Adding formal meanings to AADL with hybrid annex. In: Lanese, I., Madelaine, E. (eds.) FACS 2014. LNCS, vol. 8997, pp. 228–247. Springer, Cham (2015). https://doi.org/10.1007/978-3-319-15317-9_15
12. ATL - a model transformation technology, June 2018. http://www.eclipse.org/atl/
13. Feiler, P., Wrage, L., Hansson, J.: System architecture virtual integration: a case study. In: Embedded Real-time Software and Systems Conference (2010)
14. Delange, J., Feiler, P.: Architecture fault modeling with the aadl error-model annex. In: 2014 40th EUROMICRO Conference on Software Engineering and Advanced Applications (SEAA), pp. 361–368. IEEE (2014)
15. Feiler, P., Hudak, J.J., Delange, J., Gluch, D.: Architecture fault modeling and analysis with the error model annex, version 2 (2016)
16. Ericson, C.A.: Hazard Analysis Techniques for System Safety. Wiley, Hoboken (2005)
17. Wei, X., Dong, Y., Li, X., Eric Wong, W.: Architecture-level hazard analysis using AADL. J. Syst. Softw. **137**, 580–604 (2018)
18. Wei, X., Dong, Y., Yang, M., Hu, N., Ye, H.: Hazard analysis for AADL model. In: 2014 IEEE 20th International Conference on Embedded and Real-Time Computing Systems and Applications (RTCSA), pp. 1–10, Aug 2014
19. Gu, B., Dong, Y., Wei, X.: A qualitative safety analysis method for AADL model. In: 2014 IEEE Eighth International Conference on Software Security and Reliability-Companion, pp. 213–217, June 2014

20. Wei, X., Dong, Y., Ye, H.: QaSten: integrating quantitative verification with safety analysis for AADL model. In: 2015 International Symposium on Theoretical Aspects of Software Engineering (TASE), pp. 103–110, Sept 2015
21. Li, L., Dong, Y., Qin, Y., Zhang, F.: Design and implementation of software reconfiguration tool based on AADL. Comput. Sci. **38**(7), 121–125 (2011)
22. Qin, Y., Dong, Y.: Research on embedded software dynamic reconfigurable technology based on mode. Comput. Sci. **39**(2), 174–175 (2012)
23. Wei, X., Dong, Y., Xiao, M.: Architecture-level safety-based software reconfiguration method for integrated modular avionics systems. In IEEE International Conference on Software Quality, Reliability and Security Companion, July 2018
24. Dong, Y., Ren Wang, G., Zhang, F., Gao, L.: Reliability analysis and assessment tool for AADL model. J. Softw. **22**(6), 1252–1266 (2011)
25. Gao, L., Dong, Y., Zhang, F., Wang, G.: AADL system reliability model transformation method. Comput. Eng. **37**(14), 21–26 (2011)
26. Dingle, N.J., Knottenbelt, W.J., Suto, T.: Pipe2: a tool for the performance evaluation of generalised stochastic Petri nets. ACM SIGMETRICS Perform. Eval. Rev. **36**(4), 34–39 (2009)
27. Chang, S., Dong, Y., Zhang, F.: On reliability analysis for embedded systems with AADL behavior model **430**(4), 116–119 (2012)
28. Dong, Y., Cheng, Y., Wu,T., Ye, H.: On schedulability analysis for embedded systems with aadl model. In: 2013 13th International Conference on Quality Software, pp. 320–325, July 2013
29. Cheddar: an open-source real-time scheduling tool/simulator, June 2018. http://beru.univ-brest.fr/singhoff/cheddar/
30. Zimmermann, A.: Modelling and performance evaluation with TimeNET 4.4. In: Bertrand, N., Bortolussi, L. (eds.) QEST 2017. LNCS, vol. 10503, pp. 300–303. Springer, Cham (2017). https://doi.org/10.1007/978-3-319-66335-7_19

Characterization and Verification of Stuttering Equivalence

Xinxin Liu[✉] and Wenhui Zhang

State Key Laboratory of Computer Science, Institute of Software,
Chinese Academy of Sciences , University of Chinese Academy of Sciences,
Huairou, China
{xinxin,zwh}@ios.ac.cn

Abstract. Stuttering equivalence is an important equivalence relation
on Kripke structures. It is the equivalence which preserves all CTL*-X
properties. Two key issues concerning this equivalence are how to characterize it and how to verify whether two given states are equivalent
with respect to it. For this purpose, we propose two bisimulation style
definitions, one called ω-bisimulation which provides a concise characterization of the equality and one called stuttering bisimulation with induction which provides a verification method for establishing the equality.
We also show that stuttering bisimulation with induction coincides with
well-founded bisimulation, a notion introduced by Namjoshi for verifying
stuttering equivalence.

1 Introduction

Stuttering equivalence on Kripke structures is an important equivalence that has
the exact distinguishing strength of the set of CTL*-X properties (the computation tree logic CTL* [14] without the next operator). An important feature of
stuttering equivalence is that it is a divergence preserving equivalence with a high
level of abstraction. A main issue concerning stuttering equivalence, which has
both theoretical interest and practical implication, is how to characterize such an
equivalence in a way that two states can be shown equivalent with minimal effort.
The definition of stuttering equivalence in [3] presented it as the limit of a converging sequence of equivalences. Such a definition is not very helpful either for
equality checking or for equality proving. Here "equality checking" is the problem of deciding whether two given states are equivalent, and "equality proving"
is the problem of verifying that whether a given evidence (or a proof, e.g. a
supposed bisimulation relation) of equality two states is valid. In [11], a simpler
characterization is proposed, in which a well founded relation is used for the characterization of the stuttering equivalence. It is called well-founded bisimulation.
It is proven that well-founded bisimulation corresponds to stuttering equivalence
[11]. A difficulty with this definition is that it is not obvious how to construct
the well-founded relation, in order to be used to show the equivalence of states.
In addition, such a well-founded relation may be unnecessarily large, if it is not

© Springer Nature Switzerland AG 2018
C. Jones et al. (Eds.): Zhou-Festschrift, LNCS 11180, pp. 116–132, 2018.
https://doi.org/10.1007/978-3-030-01461-2_7

constructed carefully. In this paper, we address these difficulties by proposing a characterization of stuttering equivalence with the notion of stuttering bisimulation with induction. Firstly, we propose another characterization with the notion of ω-bisimulation which is easy to use to establish theoretical foundation. Secondly, we have a concept that uses the inductive principle instead of infinite sequence of relations and well-founded relations. Thirdly, we relate well-founded bisimulation to the new definition. Finally, we show that the new definition can be used to construct a well-founded relation that is required for showing stuttering equivalence by well-founded bisimulation, and therefore providing a method for proving the equivalence of states with well-founded bisimulation.

The paper is organized as follows. In the next section we present stuttering equivalence in terms of ω-bisimulation. In Sect. 3 we introduce the notion of stuttering bisimulation with induction to characterize stuttering equivalence. In Sect. 4 we study the relationship between stuttering bisimulation with induction and well-founded bisimulation. We discuss related works in Sect. 5, summarize and conclude in Sect. 6.

2 Stuttering Equivalence and ω-Bisimulation

In this section we establish a theoretical foundation for stuttering equivalence with the notion of ω-bisimulation. We start with some basic notions and notations.

Definition 1 *(Kripke structure and infinite runs). A Kripke structure is a tuple* $\mathcal{K} = \langle S, AP, L, \longrightarrow \rangle$ *where:*

- S *is a set of* states;
- AP *is a set of* atomic propositions *or* labels;
- $L : S \to 2^{AP}$ *is the* labeling function *which assigns each state a set of atomic propositions;*
- $\longrightarrow \subseteq S \times S$ *is the* transition relation. *An element (s, t) of* $\longrightarrow$, *usually written as* $s \longrightarrow t$, *is called a* transition. *Following the convention, we assume that* $\longrightarrow$ *is a total relation, i.e. for each $s \in S$ there exists $s' \in S$ such that* $s \longrightarrow s'$.
- *A* finite run *of $\mathcal{K}$ is a finite sequence of states, with each pair of neighbouring states connected by a transition. If ρ is a finite run of $\mathcal{K}$ with starting state s and finishing state t, we also say that ρ is a finite run from s to t, and write $first(\rho)$ for s, $last(\rho)$ for t. The length of ρ, written $length(\rho)$, is the number of transitions connecting ρ (thus $length(s) = 0$ where s is the run consists of a single state $s \in S$).*
- *An* infinite run *of $\mathcal{K}$ is an infinite sequence of states, with each pair of neighbouring states connected by a transition. If ρ is an infinite run of $\mathcal{K}$ with starting state s, we also say that ρ is an infinite run from s, and write $first(\rho)$ for s.*

Let R, R_1, R_2 be binary relations. In general, we define the *converse* R^{-1} of R and the *composition* $R_1 R_2$ of R_1 and R_2 by

$$R^{-1} = \{(s,t) \mid (t,s) \in R\},$$
$$R_1 R_2 = \{(s,t) \mid \text{there exist } (s,u) \in R_1, (u,t) \in R_2 \text{ for some } u\}.$$

Definition 2 *(Relations on finite and infinite runs). Let $\mathcal{K} = \langle S, AP, L, \longrightarrow \rangle$ be a Kripke structure, R be a binary relation on S.*

Define a binary relation $R^{\natural}$ between finite runs of $\mathcal{K}$ by induction on the lengths of the runs such that $(s_1 \ldots s_n, t_1 \ldots t_m) \in R^{\natural}$ if and only if $(s_1, t_1) \in R$ and moreover one of the following holds:

1. *$n = m = 1$;*
2. *$(s_2 \ldots s_n, t_1 \ldots t_m) \in R^{\natural}$;*
3. *$(s_1 \ldots s_n, t_2 \ldots t_m) \in R^{\natural}$;*
4. *$(s_2 \ldots s_n, t_2 \ldots t_m) \in R^{\natural}$.*

Define a binary relation $R^{\sharp}$ between infinite runs of $\mathcal{K}$ such that for two infinite runs σ, ρ of $\mathcal{K}$, $(\sigma, \rho) \in R^{\sharp}$ if and only if both of the following hold:

1. *for each finite prefix σ' of σ, there is a finite prefix ρ' of ρ with $(\sigma', \rho') \in R^{\natural}$;*
2. *for each finite prefix ρ' of ρ, there is a finite prefix σ' of σ with $(\sigma', \rho') \in R^{\natural}$.*

The intuition of $R^{\natural}$ ($R^{\sharp}$) is that it describes a relation between two finite (infinite) runs such that the states in the two sequences of the runs are pairwise related by R while making progress in lock steps modulo finite stuttering.

The following lemma shows expected homomorphic and monomorphic properties of $\natural$ and $\sharp$, which is required later in establishing transitivity of some desired equivalence relation.

Lemma 1. *Let $\mathcal{K} = \langle S, AP, L, \longrightarrow \rangle$ be a Kripke structure, R_1, R_2 be two binary relations on S. Then*

1. *$R_1{}^{\natural} R_2{}^{\natural} \subseteq (R_1 R_2)^{\natural}$;*
2. *$R_1{}^{\sharp} R_2{}^{\sharp} \subseteq (R_1 R_2)^{\sharp}$;*
3. *If $R_1 \subseteq R_2$, then $R_1{}^{\natural} \subseteq R_2{}^{\natural}$ and $R_1{}^{\sharp} \subseteq R_2{}^{\sharp}$.*

Proof. 1 can be proved by a detailed case analysis. 2 follows from 1. For 3, suppose $R_1 \subseteq R_2$, then it can be proved by induction on the total lengths of the finite runs σ and ρ that if $(\sigma, \rho) \in R_1^{\natural}$ then $(\sigma, \rho) \in R_2^{\natural}$. Then it follows immediately that in this case also $R_1{}^{\sharp} \subseteq R_2{}^{\sharp}$.   □

In [3], stuttering equivalence was originally defined as the limit of a converging sequence of equivalences. This kind of definition is not easy to work with either for theoretical foundation or for practical verification. The notion of bisimulation, proposed by Park [7], has been very successfully applied by Milner in studying equivalence relations on labeled transition systems [8]. Thus we wish to establish the theory of stuttering equivalence based on the notion of bisimulation. However, due to the consideration of infinite runs in stuttering equivalence, the bisimulation characterization of stuttering equivalence is a little more complex than that of many well-known equivalence relations. So we first ignore the issue of divergence, and present a divergence blind equivalence which is easy to describe by using bisimulation and which is also very close to stuttering equivalence.

Definition 3 *(Stuttering bisimulation, divergence blind stuttering equivalence). Let $\mathcal{K} = \langle S, AP, L, \longrightarrow \rangle$ be a Kripke structure. A stuttering bisimulation is a binary relation $R \subseteq S \times S$ such that for all $(s_0, t_0) \in R$ the following hold:*

1. *$L(s) = L(t)$;*
2. *if $s_0 \longrightarrow s_1$ then there is a finite run ρ from t_0 such that $(s_0 s_1, \rho) \in R^\natural$;*
3. *if $t_0 \longrightarrow t_1$ then there is a finite run σ from s_0 such that $(\sigma, t_0 t_1) \in R^\natural$.*

We write $s \approx_{db} t$ if there is a stuttering bisimulation R such that $(s, t) \in R$. We call $\approx_{db}$ divergence blind stuttering equivalence.

With this definition, by Lemma 1, it is routine to prove that $\approx_{db}$ is an equivalence relation, and $\approx_{db}$ is the largest stuttering bisimulation.

Definition 4 *(Divergence). Let $\mathcal{K} = \langle S, AP, L, \longrightarrow \rangle$ be a Kripke structure, $\equiv$ be an equivalence relation on S. An infinite run $\rho = s_0 s_1 \ldots s_i \ldots$ of $\mathcal{K}$ is called a divergent run with respect to $\equiv$ if $s_0 \equiv s_i$ for all i. In this case s_0 is said to be divergent with respect to $\equiv$, written $s_0 \Uparrow_\equiv$. We say that $\equiv$ is divergence preserving, if whenever $s \equiv t$ and $s \Uparrow_\equiv$ then $t \Uparrow_\equiv$.*

In discussing divergence we often omit mentioning "with respect to $\equiv$" if it is obvious from the context.

Although $\approx_{db}$ is an equivalence relation with many desired properties, it is well known that $\approx_{db}$ is not divergence preserving. This is why we call it *divergence blind* stuttering equivalence, and use the subscript *db* for it. In order to obtain divergence preserving property, it turns out that we need to strengthen the definition of divergence blind stuttering equivalence so that correspondence of all infinite runs from states are required, instead of only requiring correspondence of finite runs. The result is the following notion of ω-bisimulation.

Definition 5 *(ω-bisimulation, stuttering equivalence). Let $\mathcal{K} = \langle S, AP, L, \longrightarrow \rangle$ be a Kripke structure. An ω-bisimulation is a binary relation $R \subseteq S \times S$ such that for all $(s, t) \in R$ the following hold:*

1. *$L(s) = L(t)$;*
2. *for any infinite run σ from s, there exists an infinite run ρ from t such that $(\sigma, \rho) \in R^\sharp$;*
3. *for any infinite run ρ from t, there exists an infinite run σ from s such that $(\sigma, \rho) \in R^\sharp$.*

Define $\approx_{st} = \bigcup \{ R \mid R$ is an ω-bisimulation$\}$. We call $\approx_{st}$ stuttering equivalence, and for $s, t \in S$ we say s is stuttering equivalent to t if $s \approx_{st} t$.

The name ω-bisimulation refers to the examination of infinite runs in the definition.

Theorem 1. $\approx_{st}$ *is an equivalence relation.*

Proof. First note that $Id = \{(s,s) \mid s \in S\}$ is an ω-bisimulation. Thus $\approx_{st}$ is reflexive.

If R is an ω-bisimulation then it is easy to see from the definition that its converse R^{-1} is also an ω-bisimulation. Thus $\approx_{st}$ is symmetric.

If R_1, R_2 are two ω-bisimulations, then by Lemma 1 (2) it is easy to see that their composition $R_1 R_2$ is also an ω-bisimulation. Thus $\approx_{st}$ is transitive.   □

Theorem 2. *Let* $\mathcal{K} = \langle S, AP, L, \longrightarrow \rangle$ *be a Kripke structure. Then* $\approx_{st}$ *is the largest* ω-*bisimulation on* S.

Proof: First, we show that $\approx_{st}$ is an ω-bisimulation. For that, let $s \approx_{st} t$ for $s, t \in S$. Then there is $R \subseteq S \times S$ such that $(s,t) \in R$ and R is an ω-bisimulation. By Definition 5 the following hold:

1. $L(s) = L(t)$;
2. for any infinite run σ from s, there exists an infinite run ρ from t such that $(\sigma, \rho) \in R^{\sharp}$;
3. for any infinite run ρ from t, there exists an infinite run σ from s such that $(\sigma, \rho) \in R^{\sharp}$.

Note that $R \subseteq \approx_{st}$, and by Lemma 1 (3) $R^{\sharp} \subseteq \approx_{st}^{\sharp}$, then it is easy to see that $\approx_{st}$ is an ω-bisimulation.

It is obvious from the definition that if R is an ω-bisimulation then $R \subseteq \approx_{st}$, thus $\approx_{st}$ is the largest such.   □

This theorem shows that $\approx_{st}$ is well defined. Now we examine divergence preserving property of $\approx_{st}$.

Theorem 3. *Let* $\mathcal{K} = \langle S, AP, L, \longrightarrow \rangle$ *be a Kripke structure,* $\equiv$ *be an equivalence relation on* S. *If* $\equiv$ *is an* ω-*bisimulation, then* $\equiv$ *is divergence preserving.*

Proof: Suppose $s \equiv t$ and $s \Uparrow_{\equiv}$. Then there is a divergent run σ from s. Since $\equiv$ is an ω-bisimulation, there exists an infinite run ρ from t such that $(\sigma, \rho) \in \equiv^{\sharp}$. Then from the condition that σ is a divergent run, it is easy to see that ρ must be a divergent run, thus $t \Uparrow_{\equiv}$.   □

Corollary 1. $\approx_{st}$ *is divergence preserving.*

Proof: Follows immediately from Theorems 2 and 3.   □

The following theorem is pretty straight forward.

Theorem 4. *Let* $\mathcal{K} = \langle S, AP, L, \longrightarrow \rangle$ *be a Kripke structure,* R *be a binary relation on* S. *If* R *is an* ω-*bisimulation, then* R *is a stuttering bisimulation.*

Proof: Let $(s,t) \in R$ and $s \longrightarrow s'$, and σ be an infinite run with s, s' as its first two states (since we assume that $\longrightarrow$ is total, such a σ can always be found). Then because R is an ω-bisimulation, there is an infinite run ρ from t such that $(\sigma, \rho) \in R^\sharp$. By Definition 2, for ss', which is a finite prefix of σ, there is a finite prefix ρ' of ρ such that $(ss', \rho') \in R^\natural$. Thus R is a stuttering bisimulation.   □

Corollary 2. $\approx_{st}$ *is a stuttering bisimulation.*

Proof: Follows immediately from the above theorem and Theorem 2.   □

From Corollaries 1 and 2, it is easy to see that $\approx_{st}$ is a divergence preserving stuttering bisimulation. In fact this gives an alternative characterization of $\approx_{st}$ which we will prove in the next section: $\approx_{st}$ is the weakest equivalence which is a divergence preserving equivalence and a stuttering bisimulation.

3   Stuttering Bisimulation with Induction

Although the notion of ω-bisimulation makes stuttering equivalence quite straightforward both conceptually and intuitively, it is not very helpful in verification. This is because Definition 5 requires one to examine conditions on infinite runs, of which there are obviously too many to handle in actual verification. What we need is a characterization which can be useful in verification, something like stuttering bisimulation – the conditions to check only concern finite runs of length one. Then the following definition comes into view.

Definition 6 *(Stuttering bisimulation with induction). Let $\mathcal{K} = \langle S, AP, L, \longrightarrow \rangle$ be a Kripke structure. For a binary relation $R \subseteq S \times S$, let $\mathcal{B}_I(R)$ be the binary relation inductively defined by the following rule: for $s, t \in S$, if the following hold then $(s, t) \in \mathcal{B}_I(R)$:*

1. *whenever $s \longrightarrow s'$ then either there exists a finite run ρ from t such that $length(\rho) > 0$ and $(ss', \rho) \in R^\natural$, or $(s', t) \in R$ and $(s', t) \in \mathcal{B}_I(R)$;*
2. *whenever $t \longrightarrow t'$ then either there exists a finite run σ from s such that $length(\sigma) > 0$ and $(\sigma, tt') \in R^\natural$, or $(s, t') \in R$ and $(s, t') \in \mathcal{B}_I(R)$.*

If $R \subseteq \mathcal{B}_I(R)$, then we call R a stuttering bisimulation with induction. We write $s \approx_{si} t$ if there is a stuttering bisimulation with induction R such that $(s, t) \in R$.

Comparing the above definition with Definition 3 for stuttering bisimulation, we can find obvious similarities. The rationale behind this definition is as follows. Since $\approx_{st}$ is strictly stronger than $\approx_{db}$, and since those non-divergence preserving pairs in $\approx_{db}$ are extras for $\approx_{st}$, a natural idea to make a stuttering bisimulation like definition for $\approx_{st}$ is to strengthen the conditions of stuttering bisimulation in such a way that those non-divergence preserving pairs are excluded. The definition of stuttering bisimulation with induction did exactly that.

By using the set of ordinals $\mathcal{O}$, the following characterization of $\mathcal{B}_I(R)$ is very helpful in some of the later proofs as well as in understanding the definition of $\mathcal{B}_I(R)$.

Definition 7. Let $\mathcal{K} = \langle S, AP, L, \longrightarrow \rangle$ be a Kripke structure, R be a binary relation on S. We define $\mathcal{B}_I^\lambda(R)$ for each ordinal $\lambda \in \mathcal{O}$, as follows:

1. $\mathcal{B}_I^0(R) = \emptyset$.
2. $(s, t) \in \mathcal{B}_I^{\kappa+1}(R)$ if and only if the following hold:
   (a) whenever $s \longrightarrow s'$ then either there exists a finite run ρ from t such that $length(\rho) > 0$ and $(ss', \rho) \in R^\natural$, or $(s', t) \in R$ and $(s', t) \in \mathcal{B}_I^\kappa(R)$;
   (b) whenever $t \longrightarrow t'$ then either there exists a finite run σ from s such that $length(\sigma) > 0$ and $(\sigma, tt') \in R^\natural$, or $(s, t') \in R$ and $(s, t') \in \mathcal{B}_I^\kappa(R)$.
3. For limit ordinal λ, $(s, t) \in \mathcal{B}_I^\lambda(R)$ if and only if $(s, t) \in \mathcal{B}_I^\kappa(R)$ for some $\kappa < \lambda$.

Theorem 5. Let $\mathcal{K} = \langle S, AP, L, \longrightarrow \rangle$ be a Kripke structure, R be a binary relation on S. Then for $s, t \in S$ the following hold:

1. $\mathcal{B}_I(R) = \bigcup_{\lambda \in \mathcal{O}} \mathcal{B}_I^\lambda(R)$;
2. if λ is the least ordinal with $(s, t) \in \mathcal{B}_I^\lambda(R)$, then $\lambda = \kappa + 1$ for some $\kappa \in \mathcal{O}$.

Proof. 1 can be proved by standard fixed-point arguments. To see 2, just note that λ cannot be 0 since $\mathcal{B}_I^0(R)$ is empty, neither can it be a limit since otherwise there would exist a smaller ordinal κ with $(s, t) \in \mathcal{B}_I^\kappa(R)$.   □

In the rest of this section, our major task is to prove that the resulting relation $\approx_{si}$ is indeed the same as $\approx_{st}$.

Lemma 2. If $R_1 \subseteq R_2$, then $\mathcal{B}_I(R_1) \subseteq \mathcal{B}_I(R_2)$.

Proof. Easy to prove by induction on the definition of $\mathcal{B}_I(R_1)$, or to use the ordinal characterization and prove by induction on all $\lambda \in \mathcal{O}$.   □

This lemma shows a very nice property of the definition. It essentially says that if we consider $\mathcal{B}_I$ as a function on binary relations then it is monotonic. Then Knaster-Tarski fixed-point theorem can be applied to the complete lattice $(2^{S \times S}, \subseteq)$ to obtain $\approx_{si}$ as the maximum fixed-point of $\mathcal{B}_I$.

Theorem 6. $\approx_{si}$ is a stuttering bisimulation with induction, and it is the largest stuttering bisimulation with induction, and moreover $\approx_{si} = \mathcal{B}_I(\approx_{si})$.

Proof. The theorem is in fact an instance of Knaster-Tarski fixed-point theorem. To show that $\approx_{si}$ is a stuttering bisimulation with induction, we have to establish $\approx_{si} \subseteq \mathcal{B}_I(\approx_{si})$. Suppose that R is a stuttering bisimulation with induction, then obviously $R \subseteq \mathcal{B}_I(R)$ and $R \subseteq \approx_{si}$. According to Lemma 2, $\mathcal{B}_I$ is monotonic, thus $\mathcal{B}_I(R) \subseteq \mathcal{B}_I(\approx_{si})$, so we showed that for any stuttering bisimulation with induction R it holds that $R \subseteq \mathcal{B}_I(\approx_{si})$. Now to see $\approx_{si} \subseteq \mathcal{B}_I(\approx_{si})$, just note that $\approx_{si} = \bigcup \{R \mid R$ is a stuttering bisimulation with induction$\}$.

If R is a stuttering bisimulation with induction, then by the definition obviously $R \subseteq \approx_{si}$. Thus $\approx_{si}$ is the largest stuttering bisimulation with induction.

We have just shown above that $\approx_{si} \subseteq \mathcal{B}_I(\approx_{si})$, then since $\mathcal{B}_I$ is monotonic, $\mathcal{B}_I(\approx_{si}) \subseteq \mathcal{B}_I(\mathcal{B}_I(\approx_{si}))$. So $\mathcal{B}_I(\approx_{si})$ is a stuttering bisimulation with induction, thus $\mathcal{B}_I(\approx_{si}) \subseteq \approx_{si}$ and $\mathcal{B}_I(\approx_{si}) = \approx_{si}$.   □

Remark 1. It is clear from this theorem that $\approx_{si}$ is the greatest fixed-point of $\mathcal{B}_I$, i.e. $\approx_{si} = \nu R(\mathcal{B}_I(R))$ in μ-calculus notation. In fact, from Definition 6, it is also clear that $\mathcal{B}_I(R)$ itself is the least fixed-point of $\mathcal{F}(R)$, where for a given $R^* \subseteq S \times S$, $(s,t) \in \mathcal{F}(R)(R^*)$ if and only if the following hold:

1. whenever $s \longrightarrow s'$ then either there exists a finite run ρ from t such that $length(\rho) > 0$ and $(ss', \rho) \in R^\natural$, or $(s',t) \in R$ and $(s',t) \in R^*$;
2. whenever $t \longrightarrow t'$ then either there exists a finite run σ from s such that $length(\sigma) > 0$ and $(\sigma, tt') \in R^\natural$, or $(s,t') \in R$ and $(s,t') \in R^*$.

Then $\approx_{si} = \nu R(\mu R^*(\mathcal{F}(R)(R^*)))$, that is, $\approx_{si}$ is expressed as an alternating fixed-point (it is easy to see that $\mathcal{F}(R)$ is monotonic, thus the least fixed-point is well defined). For relations defined as an alternating fixed-point, there are efficient local algorithms to decide whether $(s,t) \in \nu R(\mu R^*(\mathcal{F}(R)(R^*)))$ where s,t are states of a Kripke structure with finite states set, see e.g. [10]. Here the localness means that the algorithm does not compute the whole of $\nu R(\mu R^*(\mathcal{F}(R)(R^*)))$ in order to decide whether $(s,t) \in \nu R(\mu R^*(\mathcal{F}(R)(R^*)))$ holds, it only computes a part $P \subseteq \nu R(\mu R^*(\mathcal{F}(R)(R^*)))$ which is big enough to decide whether $(s,t) \in \nu R(\mu R^*(\mathcal{F}(R)(R^*)))$ holds. In fact such P is just stuttering bisimulation with induction. Thus the characterization of stuttering equivalence in stuttering bisimulation with induction facilitates local decision strategy, which would give stuttering bisimulation with induction a clear advantage in verification practice.

Another important property to establish about $\approx_{si}$ is that it is an equivalence relation. Unfortunately, it is not an easy task to directly prove that $\approx_{si}$ is transitive. Here we will take an indirect approach, since anyhow we are going to establish that $\approx_{si} = \approx_{st}$ (Theorem 9). Then from the fact that $\approx_{st}$ is an equivalence relation, we immediately know that so is $\approx_{si}$.

Theorem 7. *Let $\equiv$ be an equivalence. If $\equiv$ is divergence preserving, and is a stuttering bisimulation, then $\equiv \subseteq \mathcal{B}_I(\equiv)$.*

Proof. First define a binary relation $\succ \subseteq S \times S$ such that $s \succ s'$ if and only if s is not divergent and $s \equiv s'$ and $s \longrightarrow s'$. Then it is clear that if $\equiv$ is divergence preserving, then $\succ$ is well founded, i.e. there is no infinite descending chain $s \succ s_1 \ldots \succ s_i \ldots$. Otherwise $\sigma = ss_1 \ldots s_i \ldots$ would be a divergent run from s.

Now suppose that $\equiv$ is a stuttering bisimulation, and $s \equiv t$, we will show $(s,t) \in \mathcal{B}_I(\equiv)$ by well-founded induction on $\succ$. Let $s \longrightarrow s'$ be any transition from s, we have to find a match for it that meets the requirements in Definition 6. Since $\equiv$ is a stuttering bisimulation, $s \equiv t$, then there must exist a finite run ρ from t such that $(ss', \rho) \in R^\natural$. Now we can discuss in two cases. The first case is that we can find such a ρ with $length(\rho) > 0$, then a required match for $s \longrightarrow s'$ is found. The second case is that, the only such ρ has length 0, and in this case $s' \equiv t$. Obviously t must not be a divergent state (otherwise there is a divergent run η from t, and any finite prefix ρ of η satisfies $(ss', \rho) \in R^\natural$), and since $\equiv$ is divergence preserving, then s is not divergent. Now $s \succ s'$, $s' \equiv t$, and by the induction hypothesis $(s',t) \in \mathcal{B}_I(\equiv)$, and a required match for $s \longrightarrow s'$ is also found. Thus we proved $(s,t) \in \mathcal{B}_I(\equiv)$. $\square$

Corollary 3. $\approx_{st}$ is a stuttering bisimulation with induction, and $\approx_{st}\subseteq\approx_{si}$.

Proof. From Corollaries 1, and 2, $\approx_{st}$ is a divergence preserving equivalence and it is a stuttering bisimulation. Then by Theorem 7 $\approx_{st}\subseteq \mathcal{B}_I(\approx_{st})$, thus $\approx_{st}$ is a stuttering bisimulation with induction, and $\approx_{st}\subseteq\approx_{si}$. $\qquad\square$

To establish the other direction, we need to show that $\approx_{si}$ is an ω-bisimulation.

Lemma 3. Let $\mathcal{K} = \langle S, AP, L, \longrightarrow\rangle$ be a Kripke structure, R be a binary relation on S. For all $\lambda \in \mathcal{O}$, if $(s,t) \in \mathcal{B}_I^\lambda(R)$ then the following hold

1. if σ is an infinite run from s, then there is a finite run ρ from t with $length(\rho) > 0$, and a finite prefix σ^* of σ such that $(\sigma^*, \rho) \in R^\natural$;
2. if ρ is an infinite run from t, then there is a finite run σ from s with $length(\sigma) > 0$, and a finite prefix ρ^* of ρ such that $(\sigma, \rho^*) \in R^\natural$.

Proof. Here we only show 1, because 2 can be proved in the same way. We prove by induction on $\lambda \in \mathcal{O}$. If $\lambda = 0$ there is nothing to be proved. If $\lambda = \kappa + 1$, let $(s,t) \in \mathcal{B}_I^{\kappa+1}(R)$, $\sigma = s_1 s_2 s_3 \ldots$. Then $s_1 \longrightarrow s_2$, according to the definition of $\mathcal{B}_I^{\kappa+1}(R)$, there are the following two cases. The first case is that there exists a finite run ρ from t such that $length(\rho) > 0, (s_1 s_2, \rho) \in R^\natural$, and in this case take $s_1 s_2$ as σ^*, then ρ is the required run from t. The second case is that $(s_2, t) \in R$ and $(s_2, t) \in \mathcal{B}_I^\kappa(R)$, and in this case by the induction hypothesis, for the infinite run $\sigma' = s_2 s_3 \ldots$, there is a finite run ρ from t with $length(\rho) > 0$, and there is a finite prefix $\sigma^\dagger$ of σ' such that $(\sigma^\dagger, \rho) \in R^\natural$, and in this case we take $\sigma^* = s_1\sigma^\dagger$, then $(\sigma^*, \rho) \in R^\natural$ and ρ is the required run. If λ is a limit ordinal, then there is $\kappa \in \mathcal{O}$ such that $\kappa < \lambda$ and $(s,t) \in \mathcal{B}_I^\kappa(R)$, then the induction hypothesis immediately gives a finite run ρ from t with $length(\rho) > 0$, and there is a finite prefix σ^* of σ such that $(\sigma^*, \rho) \in R^\natural$. $\qquad\square$

Theorem 8. Let $\mathcal{K} = \langle S, AP, L, \longrightarrow\rangle$ be a Kripke structure, R be a binary relation on S. If R is a stuttering bisimulation with induction, then R is an ω-bisimulation.

Proof. Suppose $R \subseteq \mathcal{B}_I(R)$, and $(s,t) \in R$ we need to prove the following:

1. if σ is an infinite run from s, then there is an infinite run ρ from t such that $(\sigma, \rho) \in R^\sharp$;
2. if ρ is an infinite run from t, then there is an infinite run σ from s such that $(\sigma, \rho) \in R^\sharp$.

Here we only prove 1, because 2 can be proved in the same way. So suppose σ is an infinite run from s. Since in this case $(s,t) \in \mathcal{B}_I(R)$, then $(s,t) \in \mathcal{B}_I^\lambda(R)$ for some $\lambda \in \mathcal{O}$, by Lemma 3 we can obtain a finite prefix σ_1 of σ and a finite run ρ_1 from t with $length(\rho_1) > 0$, such that $(\sigma_1, \rho_1) \in R^\natural$. Now we can do the same thing for $(last(\sigma_1), last(\rho_1)) \in R$ with the infinite run which is the remaining part of σ after σ_1. Repeating the process to infinity we obtain a run ρ by concatenating $\rho_1, \rho_2, \ldots$ in the obvious way. Since each ρ_i has a positive length, clearly ρ is an infinite run and it is not difficult to see that $(\sigma, \rho) \in R^\sharp$. $\square$

Finally, we are ready to prove:

Theorem 9. $\approx_{si}=\approx_{st}$.

Proof. According to Theorem 6, $\approx_{si}$ is a stuttering bisimulation with induction, then, by Theorem 8, $\approx_{si}$ is an ω-bisimulation, thus $\approx_{si}\subseteq\approx_{st}$. Then combine this with Corollary 3 we obtain $\approx_{si}=\approx_{st}$. □

Thus $\approx_{si}$ is an equivalence relation. As we promised in the end of the last section, we have to prove the following important characterization of $\approx_{si}$ and $\approx_{st}$.

Theorem 10. $\approx_{st}$ *(as well as $\approx_{si}$) is the weakest equivalence which is a stuttering bisimulation and at the same time is a divergence preserving equivalence.*

Proof. Now it is clear that $\approx_{st}$ is divergence preserving and is a stuttering bisimulation. To show that it is the weakest such, let $\equiv$ be a stuttering bisimulation and at the same time it is a divergence preserving equivalence. Then by Theorem 7 $\equiv\subseteq\mathcal{B}_I(\equiv)$, thus $\equiv\subseteq\approx_{si}=\approx_{st}$. □

Remark 2. In principle, one can "define" an equivalence relation $\simeq$ by requiring that $s \simeq t$ if and only if there exists a divergence preserving equivalence relation $\equiv$ such that $\equiv$ is a stuttering bisimulation and $s \equiv t$. However, such kind of "definition" needs to be justified in order to be meaningful. In particular, one needs to prove that the defined relation $\simeq$ is indeed an equivalence relation, and is divergence preserving, and is a stuttering bisimulation. Here Theorem 10 provides the justification for $\simeq$. In some cases this kind of justification is routine. Such examples include strong and weak bisimulation equivalences, branching bisimulation equivalence, etc. In these examples, due to the existence of obvious monotonic functions, application of Knaster-Tarski fixed-point theorem turned the justification into a routine task. In other cases it cannot be considered routine, where justification is difficult by the definition itself, and one needs to find other ways to get around. This is the case here, since from the definition itself it is not obvious how to prove that $\simeq$ is an equivalence relation, one has to construct an equivalence by other means (like $\approx_{st}$ or $\approx_{si}$), and then to use that to prove that $\simeq$ is an equivalence. It is for this reason that we do not consider the way of introducing $\simeq$ as desirable. It easily causes confusion while does not save any amount of work.

4   Well-Founded Bisimulation

In [11], the notion of well-founded bisimulation was proposed to capture stuttering equivalence. In this section we study its relationship to stuttering bisimulation with induction.

Definition 8 *(Well-founded bisimulation). Let $\mathcal{K} = \langle S, AP, L, \longrightarrow \rangle$ be a Kripke structure. Let $rank : S \times S \times S \to W$ be a total function, where $(W, \prec)$ is well-founded. A binary relation $R \subseteq S \times S$ is a well-founded bisimulation w.r.t. rank iff R is symmetric and for every $(s, t) \in R$ the following hold:*

1. $L(s) = L(t)$;
2. whenever $s \longrightarrow u$ then one of the following must hold:
   (a) $t \longrightarrow v$ for some $v \in S$ with $(u,v) \in R$;
   (b) $(u,t) \in R$ and $rank(u,u,t) \prec rank(s,s,t)$;
   (c) $(u,t) \notin R$ and $t \longrightarrow v$ for some $v \in S$ with $(s,v) \in R$ and
       $rank(u,s,v) \prec rank(u,s,t)$.

The purpose of the ternary rank function $rank(u,s,t)$, when used in case (c) in the above definition, is to enforce an order in defining the condition that the transition $s \longrightarrow u$ can be matched by a transition from t. In case (b), the rank function is used to enforce an order in defining the condition that the transition $s \longrightarrow u$ can be matched by default. In principle the two well founded orders in case (b) and case (c) of the definition are different: the former being an order between pairs of states and latter an order between triples of states. It is just a coincidence that the function $rank$ can serve both purpose.

First, we show that every well-founded bisimulation is a stuttering bisimulation with induction.

Theorem 11. *Let $\mathcal{K} = \langle S, AP, L, \longrightarrow \rangle$ be a Kripke structure. If R is a well-founded bisimulation on $\mathcal{K}$ with some well-founded set $(W, \prec)$ and total function rank, then R is a stuttering bisimulation with induction.*

Proof. We first establish the following fact by well-founded induction on $\prec$:

> If $(s,t) \in R$ and $s \longrightarrow u$ and $(u,t) \notin R$, then there exists a finite run ρ such that $length(\rho) > 0$ and $(su, \rho) \in R^\natural$.

To show that, suppose $(s,t) \in R$ and $s \longrightarrow u$ and $(u,t) \notin R$. Since R is a well-founded bisimulation, one of the conditions in $(a), (b), (c)$ of Definition 8 must hold. However because $(u,t) \notin R$, condition (b) is excluded, thus either (a) or (c) must hold. If (a) holds, then $t \longrightarrow v$ with $(u,v) \in R$ for some $v \in S$, clearly tv is the ρ we are looking for. If (c) holds, then $t \longrightarrow v$ for some $v \in S$ with $(s,v) \in R$ and $rank(u,s,v) \prec rank(u,s,t)$. Now we have two subcases to discuss: $(u,v) \in R$ and $(u,v) \notin R$. In the first subcase, again tv is the ρ we are looking for. In the second subcase, because $(s,v) \in R$, $s \longrightarrow u$, $(u,v) \notin R$, and $rank(u,s,v) \prec rank(u,s,t)$, by the induction hypothesis there is a finite run ρ' from v such that $length(\rho') > 0$ and $(su, \rho') \in R^\natural$. Let $\rho = t\rho'$, clearly $(su, \rho) \in R^\natural$.

Now suppose $(s,t) \in R$, we show $(s,t) \in \mathcal{B}_I(R)$ by well-founded induction as follows. Let $s \longrightarrow u$, then we have two cases to discuss: $(u,t) \notin R$ and $(u,t) \in R$. In the first case, by the fact we proved above there is a finite run ρ from t with $length(\rho) > 0$ and $(su, \rho) \in R^\natural$. In the second case, by the condition that R is a well-founded bisimulation, one of the conditions in $(a), (b), (c)$ of Definition 8 must hold. However (c) is clearly excluded because in this case $(u,t) \in R$. So we have two subcases to discuss. If (a) holds, then $t \longrightarrow v$ with $(u,v) \in R$ for some $v \in S$, clearly $(su, tv) \in R^\natural$. If (b) holds, then $(u,t) \in R$ and $rank(u,u,t) \prec rank(s,s,t)$, by the induction hypothesis $(u,t) \in \mathcal{B}_I(R)$. Thus, for the given (s, t), we showed that whenever $s \longrightarrow u$ then either there is a finite run ρ from t such that $length(\rho) > 0$ and $(su, \rho) \in R^\natural$, or $(u, t) \in R$ and $(u, t) \in \mathcal{B}_I(R)$, hence $(s, t) \in \mathcal{B}_I(R)$.   □

Next, we show that a symmetric stuttering bisimulation with induction is a well-founded bisimulation.

Theorem 12. *Let* $\mathcal{K} = \langle S, AP, L, \longrightarrow \rangle$ *be a Kripke structure,* R *be a symmetric binary relation on* S. *If* R *is a stuttering bisimulation with induction, then* R *is a well-founded bisimulation with some well-founded set* $(W, \prec)$ *and total function* rank.

Proof. Define $rank : S \times S \times S \rightarrow \mathcal{O}$ as follows:

1. For $s, t \in S$, if $(s, t) \in \mathcal{B}_I(R)$ then $rank(s, s, t) = \lambda$ where λ is the least ordinal such that $(s, t) \in \mathcal{B}_I^\lambda(R)$ (by Theorem 5 $\lambda = \kappa + 1$ for some $\kappa \in \mathcal{O}$), if $(s, t) \notin \mathcal{B}_I(R)$ then $rank(s, s, t) = 0$;
2. For $u, s, t \in S$ with u, s being two different states, then $rank(u, s, t) = l$, where l is the length of the shortest finite run ρ from t such that $length(\rho) > 0$ and $(su, \rho) \in R^\natural$ if such a ρ exists, otherwise let $l = 0$ (in fact just let l be any value will do in this case).

Suppose R is a stuttering bisimulation with induction and R is symmetric, we will show that with $(\mathcal{O}, <)$ and $rank$ defined above, R is a well-founded bisimulation. Let $(s, t) \in R$. Since R is a stuttering bisimulation with induction, thus $(s, t) \in \mathcal{B}_I(R)$, and let $rank(s, s, t) = \lambda = \kappa + 1$, so $(s, t) \in \mathcal{B}_I^{\kappa+1}(R)$. First note that in this case $L(s) = L(t)$. Suppose $s \longrightarrow u$, since $(s, t) \in \mathcal{B}_I^{\kappa+1}(R)$, two of the following will happen. Either there exists a finite run ρ from t such that $length(\rho) > 0$ and $(su, \rho) \in R^\natural$, or $(u, t) \in R$ and $(u, t) \in \mathcal{B}_I^\kappa(R)$. In the latter case, obviously $rank(u, u, t) < \lambda$, so condition (b) of Definition 8 is satisfied. In the former case, according to the definition of $rank(u, s, t)$, there is $l > 0$ and $rank(u, s, t) = l$. We distinguish two subcases. The first subcase is that $l = 1$, then let $\rho = tv$, and clearly $t \longrightarrow v, (u, v) \in R$, condition (a) of Definition 8 is satisfied. The second subcase is that $l > 1$, then according to the definition of $rank(u, s, t)$ there is $\rho = tvv_1 \ldots$ which is the shortest finite run from t such that $length(\rho) = l$ and $(su, \rho) \in R^\natural$. With a detailed case analysis it is not difficult to see that $(s, v) \in R$, and $rank(u, s, v) \le l - 1 < rank(u, s, t)$, and condition (c) of Definition 8 is satisfied.   □

Theorems 11 and 12 not only imply that well-founded bisimulation and (symmetric) stuttering bisimulation with induction both characterize the same relation, i.e. stuttering equivalence, but also claim that the two notions are essentially the same thing. From the point of view of verification practice, each of the two notions has its own advantages. As explained in *Remark 1*, stuttering bisimulation with induction is presented as an alternating fixed-point of some monotonic function on the complete lattice of binary relations, thus existing efficient local correctness checking strategies can be applied to decide whether some given pairs of states are stuttering equivalent. With given well-founded set and function $rank$, the conditions of well-founded bisimulation is easy to verify.

So a well-founded bisimulation R can be used as a proof that the pairs in the relation are stuttering equivalent. In other words, stuttering bisimulation with induction is more useful for equality checking, while well-founded bisimulation is better suited for equality proving. In fact the two can be combined in such a way that first using a fast local algorithm to obtain a relation R which is a stuttering bisimulation with induction, and then using the construction in the proof of Theorem 12 on the symmetric stuttering bisimulation $R \cup R^{-1}$ to obtain a well-founded bisimulation as a proof for the equality of all pairs in R. In fact the construction can be turned into an algorithm which, for a given symmetric stuttering bisimulation with induction R on a Kripke structure with finite number of states, computes the function $rank$ for the well-founded bisimulation. We describe such an algorithm in the rest of this section.

To describe the algorithm, we need a theorem which says that often it is sufficient to stay out of limit ordinals. The following lemma is needed for proving the theorem.

Lemma 4. *If $\kappa < \lambda$ then $\mathcal{B}_I^\kappa(R) \subseteq \mathcal{B}_I^\lambda(R)$.*

The proof of the lemma is standard, and we omit it here.

Theorem 13. *Let $\mathcal{K} = \langle S, AP, L, \longrightarrow \rangle$ be a Kripke structure, R be a binary relation on S.*

1. *If $\longrightarrow$ is finite branching, i.e. $\{s \in S \mid s_0 \longrightarrow s\}$ is a finite set for all $s_0 \in S$, then whenever $(s, t) \in \mathcal{B}_I(R)$ there is a natural number n such that $(s, t) \in \mathcal{B}_I^n(R)$.*
2. *If S is finite with m states, then there exists n with $0 < n \leq m^2$ such that $\mathcal{B}_I^0(R) \subseteq \mathcal{B}_I^1(R) \ldots \subseteq \mathcal{B}_I^n(R)$ is an increasing chain and $\mathcal{B}_I(R) = \mathcal{B}_I^n(R)$.*

Proof. To prove 1, it is sufficient to prove by induction that in this case for all $\lambda \in \mathcal{O}$ if $(s, t) \in \mathcal{B}_I^\lambda(R)$ then there is a natural number n such that $(s, t) \in \mathcal{B}_I^n(R)$. If λ is a natural number, then the claim trivially holds. If λ is a limit ordinal, by Definition 7 there is $\kappa < \lambda$ such that $(s, t) \in \mathcal{B}_I^\kappa(R)$, then by the induction hypothesis there is a natural number n such that $(s, t) \in \mathcal{B}_I^n(R)$. If $\lambda = \kappa + 1$, by Definition 7 and the induction hypothesis the following hold:

1. whenever $s \longrightarrow s'$ then either there exists a finite run ρ from t such that $length(\rho) > 0$ and $(ss', \rho) \in R^\natural$, or $(s', t) \in R$ and $(s', t) \in \mathcal{B}_I^n(R)$ for some natural number n;
2. whenever $t \longrightarrow t'$ then either there exists a finite run σ from s such that $length(\sigma) > 0$ and $(\sigma, tt') \in R^\natural$, or $(s, t') \in R$ and $(s, t') \in \mathcal{B}_I^n(R)$ for some natural number n.

Now since $\longrightarrow$ is finite branching, $\{s' \mid s \longrightarrow s'\} \cup \{t' \mid t \longrightarrow t'\}$ is a finite set, we can choose the maximum among the finitely many n's, and let it be m, then by Lemma 4 the following hold

1. whenever $s \longrightarrow s'$ then either there exists a finite run ρ from t such that $length(\rho) > 0$ and $(ss', \rho) \in R^\natural$, or $(s', t) \in R$ and $(s', t) \in \mathcal{B}_I^m(R)$;

2. whenever $t \longrightarrow t'$ then either there exists a finite run σ from s such that $length(\sigma) > 0$ and $(\sigma, tt') \in R^{\natural}$, or $(s, t') \in R$ and $(s, t') \in \mathcal{B}_I^m(R)$.

So in this case $(s, t) \in \mathcal{B}^{m+1}(R)$.

In order to prove 2, note that when S has m elements, the size of the relations in the increasing chain $\mathcal{B}_I^0(R) \subseteq \mathcal{B}_I^1(R) \ldots \subseteq \mathcal{B}_I^n(R) \ldots$ is bounded by m^2. So there exists n with $0 < n \le m^2$ such that $\mathcal{B}_I^n(R) = \mathcal{B}_I^{n+1}(R)$. Then it is easy to prove by induction that for all $\lambda \in \mathcal{O}$, it holds that $\mathcal{B}_I^\lambda(R) \subseteq \mathcal{B}_I^n(R)$. Then $\mathcal{B}_I(R) = \mathcal{B}_I^n(R)$ follows easily. □

By Theorem 13, we know that when the Kripke structure is finite branching, in constructing $rank$ for the well-founded bisimulation in Theorem 12, we can always use natural numbers as the well-founded set for the well-founded bisimulation. And when the Kripke structure has only finite number of states, we can always use a finite subset of natural numbers as the well-founded set for the well-founded bisimulation, and moreover in this case there is n such that $\mathcal{B}_I(R) = \mathcal{B}_I^n(R)$.

We assume a basic procedure FindRun which takes (u, s, t) as input where $(s, t) \in R$ and $s \longrightarrow u$, and find the shortest run ρ from t such that $length(\rho) > 0$ and $(su, \rho) \in R^{\natural}$. It outputs the length of such a run if there exists one, or it outputs 0. It is not difficult to see that this is similar to looking for the shortest path in a graph, which can be implemented with time complexity polynomial to the size of the state set.

Now, for a given symmetric stuttering bisimulation R, the algorithm constructs a well-founded bisimulation as follows.

First, according to Definition 7, we use FindRun to compute $\mathcal{B}_I^k(R)$ from $k = 0$ until $k = n$ where $\mathcal{B}_I^n(R) = \mathcal{B}_I^{n+1}(R)$. It is not difficult to see that each $\mathcal{B}_I^k(R)$ can be computed with time polynomial to the size of the state set. Thus the overall time complexity for computing $\mathcal{B}_I^k(R)$ from $k = 0$ to $k = n$ is also polynomial to the size of the state set.

As the last step, we construct $rank$ as follows:

1. for (u, s, t) with u, s being different states, $(s, t) \in R$ and $s \longrightarrow u$, let $rank(u, s, t) = l$ where l is the output of FindRun(u, s, t);
2. for (s, s, t) with $(s, t) \in R$, let $rank(s, s, t) = l$ where $(s, t) \in \mathcal{B}_I^l(R)$ and $(s, t) \notin \mathcal{B}_I^{l-1}(R)$;
3. for the rest of (u, s, t), let $rank(u, s, t) = 0$.

It is not difficult to see that the total time complexity of the algorithm is polynomial to the size of the state set. According to the proof of Theorem 12, R with $rank$ is a well-founded bisimulation.

5 Related Works

The notion of stuttering bisimulation with induction is an adaptation of the notion of inductive branching bisimulation introduced in [16], which is the study of the labeled transition system version of divergence preserving stuttering equivalence. The presentation of the theory part in Sects. 3 and 4 is slightly different from the presentation in [16]. In particular, the notion of ω-bisimulation is introduced in place of the complete branching bisimulation. The new presentation is simpler and more concise for stuttering equivalence due to the complete nature of the transition relation in Kripke structures, i.e. for any state there always exists some out-going transition. As an equivalence which has the exact distinguishing strength as the set of CTL*-X properties, stuttering equivalence is certainly very important. However, it seems that it is still in need for a general rigorous formulation. It is for this purpose that we propose ω-bisimulation as a candidate for this role. From the theoretical development in this paper, it looks fit for this role. The formulation in the original paper [3] is in the form of the limit of a convergence sequence of equivalence relations, which is not easy to use in proving theorems about it. Also it is assumed for finite state systems, which makes it not general enough. In [11] the formulation of stuttering equivalence relies on a non-trivial definition of a matching relation which only appears in the appendix of the paper. The matching relation makes the formulation not easy to handle, in particular it seems not easy to establish that the final relation is indeed an equivalence (no proof has been provided in the paper).

The notion of well-founded bisimulation was introduced in [11] and studied in [9] to characterize stuttering equivalence. Due to the lack of a clear theoretical foundation for stuttering equivalence, the characterization proofs in the mentioned works left something to be desired. In [9], stuttering equivalence is characterized by the so-called divergence sensitive stutter bisimulation, which is based on the notion of $\mathcal{R}$-divergence. This characterization is similar to the kind of definition mentioned in *Remark* 2. Although the characterization proof of well-founded bisimulation was provided in [9] in terms of divergence sensitive stutter bisimulation, such characterization of stuttering equivalence itself needs further justification. Theorems 11 and 12 and their proofs in this paper provide a sound theoretical foundation for well-founded bisimulation. Another disadvantage of divergence sensitive stutter bisimulation is, since it relies on equivalence relations that satisfy certain conditions on infinite paths, it would need much effort when it is used directly as a method for proving the equivalence of states.

In [13] branching bisimulation with explicit divergence is studied in detail, which is the labeled transition system version of stuttering equivalence. Branching bisimulation with explicit divergence is defined similar to the kind of definition mentioned in *Remark* 2. In [13] the authors took serious efforts to complete the needed justification for the definition. However the proofs there were quite complicated due to the lack of good co-inductive properties of the definition.

In [15], a partition based efficient algorithm for divergence blind stuttering equivalence was presented. Also a transformation between finite Kripke structures was given in [15] such that two states are divergence blind stuttering equivalent in the transformed Kripke structure if and only if the corresponding states in the original Kripke structure are stuttering equivalent. This implies that the problem of checking stuttering equivalence can also be solved by their algorithm. Compared to the local algorithm approach mentioned in *Remark* 1, the partition based algorithm has better worst case time complexity due to the exploitation of good properties of equivalence relation. However partition algorithms are inherently global, which makes them unable to exploit early termination chances.

6 Conclusion

In this paper, we propose the notion of stuttering bisimulation with induction to characterize stuttering equivalence. It is argued that, due to its fixed-point style definition, stuttering bisimulation with induction is a good characterization for stuttering equivalence in that there are efficient local algorithms for the equality checking problem. We also use stuttering bisimulation with induction to analyze the notion of well-founded bisimulation. It is shown that stuttering bisimulation with induction and well-founded bisimulation are essentially the same thing, and as a byproduct a method for constructing the ranking function for well-founded bisimulation from a given stuttering bisimulation with induction is presented. Also a notion of ω-bisimulation is introduced to characterize stuttering equivalence, which leads to smooth development of the theory.

As we pointed out in Sect. 4, stuttering bisimulation with induction and well-founded induction are good for different things, the former is good for equality checking and latter for equality proving. In this respect an interesting future work is to combine them in a tool where a local equality decision procedure produces a stuttering bisimulation with induction, which is then used to construct the corresponding well-founded bisimulation. And the resulting well-founded bisimulation can act as a proof of equality for the elements in the stuttering bisimulation with induction.

References

1. Hennessy, M.C.B., Plotkin, G.D.: A term model for CCS. In: Dembiński, P. (ed.) MFCS 1980. LNCS, vol. 88, pp. 261–274. Springer, Heidelberg (1980). https://doi.org/10.1007/BFb0022510
2. Walker, D.J.: Bisimulation and divergence. Inf. Comput. **85**, 212–241 (1990)
3. Browne, M.C., Clarke, E.M., Grümberg, O.: Characterizing finite Kripke structures in propositional temporal logic. Theor. Comput. Sci. **59**, 115–131 (1988)
4. Browne, M.C., Clarke, E.M., Grumberg, O.: Reasoning about networks with many identical finite state processes. Inf. Comput. **81**(1), 13–31 (1989)
5. Glabbeek, R.J.: The linear time — branching time spectrum II. In: Best, E. (ed.) CONCUR 1993. LNCS, vol. 715, pp. 66–81. Springer, Heidelberg (1993). https://doi.org/10.1007/3-540-57208-2_6
6. de Nicola, R., Vaandrager, F.: Three logics for branching bisimulation. J. ACM **42**(2), 458–487 (1995)
7. Park, D.: Concurrency and automata on infinite sequences. In: Deussen, P. (ed.) GI-TCS 1981. LNCS, vol. 104, pp. 167–183. Springer, Heidelberg (1981). https://doi.org/10.1007/BFb0017309
8. Milner, R.: Communication and Concurrency. Prentice-Hall, New York (1989)
9. Baier, C., Katoen, J.-P.: Principles of Model Checking. The MIT Press, Cambridge (2008)

10. Vergauwen, B., Lewi, J.: Efficient local correctness checking for single and alternating boolean equation systems. In: Abiteboul, S., Shamir, E. (eds.) ICALP 1994. LNCS, vol. 820, pp. 304–315. Springer, Heidelberg (1994). https://doi.org/10.1007/3-540-58201-0_77

11. Namjoshi, K.S.: A simple characterization of stuttering bisimulation. In: Ramesh, S., Sivakumar, G. (eds.) FSTTCS 1997. LNCS, vol. 1346, pp. 284–296. Springer, Heidelberg (1997). https://doi.org/10.1007/BFb0058037

12. van Glabbeek, R.J., Weijland, P.: Branching time and abstraction in bisimulation semantics. J. ACM **43**(3), 555–600 (1996)

13. van Glabbeek, R.J., Luttik, B., Trcka, N.: Branching bisimilarity with explicit divergence. Fundam. Inform. **93**(4), 371–392 (2009)

14. Allen Emerson, E., Halpern, J.Y.: "Sometimes" and "Not Never" revisited: on branching versus linear time temporal logic. J. ACM **33**(1), 151–178 (1986)

15. Groote, J.F., Vaandrager, F.: An efficient algorithm for branching bisimulation and stuttering equivalence. In: Paterson, M.S. (ed.) ICALP 1990. LNCS, vol. 443, pp. 626–638. Springer, Heidelberg (1990). https://doi.org/10.1007/BFb0032063

16. Liu, X., Yu, T., Zhang, W.: Analyzing divergence in bisimulation semantics. In: Proceedings of 44th ACM SIGPLAN Symposium on Principles of Programming Languages (POPL2017), Paris (2017)

$Q|SI\rangle$: A Quantum Programming Environment

Shusen Liu[1]([✉]), Xin Wang[1], Li Zhou[1], Ji Guan[1], Yinan Li[1], Yang He[1],
Runyao Duan[1]([✉]), and Mingsheng Ying[1,2,3]([✉])

[1] Centre for Quantum Software and Information, Faculty of Engineering and
Information Technology, University of Technology Sydney, Ultimo, NSW 2007,
Australia
Shusen.Liu@student.uts.edu.au

[2] Department of Computer Science and Technology, Tsinghua University,
Beijing 100084, China

[3] State Key Laboratory of Computer Science, Institute of Software,
Chinese Academy of Sciences, Beijing 100190, China

Abstract. This paper describes a quantum programming environment,
named $Q|SI\rangle$, to support quantum programming using a quantum
extension of the **while**-language. Embedded in the .Net framework, the
$Q|SI\rangle$ platform includes a quantum **while**-language compiler and a suite
of tools to simulate quantum computation, optimize quantum circuits,
analyze and verify quantum programs. This paper demonstrates $Q|SI\rangle$ in
use. Quantum behaviors are simulated on classical platforms with a
combination of components and the compilation procedures for differ-
ent back-ends are described in detail. $Q|SI\rangle$ bridges the gap between
quantum hardware and software. As a scalable framework, this platform
allows users to code and simulate customized functions, optimize them
for a range of quantum circuits, analyze the termination of a quantum
program, and verify the program's correctness (The software of $Q|SI\rangle$ is
available at http://www.qcompiler.com.).

Keywords: Quantum programming · Quantum compilation
Quantum simulation · Quantum program analysis
Quantum program verification

1 Introduction

It is well-known that quantum computers can solve certain categories of problems much more efficiently than classical computers. For example, Shor's fac-
toring algorithm [22], Grover's search algorithm [8] and more recently Harrow,
Hassidim and Lloyd's algorithm for systems of linear equations [9] are all known
to be particularly suited quantum computation. In recent years, governments
and industries around the globe have been racing to build quantum computers.
And, as quantum hardware advances quantum software is also blossoming.

© Springer Nature Switzerland AG 2018
C. Jones et al. (Eds.): Zhou-Festschrift, LNCS 11180, pp. 133–164, 2018.
https://doi.org/10.1007/978-3-030-01461-2_8

However, just as with classical computing, once quantum computers are commercialized, programmers will certainly need a modern platform to express and implement their quantum algorithms without concern for trivialities of their circuits. In fact, such platforms will be even more helpful for quantum programmers because the counterintuitive features of quantum systems are much more likely to lead to misunderstandings. Using a programming environment means the physical implementation of quantum algorithms is less of a concern and the errors caused by misunderstandings can be (partially) avoided.

To be of any use, quantum hardware requires quantum software that is compatible with the device. Yet beyond these hardware constraints, several further barriers are limiting the practical applications of quantum software, e.g., concerning physical topology of quantum computers. For example, Veldhorst et al. [15,27] use microwave electron-spin resonance (ESR) to perform global Hadamard gate and demarcate the transitions between tick and took intervals. This rule makes quantum programming more elusive when the programmer needs to perform a local Hadamard gate. Further, IBMQ's quantum computers in the cloud [11,12] deliver several different physical topologies, each with a different back-end, and these topologies require specific low-level device commands to perform an operation. Without an appropriate compiler from software, producing a workable quantum program is a very difficult task.

Several quantum programming platforms have been developed over the last two decades. The first quantum programming language, called QCL, was proposed by Ömer [18,20] in 1998. It was implemented in C++. In 2000, Sanders and Zuliani [19] introduced qGCL as a quantum extension of Dijkstra's Guarded-Command Language (GCL) and along with pGCL, a probabilistic extension of GCL. Then, in 2003, Bettelli et al. [4] defined a quantum programming language very similar to QCL, called Q language. Q language was implemented as a C++ library. However, just in the past few years, some quantum programming platforms have emerged that are more scalable and robust. In 2013, Green et al. [7] proposed a scalable functional quantum programming language, called Quipper, using Haskell as the host language. JavadiAbhari et al. [14] defined Scafford in 2014, presenting its accompanying compilation system ScaffCC in [13]. In the same year, Wecker and Svore from QuArc (Microsoft Research Quantum Architecture and Computation team) developed LIQUi|⟩as a modern tool-set embedded within F# [28]. Smelyanskiy et al. [24] at Intel built a parallel quantum computing simulator qHiPSTER in 2016 that is able to simulate up to 40 qubits on a supercomputer with very high performance. And very recently, at the end of 2017, QuARC announced a new programming language and simulator designed specifically for full stack quantum computing, called Q#. Q#'s ability to support 32 qubits on a PC and up to 40 qubits on the Microsoft Azure Cloud platform represents a new milestone in quantum programming.

The IBMQ team at IBM have also released quantum computers and simulator for high-performance computing. 2017 saw the release of a 5-qubit quantum cloud computer along with their corresponding PythonSDK and PythonAPI tools [11,12], followed by 20 qubits in 2018. The combination of hardware and software provides general researchers with access to the most advanced cloud-based quantum computing platform. As the second renaissance in quantum computation, IBMQ has attracted great interests from both the public and private sectors.

Contributions of this paper: This paper presents a powerful and flexible new quantum programming environment called $Q|SI\rangle$ [1], named after our research center [2]. The *core* of $Q|SI\rangle$ is *a quantum programming language* and *its compiler*. The language is a quantum extension of the **while**-language, first defined in [29] followed by a careful study of its operational and denotational semantics (see also [30], Chapter 3). The language includes a measurement-based case statement and a measurement-based **while**-loop. These two program constructs are extremely convenient for describing large-scale quantum algorithms, such as quantum random walk-based algorithms.

For operations with quantum hardware, we have defined a new assembly language called f-QASM (Quantum Assembly Language with feedback) as an interactive command set. f-QASM is an extension of the QASM instruction set introduced in [26]. A feedback instruction has been added that allows the efficient implementation of measurement-based case and loop statements. A compiler then transforms the quantum **while**-program into a sequence of f-QASM instructions and further generates a corresponding quantum circuit equivalent to the program (i.e., a sequence of executable quantum gates). $Q|SI\rangle$ also contains a module for optimizing the quantum circuits as well as a module for simulating quantum programs on a classical computer. Two novel features set $Q|SI\rangle$ apart from the existing quantum programming environments - its quantum program analyzers and its quantum program verifier:

- *The quantum program analyzer.* $Q|SI\rangle$ includes several algorithms for termination analysis and computing the average running time of quantum programs developed by Ying et al. [31,34], one of the authors of this paper. In addition, the platform includes a semi-definite programming (SDP) algorithm to generate invariants of quantum **while**-loops [33], also developed by Ying. These algorithms are used for the static analysis of quantum programs to help the compiler with its optimization procedures.
- *A quantum program verifier.* A logic in the Floyd-Hoare style was established in [29] (see also [30], Chapter 4). This logic, which reasons about the correctness of quantum programs, has been written in the quantum **while**-language. Recently, a theorem prover was implemented by Liu et al. [16] for quantum Floyd-Hoare logic based on Isabelle/HOL. We intend to link $Q|SI\rangle$ with the quantum theorem prover presented in [16] to provide a facility for verifying the correctness of quantum programs.

---

[1] http://www.qcompiler.com.
[2] http://www.qsi.uts.edu.au.

2 Quantum while-Language

For convenience, a brief review of the quantum **while**-language follows. The quantum **while**-language is a pure quantum language without classical variables. It assumes only a set of quantum variables denoted by the symbols $q_0, q_1, q_2, ...$ However, in practice, almost all existing quantum algorithms involve elements of both classical and quantum computation. Therefore, $Q|SI\rangle$ has been designed such that the quantum **while**-language can be embedded into C#, which brings a significant level of convenience to the program design process. Some explanations of the quantum program constructs follow; however, for more detailed descriptions and examples, see [29] and Chapter 3 of [30]. The quantum **while**-language is generated using the following simple syntax:

$$\mathbf{S} ::= \mathbf{skip} \mid q := |0\rangle \mid \bar{q} = U[\bar{q}] \mid S_1; S_2 \mid \mathbf{if} \ (\Box m \cdot M[\bar{q}] = m \to S_m) \ \mathbf{fi}$$
$$\mid \mathbf{while} \ M[\bar{q}] = 1 \ \mathbf{do} \, \mathbf{S} \, \mathbf{od}.$$

Skip. Just like the classical **while**-language, the statement **skip** does nothing and terminates immediately.

Initialization. The initialization statement "$q := |0\rangle$" sets the quantum variable q to the basis state $|0\rangle$.

Unitary transformation The statement "$\bar{q} := U[\bar{q}]$" means that a unitary transformation (quantum gate) U is performed on quantum register $\bar{q}$ leaving the other variables unchanged.

Sequential composition. In the composition $S_1; S_2$, program S_1 is executed first as per a classical programming language. Once S_1 terminates, S_2 is executed.

Case statement. In the case statement **if** $(\Box m \cdot M[\bar{q}] = m \to S_m)$ **fi**, M is a quantum measurement with m representing its possible outcomes. To execute this statement, M is first performed on the quantum register $\bar{q}$ and a measurement outcome m is obtained with a certain probability. Then, the subprogram S_m is selected according to the outcome m and executed. The difference between a classical case statement and a quantum case statement is that the state of the quantum program variable $\bar{q}$ changes after performing the measurement.

while-Loop. In the loop **while** $M[\bar{q}] = 1$ **do** S **od**, M is a "yes-no" measurement with only two possible outcomes: 0 and 1. During execution, M is performed on the quantum register $\bar{q}$ to check the loop guard. If the outcome is 0, the program terminates. If the outcome is 1 the program executes the loop body S and continues. Note that, here, the state of the program variable $\bar{q}$ also changes after measuring M.

3 The Structure of $Q|SI\rangle$

This section provides an introduction to the basic structure of $Q|SI\rangle$, leaving the details to be described in subsequent sections. $Q|SI\rangle$ is designed to offer a unified general-purpose programming environment to support the quantum **while**-language. It includes a compiler for quantum **while**-programs, a quantum computation simulator, and a module for the analysis and verification of quantum programs. We have implemented $Q|SI\rangle$ as a deeply embedded domain-specific platform for quantum programming using the host language C#.

$Q|SI\rangle$'s framework is shown in Fig. 1.

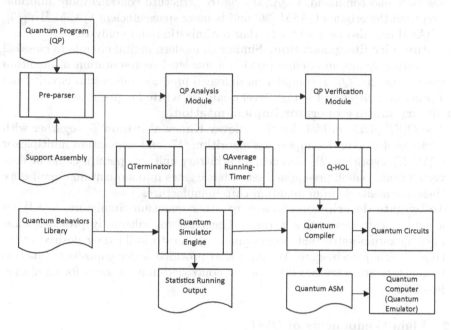

Fig. 1. Framework of $Q|SI\rangle$. Rectangle modules indicate the main stream process with respect to the execution parts in $Q|SI\rangle$, and double edged rectangles suggest the auxiliary modules. Ripple rectangles are the input and output data structures or files. QP Verification Module with Q-HOL is going to link with a theorem prover proposed by Liu et al. [16] which is still under developing.

3.1 Basic Features of $Q|SI\rangle$

The main features of $Q|SI\rangle$ are explained as follows:

Language support. $Q|SI\rangle$ is the first platform to support the quantum **while**-language. Specifically, it allows programmers to develop software with measurement-based case statements and **while**-loops. The two program constructs provide more efficient and clearer descriptions of some quantum algorithms, such as quantum walks and Grover's search algorithm.

Quantum type enriched. Compared to other simulators and analysis tools, $Q|SI\rangle$ supports quantum types beyond pure qubit states, such as density operators, mixed states, etc. These types have unified operations and can be used in different scenarios. This feature provides high flexibility to the programming process.

Dual mode. $Q|SI\rangle$ has two executable modes. "Running-time execution" mode simulates quantum behaviors in one-shot experiments. "Static execution" mode is mainly designed for quantum compilation, analysis, and verification.

f-QASM instruction set. Defined as an extension of Quantum Assembly Language (QASM) [26], f-QASM is essentially a quantum circuit description language that can be adapted for a variety purpose. In this language, every line has only one command. f-QASM's 'goto' structure contains more information than the original QASM [26] and is more space efficient QASM-HL [13]. f-QASM can also be used for further optimization and analysis.

Quantum circuits generation. Similar to modern digital circuits in classical computing, quantum circuits provide a low-level representation of quantum algorithms [26]. $Q|SI\rangle$ compiler module can produce a quantum circuit from a program written in the high-level quantum **while**-language.

Arbitrary unitary operator implementation.
The $Q|SI\rangle$ platform includes the Solovay-Kitaev algorithm [5] together with a two-level matrix decomposition algorithm [17] and a quantum multiplexor (QMUX) algorithm [21]. As such, an arbitrary unitary operator could be converted from a small pre-defined set of basic gates into a quantum circuit once these are available from quantum chip manufactures.

Gate-by-gate description. Similar to other quantum simulators, $Q|SI\rangle$ has a gate-by-gate description feature. The platform inherently provides some basic quantum gates that programmer can use to build their desired quantum circuits gate-by-gate. We have also provided a decomposition function to generate arbitrary two-dimensional controlled-unitary gates for emulation feasibility.

3.2   Main Components of $Q|SI\rangle$

The $Q|SI\rangle$ platform mainly consists of four parts.

Quantum Simulation Engine This component includes some support assemblies, a quantum mechanics library, and a quantum simulator engine. The support assemblies house the quantum types, and the quantum language semantics. More specifically, they provide a series of quantum objects, and reentrant encapsulated functions to play the role of the quantum **if** and **while** constructs. The quantum mechanics library provides the behaviors for quantum objects such as unitary transformation and measurement including the result and post-state. The quantum simulator engine is designed as an execution engine. It accepts quantum objects and their rules from the quantum mechanics library and converts them into probability programming which can be executed on a classical computer.

Quantum Program (QP) Analysis Module This module currently comprises two sub-modules to support static analysis mode: the "QTerminator" and the "QAverage Running-Timer". The former provides the terminating information, and the latter evaluates the running time of the given program. Their outputs are sent to the quantum compiler at the next stage for further use.

QP Verification Module This module is a tool for verifying the correctness of quantum programs. It is based on quantum Hoare logic, which was introduced by one of the authors in [29] and is still under development. One possibility for its future advancement is to link $Q|SI\rangle$ to the quantum theorem prover developed by Liu et al [16].

Quantum Compiler The compiler consists of a series of tools to map a high-level source program representing a quantum algorithm into the language/back-end of the targeted quantum device [26], e.g., f-QASM for $Q|SI\rangle$'s built-in simulator, OpenQASM for IBMQ quantum computers, etc. The compiler helps programmers to implement their source code without needing to consider a diverse range of devices by atuomatically constructing an executable quantum circuit. This effectively allows programmers to ignore the physical constraints of the quantum hardware their code will ultimately run on. A tool to optimize the quantum circuits will be added in the future.

3.3 Implementation of $Q|SI\rangle$

One of the basic problems during implementation is how to use probabilistic and classical algorithms to simulate quantum behaviors. To support quantum operations, $Q|SI\rangle$ has been enriched with data structures in a quantum simulation engine. Figure 2. shows the simulation procedure.

Given the quantum simulation engine involves numerous matrix computations and operations, Math.net is used for matrix computation. Math.NET has been an open-source initiative to build and maintain toolkits that support fundamental mathematics. It targets both the everyday and the advanced needs of .Net developers[3]. It includes numerical computing, computer algebra, signal processing and geometry. Math.net is also able to accelerate matrix calculations when the simulation includes a MIC device (Many Integrated Core Architecture). It should also be noted that the data in these parts are delivered by floating-points numbers with pre-defined fault-tolerant calculation while QP Analysis Module employs algebraic numbers accompanying with Symbolic Math Toolbox from Matlab library.

In static analysis mode, Roslyn is involved as an auxiliary code analysis tool. Roslyn is a set of open-source compilers and code analysis APIs for C# and Basic languages. Since our platform is embedded in the .Net framework for C# language, Roslyn is used as a parser to produce an abstract syntax tree (AST) for further analysis.

4 The Quantum Compiler

A compiler often works as a connection between different back-ends and program data/command structures. The framework of the compiler is described in Fig. 3. The compiler in $Q|SI\rangle$ produces f-QASM code for simulation purposes with its

---

[3] https://www.mathdotnet.com.

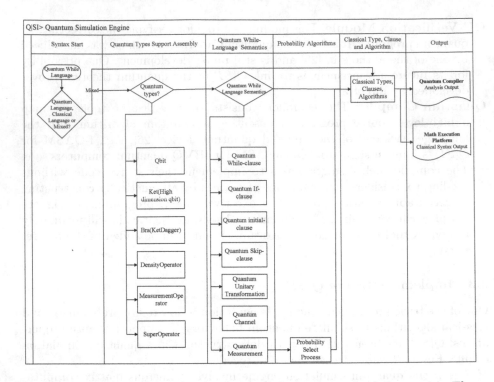

Fig. 2. $Q|SI\rangle$ The procedure for simulating in the quantum simulation engine. Three types of languages are supported: pure quantum **while**-language, classical **while**-language and a mixed language. The engine starts a support flow path when it detects the existing of the quantum part in a program. Then in the flow path, the engine checks the quantum type for each variable and operator and executes the corresponding support assembly which will be explained as a constrained object in the classical computer. As mentioned before, one of the main features of $Q|SI\rangle$ is that it supports programming in the quantum **while**-language. This feature is provided by the quantum **while**-language support assemblies. All of the behaviors considering the semantics are explained by probabilistic algorithms. The outputs are extended C# languages which can be executed directly on the .Net framework or can be explained in f-QASM and OpenQASM by the compiler.

built-in simulator. It also provides embedded Python for the IBMQ Python SDK and OpenQASM 2.0 for the IBMQ Python API. As physical quantum computers only permit several specific operations, some restrictions are imposed on the quantum circuits designs [10] and acceptable commands are generated through several conversion techniques. Other useful functions include the optimization and reconstruction procedures.

The $Q|SI\rangle$ compiler is heavily dependent on other modules. It collects data structures from the quantum simulation engine and splits the program into several parts: variables, quantum gates, quantum measurements, and the entry and exit points of each clause along with their positions. An AST (Abstract Syntax

Tree) is constructed from the program, and then the program is reconstructed as a sequence of f-QASM instructions for further use. Based on f-QASM, the compiler provides a method for decomposing the unitary operators. It can decompose an arbitrary unitary operator $U(n)$ into a sequence of basic quantum gates from a pre-defined set $\{U_1, U_2, \ldots, U_m\}$ where $U_1, U_2, \ldots, U_m \in U(2)$ (qubit gate). This corresponds to scenarios in quantum device development where people need universal computation in spite of only a few of gates, manufacturers can produce. Further, the quantum **while**-language delivers the power of loops, but it also increases the complexity of compilation. A quantum program with a loop structure is much harder to trace than one without. The QP Analysis module provides static analysis tools including a "QTerminator" for termination checking and a "QAverage Running-Timer" for computing the expected running time. In addition, a QP Verification module, still in development, is currently been designed to verify quantum programs. Once complete, programmers will be able to insert the assertions to debug program behaviors.

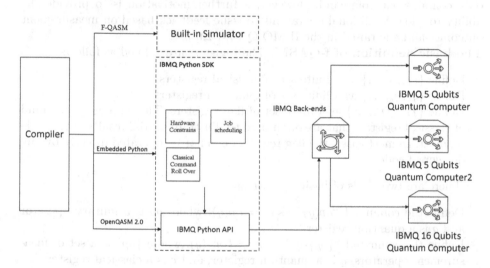

Fig. 3. The compiler of $Q|SI\rangle$ is the bridge between high-level language and low-level hardware instruction sets. f-QASM is designed for connecting the built-in simulator. Even the built-in simulator is not very powerful on the personal computer, it supports the case-statement and loop structure which are significantly different from the flattened quantum circuits description. For connecting with the IBMQ cloud quantum computer, the platform can generate two kinds of language, Embedded Python and OpenQASM 2.0. The Embedded Python is the front-end of IBMQ clients packing with an open compiler in QISKit project. It can also manage hardware resources, constraints and classical information. Moreover, the key component, Python API can be called directly with OpenQASM 2.0 to achieve better performance and compatibility with other high-level languages.

4.1 f-QASM

QASM (Quantum Assembly Language) is widely used in modern quantum simulators. It was first introduced in [26] and is defined as a technology-independent assembly language with a reduced-instruction-set but extended with a set of quantum instructions based on a model of the quantum circuit. Ying et al. [32] carefully characterize its theoretical properties. In 2014, JavadiAbhari et al. [13] defined a space-consuming flat description and denser hierarchical description QASM, called QASM-HL. Recently, Smith et al. [25] proposed a hybrid QASM for classical-quantum algorithms and applied it to Quil. Quil is the front-end of Forest which is a tool for quantum programming and simulation that works in the cloud.

We propose a specific QASM format, called f-QASM (Quantum Assembly Language with feedback). The most significant motivation behind our variation is to translate the inherent logic of quantum program written in a high-level programming language into a simple command set, where every line or period only contains one command. However, a further motivation is to provide the ability to allow conditional operations to issue feedback based on measurement outcomes-an issue raised in the IBMQ QASM 2.0 list.

The basic definition of f-QASM. The registers are defined as follows:

- Define $\{r_1, r_2, \ldots\}$ as a finite set of classical registers.
- Define $\{q_1, q_2, \ldots\}$ as a finite set of quantum registers.
- Define $\{fr_1, fr_2, \ldots\}$ as a finite set of flag registers. These are a special kind of classical registers that are often used to illustrate partial results of the code segment. In most cases, the flag registers can not be operated directly by any developed code.

There are two kinds of basic operations:

- Define the command "$op(q)$" as $q := op(q)$, where op is a unitary operator and q is a quantum register.
- Define the command "$\{op\}(q)$" as $r := \{op\}(q)$, where $\{op\}$ is a set of measurement operators, q is a quantum register, and r is a classical register.

The assembly functions are defined as:

- Define "$INIT(q)$" as $q := |0\rangle \langle 0|$, where q is a quantum register. The value of q is assigned from $\begin{bmatrix} 1 & 0 \\ 0 & 0 \end{bmatrix}$.
- Define "$OP\{q, num\}$", where q is a quantum register, $num \in \mathbb{N}$ and OP is an operator, in another functional form of $q := op(q)$. num can be 0 or other value, i.e., 0 means the unitary operator belongs to the pre-defined set of basic quantum gates which can be prepared by either the manufacturer or the user. Otherwise, num can only be used after being decomposed into basic gates, or else it is ignored.
- Define "$MOV(r_1, r_2)$", r_1 and r_2 are the classical registers. This function assigns the value of the register r_2 to the register r_1 and empties r_2.

- Define "$CMP(r_1, r_2)$" as $fr_1 = \delta(r_1, r_2)$ or as $fr_1 = (r_1 == r_2)$, where r_1, r_2 are two classical registers, and δ is the function that compares whether r_1 is equal to r_2. If r_1 is equal to r_2 then $fr_1 = 1$; otherwise, $fr_1 = 0$.
- "$JMP\ l_0$" directs the current command to go to the line indexed by l_0.
- Define "$JE\ l_0$" as the index value of fr_1 and jumping. If fr_1 is equal to 1 then the compiler executes $JMP\ l_0$, otherwise it does nothing.

f-QASM examples Some simple examples to help readers understand f-QASM follow,

Initialization $q := |0\rangle$ means the program initializes the quantum register q in the state $|0\rangle$. In f-QASM, initializing two quantum registers $Q1$ and $Q2$ in the state $|0\rangle$ would be written as

```
INIT(Q1);
INIT(Q2);
```

Unitary transformation $\bar{q} = U[\bar{q}]$ means the program performs a unitary transformation on the register q. The compiler checks whether or not the unitary matrix is a basic gate. A segment of an example program with a unitary transformation follows:

```
hGate(q1);
```

Here we support $hGate$ as a Hadamard gate performed on single qubit, i.e., $hGate = \frac{1}{\sqrt{2}} \begin{bmatrix} 1 & 1 \\ 1 & -1 \end{bmatrix}$. To transform this into an f-QASM instruction, it would be written as

```
hGate(q1, 0);
```

Sequential composition Contemporary language is not designed for concurrent programming. Thus, the sequential composition is trivial for converting the quantum **while**-language to f-QASM.

Case statement The following program segment is written as a case statement in the quantum **while**-language:

```
QIf(m(q1)
() =>
{
xGate(q1);
},
() =>
{
hGate(q1);
}
);
zGate(q1);
```

where $hGate$ is a Hadamard gate performed on single qubit, $xGate$ is a bit-flip gate performing on single qubit $xGate = \begin{bmatrix} 0 & 1 \\ 1 & 0 \end{bmatrix}$, and $zGate$ is a phase-flip gate $zGate = \begin{bmatrix} 1 & 0 \\ 0 & -1 \end{bmatrix}$. Here we assume that all the gates can be provided. M is a user-defined measurement. The compiler interprets this segment as the following f-QASM instructions:

```
MOV(r,{M}(q1));
CMP(r,0);
JE L1;
CMP(r,1);
JE L2;
L1:
xGate(q1,0);
JMP L3;
L2:
hGate(q1,0)
JMP L3;
L3:
zGate(q1,0);
```

Loop A loop construct is provided using $QWhile(M(q))$, where $QWhile$ is a keyword, M is a measurement and q is a quantum register. An example program segment with quantum **while**-loop follows:

```
QWhile(m(q1),
() =>
{
xGate(q1);
}
);
hGate(q1);
```

$hGate$ and $xGate$ are both basic gates as described above. Loop could be transformed into f-QASM as follows:

```
L1:
MOV(r,{M}(q1));
CMP(r,0);
JE L2;
XGate(q1,0);
JMP L1;
L2:
hGate(q1,0);
```

4.2   Decomposition of a General Unitary Transformation

A physical quantum computer is not like a theoretical formulation of a quantum algorithm. Theoretical algorithms allow unitary transformations to have arbitrary dimensions and qubits can be connected at will. Hirata et al. [10] proposed a conversion of quantum circuits on a Linear Nearest Neighbor (LNN) quantum computer, while Beals et al. [2] analyzed the implementation quantum circuits on the different physical topologies of a quantum computer using ancillary qubits. Considering the physical constraints of the IBMQ quantum computer, we currently use Swap gates to transfer the control qubit to a target qubit for physical implementation.

The universal gate set can be defined as follows. Given a set $\{U_1, U_2, \ldots, U_n\}$ of basic gates. If any unitary operator can be approximated to arbitrary accuracy by a sequence of gates from this set, then the set is said to be universal [17]. However, different back-ends have different universal gate sets. For general purposes, we only considering the discrete single qubit gates, $hGate = \frac{1}{\sqrt{2}} \begin{bmatrix} 1 & 1 \\ 1 & -1 \end{bmatrix}$, $sGate = \begin{bmatrix} 1 & 0 \\ 0 & i \end{bmatrix}$, $T = \begin{bmatrix} 1 & 0 \\ 0 & e^{i\pi/4} \end{bmatrix}$ and $T^\dagger \in U(2)$ and controlled-NOT gate (CNOT). In the procedure of compiler, there are two kinds of built-in decomposition algorithms. One is the QR method enlightened by [1,17], which consists of the following steps:

1. An arbitrary unitary operator is decomposed exactly into (the composition of) two-level unitary matrices, which are a sequence of unitary operators that act non-trivially only on a subspace spanned by two computational basis states. The decomposition includes a product of at most $2^{n-1}(2^n - 1)$ unitary matrices following the method in [17];
2. Each unitary operator, which only acts non-trivially on a subspace spanned by two computational basis states are further expressed using single qubit gates $(U(2))$ and the CNOT gate. This step generates $\mathcal{O}(n^2)$ gates;
3. Each single qubit gate can be decomposed into a sequence of gates from a given small set of basic (single qubit) gates using the Solovay-Kitaev theorem [5]. This step will generate $\mathcal{O}(\log^c(1/\epsilon))$ gates;
4. Check the connectivity between the control qubit and the target qubit against the physical constraints for each CNOT gate in Step 2. Using the Swap gate to transfer the control qubit to another qubit which is in a pair with the target qubit on the physical topology.

The other is the QSD method presented in [21]. This method consists of the following steps:

1. An arbitrary operator is decomposed into three multiplexed rotations and four generic $U(2^{d-1})$ operators, where d is the number of qubits;
2. Repeatedly execute step 1 until $U(4)$ is generated;
3. The $U(4)$ operator is decomposed into $U(2)$ operators with two extra CNOT gates;

4. Each single qubit gate in $U(2)$ is decomposed into gates from a given small set of basic (single qubit) gates using the Solovay-Kitaev theorem [5];
5. Check the connectivity between the control qubit and the target qubit against the physical constraints for each CNOT gate in Step 2. Swap gate is used to transfer the control qubit to another qubit which is in a pair with the target qubit on the physical topology.

5   The Quantum Simulator

5.1   Quantum Types

Data types can be extended from classical computing to quantum computing. For example, quantum generalizations of boolean and integer variables were introduced in [29]. The state space of a quantum boolean variable is the 2-dimensional Hilbert space **Boolean** $= \mathcal{H}_2$, and the state space of a quantum integer variable is the infinite-dimensional Hilbert space **integer** $= \mathcal{H}_\infty$. In $Q|SI\rangle$, every kind of quantum variable has its initialization method and operations. Currently, $Q|SI\rangle$ contains only finite-dimensional quantum variables, but infinite-dimensional variables will be added in the future. The quantum types used in $Q|SI\rangle$ are presented in Fig. 4.

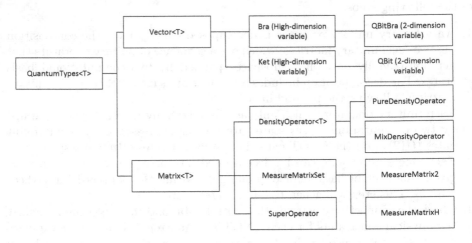

Fig. 4. $Q|SI\rangle$ Quantum types layer

Each quantum type is defined as a subclass of one virtual base class called *QuantumTypes*⟨T⟩, which houses the quantum objects. Within *QuantumTypes*⟨T⟩, there are two extended virtual base classes: *Vector*⟨T⟩, contains the quantum variables;these share some vector rules, and *Matrix*⟨T⟩, which represents a class of quantum operators that share some operator rules.

Quantum variables come in two basic types: *Ket* is used to denote a quantum variable of arbitrary dimensions, and *Bra* is the conjugate transpose of *Ket*. Two specialized (sub)types *QBit* and *QBitBra* are provided as 2-dimensional quantum variables. Note that these two variables are compatible when the boolean type is considered to be a subtype of an integer. In addition, *Ket* and *QBit* types must accept a few rules:

Normalized states For example, a qubit can be written as $|\psi\rangle = \alpha|0\rangle + \beta|1\rangle$, which returns a result of 0 with a probability of $|\alpha|^2$ or a result of 1 with a probability of $|\beta|^2$ when it is measured on a computational basis. Since these probabilities must sum to 1, it obeys $|\alpha|^2 + |\beta|^2 = 1$. Thus, the length of a vector should be normalized to 1 during initialization and computation. For convenience, $Q|SI\rangle$ provides a function *QBit.NormlizeSelf()* to keep the norm of the variable types *QBit* and *Ket*.

Hidden states It is well-known that the information of a *QBit* or a *Ket* cannot be extracted until the state is measured. However, as indicated by Nielsen and Chuang in [17], although "nature evolves a closed quantum system of qubits, not performing any 'measurements', she apparently does keep track of all the continuous variables describing the state, like α and β ". In $Q|SI\rangle$, we use a black box trick to simulate quantum computing, where each quantum state is a black box and each part within the box cooperates with the other parts, but an external viewer knows nothing. Functions and other object methods including unitary transformations and quantum channels know the exact quantum state, but this information is hidden from the viewer until it is measured. Thus, the about a state is stored in a special *"Protect"* class, to make it more difficult to access.

The matrix form is widely used in the semantics of the quantum **while**-language. There are three categorized of matrix: *DensityOperator*$\langle T\rangle$, *MeasureMatrixSet* and *SuperOperator*. *DensityOperator*$\langle T\rangle$ is also a virtual basic class with two sub-classes: *PureDensityOperator* and *MixDensityOperator*. In fact, the difference between *PureDensityOperator* and *MixDensityOperator* is that only *MixDensityOperator* accepts an ensemble, namely a set of probabilities and their corresponding states, which can be expressed by a *PureDensityOperator*$\langle T\rangle$ or a *Vector*$\langle T\rangle$. The object quantum variable ρ of a *DensityOperator*$\langle T\rangle$ must satisfy the following two conditions: (1) ρ has a trace of 1; (2) ρ is a positive operator. To ensure the object is a real density operator, every operation on a objects triggers a verification of these conditions. *MeasureMatrixSet* is a measurement containing an array of matrix $M = \{M_0, M_1, \ldots, M_n\}$ that satisfies a completeness condition $\sum_i M_i^\dagger M_i = I$, which is a very flexible way to define a quantum measurement. Specifically, a plus-minus basis $\{|+\rangle, |-\rangle\}$ and a computation basis $\{|0\rangle, |1\rangle\}$ are two built-in measurements, and a user can easily use their designed measurement. A *SuperOperator* can be used to simulate an open quantum system using an array of Kraus operators $\mathcal{E} = \{E_0, E_1, \ldots, E_n\}$ that satisfy $\sum_i E_i^\dagger E_i \leq I$ as a representation.

Simulating quantum behaviors. The basis of simulating quantum computation is to simulate the quantum behaviors as defined in the four basic postulates of quantum mechanics [17]:

- **Postulate 1**: Associated to any isolated physical system is a complex vector space with an inner product (Hilbert space) known as the state space of the system. The system is completely described by its state vector, which is a unit vector in the system's state space.

  In $Q|SI\rangle$, a Math.net function called
  $$double\ ConjugateDotProduct(Vector\langle T\rangle\ other)$$
  supports the inner product.

- **Postulate 2**: The evolution of a closed quantum system is described by a unitary transformation. That is, the state $|\psi\rangle$ of the system at time t_1 is related to the state $|\psi'\rangle$ of the system at time t_2 by a unitary operator U which depends only on the time t_1 and t_2. $|\psi'\rangle = U|\psi\rangle$.

  To simulate this feature in $Q|SI\rangle$, we have added a function called *UnitaryTrans* to some of our quantum types such as *QBit*, *Ket* and *DensityOperator*$\langle T\rangle$ in a closed quantum system. In addition, the static global function *SuperMatrixTrans* describes the dynamics of an open quantum system as a super-operator $\mathcal{E}$.

- **Postulate 3**: Quantum measurements are described by a collection $\{M_m\}$ of measurement operators. These are operators acting on the state space of the system being measured. The index m refers to the measurement outcomes that may occur in the experiment. If the state of the quantum system is $|\psi\rangle$ before the measurement, then the probability that the result m occurs is given by $p(m) = \langle\psi|M_m^\dagger M_m|\psi\rangle$ and the state of the system after the measurement is $\frac{M_m|\psi\rangle}{\langle\psi|M_m^\dagger M_m|\psi\rangle}$.

  Quantum measurements are simulated with a modified Monte Carlo method. A detailed description is provided in the next subsection.

- **Postulate 4**: The state space of a composite physical system is the tensor product of the state spaces of the component physical systems. Moreover, if we have systems numbered 1 through n, and system number i is prepared in the state $|\psi\rangle$, then the joint state of the total system is $|\psi_1\rangle \otimes |\psi_2\rangle \otimes \cdots$

  The tensor product method relies on a function called *void KroneckerProduct (Matrix$\langle T\rangle$ other, Matrix$\langle T\rangle$ result)*, which is embedded in Math.net.

Simulating measurement with pseudo-random number sampling. A pseudo-random number sampling method simulates quantum measurement in $Q|SI\rangle$. This is a numerical experiment that generates and distributes pseudo-random numbers according to a given probability distribution [6].

Let a quantum measurement be described by a collection of bounded linear operators $\{M_m\}$ that satisfy the completeness condition $\sum_m M_m^\dagger M_m = I$. m

denotes the measurement results, and P denotes the corresponding probability set, where $P = \{p_1, p_2, \ldots, p_m\}$. The indexed variable set is denoted as Y and can be settled to a value of $\{0, 1\}$. The current system state is assumed to be the quantum state $|\psi\rangle$, the indexed variables are $Y_1, \ldots, Y_m$ and the probabilities are $\Pr[Y_i = 1] = p_i$ where $p_i = \langle\psi|M_i^\dagger M_i|\psi\rangle$, $P = \{p_1, \ldots, p_m\}$. A uniform distribution X from $Q|SI\rangle$ is used to simulate a random variable Y.

Math.net provides a random variable X called *RandomSource* which is uniformly distributed between $(0, 1)$. The interval $[0, 1]$ is then divided into m intervals as $[0, p_1], (p_1, p_1 + p_2], \ldots, (\sum_{i=1}^{m-1} p_i, 1]$. The width of interval i equals the probability p_i.

Finally, measurement triggers the following strategy:

1. Given a measurement $\{M_m\}$ and the current quantum state $|\psi\rangle$, $Q|SI\rangle$ computes the set $P = \{p_1, p_2, \ldots, p_m\}$, where $p_i = \langle\psi|M_i^\dagger M_i|\psi\rangle$. This step provides the probability distribution Y: $\Pr[Y = i] = p_i$.
2. $Q|SI\rangle$ checks the elements of P. If there exists any $p_i = 0$, discard the index i in the next step. If there exists any $p_i = 1$, return the index i as the final result and skip the following steps.
3. Assuming P' is a set with the same quantity as P, $Q|SI\rangle$ accumulates the distribution from P to P' with the rules: for each p_i in P', $p_i' = \sum_i p_i$.
4. Draw a number x which is a uniformly pseudo-random number distributed between $(0, 1)$.
5. Find p_i', such that $p_{i-1}' \leq x$ and $p_i' \geq x$ and return the index i. It should be noted that $i = 1$ in the case of $x < p_1'$ and $i = m$ in the case of $x > p_{m-1}'$.

The P distribution of the Y variable where $p_i = \Pr(0 < Y \leq p_i') = \sum_i p_i'$ is a simulated distribution using the uniform distribution variable X. This method of pseudo-random number sampling was developed for Monte-Carlo simulations and its quality is determined by the quality of the pseudo-number.

After i is randomly chosen with a distribution $P = \{p_1, \ldots, p_m\}$, the function returns the value for i and the quantum state is modified as an atom operation. According to quantum mechanics, the state $|\psi\rangle$ will be changed into $|\psi'\rangle = \frac{M_i|\psi\rangle}{\sqrt{\langle\psi|M_i^\dagger M_i|\psi\rangle}}$.

Simulating the operational semantics of the quantum while-language. Simulating the computation of a program written in the quantum **while**-language is based on simulating the operational semantics of the language. To clearly delineate the different types of coding in the quantum simulation engine for mixed classic-quantum programs, quantum **if**-clauses are denoted as **cif** and quantum **while**-clauses are denoted as **cwhile**. The related methods for simulating these two functions are encapsulated in the Quantum Mechanics Library.

The execution of a quantum program can be conveniently described in terms of transitions between configurations.

Definition 1. A quantum configuration is a pair $\langle S, \rho\rangle$, where:

– S is a quantum program or the empty program E (termination);

- ρ is a partial density operator that is used to indicate the (global) state of quantum variables.

With the preparations in the previous subsections, we are able to simulate the transition rules that define the operational semantics of the quantum while-language:

Skip

$$\overline{\langle \mathbf{skip}, \rho \rangle \to \langle \mathbf{E}, \rho \rangle} .$$

The statement **skip** does nothing and terminates immediately. Both the I-identity operation and the null clause must satisfy this procedure requirement to be simulated in $Q|SI\rangle$.

Initialization

$$\overline{\langle q := |0\rangle, \rho \rangle \to \langle \mathbf{E}, \rho_0^q \rangle} ,$$

where

$$\rho_0^q = \begin{cases} |0\rangle_q \langle 0| \rho |0\rangle_q \langle 0| + |0\rangle_q \langle 1| \rho |1\rangle_q \langle 0| & \text{if } type(q) = Boolean, \\ \sum_{n=-\infty}^{\infty} |0\rangle_q \langle n| \rho |n\rangle_q \langle 0| & \text{if } type(q) = Integer. \end{cases}$$

The initialization statement "$q := |0\rangle$" sets the quantum variable q to the basis state $|0\rangle$.

Initialization has two forms in $Q|SI\rangle$. When the variable q is a $QBit$, it is explained as $[\![q := |0\rangle]\!](\rho) = |0\rangle \langle 0| \rho |0\rangle \langle 0| + |0\rangle \langle 1| \rho |1\rangle \langle 0|$; otherwise, it is explained as $[\![q := |0\rangle]\!](\rho) = \sum_{n=0}^{d} |0\rangle \langle n| \rho |n\rangle \langle 0|$, where d is the dimension of the quantum variable q. Moreover, a more flexible initialization method is provided with the help of unitary transformation.

Unitary Revolution

$$\overline{\langle \bar{q} := U[\bar{q}], \rho \rangle \to \langle \mathbf{E}, U\rho U^\dagger \rangle} .$$

The statement "$\bar{q} := U[\bar{q}]$" means that the unitary gate U is performed on the quantum register $\bar{q}$ leaving other variables unchanged.

A corresponding method named

$$QuantumTypes\langle T\rangle.UnitaryTrans(Matrix\langle T\rangle\ other)$$

has been designed to perform this function on $QBit$, Ket, $DensityOperator\langle T\rangle$ objects. This function accepts a unitary operator and performs the operator on the variable with null returns. We have also provided a global function named

$$UnitaryGlobalTrans(QuantumType\langle T\rangle, Matrix\langle T\rangle)$$

that perform an arbitrary unitary matrix on quantum variables.

The quantum **while**-language does not include any assignment claim for a pure state because a unitary operator U exists for any pure state $|\psi\rangle$ that satisfies $|\psi\rangle = U|0\rangle$. Therefore, any pure state can be produced from a combination of an initialization clause and a unitary transformation clause. However, for convenience, $Q|SI\rangle$ provides a flexible state claim to initialize a *QBit*, or a *Ket* using a vector, and to initialize a *DensityOperator$\langle T\rangle$* using a positive matrix.

Sequential composition

$$\frac{\langle S_1, \rho\rangle \to \langle S_1', \rho\rangle}{\langle S_1; S_2, \rho\rangle \to \langle S_1'; S_2, \rho'\rangle}.$$

The current version of the quantum **while**-language is not designed for concurrent programming. Thus sequential composition is spontaneous.

Case Statement

$$\frac{}{\langle \mathbf{if}(\Box m \cdot M[\bar{q}] = m \to S_m)\mathbf{fi}, \rho\rangle \to \langle S_m, M_m \rho M_m^\dagger\rangle},$$

for each possible outcome m of measurement $M = \{M_m\}$.

The first step in executing of the case statement is to perform a measurement M on the quantum variable $\bar{q}$ and observe the output result index. The corresponding subprogram S_m is then chosen according to the index.

Case statements in $Q|SI\rangle$ use an encapsulated function with the prototype

$$\mathbf{cif}(QuantumTypes\langle T\rangle, MeasureMatrixSet, Func\langle T\rangle, Func\langle T\rangle \dots).$$

By default, the $Func\langle T\rangle$ sequence is a subprogram corresponding to a measurement output index, i.e., the nth $Func\langle T\rangle$ corresponds to the nth measurement output index. However, we have also considered cases where the user has not provided a corresponding subprogram for every measurement output index. In these situations, the strategy is to automatically skip that clause if the outcome index exceeds the $Func\langle T\rangle$ number. In fact, this leaves nothing to be done on the variables excepted for a measurement.

Another difference between a classical and a quantum case statement is that the quantum case statement variables must be modified into a state that corresponds to the measurement output index after performing a measurement. The function that returns the measurement result is named

$$int\ Measu2ResultIndex(MeasureMatrixSet).$$

It then goes to the correct subprogram and will inherently call the

$$void\ StateChange(int),$$

which changes the variable $\bar{q}$ to the corresponding state after the measurement.

Loop Statement

$$(L0) \quad \overline{\langle \mathbf{while}(M[\bar{q}] = 1)\mathbf{do}\,S\,\mathbf{od}, \rho \rangle \to \langle \mathbf{E}, M_0 \rho M_0^\dagger \rangle},$$

$$(L1) \quad \overline{\langle \mathbf{while}(M[\bar{q}] = 1)\mathbf{do}\,S\,\mathbf{od}, \rho \rangle \to \langle S; \mathbf{while}(M[\bar{q}] = 1)\mathbf{do}\,S\,\mathbf{od}, M_1 \rho M_1^\dagger \rangle}.$$

An encapsulated function is used to implement this loop statement in $Q|SI\rangle$ with the prototype

$$\mathbf{cwhile}(QuantumTypes\langle T \rangle, MeasureMatrixSet, int, Func\langle T \rangle).$$

This function accepts quantum types, a measurement, and an integer. Then, it compares the measurement result with the given integer in the guard. If the guard has a value of '1', it enters into the loop body; otherwise, it terminates. In addition, the state changes after being measured in the guard. The function

$$int\ Measu2ResultIndex(MeasureMatrixSet)$$

is called to return the result to the guard index and go to the correct subprogram. Then, the *void StateChange(int)* is inherently called as per the case statement.

6   Experiments

Here, we present three experiments to show the power of $Q|SI\rangle$ quantum programming environment: Qloop, BB84 and Grover's search algorithm. Further details are available in the Appendices.

Qloop The Qloop case is a "Hello world" example that includes a quantum channel, a quantum measurement, a quantum **while**-clause and some quantum variables. Essentially, this experiment can be regarded as a simplified quantum walk to illustrate the three main features of the $Q|SI\rangle$ platform - super-operators, unitary transformations and quantum measurement.

The basic idea of a Qloop is to perform a super-operator on a quantum state and leave the state changed. A counter is used to record the number of times the state enters different branches. A measurement is taken for every shot, and the resulting counter should indicate the predicted probability of the state.

BB84 BB84 is a quantum key distribution (QKD) protocol developed by Bennett and Brassard in 1984 [3]. The protocol is an already-proven security protocol [23] that relies on the no-cloning theorem. Using this protocol Alice and Bob reach agreement over a classical key string that can be used to encrypt classical bits.

Several different scenarios are considered in this experiment. The simple BB84 case outlines the basic communications procedure between two clients: Alice and Bob. The multi-client BB84 case illustrates a more practical example where one Alice generates the raw keys, while many Bobs make an agreement key with Alice. The most interesting case is the BB84 protocol in a channel with quantum noise. Because no real quantum systems are ever perfectly closed, super-operators can serve as a key tool for describing the dynamics of open quantum systems. This case explores the influential factors in QKD, revealing that package length and sampling percentages are crucial to real QKD protocols given quantum noise. Different parameters in different channels are tested with $Q|SI\rangle$, each of which can be adjusted for practical purposes when using this protocol.

Grover's search algorithm Grover's search algorithm is an impressive algorithm in the quantum domain. It uses an oracle to solve search task in disorderly databases consisting of N elements, indexed by number $0, 1, \ldots, N-1$. The oracle finds its answers according to position and can find solutions with a high probability within $O(1/N)$ errors and $O(\sqrt{N})$ steps.

A more general multi-object Grover's search is also considered that supposes there is more than one answer (position) for the oracle to find. In this case, we use a blind box strategy that reverses the proper position of the answer. This experiment reveals that Grover's algorithm leads to an avalanche of errors in a multi-object setting, as an indication that the algorithm needs be modified in some way.

7 Conclusions

This paper presents a new software platform, called $Q|SI\rangle$, for programming with quantum computers. In a sense, $Q|SI\rangle$ the potential to enrich and expand the applications where quantum hardware is useful, as: the abundant quantum types, case-statements and loops, $Q|SI\rangle$ provides users to perform experiments beyond the standard flattened quantum circuits. $Q|SI\rangle$ includes an embedded quantum **while**-language, a quantum simulator, and toolkits for quantum program analysis and verification. Combined, these modules create a platform that can be used to simulate quantum algorithms, analyze the termination and average running time of quantum programs, and verify a program's correctness.

Throughout the paper, we demonstrate how to use $Q|SI\rangle$ to simulate quantum behaviors on classical platforms and how to generate instructions for real quantum hardware. We show how to simulate measurement with pseudo-random number sampling, and the method for generating the syntax and semantics of the quantum **while**-language.

Active development of $Q|SI\rangle$ is ongoing. The current implementation of the tensor products is a clumsy way to emulate quantum circuits. In future development, we may need to consider a timing-based and entanglement analysis inspired by [13] to extend $Q|SI\rangle$'s quantum computing power. The termination and average running time modules need to be unified into one format for syntax, and we are considering how to split classical and quantum coding for verification purposes.

Interfaces for different quantum computation programs, such as LIQU$i|\rangle$, ScaffCC and even other quantum computation platforms, such as Microsoft

Azure (Simulator) also need to be considered as these diversified platforms often can provide different views of one quantum program.

Acknowledgments. We are grateful to Professors Michael Blumenstein, Ian Burnett, Yuan Feng, and Glenn Wightwick for their helpful discussions and their strong supports of this project. We also acknowledge use of the IBM Q experience for this work. The views expressed are those of the authors and do not reflect the official policy or position of IBM or the IBM Q experience team.

A   Setup and Configuration of $Q|SI\rangle$

$Q|SI\rangle$ mainly relies on IDE (Visual Studio) to provide the details of the program. After coding a program using $Q|SI\rangle$, the programmer needs to build and compile it. This feature is considered to be an essential component because a smarter IDE is a basic way of ensuring the syntax is correct as programs grow in size and complexity. This feature is unlike IScasMC or QPAT which are not able to execute a program.

NuGet is a part of the .Net development platform and is used in $Q|SI\rangle$ to manage the packages. All packages used to provide functions, such as matrix computation, random number generation, and Roslyn, etc., can be automatically controlled by *NuGet*. To access all the essential packages, a user needs only to add the NuGet feed v3 "https://api.nuget.org/v3/index.json" to their Visual Studio 2017 configuration. This will add the package resources and automatically configure them for the platform.

$Q|SI\rangle$ is compatible with any version of Visual Studio 2015 and later. However, we recommend the Enterprise version of Visual Studio 2017 because of its premium features, e.g., the ability to draw quantum circuits with DGML tools, the most up-to-date Math.net, etc. Examples are stored in the sub-folder UnitTest. All entry-level examples can be found in the 'Program.cs' file in UnitTest.

B   Experiment-Qloop Case

The first example showcases the Qloop case. It uses quantum channels, measurement, quantum **while**-clause and quantum variables. The Qloop case can also be treated as a simplified quantum walk. The flow path is shown in Fig. 5.

B.1   Input and Output

Input:

- $\rho_0 := |+\rangle \langle+|$;
- $\mathcal{E} := \{E_0 = |0\rangle \langle0| + |1\rangle \langle1| /\sqrt{2}, E_1 = |0\rangle \langle1| /\sqrt{2}\}$;
- $M := \{M_0 = |0\rangle \langle0|, M_1 = |1\rangle \langle1|\}$;
- $H := |+\rangle \langle0| + |-\rangle \langle1|$;
- $Counter := 0$.

Output:

- num: the number of circles is num.

B.2   Results

The Qloop experiment executes for approximately $100,000$ shots with the results shown in Fig. 6.

B.3   Features and Analysis

After calculation, it is clear that $\rho_1 = \mathcal{E}(\rho_0) = \frac{3}{4}|0\rangle\langle0| + \frac{1}{4}|1\rangle\langle1| + \frac{1}{2\sqrt{2}}|0\rangle\langle1| + \frac{1}{2\sqrt{2}}|1\rangle\langle0|$, $\rho_2 = |1\rangle\langle1|$, $\rho_1' = |+\rangle\langle+|$ and $\rho_3 = |0\rangle\langle0|$.

The three main features of this experiment include super-operators, unitary transformation, and measurement operations. In addition, processes that consider a qubit's collapse and measurement probability are inherently involved as part of quantum mechanics.

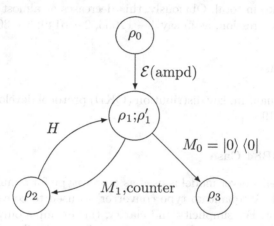

Fig. 5. Qloop

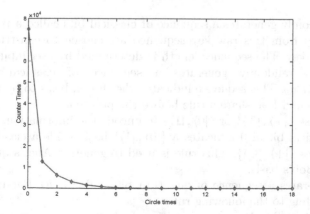

Fig. 6. Qloop data

- Super-operator operation. The initial state passes through a quantum channel and becomes ρ_1. Let M be performed on the state ρ_1 in each shot. There is a $\frac{3}{4}$ probability that the state will change to ρ_3 and then terminate. Likewise, there is a $\frac{1}{4}$ probability of moving in a circle and having the process recorded by the counter. So if the program is executed many times, such as in a $100,000$ shot experiment, the counter should show that the state enters the circle about $25,000$ times.
- Measurement operations and unitary transformations. After the first measurement, ρ_1 may change to ρ_2 and continue, or it may change to ρ_3 and terminates. If the state changes to ρ_2 after a Hadamard operator which is a unitary transformation, it becomes $\rho_1' = |+\rangle\langle+|$ and the counter records the circle once. When a measurement M is performed on the state, we can assert that almost half the time ρ_1' becomes $|0\rangle\langle0|$ and the other half of the time it becomes $|1\rangle\langle1|$. If the result is $|1\rangle\langle1|$, it will enter into the loop body again be recorded by the counter. The counter number shows how many circles the state enters into in total. Obviously, this decreases at almost half the rate of a geometric progression, as in say $1 - 12556, 2 - 6140, 3 - 3095, \ldots$

C   BB84 Case

BB84 is a basic quantum key distribution (QKD) protocol developed by Bennett and Brassard in 1984 [3].

C.1   Simple BB84 Case

In this case, a client-server model is used as a prototype for a multi-user communication protocol. A "quantum type converter" is used to convert a 'Ket' into a density operator. For simplicity and clarity, this example only consider 'Ket' quantum types, not quantum channels or Eves. The entire flow path is shown in Fig. 7.

1. Alice randomly generates a sequence of classical bits called a $rawKeyArray$. Candidates from this raw key sequence are chosen to construct the final agreement key. The sequence length is determined by user input.
2. Alice also randomly generates a sequence of classical bits called $basisRawArray$. This sequence indicates the chosen basis to be used in next step. Alice and Bob share a rule before the protocol:
   - They use $\{|+\rangle, |-\rangle\}$ or $\{|0\rangle, |1\rangle\}$ to encode the information.
   - A classical bit of 0 indicates a $\{|0\rangle, |1\rangle\}$ basis while a classical bit of 1 indicates $\{|+\rangle, |-\rangle\}$. This rule is used to generate Alice's qubits and to check Bob's basis.
3. Alice generates a sequence of quantum bits called a $KetEncArray$, one by one according to the following rules:
   - If the $basisRawArray[i]$ in position [i] is 0 and the $rawKeyArray[i]$ in position [i] is 0, $KetEncArray[i]$ would be $|0\rangle$.

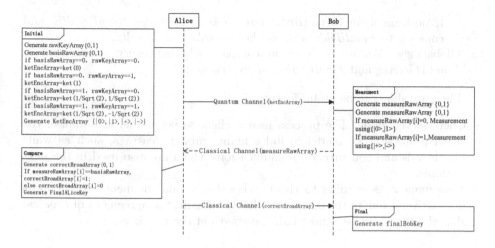

Fig. 7. Simple BB84 protocol

- If the *basisRawArray[i]* in position [i] is 0 and the *rawKeyArray[i]* in position [i] is 1, *KetEncArray[i]* would be $|1\rangle$.
- If the *basisRawArray[i]* in position [i] is 1 and the *rawKeyArray[i]* in position [i] is 0, *KetEncArray[i]* would be $|+\rangle$.
- If the *basisRawArray[i]* in position [i] is 1 and the *rawKeyArray[i]* in position [i] is 1, *KetEncArray[i]* would be $|-\rangle$.

4. Alice sends the *KetEncArray* through a quantum channel. In this case, she sends it through the I channel.
5. Bob receives the *KetEncArray* through the quantum channel.
6. Bob randomly generates a sequence of classical bits called *measureRawArray* to indicate the chosen basis to be used in next step.
7. Bob generates a sequence of classical bits called *tempResult*, using quantum measurement according to the rules:
   - If the *measureRawArray[i]* in [i] position is a classical bit 0, Bob uses a $\{|0\rangle, |1\rangle\}$ basis to measure the *KetEncArray[i]* while a classical bit 1 indicates using a $\{|+\rangle, |-\rangle\}$ basis.
8. Bob broadcasts the *measureRawArray* to Alice using a classical channel.
9. Alice generates a sequence of classical bits called *correctBroadArray*, by comparing Bob's basis *measureRawArray* and her basis *basisRawArray*. If the position [i] is correct, the *correctBroadArray[i]* would be 1; otherwise, it would be 0.
10. Alice sends the sequence *correctBroadArray* to Bob.
11. Alice generates a sequence of classical bits called *FinalALiceKey* using the rule:
    - If position [i] in *correctBroadArray[i]* is 1, she keeps *rawKeyArray[i]* and copies it to *FinalALiceKey* , else she discards *rawKeyArray[i]*.
12. Bob generates a sequence of classical bits called *FinalBobKey* using the rule:

- If position [i] in *correctBroadArray[i]* is 1, he keeps *tempResult[i]* and copies it to *FinalBobKey[i]*, else he discards *tempResult[i]*.
13. GlobalView: We use a function compare whether every position [i] in *FinalALiceKey* and *FinalBobKey[i]* are the same.

This case shows some useful features,

- Client-server mode. The process uses a client-server model to simulate the BB84 protocol. The model includes many implicit features, such as waiting threads and concurrent communications which are also used in the next example.
- Measurement. According to theory, choosing a random measurement basis may arrive at half of the correct result. As a result, the agreement of classical shared bits should be almost half the length of the raw keys.

C.2   BB84 Case, Multi-client

The multi-client BB84 model offers a more attractive and practical example. In this model, one Alice generates the raw keys while many Bobs construct an agreement key with Alice.

In this case, users can specify the number of clients. Also, a typical BB84 flow path would occur for every client-server pair of this model.

This case highlights:

- The threads model. Many clients are generated and communicate with Alice. Each of them finally reaches an agreement.
- Measurement threads. In this case, Alice generates raw keys, and Bob measures the quantum bits. However, this raises a serious question that about clients generate raw keys while a server conducts the measurement: How can we ensure the server correctly and fairly conducts the measurement for the client.

C.3   BB84 Case with Noise

A practical topic for the $Q|SI\rangle$ to consider is the BB84 model with noisy quantum channels. Noisy quantum operations are the key tools for describing the dynamics of open quantum systems.

In this example, different channels such as bit flip, depolarizing, amplitude damping and I-identity channels are described by quantum operations performed as the evolution of quantum systems in a wide variety of circumstances. Alice and Bob use these quantum channels to communicate with each other via the BB84 protocol as Fig. 7 shows. However, during communication, verification steps also need to be considered.

Input and output In this example, the basic quantum channels are defined as follows:

a deplarizing channel with a noise parameter of $p = 0.5$,

$$\mathcal{E} := \left\{ \begin{bmatrix} \frac{\sqrt{5}}{\sqrt{8}} & 0 \\ 0 & \frac{\sqrt{5}}{\sqrt{8}} \end{bmatrix}, \begin{bmatrix} 0 & \frac{1}{\sqrt{8}} \\ \frac{1}{\sqrt{8}} & 0 \end{bmatrix} \begin{bmatrix} 0 & \frac{-i}{\sqrt{8}} \\ \frac{i}{\sqrt{8}} & 0 \end{bmatrix} \begin{bmatrix} \frac{1}{\sqrt{8}} & 0 \\ 0 & -\frac{1}{\sqrt{8}} \end{bmatrix} \right\};$$

an amplitude damping channel with a noise parameter of $\gamma = 0.5$,

$$\mathcal{E} := \left\{ \begin{bmatrix} 1 & 0 \\ 0 & \frac{1}{\sqrt{2}} \end{bmatrix}, \begin{bmatrix} 0 & \frac{1}{\sqrt{2}} \\ 0 & 0 \end{bmatrix} \right\};$$

a bit flip channel with a noise parameter of $p = 0.25$,

$$\mathcal{E} := \left\{ \begin{bmatrix} \frac{1}{2} & 0 \\ 0 & \frac{1}{2} \end{bmatrix}, \begin{bmatrix} 0 & \frac{\sqrt{3}}{2} \\ \frac{\sqrt{3}}{2} & 0 \end{bmatrix} \right\};$$

a bit flip channel with a noise parameter of $p = 0.5$,

$$\mathcal{E} := \left\{ \begin{bmatrix} \frac{1}{\sqrt{2}} & 0 \\ 0 & \frac{1}{\sqrt{2}} \end{bmatrix}, \begin{bmatrix} 0 & \frac{1}{\sqrt{2}} \\ \frac{1}{\sqrt{2}} & 0 \end{bmatrix} \right\};$$

bit flip channel with noise parameter $p = 0.75$,

$$\mathcal{E} := \left\{ \begin{bmatrix} \frac{\sqrt{3}}{2} & 0 \\ 0 & \frac{\sqrt{3}}{2} \end{bmatrix}, \begin{bmatrix} 0 & \frac{1}{2} \\ \frac{1}{2} & 0 \end{bmatrix} \right\}.$$

The flow path follows the simple BB84 protocol shown in Fig. 7. The only differences are in Step 4 and the addition of a sampling step.

- Alice sends the *KetEncArray* through a quantum channel. In this case, it is one of the channels mentioned above.
- Sampling check step: Alice randomly publishes some sampling positions with the bits against these positions in her key string. Bob checks these bits against his key strings. If all the bits in these sampling strings are the same, he believes the key distribution is a success; otherwise, the connection fails.

To use a statistical quantity to characterize success in a channel with the BB84 protocol, we executed a 100-shot experiment for each channel. In every shot for every channel, different sampling percentages and package lengths were considered. The results provided in Fig. 8 shows the trade-off between success times, different sampling proportions and package lengths for each of the quantum channels.

Results. Success times for different sampling percentages in different channels over 100 shots (see Fig. 8).

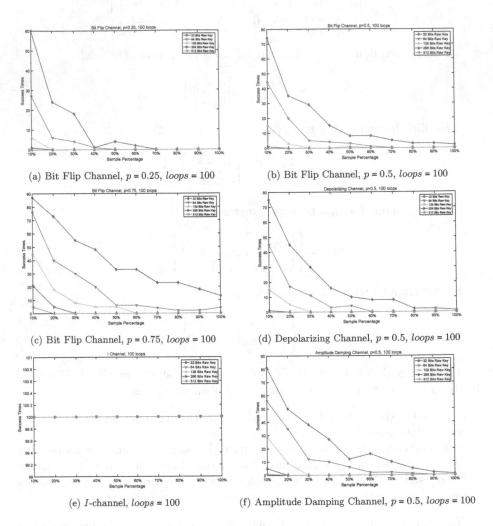

(a) Bit Flip Channel, $p = 0.25$, *loops* = 100

(b) Bit Flip Channel, $p = 0.5$, *loops* = 100

(c) Bit Flip Channel, $p = 0.75$, *loops* = 100

(d) Depolarizing Channel, $p = 0.5$, *loops* = 100

(e) *I*-channel, *loops* = 100

(f) Amplitude Damping Channel, $p = 0.5$, *loops* = 100

Fig. 8. Statistics of success communication via BB84 with channels

Features and Analysis'. The example generates some 'erroneous' bits during communication due to quantum channels which cause a connection failure. Additionally, not all error bits can be found in the sampling step because, in theory, almost half the bits are invalid in the measurement step. Further, the sampling step is also a probability verification step which means it does not use all the agreed bits to verify the communication procedure.

Subfigures (a), (b) and (c) in Fig. 8 are bit flip channels with different probabilities. Overall, the number of successful shots increases as p increases and the raw key length shortens. This is because p is a reflection of the percentage of information that remains in the bit flip channel and an increase in p means fewer errors in communication. A shorter raw key length ensures fewer bits are sampled. Sub-figure (d),(e) and (f) illustrate the communication capacity of the BB84 protocol in the other three channels. Note that the I-identity channel has a 100% success rate, which means it is a noiseless channel and can keep information intact during the transfer procedure.

D   Grover's Search Algorithm

Grover's search algorithm is a well-known quantum algorithm. It solves searching problems in databases consisting of N elements, indexed by number $0, 1, \ldots, N-1$ with an oracle provides the answer as a position. This algorithm can find solutions with a probability of $O(1)$ within $O(\sqrt{N})$ steps.

D.1   A Simple Grover's Search Algorithm

In this example, we assume there is only one answer to the question, i.e., the oracle will only reverse one position at a time. Further, the oracle is assumed to be working as a black box and can reverse the correct position of the answer. After querying the oracle $r = \frac{\pi}{4}\sqrt{N}$ times with the corresponding phase rotations, the quantum state contains the correct information to answer the question.

Input and output. Input:

- The total number of spaces N. For convenience, we have restricted $N = 2^n$.
- The correct position of the search that is used to construct the oracle.

  Output:

- The final position of the measurement result.
- Oracle time r.

Results. The simple Grover's search algorithm has only one result, and the final measurement result shows the correct answer to the searching problem.

Features and analysis. Suppose $|\alpha\rangle = \frac{1}{\sqrt{N-1}}\sum_x'' |x\rangle$ is not the solution but rather $|\beta\rangle = \sum_x' |x\rangle$ is the solution where $\sum_x'$ indicates the sum of all the solutions. The initial state $|\psi\rangle$ may be expressed as

$$|\psi\rangle = \sqrt{\frac{N-1}{N}} |\alpha\rangle + \sqrt{\frac{1}{N}} |\beta\rangle .$$

Every rotation makes the θ to the solution where

$$\sin\theta = \frac{2\sqrt{N-1}}{N} .$$

When N is larger, the gap between the measurement result and the real position number is less than $\theta = \arcsin\frac{2\sqrt{N-1}}{N} \approx \frac{2}{\sqrt{N}}$. Therefore, it is almost impossible to generate the wrong answer within r times.

D.2   Multi-object Grover's Search Algorithm

This experiment considers a more general Grover's search algorithm: a multi-object Grover's search algorithm. This case supposes that there may be more than one correct answer (position) for the oracle to find. We use a strategy that adds a blind box to reverse the proper position of the answer. This experiment reveals that Grover's algorithm leads to an avalanche of error in a multi-object setting, indicating that algorithm needs to be modified in some way.

A new blind box (a unitary gate) is added, which reverses the proper position of the answer. In short, the oracle is a matrix where all the diagonal elements are 1, but all the answer positions are −1. Thus, the blind box is a diagonal matrix where all elements are 1, and all the answer position that have been found are −1. When these two boxes are combined, we create a new oracle with the answers to all the questions except for the ones that were found in previous rounds.

Input and output The input is

- The total number of spaces N. For convenience, we have restricted $N = 2^n$.
- All correct positions of the search.

   The output is

- The final position of the measurement result.
- Oracle time r.

Results The measurement shows different probabilities of the final result. The theory holds that if we have multiple-answers, the state after r times oracles and phase gates becomes a state near to both. For example, if the answers are $|2\rangle, |14\rangle \in \mathcal{H}_{64}$, the state before the measurement is expected to be almost $\frac{1}{\sqrt{2}}(|2\rangle + |14\rangle)$. We should get $|2\rangle$ or $|14\rangle$ the first time and the other one the next time. However, we get results other than $|2\rangle$ and $|14\rangle$ with high probability, which indicates that the multi-object search algorithm is not very good.

Features and analysis It worth noting that due to multi-objects, the real state after using Grover's search algorithm becomes $a(|2\rangle + |14\rangle) + b(|1\rangle + |3\rangle + |4\rangle + |5\rangle + ...)$ where $a, b \in \mathcal{C}$ and $|a|^2 + |b|^2 = 1$. However, b cannot be ignored even if it is very small. An interesting issue occurs when the wrong position index is found. If the wrong index is measured, the algorithm creates an incorrect blind box and reverses the wrong position of the oracle, i.e., it adds a new answer to the questions. In next round, the proportion of correct answers is further reduced. In the last example, we would measured an incorrect answer, say $|5\rangle$. After the new procedure, the state would become: $a(|2\rangle + |14\rangle + |5\rangle) + b(|1\rangle + |3\rangle + |4\rangle + |5\rangle + ...)$, making it even harder to find the correct answer.

References

1. Barenco, A., Bennett, C.H., Cleve, R., DiVincenzo, D.P., Margolus, N., Shor, P., Sleator, T., Smolin, J.A., Weinfurter, H.: Elementary gates for quantum computation. Phys. Rev. A **52**(5), 3457 (1995)

2. Beals, R., Brierley, S., Gray, O., Harrow, A.W., Kutin, S., Linden, N., Shepherd, D., Stather, M.: Efficient distributed quantum computing. In: Proc. R. Soc. A. vol. 469, p. 20120686. The Royal Society (2013)
3. Bennett, C.H., Brassard, G.: Quantum cryptography: public key distribution and coin tossing. Theor. Comput. Sci. **560**, 7–11 (2014)
4. Bettelli, S., Calarco, T., Serafini, L.: Toward an architecture for quantum programming. Eur. Phys.J. D-Atomic, Mol. Opt. Plasma Phys. **25**(2), 181–200 (2003)
5. Dawson, C.M., Nielsen, M.A.: The solovay-kitaev algorithm. arXiv preprint quant-ph/ arXiv:0505030 (2005)
6. Devroye, L.: Sample-based non-uniform random variate generation. In: Proceedings of the 18th conference on Winter simulation, pp. 260–265 (1986)
7. Green, A.S., Lumsdaine, P.L., Ross, N.J., Selinger, P., Valiron, B.: Quipper: a scalable quantum programming language. In: ACM SIGPLAN Notices, vol. 48, pp. 333–342. ACM (2013)
8. Grover, L.K.: A fast quantum mechanical algorithm for database search. In: Proceedings of the twenty-eighth annual ACM symposium on Theory of computing, pp. 212–219. ACM (1996)
9. Harrow, A.W., Hassidim, A., Lloyd, S.: Quantum algorithm for linear systems of equations. Phys. Rev. Lett. **103**(15), 150502 (2009)
10. Hirata, Y., Nakanishi, M., Yamashita, S., Nakashima, Y.: An efficient conversion of quantum circuits to a linear nearest neighbor architecture. Q. Inf. Comput. **11**(1&2), 142–166 (2011)
11. qubit backend: IBM QX team,: ibmqx3 backend specification. Retrieved from https://ibm.biz/qiskit-ibmqx3 (2017)
12. qubit backend: IBM QX team,: ibmqx2 backend specification. Retrieved from https://ibm.biz/qiskit-ibmqx2 (2017)
13. JavadiAbhari, A., et al.: Scaffcc: a framework for compilation and analysis of quantum computing programs. In: Proceedings of the 11th ACM Conference on Computing Frontiers, p. 1 (2014)
14. JavadiAbhari, A., Patil, S., Kudrow, D., Heckey, J., Lvov, A., Chong, F.T., Martonosi, M.: Scaffcc: scalable compilation and analysis of quantum programs. Parallel Comput. **45**, 2–17 (2015)
15. Jones, C., Gyure, M.F., Ladd, T.D., Fogarty, M.A., Morello, A., Dzurak, A.S.: A logical qubit in a linear array of semiconductor quantum dots. arXiv preprint arXiv:1608.06335 (2016)
16. Liu, T., Li, Y., Wang, S., Ying, M., Zhan, N.: A theorem prover for quantum hoare logic and its applications. arXiv preprint arXiv:1601.03835 (2016)
17. Nielsen, M.A., Chuang, I.L.: Quantum Computation and Quantum Information. Cambridge University Press, Cambridge (2010)
18. Ömer, B.: A procedural formalism for quantum computing (1998)
19. Sanders, J.W., Zuliani, P.: Quantum programming. In: Backhouse, R., Oliveira, J.N. (eds.) MPC 2000. LNCS, vol. 1837, pp. 80–99. Springer, Heidelberg (2000). https://doi.org/10.1007/10722010_6
20. Selinger, P.: A brief survey of quantum programming languages. In: Kameyama, Y., Stuckey, P.J. (eds.) FLOPS 2004. LNCS, vol. 2998, pp. 1–6. Springer, Heidelberg (2004). https://doi.org/10.1007/978-3-540-24754-8_1
21. Shende, V., Bullock, S., Markov, I.: Synthesis of quantum-logic circuits. IEEE Trans. Comput.-Aided Des. Integr. Circuits Syst. **25**(6), 1000–1010 (2006)
22. Shor, P.W.: Polynomial-time algorithms for prime factorization and discrete logarithms on a quantum computer. SIAM Rev. **41**(2), 303–332 (1999)

23. Shor, P.W., Preskill, J.: Simple proof of security of the bb84 quantum key distribution protocol. Phys. Rev. Lett. **85**(2), 441 (2000)

24. Smelyanskiy, M., Sawaya, N.P., Aspuru-Guzik, A.: qhipster: the quantum high performance software testing environment. arXiv preprint arXiv:1601.07195 (2016)

25. Smith, R.S., Curtis, M.J., Zeng, W.J.: A practical quantum instruction set architecture. arXiv preprint arXiv:1608.03355 (2016)

26. Svore, K.M., Aho, A.V., Cross, A.W., Chuang, I., Markov, I.L.: A layered software architecture for quantum computing design tools. IEEE Comput. **39**(1), 74–83 (2006)

27. Veldhorst, M., Yang, C., Hwang, J., Huang, W., Dehollain, J., Muhonen, J., Simmons, S., Laucht, A., Hudson, F., Itoh, K., et al.: A two-qubit logic gate in silicon. Nature **526**(7573), 410–414 (2015)

28. Wecker, D., Svore, K.M.: Liquid: A software design architecture and domain-specific language for quantum computing. arXiv preprint arXiv:1402.4467 (2014)

29. Ying, M.: Floyd-hoare logic for quantum programs. ACM Trans. Program. Lang. Syst. (TOPLAS) **33**(6), 19 (2011)

30. Ying, M.: Foundations of Quantum Programming. Morgan Kaufmann, Burlington (2016)

31. Ying, M., Feng, Y.: Quantum loop programs. Acta Inf. **47**(4), 221–250 (2010)

32. Ying, M., Feng, Y.: A flowchart language for quantum programming. IEEE Trans. Soft. Eng. **37**(4), 466–485 (2011)

33. Ying, M., Ying, S., Wu, X.: Invariants of quantum programs: characterisations and generation. In: Proceedings of the 44th ACM SIGPLAN Symposium on Principles of Programming Languages, pp. 818–832. ACM (2017)

34. Ying, M., Yu, N., Feng, Y., Duan, R.: Verification of quantum programs. Sci. Comput. Program. **78**(9), 1679–1700 (2013)

The Demon, the Gambler, and the Engineer
Reconciling Hybrid-System Theory with Metrology

Martin Fränzle and Paul Kröger$^{(\boxtimes)}$

Department of Computing Science, Carl von Ossietzky Universität Oldenburg,
26111 Oldenburg, Germany
{martin.fraenzle,paul.kroeger}@informatik.uni-oldenburg.de

Abstract. Hybrid discrete-continuous system dynamics arises when discrete actions, e.g. by a decision algorithm, meet continuous behaviour, e.g. due to physical processes and continuous control. Various flavours of hybrid automata have been suggested as a means to formally analyse such dynamical systems, among them deterministic automata models facilitating reasoning about their normative behaviour, nondeterministic automata under a demonic interpretation supporting worst-case analysis, and stochastic variants enabling quantitative verification. In this article, we demonstrate that all these variants provide imprecise, in the sense of either overly pessimistic or overly optimistic, verdicts for engineered systems operating under uncertain observation of their environment due to, e.g., measurement error. We argue that even the most elaborate models of hybrid automata currently available ignore wisdom from metrology and game theory concerning environmental state estimation to be pursued by a rational player, which a control system obviously ought to constitute. We consequently suggest a revised formal model, called Bayesian hybrid automata, that is able to represent state tracking and estimation in hybrid systems and thereby enhances precision of verdicts obtained from the model.

1 Introduction

Hybrid systems and their associated hybrid discrete-continuous dynamic behaviour are the result of connecting discrete and continuous dynamic processes, as in the case of embedded computers and their physical environment. An increasing number of the technical artefacts shaping our ambience are relying on such cyber-physical interaction. Within these artefacts, embedded computing

---

For their work on this subject, the authors received funding from Deutsche Forschungsgemeinschaft under grant number DFG GRK 1765, covering the Research Training Group SCARE: System Correctness under Adverse Conditions.

M. Fränzle dedicates this article to Zhou Chaochen in grateful remembrance of Zhou introducing him to the field of formal models for hybrid-system dynamics a quarter of a century ago.

© Springer Nature Switzerland AG 2018
C. Jones et al. (Eds.): Zhou-Festschrift, LNCS 11180, pp. 165–185, 2018.
https://doi.org/10.1007/978-3-030-01461-2_9

interfaces to physical environments via sensors and actuators, and these entities interact in a complex and often safety-critical manner, having sensitive variables of the environment in their sphere of control. Everyday examples include process control at all scales, ranging from household appliances over chemical processing to nuclear power plants, or embedded systems in the transportation domain, such as highly automated driving in automotive, aircraft collision avoidance protocols in avionics, or automatic train control applications on high-speed tracks.

The behaviour of such hybrid discrete-continuous systems cannot be fully understood without explicitly modelling and analysing the tight interaction of their discrete switching behaviour and their continuous dynamics, as mutual feedback confines fully separate analysis to limited cases. Tools for building such integrated models and for simulating their approximate dynamics are commercially available, e.g. Simulink with the Stateflow extension[1]. Simulation is, however, inherently incomplete and has to be complemented by *verification*, which amounts to showing that the coupled dynamics of the embedded system and its environment is well-behaved, regardless of the actual disturbance and the influences of the application context, as entering through the open inputs of the system under investigation. Basic notions of being well-behaved demand that the system under investigation may never reach an undesirable state (*safety*), that it will converge to a certain set of states (*stabilisation*), or that it can be guaranteed to eventually reach a desirable state (*progress*).

To facilitate such formal verification, corresponding mathematical models of the dynamics of hybrid systems have been proposed. The prototypical mathematical abstraction is the *hybrid automaton* [1,2] coupling a finite-state control skeleton with a continuous state-space spanned by real-valued variables. The continuous state has its dynamics governed by differential equations depending on the control-skeleton state (often called a *discrete mode*), and vice versa state dynamics of the control skeleton is controlled by predicates on the continuous state. Various flavours of hybrid automata have been suggested as a means to formally analyse different aspects of hybrid-state dynamical systems, among them deterministic hybrid automata models facilitating reasoning about their normative behaviour, nondeterministic hybrid automata under a demonic interpretation supporting worst-case analysis with respect to disturbances and measurement error, and stochastic hybrid automata variants enabling quantitative verification [3–8].

Encoding an actual hybrid system in one of the aforementioned modelling frameworks is in general considered a tedious, yet mostly straightforward activity: it is assumed that they are rich enough to accommodate adequate models of standard components, like sensors measuring physical quantities and actuators modifying such quantities, as well as standard models of physical dynamics, continuous control, and mode-switching control. All that would then be required would first be to model the particular physical system under consideration, which may involve ordinary or stochastic differential equations, second to design continuous control and model it by means of differentio-integral equations, third to

---

[1] http://www.mathworks.com/products.

design discrete control and model it by means of automata, and finally to instantiate sensor and actuator models. Building the concurrent, time-synchronous composition of the aforementioned model components completes the modelling effort. After this effort, the hybrid-automaton model could then be used to derive reliable and—if enough modelling effort was invested—accurate verdicts about the system dynamics.

In this article, we demonstrate that contrary to the intuition underlying the above modelling pragmatics, the quest for precise verdicts cannot be satisfied by even the most expressive of the aforementioned hybrid automata variants. All these variants are bound to provide safe yet inherently imprecise, in the sense of being either overly pessimistic or overly optimistic, verdicts for engineered systems operating under uncertain observation of their environment due to, e.g., measurement error. We identify the state spaces underlying the traditional hybrid automata models as the source of this deficiency, as they are spanned by a finite-dimensional vector space being the product of $\mathbb{R}$ and a finite set of control modes. Such a state space is finite-dimensional and thus cannot incorporate functions over the $\mathbb{R}^n$ as state components, which would be necessary for representing distributions, as pertinent in metrology for state estimation from uncertain measurements. We argue that consequently even the most elaborate models of hybrid automata currently available ignore wisdom from metrology and game theory concerning environmental state estimation to be pursued by a rational player, which a control system obviously ought to constitute. We consequently suggest a revised formal model, called *Bayesian hybrid automata* (BHA), that is able to represent state tracking and estimation in hybrid systems. Both the inherent imprecision of the classical automata models, i.e., their substantial pessimism or optimism in the verdicts attainable, and the enhanced precision of the revised model of BHA are rigorously demonstrated on a running example.

Organisation of the paper. In the subsequent section, we discuss related work in order to identify a current lack of models for hybrid dynamics being able to directly accommodate inference mechanisms about uncertain state observation. This would, however, not necessarily imply that current models are too weak for producing concise verdicts of system correctness, as an encoding of pertinent methods for fusing measurements could well be possible within the existing models. In Sect. 3, we therefore demonstrate by means of a running example that traditional hybrid system models are bound to fail in providing the expected verdicts. This in turn motivates us to introduce a revised model of hybrid systems, called Bayesian hybrid automata, in Sect. 4, where we also demonstrate that it is able to yield the expected verdicts. Section 5 concludes our paper.

2   Related Work

An essential characteristic of hybrid discrete-continuous systems, or hybrid systems (HS) for short, is the combination of a continuous state space that evolves over time with a number of discrete modes determining the dynamics of the continuous evolution. Modelling such systems as hybrid automata has a long tradition [1,2]. In their qualitative form, these automata can be either deterministic or nondeterministic in their evolution over time and in the choice of a discrete successor mode, thereby supporting qualitative reasoning over the normative behaviour or the worst-case behaviour of the system.

The aforementioned qualitative models do not allow to derive quantitative figures about the satisfaction of safety targets, e.g., the likelihood of eventually reaching an undesirable operational state. Probabilistic or stochastic extensions of hybrid automata, so-called stochastic hybrid automata [9], enable such a quantification by considering probability distributions over (not necessarily all) uncertain choices. Several variants of such a quantification have been studied, e.g. hybrid automata with discrete [3,5] or continuous [6] distributions over discrete transitions as well as stochastic differential dynamics within a discrete mode [7].

These models support the qualitative and quantitative analysis of systems subject to noise, yet do assume that control decisions are taken based on perfect knowledge about the current system state, as they lack pertinent means for expressing the effects of state estimation and filtering known to be central to rational strategies in games of incomplete information [10, Chaps. 9–11] and thus in optimal control under uncertainty.

Formal modelling of such systems taking rational decisions based on best estimates of the uncertain and only partially observable state of other agents inherently requires to incorporate two levels of probabilism: first, in the model of system dynamics as probabilistic occurrences of sequences of observations; second, as distributions representing the best estimations the embedded controller can make about the state of its environment based on the observations available. Consequently, such a model has to accommodate distributions over state estimations, which are themselves distributions, rather than just distributions over scalar state.

While distributions over sequences of observations can be handled by traditional stochastic automata in terms of probabilistic occurrences of execution paths, the aforementioned modelling frameworks are not yet able to reflect decisions and thus changes of behaviour based on best estimations made according to those sequences. Such a model first requires the estimations to be explicitly available in the state space for evaluations underlying decisions (e.g., in the evaluation of a transition guard) and secondly correlated observations have to be fused to obtain best estimations, e.g. in form of Bayes filters [11–13]. Such probabilistic filters are widely used in robotics, e.g. for the estimation of occupancy grids [14,15], in robust fault detection under noisy environments [16], or for estimating parameters of stochastic processes in biological tissues or molecular structures [17].

Aiming at approximating Maximum Likelihood Estimates for parameters of non-linear systems with non-Gaussian noise, Murphy [18] considers state estimation with switching Kálmán filters in presence of multiple linear dynamic models. In his setting, the time instances at which a certain linear dynamics is switched in are unknown up to a known stochastic distribution. In combination with stochastic state observations, this gives rise to state estimations in form of joint distributions, approximated by mixtures of Gaussian distributions, similar to the desired estimations. However, in addition to limited dynamics, switching between modes is based on Markovian dynamics, i.e. it is not possible to model switching based on probabilistic constraints on state estimations as necessary to model rational decisions about changing a mode as a response to the estimated behaviour of the observed state.

The consequential necessity of applying Bayesian filtering within hybrid systems implementing optimal control was already discovered by Ding et. al. [19]. They present a theoretical approach to derive optimal control policies for partially observable discrete time stochastic hybrid systems, where optimality is defined in terms of achieving the maximum probability that the system remains in a set of safe states. In order to be able to apply dynamic programming in search for an optimal solution, Ding et al. replace the partially observable system by an equivalent perfect information system via a sufficient statistics in form of a Bayes filter. This is very close to our approach in mindset, as a sufficient statistics about a Bayesian estimate of the imperfectly known actual system state is at the heart of rational decisions in control under uncertainty. The main difference is that we are trying to formulate a general model facilitating the behavioural analysis of such optimal hybrid control systems, while Ding et al. aim at the construction of such controllers wrt. a given safety goal. The latter facilitates a decomposition of the design problem into obtaining a Bayesian filtering process and developing a—then scalar-valued—control skeleton. This renders a direct integration, as pursued in this article, of state distributions and Bayesian inference mechanisms into the state space of an analytical model unnecessary.

3 Traditional Hybrid Automata Models

Hybrid automata traditionally span a finite-dimensional state space over the product of the reals and a finite set of discrete modes. This base model comes in various flavours, which are distinguished by the form of dynamics supported in both discrete transitions and continuous evolutions. In the sequel, we will employ three typical variants, namely hybrid automata with deterministic transitions, with nondeterministic transitions, and with stochastically branching transitions for modelling environmental sensing in a running example representing a simple driving scenario from the automotive domain. In all cases, we will confine the continuous dynamics in the example to piecewise constant derivatives, as its exact shape is not really relevant to the effects observed. For all three automata variants, we will analyse the verdicts that can be obtained for two typical functional requirements, one dealing with safety, the other with liveness.

3.1 Running Example

Consider the extremely simplified traffic situation depicted in Fig. 1. The ego vehicle, labelled by E, is driving along a road while another uncontrolled vehicle,

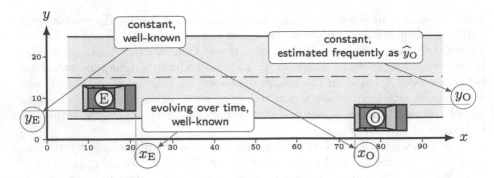

Fig. 1. Simplified traffic situation: ego vehicle E tries to pass obstacle O whenever possible while staying in its lane, or shall otherwise halt to avoid a collision.

labelled by O, is parked at some distance on the roadside. Car O possibly overlaps the lane of car E, i.e., car E is in danger of colliding with car O.

We assume that car E cannot perform a lateral evasive manoeuvre, possibly due to dense oncoming traffic. Our small system thus comprises three rigid variables y_E, x_O, and y_O describing the geometric situation as well as a continuously evolving variable x_E representing the longitudinal position of the ego car. All values except y_O are exactly known to the ego car E. The value of y_O, however, has to be determined by sensing the environment via a possibly inaccurate measurement yielding an estimate $\widehat{y}_O$ for y_O. For the sake of providing a concrete instance, we assume a normally distributed measurement error, i.e., $\widehat{y}_O \sim \mathcal{N}(y_O, \sigma^2)$, though our findings do not hinge on that particular distribution. As a further non-critical simplification we assume that car E will either drive with a pre-defined speed ($\dot{x}_E = 1$) or stand still ($\dot{x}_E = 0$) and that it can switch between these two modes instantaneously.

The overall goal is to prove that the ego car is safe and live. Liveness in this context means that car E eventually passes car O whenever $y_E > y_O$. Safety is defined as the exclusion of the possibility of a collision, i.e., that $x_E < x_O$ is invariant over time whenever $y_E \leq y_O$. These two properties can be formalised as follows using a straightforward extension of CTL featuring relational atoms over continuous signals akin to Signal Temporal Logic [20]:

$$\textbf{safe} := (y_E \leq y_O) \Rightarrow \textbf{AG}\,(x_E < x_O) \tag{1a}$$

$$\textbf{live} := (y_E > y_O) \Rightarrow \textbf{AF}\,(x_E \geq x_O) \tag{1b}$$

In the remainder of this section, we compare different classes of hybrid automata by creating a corresponding automaton for our example and analysing the resulting models wrt. the system properties above. In this comparison, our focus will be on the handling of the inaccuracy induced by the sensor system, i.e., we employ deterministic, nondeterministic, or stochastic transitions as a model of environmental sensing.

3.2 Deterministic Environmental Sensing

Initial phases of control system design address normative behaviour of the overall system in order to get the control logic right. Following this rationale, a lot of hybrid-system modelling and verification ignores implementation effects and employs idealised models of the feedback loop between controller and environment. This entails exclusion of measurement error from the analytic model, instead assuming identity between environmental variables and the variables used inside the controller for drawing decisions. In fact, it is common practice in hybrid-system modelling and verification to not even distinguish between environmental variables and their representation in the controller-internal real-time image of the world, like we do with y_O vs. $\hat{y}_O$, and instead directly refer to environmental variables in guards etc.

Before we formalise such a model for our running example, we briefly introduce hybrid automata formally akin to the definition of Kowalewski et al. [9]:

Definition 1 (Hybrid Automaton). *A hybrid automaton is a tuple* $HA = (\mathcal{M}, \mathcal{V}, \mathbf{d}, \mathbf{i}, \mathcal{T}, \mathbf{g}, \mathbf{u}, \mathcal{I})$ *where*

- $\mathcal{M} = \{m_0, m_1, \cdots, m_k\}$ *is a finite set of discrete* control modes,
- $\mathcal{V} = \{v_0, v_1, \cdots, v_n\}$ *is a finite set of* continuous variables,
- $\mathbf{d} : \mathcal{M} \times \mathbb{R}^n \to \mathbb{R}^n$ *is a* mode-dependent vector field *defining the evolution of the continuous variables in reation to the control mode,*
- $\mathbf{i} : \mathcal{M} \to 2^{\mathbb{R}^n}$ *is a function describing the* invariants *per control mode, i.e. the part of the continuous state space for which the system may remain in the corresponding control mode,*
- $\mathcal{T} \subseteq \mathcal{M} \times \mathcal{M}$ *is the* transition relation *between discrete modes,*
- $\mathbf{g} : \mathcal{T} \to 2^{\mathbb{R}^n}$ *is the* guard function *assigning each transition a subset of the continuous state space for which the transition is enabled, i.e. the transition can be taken iff the current continuous state is an element of that subset,*
- $\mathbf{u} : \mathcal{T} \times \mathbb{R}^n \to 2^{\mathbb{R}^n}$ *is the* update function *that updates the continuous state space when the transition is taken, and*
- $\mathcal{I} \subseteq \mathcal{M} \times \mathbb{R}^n$ *is the set of valid* initial states.

A tuple $(m, \mathbf{v}) \in \mathcal{M} \times \mathbb{R}^n$ *is a state of the automaton* HA *whenever* $\mathbf{v} \in \mathbf{i}(m)$. *The vector* $\mathbf{v}$ *represents the continuous part of the state space.*

Such a hybrid automaton starts from an initial state in $\mathcal{I}$ and then engages in an alternating sequence of continuous evolutions $\xrightarrow{\delta} \subseteq (\mathcal{M} \times \mathbb{R}^n)^2$, for $\delta \geq 0$, and instantaneous jumps $\xrightarrow{\tau} \subseteq (\mathcal{M} \times \mathbb{R}^n)^2$, for $\tau \in \mathcal{T}$. A continuous evolution $(m, \mathbf{x}) \xrightarrow{\delta} (m', \mathbf{x}')$ is possible iff $m' = m$ and there is a solution $\mathbf{y} : [0, \delta] \to \mathbf{i}(m)$ to the ordinary differential equation $\frac{d\mathbf{x}}{dt} = \mathbf{d}(m, \mathbf{x})$ with $\mathbf{y}(0) = \mathbf{x}$ and $\mathbf{y}(\delta) = \mathbf{x}'$. A jump $(m, \mathbf{x}) \xrightarrow{\tau} (m', \mathbf{x}')$ is possible iff $\tau = (m, m')$ and $\mathbf{x} \in \mathbf{g}(\tau) \cap \mathbf{i}(m)$ and $\mathbf{x}' \in \mathbf{u}(\tau, \mathbf{x})$.

In order to model our exemplary system as a hybrid automaton, we freely choose the initial positions of the vehicles as illustrated in Fig. 1. In addition, we introduce a clock c serving as a timer that initiates a measurement. We obtain the following automaton of which the graphical representation is shown in Fig. 2:

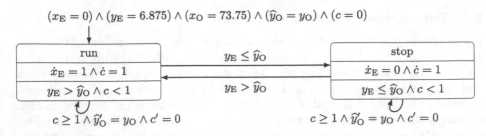

$$(x_E = 0) \wedge (y_E = 6.875) \wedge (x_O = 73.75) \wedge (\widehat{y}_O = y_O) \wedge (c = 0)$$

Fig. 2. Hybrid automaton formalising the dynamics of the running example under the assumption of ideal measurement. The ego vehicle switches between modes based on measurements that accurately reflect the true position of car O.

- $\mathcal{M} = \{\text{run}, \text{stop}\}$
- $\mathcal{V} = \{x_E, y_E, x_O, \widehat{y}_O, c\}$
- $\mathbf{d}((m, \boldsymbol{v})) =$

$$\dot{\boldsymbol{v}}_m(t) = \left(\dot{x}_E(t), \dot{y}_E(t), \dot{x}_O(t), \dot{\widehat{y}}_O(t), \dot{c}(t)\right)^T_m = \begin{cases} (0,0,0,0,1)^T & \text{iff } m = \text{stop} \\ (1,0,0,0,1)^T & \text{otherwise} \end{cases}$$

- $\mathbf{i}(m) = \begin{cases} y_E > \widehat{y}_O \wedge c < 1 & \text{iff } m = \text{run} \\ y_E \le \widehat{y}_O \wedge c < 1 & \text{otherwise} \end{cases}$
- $\mathcal{T} = \mathcal{M} \times \mathcal{M}$
- $\mathbf{g}(u) = \begin{cases} c \ge 1 & \text{iff } u = (\text{run}, \text{run}) \vee u = (\text{stop}, \text{stop}) \\ y_E \le \widehat{y}_O & \text{iff } u = (\text{run}, \text{stop}) \\ y_E > \widehat{y}_O & \text{otherwise} \end{cases}$
- $\mathbf{u}(u, \boldsymbol{v}) = \begin{cases} \left\{(x_E, y_E, x_O, y_O, 0)^T\right\} & \text{iff } u = (\text{run}, \text{run}) \vee u = (\text{stop}, \text{stop}) \\ \{\boldsymbol{v}\} & \text{otherwise} \end{cases}$
- $\mathcal{I} = \left\{\left(\text{run}, (0, 0.6875, 73.75, y_O, 0)^T\right)\right\}$

Note that the discrete transitions from mode run to mode run or from mode stop to mode stop, resp., represent taking a measurement. As measurement error is excluded from the model, this amounts to just copying the value of y_O to the variable $\widehat{y}_O$ representing the measured quantity.

Analysing the above model wrt. the desired properties (1a) and (1b) yields the following results also summarised in Table 1a:

- *Safety results:* For $y_E > y_O$, the safety property (1a) is trivially satisfied. For $y_E \le y_O$, the analysis finds the system to be safe: under the assumption of perfect knowledge, it is not possible to reach an unsafe state because the system immediately switches to stop and cannot switch to run again.
- *Liveness results:* For $y_E > y_O$, the liveness property (1b) is found to be satisfied: due to the assumption of perfect knowledge, it is not possible that the system switches to stop. Thus, the ego vehicle will eventually pass car O. For $y_E \le y_O$, the liveness property is trivially satisfied.

The analysis promises a perfect system that is safe and live. But due to the assumption of perfect knowledge, this model does not represent the true behaviour of the system and thus the results of the analysis are possibly inaccurate verdicts wrt. the real system.

It is easy to see that this is indeed the case: the verdict obtained on the idealised model obviously is optimistic. Remember that the sensor system actually is bound to yield inexact measurements. Therefore the result for the safety property for $y_E \leq y_O$ is wrong: due to the normally distributed measurement error, always eventually a measurement $y_E > \widehat{y}_O$ will arise s.t. car E can return to mode run if currently in mode stop. Hence, whenever car E detects the obstacle and stops, it will eventually continue driving until the obstacle is re-detected. For unbounded runs of the system, a collision is therefore guaranteed while for step-bounded runs a collision occurs with some positive probability which depends on the actual distances $x_O - x_E$ and $y_O - y_E$ as well as the variance of the error distribution and the number of steps. Therefore, the safety property is satisfied with some probability only, which is strictly less than 1 for bounded and 0 for unbounded runs. The unconditional safety attested by the idealised model consequently is severely optimistic.

3.3 Demonic Modelling

Responsible engineers will possibly not adopt an as optimistic perspective as above and instead refine their model. A frequent suggestion is to exploit the power of demonic nondeterminism for obtaining a safe model. In such a setting the existence of measurement errors is represented in a qualitative manner by means of nondeterministically disturbed assignments of environmental quantities to their real-time images in the controller. The systems are then rendered safe by introducing appropriate safety margins around unsafe areas of the state space into the control design.

Definition 1 of hybrid automata already incorporates nondeterminism and thus readily provides the possibility to model such a system. In order to analyse the system wrt. safety and liveness, the nondeterminism has to be resolved demonically which yields a worst case analysis. The qualitative character of the measurement error requires that the safety margin covers all possible errors.

Table 1. Analysis results for the different models. The symbol $\rightarrow$ denotes a probability converging to the given value in the long run, yet staying properly between 0 and 1 for any bounded run-length.

	safe	live
$y_E > y_O$	sat	sat
$y_E \leq y_O$	sat	sat

(a) idealised model

	safe	live
$y_E > y_O + \varepsilon + \max(e)$	sat	sat
$y_O + \varepsilon + \max(e) \geq y_E > y_O$	sat	unsat
$y_E \leq y_O \wedge \varepsilon \geq \max(e)$	sat	sat
$y_E \leq y_O \wedge \varepsilon < \max(e)$	unsat	sat

(b) demonic model

	$p(\textbf{safe})$	$p(\textbf{live})$
$y_E > y_O$	1	$\rightarrow 1$
$y_E \leq y_O$	$\rightarrow 0$	1

(c) stochastic model

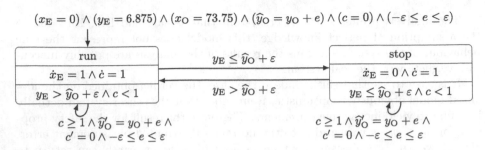

Fig. 3. Demonic hybrid automaton for the running example. The ego vehicle switches to the run mode only when progressing is safe even under worst-case measurement error.

Hence, we widen the condition for stopping by a safety margin at least as large as the maximum measurement error. This in turn requires that we confine the carrier of the measurement interval to a finite range, simply suppressing in the model the exceptionally high measurement deviations due to their low probability of occurrence. It should be noted that this constitutes an uncontrolled modelling error of its own. But even if we ignore that optimistic inaccuracy in the demonic model, the verdicts obtained from the demonic model are not fully satisfactory.

Before we discuss the verdicts, we provide the demonic model for our running example. Let $e \in [-\varepsilon, \varepsilon]$ be the measurement error. We assume the worst case value of e, i.e. $-\varepsilon$, to define an appropriate safety margin (see also Fig. 3):

$$- \mathbf{i}(m) = \begin{cases} y_E > \widehat{y}_O + \varepsilon \wedge c < 1 & \text{iff } m = \text{run} \\ y_E \leq \widehat{y}_O + \varepsilon \wedge c < 1 & \text{otherwise} \end{cases}$$

$$- \mathbf{g}(u) = \begin{cases} c \geq 1 & \text{iff } u = (\text{run}, \text{run}) \vee u = (\text{stop}, \text{stop}) \\ y_E \leq \widehat{y}_O + \varepsilon & \text{iff } u = (\text{run}, \text{stop}) \\ y_E > \widehat{y}_O + \varepsilon & \text{otherwise} \end{cases}$$

$$- \mathbf{u}(u, v) = \begin{cases} \left\{ (x_E, y_E, x_O, y_O + e, 0)^T \mid -\varepsilon \leq e \leq \varepsilon \right\} & \text{iff } u = (\text{run}, \text{run}) \\ & \vee u = (\text{stop}, \text{stop}) \\ \{v\} & \text{otherwise} \end{cases}$$

$$- \mathcal{I} = \left\{ \left(\text{run}, (0, 0.6875, 73.75, y_O + e, 0)^T \right) \mid -\varepsilon \leq e \leq \varepsilon \right\}$$

Table 1b presents the results of the analysis of the demonic model wrt. the requirement properties:

- *Safety results:* Again, for $y_E > y_O$, the safety property (1a) is trivially satisfied. Given $y_E \leq y_O$ and $\varepsilon \geq \max(e)$, the analysis finds the system to be safe: the safety margin is considered sufficient to always prevent car E from switching to mode run when this is unsafe. This constitutes an optimistic verdict neglecting the possibility of actual stochastic measurement errors sometimes exceeding ε.

If we had chosen $\varepsilon < \max(e)$ instead, the system would be considered to be unsafe: the exclusion of errors from the safety margin yields a possibility of switching to run after each measurement. Thus, a collision will eventually happen, which is detected in this framework.

– *Liveness results:* For $y_E \leq y_O$, the liveness property (1b) is trivially satisfied. For $y_E > y_O$, the liveness property is found to be satisfied only if $y_E - y_O > \varepsilon + \max(e)$. For all $y_E \in]y_O, y_O + \varepsilon + \max(e)]$, a measurement outcome blocking progress is possible. Qualitative modelling permits this outcome infinitely often in sequence, which obviously is probabilistically impossible in the original stochastic formulation of the measurement process. The demonic model thus is pessimistic with respect to liveness.

The above analysis reveals that the demonic model conditionally (depending on the safety margin chosen) is optimistic for safety and always is pessimistic for liveness. Neither problem can be resolved in a purely qualitative setting:[2] increasing the safety margin in relation to the error margin increases the pessimism concerning liveness while stabilising the optimism concerning safety, whereas even decreasing the safety margin to zero will not resolve pessimism wrt. liveness while additionally becoming pessimistic on safety. The natural suggestion thus is to advance to stochastic modelling in order to faithfully represent the stochastic nature of the repeated measurement process.

3.4   Stochastic Modelling

The aforementioned two qualitative models suffer from a lack of knowledge about the error distribution as well as about 0-1 effects in iterated stochastic trials. Therefore they cannot reconcile accurate verdicts for safety with accurate verdicts for liveness.

Stochastic hybrid automata, however, allow to consider the error distribution explicitly and thus enable the engineer to scale down the safety margin by excluding rare errors. As suggested in Sect. 2, there are different types of stochastic models. For our running example, we consider a measurement to be represented as a randomised update function copying a noisy image of y_O to $\hat{y}_O$. The probability distribution of the noise term corresponds to the error distribution in measurement.

Before we proceed to the actual model of our running example, we define a stochastic hybrid automaton by adding a stochastic transition kernel akin to [6] as follows:

Definition 2 (Stochastic Hybrid Automaton). *A stochastic hybrid automaton is a tuple* $SA = (\mathcal{M}, \mathcal{V}, \mathbf{d}, \mathbf{i}, \mathcal{T}, \mathbf{g}, \mathbf{u}, \mathcal{I})$, *where* $\mathcal{M}$, $\mathcal{V}$, $\mathbf{d}$, $\mathbf{i}$, $\mathcal{T}$, *and* $\mathbf{g}$ *are defined as in Definition 1 and*

---

[2] An accurate verdict for liveness could actually be achieved if fairness conditions were part of the automaton model, but hybrid automata tend to omit such.

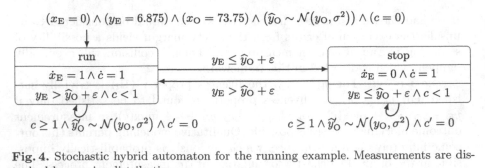

$(x_E = 0) \wedge (y_E = 6.875) \wedge (x_O = 73.75) \wedge \left(\widehat{y}_O \sim \mathcal{N}\left(y_O, \sigma^2\right)\right) \wedge (c = 0)$

run		stop	
$\dot{x}_E = 1 \wedge \dot{c} = 1$	$y_E \le \widehat{y}_O + \varepsilon$	$\dot{x}_E = 0 \wedge \dot{c} = 1$	
$y_E > \widehat{y}_O + \varepsilon \wedge c < 1$	$y_E > \widehat{y}_O + \varepsilon$	$y_E \le \widehat{y}_O + \varepsilon \wedge c < 1$	

$c \ge 1 \wedge \widehat{y}_O \sim \mathcal{N}\left(y_O, \sigma^2\right) \wedge c' = 0$ $c \ge 1 \wedge \widehat{y}_O \sim \mathcal{N}\left(y_O, \sigma^2\right) \wedge c' = 0$

Fig. 4. Stochastic hybrid automaton for the running example. Measurements are disturbed by a noise distribution.

- $\mathbf{u} : \mathcal{T} \times \mathbb{R}^n \to \mathcal{P}(\mathbb{R}^n)$, with $\mathcal{P}(\mathbb{R}^n)$ representing the set of probability distributions over $\mathbb{R}^n$, is the update function that updates the continuous state space according to a probability distribution when the transition is taken, and
- $\mathcal{I} \subseteq \mathcal{M} \times \mathcal{P}(\mathbb{R}^n)$ is the set of valid initial states.

A tuple $(m, \mathbf{v}) \in \mathcal{M} \times \mathbb{R}^n$ is a state of the automaton SA as in Definition 1.

The semantics is mostly identical to that of qualitative hybrid automata put forward in Sect. 3.2. The only difference is that the updates in jumps are now assigned a stochastic interpretation. A jump $(m, \mathbf{x}) \xrightarrow{\tau} (m', \mathbf{x}')$ is possible iff $\tau = (m, m')$ and $\mathbf{x} \in \mathbf{g}(\tau) \cap \mathbf{i}(m)$. The density associated to its continuous successor states is $\mathbf{u}(\tau, \mathbf{x})$. This induces a density on finite runs by multiplication of the step-wise densities for the individual jumps in the run; for infinite runs, a standard cylinder construction can be applied.

We create an instance of such an automaton for our example by modifying the demonic automaton as follows (see also Fig. 4):

- $\mathbf{u}(u, \mathbf{v}) = \begin{cases} (x_E, y_E, x_O, \widehat{y}_O, 0)^T & \text{iff } m = (\text{run}, \text{run}) \vee m = (\text{stop}, \text{stop}) \\ \mathbf{v} & \text{otherwise} \end{cases}$

where the (partially deterministic) joint distribution over the continuous states is represented by single vectors using $\widehat{y}_O \sim \mathcal{N}(y_O, \sigma^2)$

- $\mathcal{I} = \left\{ \left(\text{run}, (0, 0.6875, 73.75, \widehat{y}_O, 0)^T \right) \right\}$ with $\widehat{y}_O \sim \mathcal{N}(y_O, \sigma^2)$

Note that we do not require $\max(e) \le \varepsilon$ in this setup. On the contrary, we have $\max(e) > \varepsilon$ s.t. we may progress on rare measurements featuring an exceptional error and obtain a non-paralysed system with a controlled, negligible collision probability.

In contrast to the previous model, the stochastic model enables to quantify the probability that a certain execution path of the system occurs. Hence, the probability of reaching an unsafe state can be quantified which means that our analysis is about the probability that the desired properties are satisfied.

For the stochastic hybrid automaton model, the graphs in Figs. 7 and 8 show simulation results for the probabilities of bounded liveness and safety, resp., in terms of run length (watch for label "SHA" in the graphics). Table 1c presents the analysis results for runs of unbounded length.

Again, these formal verdicts are not convincing: Despite simplicity of the problem, the analysis would claim that it is perfectly impossible to build a safe system, as the probability of being safe is zero in the long run for each critical instance $y_E \leq y_O$. To the contrary, we will demonstrate in the next section that it is well possible to construct a quantitatively safe system, for any strictly positive safety target, by standard engineering means. The model of stochastic hybrid automata thus again fails to provide a reasonable representation of the design space. The repeated failure of classical hybrid automata models to provide pertinent verdicts motivates us to suggest a revised hybrid-automaton model in the next section.

4 Bayesian Hybrid Automata

In the previous section, we illustrated by means of an example that classical types of hybrid automata are inapt of adequately reflecting the behaviour of hybrid control under uncertainty. A key issue is that crucial elements of rational decision under uncertainty are not part of the model: an optimal decision, e.g. about a driving manoeuvre, would have to be based on an optimal estimation of the environmental situation, e.g. the obstacle position. In a setting of noisy measurements, such an estimate cannot be obtained from single measurements, but from a correlation of multiple stochastically independent measurements plus— if measurements are taken at different times—the system dynamics translating the measurements to other time instances. This is the field of state estimation and filtering, e.g. Kálmán filtering [21]. Such filtering, where sequences of measurements are combined in order to improve the precision of the estimate, is standard in control and robotics [13–15,22]. That such filtering also is essential to optimal hybrid control under uncertainty should thus come as no surprise and has indeed earlier been observed by Ding et al. [19]. The objective of this section is to provide a general model of such systems.

Many estimation techniques are based on Bayes filters [11], which, for instance, can be implemented for linear dynamics and normally distributed noise as Kálmán filters [21]. The main idea behind those probabilistic filters is to compute a weighted average of multiple measurements, which will converge to the true value due to the law of large numbers if the observed value is not afflicted by any dynamics, i.e., stays constant over multiple measurements. If (possibly noisy) dynamics must be considered, the idea is to compute an optimal estimate for the next measurement based on the knowledge from the last measurements by applying the dynamics on the last estimation. The prediction is then interpreted as a noisy measurement and charged against the new, again noisy, measurement.

In order to tackle the drawbacks of traditional hybrid models illustrated in Sect. 3, we suggest a new theory for stochastic hybrid systems that includes such probabilistic filters: we will extend the continuous state space of hybrid automata by *distribution variables* incorporating probability distributions that represent the estimation of a datum. Distribution variables will evolve over time according to the dynamics of the estimated datum while discrete updates will be performed in terms of a Bayes filter. Thereby, we expect an increase of the precision of data estimation over time within the model, thus reflecting data estimation techniques implemented in actual cyber-physical systems.

Based on the optimised data estimation, we then allow to model decisions, viz. guards of discrete transitions, that are optimal in the sense of using as much information as is available from such optimal state estimates: we will introduce transition guards which are satisfied if a certain constraint on the estimated datum holds with some probability, i.e., reliability. Definition 3 presents the suggested model.

Definition 3 (Bayesian Hybrid Automaton). *A Bayesian hybrid automaton is a tuple $BA = (\mathcal{M}, \mathcal{V}, \mathcal{S}, \mathbf{d}, \mathbf{i}, \mathcal{T}, \mathbf{g}, \mathbf{u}, \mathcal{I})$ where*

- $\mathcal{M} = \{m_0, m_1, \cdots, m_k\}$ *is a finite set of discrete control modes,*
- $\mathcal{V} = \{v_0, v_1, \cdots, v_n\}$ *is a finite set of continuous variables. The continuous state space spanned by it occurs in two copies: we have system variables v_i spanning the space $\mathbb{R}^n$ and we have a second variable $\hat{v}_i$ representing an estimate for the value v_i, i.e., spanning a probability distribution in $\mathcal{P}(\mathbb{R}^n)$, where $\mathcal{P}(X)$ denotes the set of density functions over X. The state space spanned by the BHA thus is $\Sigma = \mathcal{M} \times \mathbb{R}^n \times \mathcal{P}(\mathbb{R}^n)$.*
- $\mathcal{S} \subset (\{1, \ldots, n\} \times (\mathbb{R} \to \mathcal{P}(\mathbb{R})))$ *represents a set of measurement actions, where i in such a pair (i, f) represents the variable v_i to be measured and f the mapping of v_i's values to measurements,*
- $\mathbf{d} : \mathcal{M} \times \mathbb{R}^n \to \mathbb{R}^n$ *is a mode-dependent vector field defining the evolution of the continuous variables per control mode, which applies to system variables v_i and estimates $\hat{v}_i$ equally,*
- $\mathbf{i} : \mathcal{M} \to ((2^{\mathbb{R}^n})^2 \times [0, 1])$ *is a function describing the invariants per control mode, which is interpreted classically wrt. system variables, yet probabilistically wrt. estimates $\hat{v}_i$: only if $S_2 \subseteq \mathbb{R}^n$ in $((S_1, S_2), \varepsilon) = \mathbf{i}(m)$ is assigned a probability mass larger than ε by $\hat{x}$ can the mode be held,*
- $\mathcal{T} \subseteq \mathcal{M} \times \mathcal{M}$ *is the transition relation between discrete modes,*
- $\mathbf{g} : \mathcal{T} \to ((2^{\mathbb{R}^n})^2 \times [0, 1])$ *is the guard function, which is interpreted classically wrt. system variables, yet probabilistically wrt. estimates $\hat{v}_i$: only if $S_2 \subseteq \mathbb{R}^n$ in $((S_1, S_2), \varepsilon) = \mathbf{g}(\tau)$ is assigned a probability mass larger than ε by the estimates $\hat{v}$ can the transition be taken,*
- $\mathbf{u} : \mathcal{T} \times \mathbb{R}^n \to (\mathcal{P}(\mathbb{R}^n) \times 2^{\mathcal{S}})$ *is the update function that stochastically updates the continuous state space and potentially takes measurements when the transition is taken, thereby updating the estimates also, and*
- $\mathcal{I} \subseteq \Sigma$ *is the set of valid initial states.*

Such a hybrid automaton starts from an initial state in $\mathcal{I}$ and then engages in an alternating sequence of continuous evolutions $\xrightarrow{\delta} \subseteq \Sigma^2$, for $\delta \geq 0$, and instantaneous jumps $\xrightarrow{\tau} \subseteq \Sigma^2$, for $\tau \in \mathcal{T}$.

A continuous evolution $(m, \boldsymbol{x}, \hat{\boldsymbol{x}}) \xrightarrow{\delta} (m', \boldsymbol{x}', \hat{\boldsymbol{x}}')$ is possible iff $m' = m$ and has consistent effect on both the state variables x_i and their estimates $\hat{x}_i$. I.e., there is a solution $y : [0, \delta] \rightarrow \mathbf{i}(m)$ to the ordinary differential equation $\frac{d x}{dt} = \mathbf{d}(m, x)$ with $y(0) = x$ and $y(\delta) = x'$. Likewise, $\hat{x}'$ is the distribution resulting from an initial distribution $\hat{x}$ by following the evolution $\frac{d x}{dt} = \mathbf{d}(m, x)$ for δ time units. We obviously also require that the invariant is respected as follows: First, the system variables x_i respect the invariant S_1 in $((S_1, S_2), \varepsilon) = \mathbf{i}(m)$, i.e., $\forall t \in [0, \delta] : y(t) \in S_1$. Second, the estimate variables $\hat{x}_i$ invariantly assign a likelihood of at least ε to the required invariant set S_2 by demanding $\forall t \in [0, \delta] :$ $\int \chi_{S_2} d\hat{y}(t) \geq \varepsilon$, where χ_{S_2} is the characteristic function of S_2.

A jump $(m, x, \hat{x}) \xrightarrow{\tau} (m', x', \hat{x}')$ is possible iff $\tau = (m, m')$ and $x \in S_1$ and $\int \chi_{S_2} d\hat{x} \geq \varepsilon$, where $((S_1, S_2), \varepsilon) = \mathbf{g}(\tau)$ and χ_{S_2} is the characteristic function of S_2. Thus, a transition is enabled only if the guard condition applies to the system variables x_i in the sense of $(x_1, \ldots, x_n) \in S_2$ and, furthermore, a probability evaluation of the guard condition S_2 on the estimates provides sufficient evidence, namely likelihood ε at least, for the guard condition $(\hat{x}_1, \ldots, \hat{x}_n) \in S_2$. Note that S_1 need not—and in general will not—coincide. The transition effect then is to pursue an update $(P, R) = \mathbf{u}(\tau, x)$ as follows: x' is drawn according to the density P and $\hat{x}' = \bigwedge_{(i,f) \in R} BayesianUpdate(\hat{x}, f(\hat{x}_i))$, where $BayesianUpdate(A, B)$ denotes a Bayesian update of the prior distribution A by the likelihood function B obtained via the measurement taken on $\hat{x}_i$.

Note that Bayesian hybrid automata introduce an additional dimension of randomness: first, there is a probability distribution over the assignment effect to system variables, as for stochastic hybrid automata. The second dimension of randomness lies in the distribution variables: they incorporate probability distributions representing data estimations.

Such a model thus comprises distributions over estimations where each estimation is a distribution over the domain of the estimated datum. Traditional stochastic automata, in contrast, incorporate distributions over scalar values only. Even Ding et al. [19] employ this kind of traditional models although they use filter techniques to estimate the state of a partially observable hybrid system in order to generate an optimal control policy. Being focused on synthesizing an optimal rational control policy in a particular setting rather than trying to verify an existing, potentially not completely rational policy, they avoid the problem of having to incorporate a general model of state estimation into their system description.

When instantiating our setting of Bayesian hybrid automata to our running example, we note that due to the lacking (and thus trivially linear) dynamics of y_O, optimal Bayesian state inference can be obtained by Kálmán filtering. We exploit the fact that a normal distribution, as underlying Kálmán filtering, can be fully described by its mean value and variance and model our exemplary system as Bayesian hybrid automaton with such a filter as follows (see Fig. 5 for the graphical representation):

- $\mathcal{M} = \{\text{run}, \text{stop}\}$
- $\mathcal{V} = \{v_0 = (x_E, \hat{x}_E), v_1 = (y_E, \hat{y}_E), v_2 = (x_O, \hat{x}_O), v_3 = (y_O, \hat{y}_O), v_4 = (c, \hat{c})\}$
  where each $\hat{v}_i$ is represented as a pair $(\mu_{(\hat{v}_i)}, \sigma^2_{(\hat{v}_i)})$ that represents the mean μ and the variance σ^2 of a normal distribution

$$(x_E = 0) \wedge (y_E = 6.875) \wedge (x_O = 73.75) \wedge (y_O = 8.1) \wedge (\hat{y}_O \leftarrow \mathcal{N}(y_O, 10^2)) \wedge (c = 0)$$

Fig. 5. Bayesian hybrid automaton for the running example. The notation $v \leftarrow d$, where d is a distribution representing the result of a measurement process, denotes a Bayesian update to the state estimation represented by estimation variables $\hat{y}_O, \cdots$ based on a measurement taken.

- $\mathcal{S} = \{(3, \mathcal{N}(y_O, 10))\}$
- $\mathbf{d}((m, \boldsymbol{v})) =$

$$\dot{\boldsymbol{v}}_m(t) = (\dot{x}_E(t), \dot{y}_E(t), \dot{x}_O(t), \dot{y}_O(t), \dot{c}(t))_m^T = \begin{cases} (0,0,0,0,1)^T & \text{iff } m = \text{stop} \\ (1,0,0,0,1)^T & \text{otherwise} \end{cases}$$

- $\mathbf{i}(m) = \begin{cases} p(y_E > y_O) \geq \varepsilon \wedge c < 1 & \text{iff } m = \text{run} \\ p(y_E \leq y_O) \geq \varepsilon \wedge c < 1 & \text{otherwise} \end{cases}$

  where $p(y_E \lessgtr y_O)$ is the probability mass that $y_E \lessgtr y_O$ holds according to $\hat{y}_E$ and $\hat{y}_O$
- $\mathcal{T} = \mathcal{M} \times \mathcal{M}$
- $\mathbf{g}(u) = \begin{cases} c \geq 1 & \text{iff } u = (\text{run}, \text{run}) \vee u = (\text{stop}, \text{stop}) \\ p(y_E \leq y_O) \geq \varepsilon & \text{iff } u = (\text{run}, \text{stop}) \\ p(y_E > y_O) \geq \varepsilon & \text{otherwise} \end{cases}$

  where p is defined as for the invariants
- $\mathbf{u}(u, \boldsymbol{v}) = \begin{cases} \left((x_E, y_E, x_O, y_O, 0)^T, \{(3, y_O \mapsto \mathcal{N}(y_O, 10^2))\}\right) \\ \qquad\qquad \text{iff } u = (\text{run}, \text{run}) \vee u = (\text{stop}, \text{stop}) \\ (\boldsymbol{v}, \emptyset) \qquad\qquad\qquad\qquad\qquad\qquad \text{otherwise} \end{cases}$

  where the function *BayesianUpdate* introduced in the description of the semantics of $\mathbf{u}$ above is defined as a single-dimensional Kálmán filter updating the marginal distribution $\hat{y}_O$ and the distribution over the system variables is a Dirac-distribution abbreviated in form of a single value according to the deterministic update of those variables in our example
- $\mathcal{I} = \left\{ \left(\text{run}, (0, 0.6875, 73.75, 8.1, 0)^T, \hat{\boldsymbol{v}}\right) \right\}$ where $\hat{\boldsymbol{v}}$ spans a distribution over $\mathbb{R}^n$ with the marginal $\hat{y}_O = \mathcal{N}(8.1, 10^2)$

Figure 6 illustrates how our model works for a situation where $y_E < y_O$, i.e. the ego vehicle has to stop in order to avoid a collision. The precision of the estimation of y_O, viz. the variance of the distribution $\hat{y}_O$, correlates to the accuracy of the sensing system after a first measurement. After this initial measurement, the ego vehicle is in mode stop since probability mass $\int_{-\infty}^{y_E} \hat{y}_O < \varepsilon$. Figure 6b indicates the estimation after several measurements. Due to the Kálmán filter,

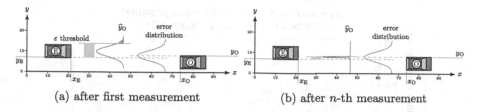

| (a) after first measurement | (b) after n-th measurement |

Fig. 6. Graphical illustration of filtered data-estimation for the running example. The distribution $\widehat{y}_O$ represents the current estimation of y_O while the error distribution illustrates the measurement error. The ε threshold indicates the probability mass defined as threshold for switching the mode: as long as the plotted line is above y_E, the ego vehicle will remain in mode stop. Thus, the shaded probability mass above that line represents the admissible probability of an estimation error regarding $y_E > y_O$.

the precision of the estimation increased and the mean of the estimation converged towards y_O.

Note that still every measurement can comprise an error that is sufficient to switch to mode run. The shaded area under $\widehat{y}_O$ above the ε threshold indicates the admissible probability that the estimation is wrong enough to continue travelling. However, the higher the precision of the estimation becomes, the higher is the measurement error that is required to continue travelling. Due to the normal distribution, the larger the error is, the smaller is the probability that such an error occurs. This implies that the probability of further movements—and thus, of a future collision—decreases over time when $y_E < y_O$. In contrast, the probability of moving forward in the stochastic hybrid-automaton model depends on the current measurement only and thus is constant, which implies that the probability of a collision is 1 in the long run when $y_E < y_O$.

We did a statistical evaluation of the suggested model in comparison to a traditional stochastic model by simulating runs of the BHA and the SHA for our running example. The minimum degree of belief in a safe state was chosen as $\varepsilon = 0.9$ for the BHA. For the SHA, we chose a safety margin ε that meets the same requirements, i.e., a measurement has to satisfy $p(y_E > y_O) \geq 0.9$ in order to force the system to switch to or stay in mode run. Measurements were performed according to the normal distribution $\mathcal{N}(8.1, 10^2)$. Each sequence of measurement outcomes was applied to a run of a BHA and a run of a SHA.

We created two scenarios for which we carried out the comparison. In the first scenario, we set $y_E > y_O$ such that a collision is impossible. In this scenario, we compared the models regarding the liveness property. For the second scenario, we chose to compare models regarding the safety property by setting $y_E < y_O$.

We simulated each model instance 3000 times for each scenario. For the simulation, time was discretised s.t. the discrete time instance t_d refers to the continuous time instance t just before the t_d-th continuous evolution is carried out, i.e. after each measurement and—if executed—mode change. At each discrete time instance t_d, we observed whether the ego vehicle moved forward or stopped as well as whether car E collided with car O or passed it, respectively.

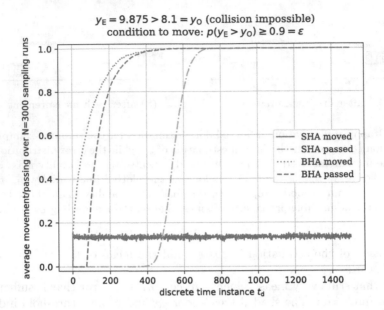

Fig. 7. Experimental evaluation by simulation of the stochastic and the Bayesian model in a safe situation ($y_E > y_O$). The Bayesian hybrid automaton allows car E to pass car O much earlier than in the traditional stochastic model, i.e., performs better wrt. the liveness property (dashed vs. dash-dotted line). It also permits smoother movement once enough evidence for safety of the situation has been accumulated (dotted vs. solid line).

Figures 7 and 8 present the results of the simulations in form of an average over the 3000 simulation runs.

For the stochastic hybrid-automaton model, both scenarios yield an almost constant positive rate of continuing movement for each time instant (solid graphs). This rate is the average $(\sum_{i=1}^{3000} \mathbf{1}_{i,t_d})/(3000)$ where $\mathbf{1}_{i,t_d} = 1$ iff car E moved at time t_d and 0 otherwise. The constancy of the rate is a result of the memoryless decision making of the traditional models: for each time instance t_d, the decision to continue driving is made based on the current measurement and the constant sensor precision only. The difference of those probabilities between Figs. 7 and 8 is a result of the different distance $|y_O - y_E|$ between the ego vehicle and car O. The dash-dotted graphs show the average rate of passing (Fig. 7) and colliding (Fig. 8) with car O at time t_d. The constant rate of moving results in surely eventually passing car O for the first scenario as well as surely eventually colliding with car O for the second scenario. Note that the distance $|x_O - x_E| = 73.75$ and the "driving speed" is 1. Thus, it takes about 6 to 10 times longer than necessary to pass car O in case of $y_E > y_O$.

The BHA shows a different behaviour: for the $y_E > y_O$ setting, we observed a fast-growing movement rate while we observed a rapidly decreasing movement rate in the second setting (dotted graphs). This behaviour results from

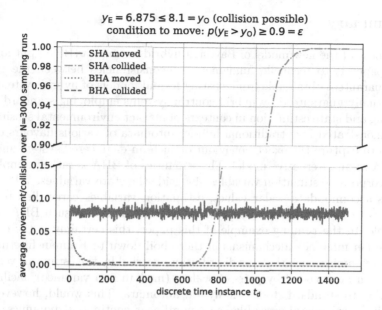

Fig. 8. Experimental evaluation by simulation of the stochastic and the Bayesian model in an unsafe situation ($y_E < y_O$). In the Bayesian hybrid automaton, the collision probability stabilises at a low level, whereas it diverges to 1 in the stochastic (dashed vs. dash-dotted line). The reason is that movements are blocked in the BHA once enough evidence has been accumulated, while the SHA permits a constant positive rate of movement due to the stochastic independence of measurements (dotted vs. solid line).

the filtering algorithm, which yields an increasing precision of the estimation $\widehat{y}_O$ by accumulating knowledge from the history of measurements. This precision is taken into account for decisions. The increase of the precision is reflected by the increasing/decreasing movement rate: the more precise the estimation, i.e. the more measurements are already taken, the larger has the measurement error to be in order to manipulate the estimation s.t. a "wrong" decision is made. Since the measurement error is normally distributed, large errors occur less frequently than small ones. Thus, the more measurements are taken, i.e., the further time has proceeded, the more likely is a "correct" decision, i.e. the more likely is that car E continues driving in case of $y_E > y_O$ and stops in case of $y_E \leq y_O$, respectively. As a result, for the first scenario, the ego vehicle passes the obstacle substantially earlier (dashed graph)—often almost at the earliest time possible—than in the stochastic model. In the second scenario, the collision probability remains negligible small over the whole observation period instead of rapidly converging to 1.

5 Summary

The purpose of the new model of Bayesian hybrid automata (BHA) put forward in this paper is to reconcile fundamental inconsistencies between the performance guarantees obtainable from existing formal models of hybrid systems and those actually guaranteed by hybrid control systems employing standard forms of filtering and state estimation in contexts of inexact environmental sensing. We have demonstrated how traditional hybrid automata of various flavours drastically fail to capture the exact behaviour of such an engineered system and suggest BHA as an alternative model. The semantics of BHA is rather complex, as BHA incorporate estimation variables alongside the state variables. While state variables accommodate scalar values, estimation variables carry distributions. It remains to be investigated under which special conditions such BHA remain analysable. In the running example of this paper, this certainly is the case, as the Bayesian inference mechanisms in there boil down to Kálmán filtering due to linear dynamics, such that the distributions carried by the estimator variables actually can be encoded by pairs of scalars (median and variance), facilitating a reduction to standard stochastic hybrid automata. This would, however, not employ in more general cases like, e.g., non-linear continuous dynamics. Automatic analysis techniques for BHA are therefore subject of further research. Due to the complexity of the state space, we aim for statistical analysis first, while planning for exploring the possibilities for closed-form analysis in the long.

References

1. Alur, R., Courcoubetis, C., Henzinger, T.A., Ho, P.: Hybrid automata: an algorithmic approach to the specification and verification of hybrid systems. In: [23], pp. 209–229 (1993)
2. Nerode, A., Kohn, W.: Models for hybrid systems: automata, topologies, controllability, observability. In: [23], pp. 317–356 (1993)
3. Sproston, J.: Decidable model checking of probabilistic hybrid automata. In: Joseph, M. (ed.) FTRTFT 2000. LNCS, vol. 1926, pp. 31–45. Springer, Heidelberg (2000). https://doi.org/10.1007/3-540-45352-0_5
4. Davis, M.: Markov Models and Optimization. Chapman & Hall, London (1993)
5. Fränzle, M., Hermanns, H., Teige, T.: Stochastic satisfiability modulo theory: a novel technique for the analysis of probabilistic hybrid systems. In: Egerstedt, M., Mishra, B. (eds.) HSCC 2008. LNCS, vol. 4981, pp. 172–186. Springer, Heidelberg (2008). https://doi.org/10.1007/978-3-540-78929-1_13
6. Fränzle, M., Hahn, E.M., Hermanns, H., Wolovick, N., Zhang, L.: Measurability and safety verification for stochastic hybrid systems. In Caccamo, M., Frazzoli, E., Grosu, R. (eds.) Proceedings of the 14th ACM International Conference on Hybrid Systems: Computation and Control, HSCC 2011, 12–14 April 2011, pp. 43–52. ACM, Chicago (2011)
7. Hu, J., Lygeros, J., Sastry, S.: Towards a theory of stochastic hybrid systems. In: Lynch, N., Krogh, B.H. (eds.) HSCC 2000. LNCS, vol. 1790, pp. 160–173. Springer, Heidelberg (2000). https://doi.org/10.1007/3-540-46430-1_16

8. Bujorianu, L., Lygeros, J.: Toward a general theory of stochastic hybrid systems. Stochastic Hybrid Systems: Theory and Safety Critical Applications. LNCIS, vol. 337, pp. 3–30. Springer, Berlin (2006)
9. Kowalewski, S., et al.: Hybrid Automata, pp. 57–86. Cambridge University Press, Cambridge (2009)
10. Maschler, M., Solan, E., Zamir, S.: Game Theory. Cambridge University Press, Cambridge (2013)
11. Barber, D.: Bayesian Reasoning and Machine Learning. Cambride University Press, Cambridge (2012)
12. Langseth, H., Nielsen, T.D., Rum, R., Salmern, A.: Inference in hybrid Bayesian networks. Reliab. Eng. Syst. Saf. **94**(10), 1499–1509 (2009)
13. Mahler, R.P.S.: Multitarget bayes filtering via first-order multitarget moments. IEEE Trans. Aerosp. Electron. Syst. **39**(4), 1152–1178 (2003). October
14. Elfes, A.: Using occupancy grids for mobile robot perception and navigation. Computer **22**(6), 46–57 (1989). June
15. Coué, C., Pradalier, C., Laugier, C., Fraichard, T., Bessiere, P.: Bayesian occupancy filtering for multitarget tracking: an automotive application. Int. J. Robot. Res. **25**(1), 19–30 (2006). voir basilic : http://emotion.inrialpes.fr/bibemotion/2006/CPLFB06/
16. Combastel, C.: Merging kalman filtering and zonotopic state bounding for robust fault detection under noisy environment. IFAC-PapersOnLine 48(21) (2015) 289–295; In: 9th IFAC Symposium on Fault Detection, Supervision andSafety for Technical Processes SAFEPROCESS 2015
17. Sherlock, C., Golightly, A., Gillespie, C.S.: Bayesian inference for hybrid discrete-continuous stochastic kinetic models. Inverse Probl. **30**(11), 114005 (2014). November
18. Murphy, K.P.: Switching kalman filters. Technical report (1998)
19. Ding, J., Abate, A., Tomlin, C.: Optimal control of partially observable discrete time stochastic hybrid systems for safety specifications. In: 2013 American Control Conference, pp. 6231–6236 (2013)
20. Donzé, A., Maler, O.: Robust satisfaction of temporal logic over real-valued signals. In: Chatterjee, K., Henzinger, T.A. (eds.) FORMATS 2010. LNCS, vol. 6246, pp. 92–106. Springer, Heidelberg (2010). https://doi.org/10.1007/978-3-642-15297-9_9
21. Kalman, R.E.: A new approach to linear filtering and prediction problems. Trans. ASME-J. Basic Eng. 82(Series D), 35–45 (1960)
22. Thrun, S.: Probabilistic robotics. Commun. ACM **45**(3), 52–57 (2002). March
23. Grossman, R.L., Nerode, A., Ravn, A.P., Rischel, H. (eds.): HS 1991-1992. LNCS, vol. 736. Springer, Heidelberg (1993). https://doi.org/10.1007/3-540-57318-6

Linking Theories of Probabilistic Programming

He Jifeng$^{(\boxtimes)}$

Shanghai Key Laboratory of Trustworthy Computing, East China
Normal University, Shanghai, China
jifeng@sei.ecnu.edu.cn

Abstract. Formal methods advocate the critical role played by the algebraic approach in specification and implementation of programs. Traditionally, a top-down approach (with denotational model as its origin) links the algebra of programs with the denotational representation by establishment of the *soundness* and *completeness* of the algebra against the given model, while a bottom-up approach (a journey started from operational model) introduces a variety of bisimulations to establish the equivalence relation among programs. This paper follows up a new way presented in [1] to handle probabilistic programming. Our approach takes an algebra of probabilistic programs as its foundation, and then generates both denotational model and transition system, and explores the consistency among three types of representations.

1 Introduction

Formal methods [4,5,9] advocate the critical role played by the algebra of programs in specification and implementation of programs [6,8]. Study leads to the conclusion that both the top-down approach (with denotational model as its origin) [2,3,11] and the bottom-up approach (a journey started from operational model) [10] can meet in the middle.

This paper proposes a new roadmap for linking theories of probabilistic programming. Our new journey consists of the following steps:

Step 1: First we present an algebraic framework for a probabilistic programming language, which provides a set of algebraic laws for probabilistic programs, and introduces the concept of finite normal form. This paper then defines the refinement relation $\sqsubseteq_A$, and demonstrates how to reduce finite programs into finite normal form, and to transform an infinite program into an ascending chain of finite normal forms.

Step 2: Within the given program algebra we discuss the algebraic properties of the test operator $\mathcal{T}$ which composes test case tc and testing program P in

$$\mathcal{T}(tc,\ P)\ =_{df}\ (tc; P)$$

© Springer Nature Switzerland AG 2018
C. Jones et al. (Eds.): Zhou-Festschrift, LNCS 11180, pp. 186–210, 2018.
https://doi.org/10.1007/978-3-030-01461-2_10

where tc is represented by a total constant assignment

$$x, y, .., z := a, b, .., c$$

Based on the algebra of test, this paper identifies a probabilistic program P as a binary relation $[P]$ which relates the test case with the final observation

$$[P] =_{df} \{(tc, \ obs) \mid T(tc, P) \sqsubseteq_A obs\}$$

and selects the set inclusion as the refinement relation $\sqsubseteq_{rel}$

$$P \sqsubseteq_{rel} Q =_{df} ([P] \supseteq [Q])$$

We establish the consistency of the denotational model against the algebraic framework by proof of

$$\sqsubseteq_{rel} = \sqsubseteq_A$$

Step 3: We propose an algebraic definition of the *consistency* of step relation of the transition system of programs such that any consistent transition system $(O, \sqsubseteq_O)$ satisfies

$$\sqsubseteq_O = \sqsubseteq_A$$

The paper is organised in the following way:

Section 2 is devoted to the algebraic framework of a probabilistic programming language with a collection of algebraic laws. Section 3 shows the normal forms of the finite and infinite probabilistic programs and proves that any probabilistic program can be converted into normal form with algebraic laws. Section 4 presents a test-based model, where each program is identified as a binary relation between test case and visible observation recorded during the execution of the test. It is shown that the refinement relation $\sqsubseteq_{rel}$ in the test model is equivalent to the algebraic refinement $\sqsubseteq_A$. Section 5 proposes a formal definition for the consistency of step relation of transition system against the algebra of programs. Moreover, it provides a transition system for the probabilistic programming language, and establishes its correctness. The paper ends with a short summary.

2   Probabilistic Programming Language

This section is going to construct an algebraic framework for the probabilistic programming language introduced in [12]

$$
\begin{aligned}
P ::=\ & \perp \mid \textbf{skip} \mid var := exp \\
& \mid P \lhd bexp \rhd P \\
& \mid P \, ; P \\
& \mid \oplus \{\underline{G}\} \\
& \mid \mu X \bullet P(X)
\end{aligned}
$$

$\oplus(\underline{G})$ denotes the probabilistic choice with a list of weighted alternatives $\underline{G}$ as its argument

$$\underline{G} ::= <> \mid \alpha(v) : P, \underline{G}$$

where the expression $\alpha(v)$ maps any given value of program variable v to a non-negative real number.

2.1   Probabilistic Choice

This section presents the algebraic properties of the probabilistic choice, which plays a crucial role in construction of normal form for the probabilistic language, and provides an elegant representation for finite observation. Later we are also going to use these algebraic laws to show that any finite program can be converted into a probabilistic choice.

The probabilistic choice is commutative.

($\oplus$-1) $\oplus\{\beta_1 : P_1, ..., \beta_m : P_m\}$ $=_A$ $\oplus\{\beta_{\rho(1)} : P_1, ..., \beta_{\rho(m)} : P_m\}$

where ρ is an arbitrary permutation of the list $< 1, ..., m >$.

The alternative $(1 - \beta) : \bot$ can be added to the probabilistic choice construct where $\beta =_{df} \Sigma_i \beta_i$.

($\oplus$-2) $\oplus\{\beta_1 : P_1, ..., \beta_m : P_m\}$ $=_A$ $\oplus\{\beta_1 : P_1, ..., \beta_k : P_k, (1 - \beta) : \bot\}$

The probabilistic choice operator becomes void whenever it contains an alternative with the probability 1.

($\oplus$-3) $\oplus\{1 : Q\}$ $=_A$ Q

Corollary. $\oplus\{\}$ $=_A$ $\bot$

Proof. From $\oplus$-2 and $\oplus$-3.

The next law shows how to eliminate the nested choices.

($\oplus$-4) Let $P = \oplus\{\beta_1 : P_1, ..., \beta_m : P_m\}$, then

$\oplus\{\alpha : P, \underline{G}\}$
$=_A$ $\oplus \{(\alpha \cdot \beta_1) : P_1, ..., (\alpha \cdot \beta_k) : P_k, \underline{G}\}$

The probabilistic choice operator distributes over sequential composition.

(⊕-5) $\oplus\{\beta_1 : P_1, ..., \beta_m : P_m\}; Q$
$=_A \quad \oplus\{\beta_1 : (P_1; Q), ..., \beta_k : (P_k; Q)\}$

Assignment distributes through the probabilistic choice.

(⊕-6) $(v := e); \oplus\{\beta_1 : P_1, ..., \beta_m : P_m\}$

$=_A \quad \oplus\{\beta_1[e/v] : (v := e; P_1), ..., \beta_k[e/v] : (v := e; P_k)\}$

Two alternatives with the same guarded program can be merged.

(⊕-7) $\oplus\{\alpha : Q, \beta : Q, \underline{G}\} \quad =_A \quad \oplus\{(\alpha + \beta) : Q, \underline{G}\}$

Any alternative with zero probability can be removed.

(⊕-8) $\oplus\{0 : Q, \underline{G}\} \quad =_A \quad \oplus\{\underline{G}\}$

2.2 Conditional Choice

Conditional choice can be seen as a special form of probabilistic choice.

cond-1 $(P \lhd b \rhd Q) \quad =_A \quad \oplus\{(1 \lhd b \rhd 0) : P, (0 \lhd b \rhd 1) : Q\}$

From Law **cond**-1 and the laws of probabilistic choice presented in the previous section, we can derive the following set of well-known properties of conditional choice:

Theorem 2.1.
(1) $P \lhd b \rhd P =_A P$
(2) $P \lhd b \rhd Q =_A Q \lhd \neg b \rhd P$
(3) $(P \lhd b \rhd Q) \lhd c \rhd R =_A P \lhd b \wedge c \rhd (Q \lhd c \rhd R)$
(4) $P \lhd b \rhd (Q \lhd c \rhd R) =_A (P \lhd b \rhd Q) \lhd c \rhd (P \lhd b \rhd R)$
(5) $P \lhd true \rhd Q =_A P =_A Q \lhd false \rhd P$
(6) $(P \lhd b \rhd Q); R =_A (P; R) \lhd b \rhd (Q; R)$
(7) $(v := e); (P \lhd b \rhd Q) =_A ((v := e); P) \lhd b[e/v] \rhd ((v := e); Q)$

Proof.
For any finite program P:
  (1) $P \lhd b \rhd P$ $\{cond - 1\}$
  $=_A \quad \oplus\{(1 \lhd b \rhd 0) : P, (0 \lhd b \rhd 1) : P\}$ $\{\oplus - 7\}$
  $=_A \quad \oplus\{1 : P\}$ $\{\oplus - 3\}$
  $=_A \quad P$

  (2) $P \lhd b \rhd Q$ $\{cond - 1\}$
  $=_A \quad \oplus\{(1 \lhd b \rhd 0) : P, (0 \lhd b \rhd 1) : Q\}$ $\{\oplus - 1\}$
  $=_A \quad \oplus\{(1 \lhd \neg b \rhd 0) : Q, (0 \lhd \neg b \rhd 1) : P\}$ $\{cond - 1\}$
  $=_A \quad Q \lhd \neg b \rhd P$

(3) $(P \lhd b \rhd Q) \lhd c \rhd R$ {cond − 1}

$=_A$ $\oplus \left\{ \begin{array}{l} (1 \lhd c \rhd 0) : \oplus\{(1 \lhd b \rhd 0) : P,\ (0 \lhd b \rhd 1) : Q), \\ (0 \lhd c \rhd 1) : R \end{array} \right\}$ {⊕ − 4}

$=_A$ $\oplus \left\{ \begin{array}{l} (1 \lhd b \wedge c \rhd 0) : P, \\ Let(1 \lhd \neg b \wedge c \rhd 0) : Q, \\ (1 \lhd \neg c \rhd 0) : R \end{array} \right\}$ {⊕ − 4}

$=_A$ $\oplus \left\{ \begin{array}{l} (1 \lhd b \wedge c \rhd 0) : P, \\ (0 \lhd b \wedge c \rhd 1) : \oplus\{(1 \lhd c \rhd 0) : Q,\ (0 \lhd c \rhd 1) : R\} \end{array} \right\}$ {cond − 1}

$=_A$ $P \lhd b \wedge c \rhd (Q \lhd c \rhd R)$

(4) $P \lhd b \rhd (Q \lhd c \rhd R)$ {cond − 1}

$=_A$ $\oplus \left\{ \begin{array}{l} (1 \lhd b \rhd 0) : P, \\ (0 \lhd b \rhd 1) : \oplus\{(1 \lhd c \rhd 0) : Q,\ (0 \lhd c \rhd 1) : R\} \end{array} \right\}$ {⊕ − 4}

$=_A$ $\oplus \left\{ \begin{array}{l} (1 \lhd b \rhd 0) : P, \\ (1 \lhd \neg b \wedge c \rhd 0) : Q, \\ (1 \lhd \neg b \wedge \neg c \rhd 0) : R \end{array} \right\}$ {⊕ − 7}

$=_A$ $\oplus \left\{ \begin{array}{l} (1 \lhd b \wedge c \rhd 0) : P, \\ (1 \lhd b \wedge \neg c \rhd 0) : P, \\ (1 \lhd \neg b \wedge c \rhd 0) : Q, \\ (1 \lhd \neg b \wedge \neg c \rhd 0) : R \end{array} \right\}$ {⊕ − 1 and cond − 1}

$=_A$ $\oplus \left\{ \begin{array}{l} (1 \lhd c \rhd 0) : (P \lhd b \rhd Q), \\ (0 \lhd \neg c \rhd 1) : (P \lhd b \rhd R) \end{array} \right\}$ {cond − 1}

$=_A$ $(P \lhd b \rhd Q) \lhd c \rhd (P \lhd b \rhd R)$

(5) $P \lhd true \rhd Q$ {cond − 1}

$=_A$ $\oplus\{(1 \lhd true \rhd 0) : P,\ (1 \lhd true \rhd 1) : Q\}$ {⊕ − 8}

$=_A$ $\oplus\{1 : P\}$ {⊕ − 3}

$=_A$ P {⊕ − 1, 3 and 8}

$=_A$ $\oplus\{0 : Q,\ 1 : P\}$ {calculation}

$=_A$ $\oplus\{(1 \lhd false \rhd 0) : Q,\ (0 \lhd false \rhd 1) : P\}$ {cond − 1}

$=_A$ $Q \lhd false \rhd P$

(6) From **cond**-1 and ⊕-5.

(7) From **cond**-1 and ⊕-6.

The probabilistic choice operator distributes over conditional.

Theorem 2.2.

Let $P = \oplus\{\beta_1 : P_1, ..., \beta_m : P_m\}$, then
$(P \lhd b \rhd Q) =_A \oplus \{\beta_1 : (P_1 \lhd b \rhd Q), ..., \beta_k : (P_k \lhd b \rhd Q)\}$
provided that $\Sigma_i \beta_i = 1$

Proof.

$P \lhd b \rhd Q$ {cond − 1}

$=_A \oplus\{(1 \lhd b \rhd 0) : P,\ (0 \lhd b \rhd 1); Q\}$ {⊕ − 4}

$=_A \oplus \left\{ \begin{array}{l} (\beta_1 \lhd b \rhd 0) : P_1, \\ ...., \\ (\beta_m \lhd b \rhd 0) : P_m, \\ (0 \lhd b \rhd 1) : Q \end{array} \right\}$ {(⊕ − 7) and assumption:$\sigma_i \beta_i = 1$}

$$=_A \quad \oplus \left\{ \begin{array}{l} (\beta_1 \lhd b \rhd 0) : P_1, \\ ...., \\ (\beta_m \lhd b \rhd 0) : P_m, \\ (0 \lhd \neg b \rhd \beta_1) : Q, \\ ...., \\ (0 \lhd b \rhd \beta_m) : Q \end{array} \right.$$

$$=_A \quad \oplus \left\{ \begin{array}{l} \beta_1 : (P_1 \lhd b \rhd Q), \\ ...., \\ \beta_m : (P_m \lhd b \rhd Q) \end{array} \right\}$$

$\{cond - 1\}$

2.3 Sequential Composition

Sequential composition in the probabilistic programming language inherits the algebraic laws of its counterpart in the conventional programming language. It is associative, and has $\perp$ as its zero, and *skip* as its unit.

seq-1. $P; (Q; R) =_A (P; Q); R$

seq-2. $\perp; Q =_A \perp =_A P; \perp$

seq-3. $\textbf{skip}; Q =_A Q =_A Q; \textbf{skip}$

2.4 Total Assignment

An assignment is a total one if all the variables of the program appear on the left hand side in some standard order

$$x, y, .., z := e, f, ..., g$$

A non-total assignment $x := e$ can be transformed to a total assignment by addition of identity assignments

asgn-1. $(x := e) =_A (x, y, .., z := e, y, ..., z)$

For the notational simplicity we will use v to stand for the list $x, y, .., z$ of program variables and $v := e$ for a total assignment.

The list of variables may be sorted into any desired order, provided that the right hand side is subject tote same permutation.

asgn-2. $(x, y, .. := e, f, ..) =_A (y, x, .. := f, e, ..)$

The following law enables us to eliminate sequential composition between total assignments

asgn-3. $(v := e; v := f(v)) =_A (v := f(e))$

where the expression $f(e)$ is easily calculated by substituting the expression in the list e for the corresponding variables in the list v.

The following law deals with the conditional of total assignments

asgn-4. $((v := e) \lhd b \rhd (v := f))$ $=_A$ $(v := (e \lhd b \rhd f))$

where the conditional expression $e \lhd b \rhd f$ is defined mathematically:

$$e \lhd b \rhd f \begin{cases} =_{df} e & \text{if } b \\ =_{df} f & \text{if } \neg b \end{cases}$$

Finally, we need a law that determines when two total assignments are equal.

asgn-5. $(v := f)$ $=_A$ $(v := g)$ iff $\forall v \bullet f(v) = g(v)$

3   Normal Form Reduction

This section is devoted to the concept of normal form. It will deal with the following issues:

- Transform a finite program into a finite normal form based on the algebraic laws of the previous section.
- Introduce the least upper bound operator for an ascending chain of finite normal forms.
- Establish the continuity of programming combinators.
- Verify the continuity of the recursion operator.
- Convert an infinite program into an ascending chain of finite normal forms.

First we introduce the concept of finite normal form.

3.1   Finite Normal Form

Definition 3.1 (finite normal form).
A finite normal form is a probabilistic choice with total assignments as its alternatives:
$$\oplus \{\beta_1 : (v := e_1), \, ... , \beta_k : (v := e_k)\}$$

Theorem 3.2. Let $S_1 = \oplus \{\beta_1 : (v := e_1), .., \beta_m : (v := e_m)\}$ and $S_2 = \oplus \{\alpha_1 : (v := f_1), .., \alpha_n : (v := f_n)\}$.
Then

$$(1) \ S_1; S_2 =_A \oplus \begin{cases} (\beta_1 \cdot \alpha_1) : (v := f_1(e_1)), \\ ..., \\ (\beta_1 \cdot \alpha_n) : (v := f_n(e_1)), \\ ... \\ (\beta_m \cdot \alpha_1) : (v := f_1(e_m)), \\ ..., \\ (\beta_m \cdot \alpha_n) : (v := f_n(e_m)) \end{cases}$$

$$(2)\ S_1 \lhd b \rhd S_2\ =_A\ \oplus \left\{ \begin{array}{l} (\beta_1 \lhd b \rhd 0) : (v := e_1), \\ \dots\dots, \\ (\beta_m \lhd b \rhd 0) : (v := e_m), \\ (\alpha_1 \lhd \neg b \rhd 0) : (v := f_1), \\ \dots\dots, \\ (\alpha_n \lhd \neg b \rhd 0) : (v := f_n) \end{array} \right\}$$

Proof.

$$(1)\quad S_1; S_2 \qquad\qquad\qquad \{\oplus - 5\}$$
$$=_A\ \oplus\{\beta_1 : (v := e_1; S_2), \dots, \beta_m : (v := e_m; S_2)\} \qquad \{\oplus - 6\}$$

$$=_A\ \oplus \left\{ \begin{array}{l} \beta_1 : \oplus \left\{ \begin{array}{l} \alpha_1[e_1/v] : (v := e_1; v := f_1), \\ \dots, \\ \alpha_n[e_1/v] : (v := e_1; v := f_n) \end{array} \right\}, \\ \dots\dots, \\ \beta_m : \oplus \left\{ \begin{array}{l} \alpha_1[e_m/v] : (v := e_m; v := f_1), \\ \dots, \\ \alpha_n[e_m/v] : (v := e_m; v := f_n) \end{array} \right\} \end{array} \right\} \qquad \{\mathbf{asgn} - 3\}$$

$$=_A\ \oplus \left\{ \begin{array}{l} \beta_1 : \oplus \left\{ \begin{array}{l} \alpha_1[e_1/v] : (v := f_1(e_1)), \\ \dots, \alpha_n[e_1/v] : (v := f_n(e_1)) \end{array} \right\}, \\ \dots\dots, \\ \beta_m : \oplus \left\{ \begin{array}{l} \alpha_1[e_m/v] : (v := f_1(e_m)), \\ \dots, \\ \alpha_n[e_m/v] : (v := f_n(e_m)) \end{array} \right\} \end{array} \right\} \qquad \{\oplus - 4\}$$

$$=_A\ \oplus \left\{ \begin{array}{l} (\beta_1 \cdot \alpha_1) : (v := f_1(e_1)), \\ \dots, \\ (\beta_1 \cdot \alpha_n) : (v := f_n(e_1)), \\ \dots \\ (\beta_m \cdot \alpha_1) : (v := f_1(e_m)), \\ \dots, \\ (\beta_m \cdot \alpha_n) : (v := f_n(e_m)) \end{array} \right\}$$

$$(2)\quad S_1 \lhd b \rhd S_2 \qquad\qquad\qquad \{\mathbf{cond} - 1\}$$
$$=_A\ \oplus\{(1 \lhd b \rhd 0) : S_1,\ (1 \lhd \neg b \rhd 0) : S_2\} \qquad \{\oplus - 4\}$$

$$=_A\ \oplus \left\{ \begin{array}{l} (\beta_1 \lhd b \rhd 0) : (v := e_1), \\ \dots\dots, \\ (\beta_m \lhd b \rhd 0) : (v := e_m), \\ (\alpha_1 \lhd \neg b \rhd 0) : (v := f_1), \\ \dots\dots, \\ (\alpha_n \lhd \neg b \rhd 0) : (v := f_n) \end{array} \right\}$$

Theorem 3.3. Assume that $S_i\ =\ \oplus \{\alpha_{i,1} : (v := e_{i,1}), \dots, \alpha_{i,k_i} : (v := e_{i,k_i})\}$ for $1 \leq i \leq n$. Then

$$\oplus\{\beta_1 : S_1, ..., \beta_n : S_n\} \quad =_A \quad \oplus \left\{ \begin{array}{l} (\beta_1 \cdot \alpha_{1,1}) : (v := e_{1,1}), \\ ......, \\ (\beta_1 \cdot \alpha_{1,k_1}) : (v := e_{1,k_1}), \\ ......, \\ (\beta_n \cdot \alpha_{n,1}) : (v := e_{n,1}), \\ ......, \\ (\beta_n \cdot \alpha_{n,k_n}) : (v := e_{n,k_n}) \end{array} \right\}$$

Proof: Similar to Theorem 3.2(1).

Theorem 3.4 (finite normal reduction).
Any finite program can be converted into a finite normal form.

Proof.
Basic case:
(1) From $\oplus$-3, we have $(v := e) \ =_A \ \oplus\{1 : (v := e)\}$
(2) From Corollary of $\oplus$-3, it follows that $\bot =_A \oplus\{\}$

induction: The conclusion follows from Theorems 3.2 and 3.3.
The following law permits comparison of finite normal forms
norm-1. Let $S_1 = \oplus\{\beta_1(v) : (v := e_1(v)), \ .., \ \beta_m(v) : (v := e_m(v))\}$
and $S_2 = \oplus\{\alpha_1(v) : (v := f_1(v)), \ ..., \ \alpha_n(v) : (v := f_n(v))\}$.
Then $S_1 \sqsubseteq_A S_2$ **iff**
$\forall c, d \bullet (\Sigma_i\{\beta_i(c) \mid e_i(c) = d\} \leq \Sigma_j\{\alpha_j(c) \mid f_j(c) = d\})$

Theorem 3.5. $S_1 \sqsubseteq_A S_2$ iff for all constants c

$$((v := c); S_1) \sqsubseteq_A ((v := c); S_2)$$

Proof. From $\oplus$-6 and **norm-1**.

Corollary. Assume that

$$T_1 = \oplus\{\beta_1 : (v := c_1), .., \beta_n : (v := c_m)\}$$
$$T_2 = \oplus\{\alpha_1 : (v := d_1), .., \alpha_n : (v := d_n)\}$$

where all β_i and α_j are constants, and furthermore both $\{c_1, .., c_m\}$ and $\{d_1, .., d_n\}$ are lists of distinct constants.
Then $T_1 \sqsubseteq_A T_2$ iff there exists an injective mapping ϕ from $\{1, .., m\}$ to $\{1, .., n\}$ such that

$$\forall i \bullet (c_i = d_{\phi(i)}) \ \wedge \ (\beta_i \leq \alpha_{\phi(i)})$$

The next theorem shows that all programming combinators F satisfy

$$F(S_1) \sqsubseteq_A F(S_2)$$

whenever both S_1 and S_2 are finite normal forms, and $S_1 \sqsubseteq_A S_2$

Theorem 3.6.
If S_1 and S_2 are finite normal forms satisfying $S_1 \sqsubseteq_A S_2$, then
(1) $(S_1 \lhd b \rhd R) \sqsubseteq_A (S_2 \lhd b \rhd R)$
provided that R is a finite program.
(2) $\oplus\{\gamma : S_1, \underline{G}\} \sqsubseteq_A \oplus\{\gamma : S_2, \underline{G}\}$
where $\underline{G} = \xi_1 : R_1, .., \xi_n : R_n$ and all R_i are finite.
(3) $(S_1; R) \sqsubseteq_A (S_2; R)$ provided that R is a finite program.
(4) $(R; S_1) \sqsubseteq_A (R; S_2)$ provided that R is a finite program.

Proof. From $\oplus$-6 we can transform $(v := c); S_1$ and $(v := c); S_2$ into the following form

$$(v := c); S_1 =_A \oplus\{\beta_1 : (v := c_1), .., \beta_m : (v := c_m)\}$$
$$(v := c); S_2 =_A \oplus\{\alpha_1 : (v := d_1), ..., \alpha_n : (v := d_n)\}$$

where all β_i and α_j are constants, and furthermore both $\{c_1, .., c_m\}$ and $\{d_1, .., d_n\}$ are lists of distinct constants. From Corollary of Theorem 3.5 it follows that there exists an injective mapping ϕ from $\{1, .., m\}$ to $\{1, .., n\}$ satisfying

$$\forall i \bullet (c_i = d_{\phi(i)}) \land (\beta_i \leq \alpha_{\phi(i)})$$

Proof of (1).

Case 1:$b[c/v] = true$
$$\begin{aligned}
&(1) \quad (v := c); (S_1 \lhd b \rhd R) &\{\text{Theorem 2.1(5)}\} \\
&\equiv_A \quad (v := c); S_1 &\{\text{Theorem 3.5}\} \\
&\sqsubseteq_A \quad (v := c); S_2 &\{\text{Theorem 2.1(5)}\} \\
&=_A \quad (v := c); (S_2 \lhd b \rhd R)
\end{aligned}$$

Case 2: $b[c/v] = false$. From Theorem 2.1 it follows that

$$(v := c); (S_1 \lhd b \rhd R) =_A (v := c); R =_A (v := c); (S_2 \lhd b \rhd R)$$

The conclusion follows from Theorem 3.5.

Proof of (2). From Theorem 3.4 it follows that all R_i can be transformed into finite normal forms:

$$R_i =_A \oplus \{\rho_{i,1}(v) : (v := f_{i,1}), ..., \rho_{i,k_i}(v) : (v := f_{i,k_i})\}$$

for $i \in \{1, .., n\}$.
From Theorem 3.3 it follows that
$(v := c); \oplus\{\gamma : S_1, \underline{G}\} =_A$

$$\oplus \left\{ \begin{array}{l} (\gamma(c) \cdot \beta_1) : (v := c_1), ..., (\gamma(c) \cdot \beta_m) : (v := c_m), \\ (\xi_1(c) \cdot \rho_{1,1}(c)) : (v := f_{1,1}(c)), ..., (\xi_1(c) \cdot \rho_{1,k_1}(c)) : (v := f_{1,k_1}(c)), \\ ......, \\ (\xi_n(c) \cdot \rho_{n,1}(c)) : (v := f_{n,1}(c)), ..., (\xi_n(c) \cdot \rho_{n,k_n}(c)) : (v := f_{n,k_n}(c)) \end{array} \right\}$$

$(v := c); \oplus\{\gamma : S_2, \underline{G}\} =_A$

$$\oplus \left\{ \begin{array}{l} (\gamma(c) \cdot \alpha_1) : (v := d_1), ..., (\gamma(c) \cdot \alpha_n) : (v := d_n), \\ (\xi_1(c)\rho_{1,1}(c)) : (v := f_{1,1}(c)), ..., (\xi_1(c) \cdot \rho_{1,k_1}(c)) : (v := f_{1,k_1}(c)), \\ ....., \\ (\xi_n(c) \cdot \rho_{n,1}(c)) : (v := f_{n,1}(c)), ..., (\xi_n(c) \cdot \rho_{n,k_n}(c)) : (v := f_{n,k_n}(c)) \end{array} \right\}$$

Then for any constant r

$$\begin{array}{lll} & \Sigma \left(\begin{array}{l} \{(\gamma(c) \cdot \beta_i) \mid (c_i = r)\} \\ \cup \{(\xi_i(c) \cdot \rho_{i,j}(c)) \mid (f_{i,j} = r)\} \end{array} \right) & \{\forall i \bullet (c_i = d_{\phi(i)})\} \\ = & \Sigma \left(\begin{array}{l} \{(\gamma(c) \cdot \beta_i) \mid (d_{\phi(i)} = r)\} \\ \cup \{(\xi_i(c) \cdot \rho_{i,j}(c)) \mid (f_{i,j} = r\} \end{array} \right) & \{\forall i \bullet (\beta_i \leq \alpha_{\phi(i)})\} \\ \leq & \Sigma \left(\begin{array}{l} \{(\gamma(c) \cdot \alpha_{\phi(i)}) \mid (d_{\phi(i)} = r)\} \\ \cup \{(\xi_i(c) \cdot \rho_{i,j}(c)) \mid (f_{i,j} = r)\} \end{array} \right) & \{(\Sigma X) \leq (\Sigma (X \cup Y))\} \\ \leq & \Sigma \left(\begin{array}{l} \{(\gamma(c) \cdot \alpha_l) \mid (d_l = r)\} \\ \cup \{(\xi_i(c) \cdot \rho_{i,j}(c)) \mid (f_{i,j} = r)\} \end{array} \right) & \end{array}$$

which leads to the conclusion

$$(v := c); \oplus\{\gamma : S_1, \underline{G}\} \sqsubseteq_A (v := c); \oplus\{\gamma : S_2, \underline{G}\}$$

Proof of (3). From Theorem 3.4 we can convert R into a finite normal form

$$R =_A \oplus \{\rho_1(v) : (v := f_1), ..., \rho_n(v) : (v := f_n)\}$$

From $\oplus$-5 and 6 we obtain
$(v := c); S_1; R =_A$

$$\oplus \left\{ \begin{array}{l} \beta_1 \cdot \rho_1(c_1) : (v := f_1(c_1)), ..., \beta_1 \cdot \rho_n(c_1) : (v := f_n(c_1)), \\ ....., \\ \beta_m \cdot \rho_1(c_m) : (v := f_1(c_m)), ..., \beta_m \cdot \rho_n(c_m) : (v := f_n(c_m)) \end{array} \right\}$$

$(v := c); S_2; R =_A$

$$\oplus \left\{ \begin{array}{l} (\alpha_1 \cdot \rho_1(d_1)) : (v := f_1(d_1)), ..., (\alpha_1 \cdot \rho_n(d_1)) : (v := f_n(d_1)), \\ ....., \\ (\alpha_n \cdot \rho_1(d_n)) : (v := f_1(d_n)), ..., (\alpha_n \cdot \rho_n(d_n)) : (v := f_n(d_n)) \end{array} \right\}$$

Then for any constant r we have

$$\begin{array}{lll} & \Sigma_{i,j}\{\beta_i \cdot \rho_j(c_i) \mid f_j(c_i) = r\} & \{\forall i \bullet (c_i = d_{\phi(i)})\} \\ = & \Sigma_{i,j}\{\beta_i \cdot \rho_j(d_{\phi(i)}) \mid f_j(d_{\phi(i)}) = r\} & \{\forall i \bullet (\beta_i \leq \alpha_{\phi(i)})\} \\ \leq & \Sigma_{i,j}\{\alpha_{\phi(i)} \cdot \rho_j(d_{\phi(i)}) \mid f_j(d_{\phi(i)}) = r\} & \{\Sigma X \leq \Sigma (X \cup Y)\} \\ \leq & \Sigma_{i,j}\{\alpha_i \cdot \rho_j(d_i) \mid f_j(d_i) = r\} & \end{array}$$

which leads to the conclusion that

$$(v := c); S_1; R \sqsubseteq_A (v := c); S_2; R$$

3.2   Infinite Normal Form

Definition 3.2 (infinite normal form).
An infinite normal form is represented by an infinite sequence of finite normal forms

$$S = \{S_i \mid i \in Nat\}$$

where each S_{i+1} is a more accurate description than its predecessor

$$(S_{i+1} \sqsupseteq_A S_i) \qquad \text{for all } i \in Nat$$

This is called ascending chain condition. It is this type of chain that will be taken as the normal form for programs that contains recursion. The exact behaviour of the normal form is captured by the least upper bound of the whole sequence, written

$$\bigsqcup S$$

The least upper bound operator is characterised by two laws:

norm-2. $\bigsqcup S \sqsubseteq_A Q$ iff $\forall i \bullet (S_i \sqsubseteq_A Q)$
norm-3. If P is a finite normal form, then $P \sqsubseteq_A \bigsqcup T$ iff

$$\forall c, \exists j \bullet ((v := c); P) \sqsubseteq_A ((v := c); T_j)$$

The following theorem states that $\bigsqcup S$ is actually the least upper bound of the ascending chain with respect to the refinement order $\sqsubseteq_A$.

Theorem 3.7.
(1) $S_i \sqsubseteq_A \bigsqcup S$ for all $i \in Nat$.
(2) If $S_i \sqsubseteq_A Q$ for all $i \in Nat$ then $\bigsqcup S \sqsubseteq_A Q$

Proof. (1) From **norm-3**.
(2) From **norm-2**.

3.3   Continuity

This section deals with the continuity of programming combinators (including recursion) before we show how to transform a program into an ascending chain of finite normal form.

Definition 3.3 (continuity).
An operator is continuous if it distributes through least upper bound of descending chains.

The following laws explore the continuity of finite programming combinators.

norm-4. $(\bigsqcup S) \triangleleft b \triangleright P =_A \bigsqcup_i (S_i \triangleleft b \triangleright P)$
norm-5. $(\bigsqcup S); P =_A \bigsqcup_i (S_i; P)$
norm-6. $P; (\bigsqcup S) =_A \bigsqcup_i (P; S_i)$
provided that P is a finite normal form.
norm-7. $\oplus\{\alpha : (\bigsqcup S), \underline{G}\} =_A \bigsqcup_i \oplus\{\alpha : S_i, \underline{G}\}$
The next concern is how to eliminate the nested least upper bound operators.
norm-8. $\bigsqcup_k (\bigsqcup_l S_{k,l}) =_A \bigsqcup_i S_{i,i}$
provided that $(S_{k,i+1} \sqsubseteq_A S_{k,i})$ and $(S_{i+1,l} \sqsubseteq_A S_{i,l})$ for all i, k and l.

Law **norm-8** lays down the foundation for computation of normal forms by eliminating programming operators.

Theorem 3.8 (Continuity of finite programming combinators).
(1) $(\bigsqcup S) \lhd b \rhd (\bigsqcup T) =_{df} \bigsqcup_i (S_i \lhd b \rhd T_i)$
(2) $(\bigsqcup S) ; (\bigsqcup T) =_{df} \bigsqcup_i (S_i ; T_i)$
(3) $\oplus \{\alpha : (\bigsqcup S), .., \beta : (\bigsqcup T)\} =_{df} \bigsqcup_i \oplus \{\alpha : S_i, ..., \beta : T_i\}$

Proof.

(2) $(\bigsqcup S); (\bigsqcup T)$	$\{norm - 5\}$
$=_A \bigsqcup_i (S_i; \bigsqcup T)$	$\{norm - 6\}$
$=_A \bigsqcup_i \bigsqcup_j (S_i; T_j)$	$\{norm - 8\}$
$=_A \bigsqcup_i (S_i; T_i)$	

The continuity theorem ensures that ascending chains constitute a valid normal form for all the combinators of our probabilistic language, and the stage is set for treatment of recursion.

3.4   Recursion

Consider first an innermost recursive program

$$\mu X \bullet P(X)$$

where $P(X)$ contains X as its only free identifier. Because X is certainly not in normal form, it is impossible to express $P(X)$ in normal form. However, all other components of $P(X)$ are expressible in finite normal form, and all its combinators permit reduction to finite normal form. So if X were replaced by $\bot$, $P(\bot)$ can be reduced to finite normal form, and so on $P(\bot)$, $P^2(\bot)$,.., Furthermore from Theorem 3.6 it follows that P is monotonic, this constitutes an ascending chain of finite normal forms.

rec-1. $\mu X \bullet P(X) =_A \bigsqcup_n P^n(\bot)$ provided that P is continuous.
where $P^0(X) =_{df} \bot$ and $P^{n+1}(X) =_{df} P(P^n(\bot))$.
Finally we are going to show that the μ operator is also continuous.

Theorem 3.9 (Continuity of the recursion operator).
If $S_i(X)$ contains X as its only free recursive identifier for all i,
and that all S_i are continuous and they form an ascending chain for all finite normal forms X:

$$S_{i+1}(X) \sqsupseteq_A S_i(X) \qquad \text{for all } i \in Nat$$

then $\mu X \bullet \bigsqcup_i S_i(X) =_A \bigsqcup_i \mu X \bullet S_i(X)$

Proof. Let $P(X) =_{df} \bigsqcup_i S_i(X)$. By induction we are going to establish for all $n \in Nat$

$$P^n(\bot) =_A \bigsqcup_i S_i^n(\bot) \qquad (*)$$

Base case: $n = 0$

$$P^0(\bot) =_A \bot =_A \bigsqcup_i \bot =_A \bigsqcup_i S_i^0(\bot)$$

Induction:

$$P^{n+1}(\bot)$$
$$=_A \bigsqcup_i S_i(P^n(\bot)) \qquad \{\text{induction hypothesis}\}$$
$$=_A \bigsqcup_i S_i(\bigsqcup_j S_j^n(\bot)) \qquad \{S_i \text{ is continuous}\}$$
$$=_A \bigsqcup_i \bigsqcup_j S_i(S_j^n(\bot)) \qquad \{\text{norm} - 8\}$$
$$=_A \bigsqcup_i S_i(S_i^n(\bot)) \qquad \{\text{Def of } S_i^{n+1}\}$$
$$=_A \bigsqcup_i S_i^{n+1}(\bot)$$

with $\{\text{Def of } P^{n+1}\}$ for the first line.

which leads to the conclusion:

$$\mu X \bullet P(X) \qquad \{\text{rec} - 1\}$$
$$=_A \bigsqcup_n P^n(\bot) \qquad \{\text{Conclusion } (*)\}$$
$$=_A \bigsqcup_n (\bigsqcup_i S_i^n(\bot)) \qquad \{\text{norm} - 8\}$$
$$=_A \bigsqcup_i (\bigsqcup_n S_i^n(\bot)) \qquad \{\text{rec} - 1\}$$
$$=_A \bigsqcup_i \mu X \bullet S_i(X)$$

Now we reach the stage to eliminate the recursion operator.

Theorem 3.10.

Any recursive program $\mu X \bullet F(X)$ can be converted into the least upper bound of an ascending chain.

Proof.

$$\mu X \bullet F(X, \mu Y.G_1(Y), ..., \mu Y \bullet G_m(Y)) \qquad \{\text{rec} - 1\}$$
$$=_A \mu X \bullet F(X, \bigsqcup_n G^n(\bot), .., \bigsqcup_n G_m^n(\bot)) \qquad \{\text{Theorem 3.8}\}$$
$$=_A \mu X \bullet \bigsqcup_n (F(X, G^n(\bot), .., G_m^n(\bot))) \qquad \{\text{Theorem 3.9}\}$$
$$=_A \bigsqcup_n \mu X \bullet F(X, G^n, .., G_m^n(\bot)) \qquad \left\{ \begin{array}{l} \text{rec} - 1 \ \text{ and let} \\ F_n =_{df} F(X, G^n(\bot), .., G_m^n(\bot)) \end{array} \right\}$$
$$=_A \bigsqcup_n \bigsqcup_m F_n^m(\bot) \qquad \{\text{norm} - 8\}$$
$$=_A \bigsqcup_n F_n^n(\bot)$$

Theorem 3.11.
(1) If $P \sqsubseteq_A Q$, then
(a) $(P \lhd b \rhd R) \sqsubseteq_A (Q \lhd b \rhd R)$
(b) $(P; R) \sqsubseteq_A (Q; R)$
(c) $\oplus\{\gamma : P, \xi_1 : U_1, ..., \xi_l : U_l\} \sqsubseteq_A \oplus\{\gamma : Q, \xi_l : U_l\}$
(d) $(R; P) \sqsubseteq_A (R; Q)$
(2) If $P(S) \sqsubseteq_A Q(S)$ for any finite normal form S, then
$$\mu X \bullet P(X) \sqsubseteq_A \mu X \bullet Q(X)$$

Proof: From Theorems 3.4 and 3.10 we can transform P, Q and R into descending chain of finite normal forms:

$$P =_A \bigsqcup_i P_i, \qquad Q =_A \bigsqcup_j Q_j \qquad R =_A \bigsqcup_k R_k$$

From Definition 3.2 it follows that for any constant c there exists a mapping ψ_c satisfying $\forall i \bullet (i \le \psi_c(i))$, and

$$\forall i \bullet ((v := c); P_i) \sqsubseteq_A ((v := c); Q_{\psi_c(i)}) \qquad (*)$$

Proof of 1.(a): From $(*)$ and Theorem 3.6(1) we reach the conclusion

$$\forall i \bullet ((v := c); (P_i \lhd b \rhd R_i)) \sqsubseteq_A ((v := c); (Q_{\psi_c(i)} \lhd b \rhd R_{\psi_c(i)}))$$

which implies

$$
\begin{array}{ll}
(P \lhd b \rhd R) & \{\text{Theorem 3.8}\} \\
=_A \bigsqcup_i (P_i \lhd b \rhd R_i) & \{\textbf{norm } 2 \text{ and } 3\} \\
\sqsubseteq_A \bigsqcup_j (Q_j \lhd b \rhd R_j) & \{\text{Theorem 3.8}\} \\
=_A (Q \lhd b \rhd R) &
\end{array}
$$

Proof of 1.(b): From $(*)$ and Theorem 3.6(3)(4) we reach the conclusion

$$\forall i \bullet ((v := c); (P_i; R_i)) \sqsubseteq_A ((v := c); (Q_{\psi_c(i)}; R_{\psi_c(i)}))$$

which implies

$$
\begin{array}{ll}
(P; R) & \{\text{Theorem 3.8}\} \\
=_A \bigsqcup_i (P_i; R_i) & \{\textbf{norm } 2 \text{ and } 3\} \\
\sqsubseteq_A \bigsqcup_j (Q_j; R_j) & \{\text{Theorem 3.8}\} \\
=_A (Q; R) &
\end{array}
$$

Proof of 1.(c): From Theorems 3.4 and 3.10 there exists a family $\{\{U_{i,n} \ n \in Nat\} \mid 1 \le i \le l\}$ of ascending chains such that for all i, $U_i =_A \bigsqcup_j U_{i,j}$. Then we have

$$
(v := c); \oplus \left\{ \begin{array}{l} \gamma : P_i, \\ \xi_1 : U_{1,i}, \\ ..., \\ \xi_l : U_{l,i} \end{array} \right\} \qquad \{\oplus - 6\}
$$

$$
=_A \oplus \left\{ \begin{array}{l} \gamma(c) : ((v := c); P_i)), \\ \xi_1(c) : ((v := c); U_{1,i}), \\ ..., \\ \xi_l(c) : ((v := c); U_{l,i}) \end{array} \right\} \qquad \{\text{Theorem 3.6}\}
$$

$$
\sqsubseteq_A \oplus \left\{ \begin{array}{l} \gamma(c) : ((v := c); Q_{\psi_c(i)}), \\ \xi_1(c) : ((v := c); U_{1,i}), \\ ..., \\ \xi_l(c) : ((v := c); U_{l,i}) \end{array} \right\} \qquad \{(i \le \psi_c(i)) \implies \forall j \bullet (U_{j,i} \sqsubseteq_A U_{j, \psi_c(i)}\}
$$

$$
\sqsubseteq_A \oplus \left\{ \begin{array}{l} \gamma(c) : ((v := c); Q_{\psi_c(i)}), \\ \xi_1(c) : ((v := c); U_{1, \psi_c(i)}), \\ ..., \\ \xi_l(c) : ((v := c); U_{l, \psi_c(i)}) \end{array} \right\} \qquad \{\oplus - 6\}
$$

$$
=_A (v := c); \oplus \left\{ \begin{array}{l} \gamma : Q_{\psi_c(i)}, \\ \xi_1 : U_{1, \psi_c(i)}, \\ ..., \\ \xi_l : U_{l, \psi_c(i)} \end{array} \right\}
$$

which leads to the conclusion.

Proof of 1.(d): Assume that

$$R_i =_A \oplus \{\xi_{i,1} : (v := e_{i,1}), ..., \xi_{i,n_i} : (v := e_{i,n_i} : (v := e_{i,n_i})\}$$

Define $\Phi_c(i) =_{df} \mathbf{max}(\psi_{e_{i,1}(c)}(i), ..., \psi_{e_{i,n_i}(c)}(i))$. Then we have

$$(v := c); R_i; P_i \qquad \{\oplus - 5 \text{ and } 6\}$$

$$=_A \oplus \left\{ \begin{array}{l} x_{i,1}(c) : (v := e_{i,1}(c)); P_i), \\ ...., \\ x_{i,n_i} : (v := e_{i,n_i}; P_i) \end{array} \right\} \qquad \{\text{Conclusion } 1(c)\}$$

$$\sqsubseteq_A \oplus \left\{ \begin{array}{l} x_{i,1}(c) : (v := e_{i,1}(c)); Q_{\psi_{e_{i,1}(c)}(i)}, \\ ...., \\ x_{i,n_i} : (v := e_{i,n_i}; Q_{\psi_{e_{i,n_i}}(c)(i)}, \end{array} \right\} \qquad \{\text{Def of } \Phi \text{ and Conclusion } 1(c)\}$$

$$\sqsubseteq_A \oplus \left\{ \begin{array}{l} x_{i,1}(c) : (v := e_{i,1}(c)); Q_{\Phi_c(i)}, \\ ...., \\ x_{i,n_i} : (v := e_{i,n_i}; Q_{\Phi_c(i)}, \end{array} \right\} \qquad \{\oplus - 6\}$$

$$=_A (v := c); R_i; Q_{\Phi_c(i)} \qquad \{i \leq \Phi_c(i)\}$$

$$\sqsubseteq_A (v := c); R_{\Phi_c(i)}; Q_{\Phi_c(i)}$$

which leads to the conclusion.

4   Testing Programs

An operational approach usually defines the relationship between a program and its possible execution by machine. In an abstract way, a computation consists of a sequence of individual steps with the following features:

- each step takes the machine from one state to a closely similar state;
- each step is drawn from a very limited repertoire.

In a stored program computer, the machine states are represented as pairs

$$(s, \ P)$$

where

(1) s is a text, defining the *data state* as an assignment of constant to all variables of the alphabet

$$x, y, ..., z := a, b, ..., c$$

(2) P is a program text, representing the rest of the program that remains to be executed. When this becomes the empty text ϵ, there is no more program to be executed. The machine state

$$(t, \ \epsilon)$$

is the last state of any execution sequence that contains it, and t presents the final value of the variables in the end of execution.

The following lemma indicates that data states are the best programs.

Lemma 4.1.
$(s \sqsubseteq_A P)$ implies $(s =_A P)$.

Definition 4.1 (Probabilistic state).
Let $S_i =, \oplus\{\xi_{i,1} : (v := c_{i,1}), .. \xi_{i,m_i} : (v := c_{i,m_i})\}$ be a finite normal form for all $i \in Nat$ in which all $\xi_{i,j}$ and $c_{i,j}$ are constants,

and $c_{i,l} \neq c_{i,m}$ for all $l \neq m$.

If $S_i \sqsubseteq_A S_{i+1}$ for all $i \in Nat$, then

$$\bigsqcup_i S_i$$

is called a probabilistic state.

The execution of program $(s; P)$ can be seen as a *test* on P with the test case s. The result of such a testing gives rise to a set of possible outcomes. We are then able to compare the behaviours of two programs based on testing.

Formally, the test operator for our probabilistic programming language is defined by

$$\mathcal{T}(s,\, P) =_{df} (s; P)$$

When $\bot$ is taken as the test case, we obtain

$$\mathcal{T}(\bot,\, P) =_A \bot$$

Execution of a test will deliver a probabilistic state.

Theorem 4.1. For any test $\mathcal{T}(s,\, P)$, there exists a probabilistic state t such that

$$\mathcal{T}(s,\, P) =_A t$$

Proof. From Theorem 3.4 it follows that any finite program P can be converted into a finite normal form:

$$P =_A \oplus\{\beta_1 : (v := e_1), ..., \beta_m : (v := e_m)\}$$

The conclusion is derived from $\oplus - 6$.

For any program P there exists an ascending chain $S = \{S_i \mid i \in Nat\}$ of finite normal form such that

$$P =_A \bigsqcup S$$

The conclusion follows from **norm** $- 6$.

Corollary.

$P \sqsubseteq_A Q$ iff for all test case s

$$\mathcal{T}(s,\, P) \sqsubseteq_A \mathcal{T}(s,\, Q)$$

Definition 4.2.

A program P can be identified as a binary relation $[P]$ between test case s and a final probabilistic data state t it may enter in the end of testing

$$[P] =_{df} \{(s,\, t) \mid \mathcal{T}(s,\, P) \sqsubseteq_A t\}$$

As usual we define the refinement relation $\sqsubseteq_{rel}$ on the relational model by the set inclusion

$$P \sqsubseteq_{rel} Q =_{df} ([P] \supseteq [Q])$$

Theorem 4.2.
$\sqsubseteq_{rel} = \sqsubseteq_A$

Proof.

$$
\begin{array}{lll}
& P \sqsubseteq_A Q & \{\text{Corollary of Theorem 4.1}\} \\
\equiv & \forall s \bullet T(s, P) \sqsubseteq_A T(s, Q) & \{\text{Theorem 4.1}\} \\
\equiv & \forall s, t \bullet (T(s, Q) \sqsubseteq_A t) \implies (T(s, P) \sqsubseteq_A t) & \{\text{Definition 4.2}\} \\
\equiv & [Q] \subseteq [P] & \{\text{Definition of } \sqsubseteq_{rel}\} \\
\equiv & P \sqsubseteq_{rel} Q &
\end{array}
$$

Theorem 4.3.

(1) $[P \lhd b \rhd Q](v := c) = [P](v := c) \lhd b[c/v] \rhd [Q](v := c)$

(2) $[\oplus\{\beta_1 : P_1, .., \beta_m : P_m\}](v := c) = \left\{ \begin{array}{l} \oplus\{\beta_1[c/v] : t_1, .., \beta_m[c/v] : t_m\} \mid \\ \forall i \bullet t_i \in [P_i](v := c) \end{array} \right\}$

(3) $[P; Q] = [P] \circ [Q] \uparrow$

where $[Q] \uparrow$ is defined inductively:

$$[Q] \uparrow (v := c) =_{df} [Q](v := c)$$

$$[Q] \uparrow (\oplus\{\rho_1 : (v := c_1), .., \rho_m : (v := c_m)\}) =_{df} \left\{ \begin{array}{l} \oplus\{\rho_1 : t_1, .., \rho_m : t_m\} \mid \\ \forall i \bullet t_i \in [Q] \uparrow (v := c_i) \end{array} \right\}$$

$$[Q] \uparrow (\bigsqcup_i t_i) =_{df} \{\bigsqcup_i u_i \mid \forall i \bullet u_i \in [Q] \uparrow (t_i)\}$$

(4) $[\mu X \bullet P(X)] = \bigcap_n [P^n(\bot)]$

Proof of (3)

$$
\begin{array}{lll}
& (s, t) \in [P; Q] & \{\text{Definition 2.1}\} \\
\equiv & T(s, (P; Q)) \sqsubseteq_A t & \{\text{Theorem 4.1}\} \\
\equiv & \exists u \bullet T(s, P) =_A u \wedge (u; Q) \sqsubseteq_A t & \{\text{Def of } [Q] \uparrow\} \\
\equiv & \exists u \bullet T(s, P) =_A u \wedge (u, t) \in [Q] \uparrow & \{\text{Theorem 3.11}\} \\
\equiv & \exists u \bullet (T(s, P) \sqsubseteq_A u) \wedge (u, t) \in [Q] \uparrow & \{\text{Definition 4.2}\} \\
\equiv & \exists u \bullet ((s, u) \in [P] \wedge (u, t) \in [Q] \uparrow) & \{\text{Def of relational composition}\} \\
\equiv & (s, t) \in ([P] \circ [Q] \uparrow) &
\end{array}
$$

5   Operational Approach

This section provides an operational semantics for our probabilistic programming language. We will introduce the concept of the *consistency* of an operational framework with respect to the algebra of programs, and present a transition system for the probabilistic language. This section also explores the link between the consistent transition system with the normal form representation of probabilistic programs.

There are two types of transitions for our language

(1) Transition $(s, P) \to (t, Q)$ means P transfers to Q with the data state s replaced by t.

We define the concept of *divergence*, being a machine state that can lead to an infinite execution

$$\mathbf{divergence}(s, P) =_{df} \forall n \exists t, Q \bullet ((s, P) \to_n (t, Q))$$

where $\rightarrow_0 =_{df} id$, and $\rightarrow_{n+1} =_{df} (\rightarrow; \rightarrow_n)$.

(2) Transition $(s, P) \xrightarrow{r} (s, Q)$ (where $0 < r \leq 1$ means Q is chosen by P to be executed with the probability r, whereas the data state remains unchanged.

We examine the concept of *finitary*, being a machine state that can only engage in finite number of probabilistic choices

$$\mathbf{finitary}(s, P) =_{df} \exists n \, \forall t, Q, r, m \bullet \left(\begin{array}{c} (s, P) \xrightarrow{r}_m (t, Q) \wedge m > n \\ \implies \mathbf{divergence}(t, Q) \end{array} \right)$$

where $\xrightarrow{r}_1 =_{df} \xrightarrow{r}$

and $\xrightarrow{r}_{n+1} =_{df} (\rightarrow; \xrightarrow{r}_n) \cup \{(\xrightarrow{r_1}; \xrightarrow{r_2}_n) \mid r_1 \cdot r_2 = r\}$

and $\xrightarrow{r}_* =_{df} \bigcup_n \xrightarrow{r}_n$

Definition 5.1. A transition system is *consistent* with respect to the algebraic semantics if for all machine states (s, P)

(1) **divergence**(s, P) implies $\mathcal{T}(s, P) =_A \bot$, and

(2) **finitary**(s, P) if P does not contain μ operator.

(3) $\mathcal{T}(s, P) =_A \oplus \{r : \mathcal{T}(t, Q) \mid (s, P) \xrightarrow{r} (t, Q)\}$,

where we extend the definition of the test operator to deal with the empty program text ϵ by

$$\mathcal{T}(s, \epsilon) =_{df} s$$

Theorem 5.1. Let $\rightarrow$ be a consistent transition system.

If **finitary**(s, P), then there exists n such that

$$\mathcal{T}(s, P) =_A \oplus \{r : t \mid \exists m \bullet (m \leq n) \wedge (s, P) \xrightarrow{r}_m (t, \epsilon)\}$$

Otherwise

$$\mathcal{T}(s, P) =_A \bigsqcup_n \oplus \{r : t \mid \exists m \bullet (m \leq n) \wedge (s, P) \xrightarrow{r}_m (t, \epsilon)\}$$

Proof. (1) Assume that **finitary**(s, P). For $k > 0$ define

$$\mathbf{finitary}_k(s, P) =_{df} \forall (t, Q), \forall r, m \bullet \left(\begin{array}{c} (s, P) \xrightarrow{r}_m (t, Q) \wedge m > k \\ \implies \mathbf{divergence}(t, Q) \end{array} \right)$$

The following inductive proof is based on the length of transition sequences

Basic case: **finitary**$_1(s, P)$.

The conclusion directly follows from (1) and (3) of Definition 5.1.

Induction step: **finatary**$_{k+1}(s, P)$.

From the definition of **finitary**$_{n+1}$ it follows that

$$(s, P) \xrightarrow{r} (t, Q) \implies \mathbf{finitary}_k(t, Q) \qquad (*)$$

$$T(s, P) \qquad \qquad \{\text{Def } 5.1(3)\}$$
$$=_A \quad \oplus \{r : T(u, Q) \mid (s, P) \xrightarrow{r} (u, Q)\} \qquad \{(*) \text{ and inductive hypothesis}\}$$
$$=_A \quad \oplus \begin{cases} r : \oplus \{\lambda : t \mid \exists m \bullet (m \leq n) \wedge \\ (s, P) \xrightarrow{r} (u, Q) \wedge (u, Q) \xrightarrow{\lambda}_m (t, \epsilon)\} \end{cases} \qquad \{\oplus - 4 \text{ Let } l = n + 1\}$$
$$=_A \quad \oplus \{\beta : t \mid \exists m \leq l \bullet (s, P) \xrightarrow{\beta} (t, \epsilon)\}$$

(2) Consider the case where $\neg\textbf{finitary}(s, P)$.
First we are going to establish the inequality

$$T(s, P) \sqsupseteq_A \bigsqcup_n \oplus \{r : t \mid \exists m \leq n \bullet (s, P) \xrightarrow{r}_m (t, \epsilon)$$

By **norm-2** we are required to prove for all n

$$T(s, P) \sqsupseteq_A \oplus\{r : t \mid \exists m \bullet (m \leq n) \wedge (s, P) \xrightarrow{r}_m (t, \epsilon)\}$$

Basic case: $n = 1$.
$$T(s, P) \qquad \qquad \{\text{Def } 5.1(3)\}$$
$$=_A \quad \oplus \begin{cases} \{\lambda : T(t, Q) \mid (s, P) \xrightarrow{\lambda} (t, Q)\} \cup \\ \{\beta : t \mid (s, P) \xrightarrow{\beta} (t, \epsilon)\} \end{cases} \qquad \{\text{Theorem } 3.11(c)\}$$
$$\sqsupseteq_A \quad \oplus \begin{cases} \{\lambda : \bot \mid (s, P) \xrightarrow{\lambda} (t, Q)\} \cup \\ \{\beta : t \mid (s, P) \xrightarrow{\beta} (t, \epsilon)\} \end{cases} \qquad \{\oplus - 2\}$$
$$=_A \quad \oplus \{r : t \mid (s, P) \xrightarrow{r} (t, \epsilon)\}$$

Induction:
$$T(s, P) \qquad \qquad \{\text{Def } 5.1(3)\}$$
$$=_A \quad \oplus \begin{cases} \{\lambda : T(t, Q) \mid (s, P) \xrightarrow{\lambda} (t, Q)\} \cup \\ \{\beta : t \mid (s, P) \xrightarrow{\beta} (t, \epsilon)\} \end{cases} \qquad \{\text{inductive hypothesis}\}$$
$$\sqsupseteq_A \quad \oplus \begin{cases} \{\lambda : \oplus\{\gamma : u \mid (s, P) \xrightarrow{\lambda} (t, Q) \wedge \\ \exists m \leq n \bullet (t, Q) \xrightarrow{\gamma}_m (u, \epsilon)\}\} \cup \\ \{\beta : t \mid (s, P) \xrightarrow{\beta} (t, \epsilon)\} \end{cases} \qquad \{\text{Def } \xrightarrow{r}_n\}$$
$$=_A \quad \oplus \{r : t \mid \exists m \leq n + 1 \bullet (s, P) \xrightarrow{r}_m (t, \epsilon)\}$$

Now we are going to prove the inequality

$$T(s, P) \sqsubseteq_A \bigsqcup_n \oplus\{r : t \mid \exists m \bullet (m \leq n) \wedge (s, P) \xrightarrow{r}_m (t, \epsilon)\}$$

From Definition 5.1 (2) we conclude that P must contain μ operator. Let us begin with the simplest case:

$$P = \mu X \bullet F(X)$$

where $F(X)$ does not refer to μ operator. Clearly from Definition 5.1(2) we have for all n
(i) $\textbf{finitary}(F^n(\bot))$
By induction it can be shown that
(ii) $(s, F^n(\bot)) \xrightarrow{\lambda}_m (t, \epsilon) \implies \exists k \leq n \bullet (s, \mu X \bullet F(X)) \xrightarrow{\lambda}_{m+k} (t, \epsilon)$
From (i) it follows that for all n there exists k_n such that

$$\mathcal{T}(s, F^n(\bot)) \qquad\qquad \{\mathbf{finitary}(F^n(\bot))\}$$

$$=_A \quad \oplus\{r:t \mid \begin{pmatrix} \exists m \bullet (m \le k_n) \wedge \\ (s, F^n(\bot)) \xrightarrow{r}_m (t, \epsilon) \end{pmatrix}\} \qquad \{(ii) \text{ and Corollary of } \mathbf{norm}-1\}$$

$$\sqsubseteq_A \quad \oplus\{r:t \mid \begin{pmatrix} \exists m \bullet (m \le (k_n+n)) \wedge \\ (s, \mu X \bullet F(X)) \xrightarrow{r}_m (t, \epsilon) \end{pmatrix}\} \qquad \{\mathbf{norm}-3\}$$

$$\sqsubseteq_A \quad \bigsqcup_n \oplus\{r:t \mid \begin{pmatrix} \exists m \bullet (m \le n) \wedge \\ (s, \mu X \bullet F) \xrightarrow{r}_m (t, \epsilon) \end{pmatrix}\}$$

which leads to the conclusion

$$\mathcal{T}(s, \mu X \bullet F(X)) \qquad\qquad \{\text{Theorem 3.8 and } \mathbf{rec}-1\}$$

$$=_A \quad \bigsqcup_n \mathcal{T}(s, F^n(\bot)) \qquad\qquad \{\text{previous conclusion}\}$$

$$\sqsubseteq_A \quad \bigsqcup_n \oplus\{r:t \mid \begin{pmatrix} \exists m \bullet (m \le n) \wedge \\ (s, \mu X \bullet F) \xrightarrow{r}_m (t, \epsilon) \end{pmatrix}\}$$

Finally let us examine the case where

$$P = F(\mu X \bullet Q(X), .., \mu X \bullet R(X))$$

In a similar way we can prove

$$\bullet \; \mathcal{T}(s, F(\mu X \bullet Q(X), .., \mu X \bullet R(X))) \qquad \{\text{Theorem 3.8}\}$$

$$=_A \quad \bigsqcup_n \mathcal{T}(s, F(Q^n(\bot), .., R^n(\bot))) \qquad \{\mathbf{finitary}(F(Q^n(\bot), .., R^n(\bot)))\}$$

$$=_A \quad \bigsqcup_n \oplus\{r:t \mid \begin{pmatrix} \exists m \bullet (m \le n_k) \wedge \\ (s, F(Q^n(\bot), ...)) \\ \xrightarrow{r}_m (t, \epsilon) \end{pmatrix}\} \qquad \{\text{proof for } (P = \mu X \bullet F(X))\}$$

$$\sqsubseteq_A \quad \bigsqcup_n \oplus\{r:t \mid \begin{pmatrix} \exists m \bullet (m \le n) \wedge \\ (s, P) \\ \xrightarrow{r}_m (t, \epsilon) \end{pmatrix}\}$$

We propose the following transition system for our probabilistic programming language.

Definition 5.2.

(1) Assignment

$((v := c), v := e) \to ((v := e[c/v]), \epsilon)$.

(2) Probabilistic Choice

(a) $((v := c), \oplus \{r_1 : P_1, .., r_m; P_m\}) \xrightarrow{r_k[c/v]} ((v := c), P_k)$
provided that $r_k[c/v] > 0$

(b) $((v := c), \oplus \{r_1 : P_1, .., r_m; P_m\}) \xrightarrow{1-\sum_k r_k[c/v]} ((v := c), \bot)$
provided that $\sum_k r_k[c/v] < 1$.

(3) Conditional

(a) $((v := c), P \triangleleft b \triangleright Q) \to ((v := c), P)$ if $b[c/v] = true$

(b) $((v := c), P \triangleleft b \triangleright Q) \to ((v := c), Q)$ if $b[c/v] = false$

(4) Composition

(a) $(s, P; Q) \xrightarrow{r} (t, R; Q)$ if $(s, P) \xrightarrow{r} (t, R)$

(b) $(s, P; Q) \to (t, R; Q)$ if $(s, P) \to (t, R)$

(c) $(s, P; Q) \xrightarrow{r} (t, Q)$ if $(s, P) \xrightarrow{r} (t, \epsilon)$

(d) $(s, P; Q) \to (t, Q)$ if $(s, P) \to (t, \epsilon)$

(5) Recursion

$(s, \mu X \bullet P(X)) \to (s, P(\mu X \bullet P(X)))$

(6) Chaos

$(s, \bot) \to (s, \bot)$

We are going to show that Definition 5.2 gives a consistent transition system. First, we show that the given transition system satisfies Definition 5.1(3)

Lemma 5.2. $T(s, P) =_A \oplus \{r : T(t, Q) \mid (s, P) \xrightarrow{r} (t, Q)\}$

Proof. Direct from the following properties of the test operator T:

(1) From $\oplus$-6 it follows that
$T((v := c), \oplus\{r_1 : P_1, .., r_n : P_n\} =_A \oplus \{r_1[c/v] : T((v := c), P_1), ..., r_n[c/v] : T((v := c), P_n)\}$

(2) From Theorem 2.1(7) we obtain
$T((v := c), (P \triangleleft b \triangleright Q)) =_A T((v := c), P) \triangleleft b[c/v] \triangleright T((v := c), Q)$

(3) From Theorem 4.1 we have
$T((v := c), (P; Q)) =_A \oplus \{r_1 : T((v := d_1), Q), ..., r_m : T((v := d_m), Q)\}$
provided that $T((v := c), P) =_A \oplus \{r_1 : (v := d_1), .., r_m : (v := d_m)\}$

(4) $T(s, \mu X \bullet P(X)) =_A T(s, P(\mu X \bullet P(X)))$

Next we deal with the condition (1) of Definition 5.1.

Lemma 5.3. If P is a finite program, then

$$\mathbf{divergence}(s, P) \implies T(s, P) =_A \bot$$

Proof. We give an induction proof based on the structure of program text P:
Base case: Clearly the conclusion holds for the case $P = v := e$ and $P = \bot$
Inductive step:

$\mathbf{divergence}((v := c), (P \triangleleft b \triangleright Q))$ {Rule (3) in Definition 5.2}

$\implies \begin{pmatrix} \mathbf{divergence}((v := c), P) \\ \triangleleft b[c/v] \triangleright \\ \mathbf{divergence}((v := c), Q) \end{pmatrix}$ {Induction hypothesis}

$\implies \begin{pmatrix} (T((v := c), P) =_A \bot) \\ \triangleleft b[c/v] \triangleright \\ (T((v := c), Q) =_A \bot) \end{pmatrix}$ {Theorem 2.1(7)}

$\implies T((v := c), (P \triangleleft b \triangleright Q)) =_A \bot$

$\mathbf{divergence}((v := c), \oplus \{r_1 : P_1, .., r_n : P_n\})$ {Rule (2) in Definition 5.2}
$\implies \Sigma\{(r_k[c/v]) \mid \mathbf{divergence}((v := c), P_k)\} = 1$ {Induction hypothesis}
$\implies \Sigma\{(r_k[c/v]) \mid T((v := c), P_k) =_A \bot\} = 1$ {$\oplus - 3$ and 6}
$\implies T((v := c), \oplus \{r_1 : P_1, .., r_n : P_n\}) =_A \bot$

Finally we are going to tackle infinite programs.

Lemma 5.4. If $(s, G(Q)) \to_* (t, \epsilon)$,
then either $\mathbf{divergence}(s, G(\bot))$ or $(s, G(\bot)) \to_* (t, \epsilon)$.

Proof. Induction on the structure of G
Base case. $G(Q) = Q$ From Rule (6)

$$(s, \bot) \to (s, \bot)$$

in Definition 5.2.
Inductive step:
(1) $G(Q) = G_1(Q) \triangleleft b \triangleright G_2(X)$

$$(s,\ G(Q)) \to_* (t,\ \epsilon) \qquad\qquad \{\text{Rule (3) in Def 5.2}\}$$

$$\implies \begin{pmatrix} (s,\ G_1(Q)) \to_* (t,\ \epsilon) \\ \lhd(s;b)\rhd \\ (s,\ G_2(Q)) \to_* (t,\ \epsilon) \end{pmatrix} \qquad\qquad \{\text{Induction hypothesis}\}$$

$$\implies \begin{pmatrix} \mathbf{divergence}(s,\ G_1(\bot)) \ \lor\ (s,\ G_1(\bot)) \to_* (t,\ \epsilon) \\ \lhd(s;b)\rhd \\ \mathbf{divergence}(s,\ G_2(\bot)) \ \lor\ (s,\ G_2(\bot)) \to_* (t,\ \epsilon) \end{pmatrix} \quad \{\text{Rule (3) in Def 5.2}\}$$

$$\implies \mathbf{divergence}(s.\,G(\bot)) \lor (s,\ G(\bot)) \to_* (t,\ \epsilon)$$

(2) $G(Q) = \oplus\{\alpha_1 : G_1(Q),\ \dots \alpha_k : G_k(Q)\}$. Similar to Case (1).

(3) $G(Q) = G_1(Q); G_2(Q)$

$$(s,\ G(Q)) \to_* (t,\ \epsilon) \qquad\qquad \{\text{Rule (4) in Def 5.2}\}$$

$$\implies \exists u \bullet \begin{pmatrix} (s,\ G_1(Q)) \to_* (u,\ \epsilon)\ \lor \\ (u,\ G_2(Q)) \to_* (t,\ \epsilon) \end{pmatrix} \qquad\qquad \{\text{Induction hypothesis}\}$$

$$\implies \exists u \bullet \begin{pmatrix} \mathbf{divergence}(s,\ G_1(\bot)) \ \lor \\ (s,\ G_1(\bot)) \to_* (u,\ \epsilon)\ \lor \\ \mathbf{divergence}(u,\ G_2(\bot)) \ \lor \\ (u,\ G_2(\bot)) \to_* (t,\ \epsilon) \end{pmatrix} \qquad \{\text{Rule (4) in Def 5.2}\}$$

$$\implies \mathbf{divergence}(s.\,G(\bot)) \lor (s,\ G(\bot)) \to_* (t,\ \epsilon)$$

(4) $G(Q) = \mu X \bullet P(Q,\ X)$

$$(s,\ \mu X \bullet P(Q,\ X)) \to_* (t,\ \epsilon) \qquad\qquad \{\text{Rule (5) in Def 5.2}\}$$

$$\implies (s,\ P(Q,\ \mu X \bullet P(Q,\ X))) \to_* (t,\ \epsilon) \qquad \{\text{Induction hypothesis}\}$$

$$\implies \begin{pmatrix} \mathbf{divergence}(s,\ P(\bot,\ \mu X \bullet P(\bot,\ X)))\ \lor \\ (s,\ P(\bot,\ \mu X \bullet P(\bot,\ X))) \to_* (t,\ \epsilon) \end{pmatrix} \quad \{\text{Rule (5) in Def 5.2}\}$$

$$\implies \begin{pmatrix} \mathbf{divergence}(s,\ \mu X \bullet P(\bot,\ X))\ \lor \\ (s,\ \mu X \bullet P(\bot,\ X)) \to_* (t,\ \epsilon) \end{pmatrix}$$

Lemma 5.5.

(1) $\mathbf{divergence}(s,\ F(P)) \implies \mathbf{divergence}(s,\ \mathcal{F}(\bot))$

(2) $\mathbf{divergence}(s,\ F(\mu X \bullet P(X))) \implies \mathbf{divergence}(s,\ F(P(\mu X \bullet P(X))))$

Proof. (1) Based on induction on the structure of F.

Base case: $F(X) = X$. The conclusion follows from the Rule (6) in Definition 5.2.

Inductive Step:

$$\mathbf{divergence}(s,\ F_1(Q) \lhd b \rhd F_2(Q)) \qquad\qquad \{\text{Rule (3) in Def 5.2}\}$$

$$\implies \begin{pmatrix} \mathbf{divergence}(s,\ F_1(Q)) \\ \lhd(s;b)\rhd \\ \mathbf{divergence}(s,\ F_2(Q)) \end{pmatrix} \qquad\qquad \{\text{induction hypothesis}\}$$

$$\implies \begin{pmatrix} \mathbf{divergence}(s,\ F_1(\bot)) \\ \lhd(s;b)\rhd \\ \mathbf{divergence}(s,\ F_2(\bot)) \end{pmatrix} \qquad\qquad \{\text{Rule (3) in Def 5.2}\}$$

$$\implies \mathbf{divergence}((s,\ (F_1(\bot) \lhd b \rhd F_2(\bot))))$$

$$\mathbf{divergence}(s,\ F_1(Q); F_2(Q)) \qquad\qquad \{\text{Rule (4) in Def 5.2}\}$$

$$\implies \mathbf{divergence}(s,\ F_1(Q)) \lor$$
$$\exists t \bullet (s,\ F_1(Q)) \to_* (t,\ \epsilon) \land \mathbf{divergence}(t,\ F_2(Q)) \qquad \{\text{Lemma 5.4}\}$$

$$\implies \begin{pmatrix} \mathbf{divergence}(s,\ F_1(\bot)) \lor \\ (s,\ F_1(\bot)) \to_* (t,\ \epsilon) \land \mathbf{divergence}(t,\ F_2(\bot)) \end{pmatrix} \quad \{\text{Rule (4) in Def 5.2}\}$$

$$\implies \mathbf{divergence}(s,\ F_1(\bot); F_2(\bot))$$

Lemma 5.6.

$$\mathbf{divergence}(s,\ F(\mu X \bullet P(X)) \implies \mathcal{T}(s,\ F(\mu X \bullet P(X))) =_A \bot$$

Proof.

$$\textbf{divergence}(s,\ F(\mu X \bullet P(X))) \qquad \qquad \{\text{Lemma } 5.5(2)\}$$
$$\implies \forall n \bullet \textbf{divergence}(s,\ F(P^n(\mu X \bullet P(X)))) \qquad \{\text{Lemma } 5.5(1)\}$$
$$\implies \forall n \bullet \textbf{divergence}(s,\ F(P^n(\bot))) \qquad \qquad \{\text{Lemma } 5.3\}$$
$$\implies \forall n \bullet \mathcal{T}(s,\ F(P^n(\bot))) =_A \bot \qquad \qquad \{\text{Theorem } 3.8\}$$
$$\implies \mathcal{T}(s,\ F(\mu X \bullet P(X))) =_A \bot$$

Lemma 5.7.

If P is finite, then $\textbf{fnitary}(s, P)$ holds for all states s

Proof. On structural induction

Combining Lemmas 5.2, 5.6 and 5.7 we conclude

Theorem 5.8.

The transition system defined in Definition 5.2 is consistent.

6   Conclusions

This paper begins with an algebraic framework for our probabilistic programming language, and then shows how to deliver the corresponding denotational and operational representations consistently. The main contributions include:

- Clarify the type of observations we are able to record during the execution of a probabilistic programs:
  - The behaviour of a program cannot simply be modelled as a relation between the initial data state and a finite distribution on the possible final data states.
  - The normal approach permits us to distinguish a program which can terminate and deliver a final distribution function from a program which can only generate an approximate distribution function during its everlasting execution.
- The test algebra lays down the foundation for construction of a denotational framework for our probabilistic programming language.
- The consistency of an operational approach against the algebra of programs can be formalised and validated within the algebra of programs.

The language we put forward in this paper has not included the nondeterministic choice operator given in the traditional programming languages. As a result, we lose the case where the probabilistic choice can be identified as a refinement of the nondeterministic choice. Moreover, the refinement order in the conventional languages was directly induced from the choice operator, whereas we were forced to adopt an inductive definition in Sects. 1 and 2 based on finite and infinite normal forms. Consequently, it makes the proof of monotonicity of programming combinators in this paper look cumbersome.

In future, we will investigate a language armed with both probabilistic and nondeterministic choice operators, and follow up the algebraic approach advocated in this paper to explore the links among various programming presentations for the probabilistic languages.

References

1. Jifeng, H., Qin, L.: A new roadmap for linking theories of programming and its applications on GCL and CSP. Sci. Comput. Program. Elsevier **162**, 3–34 (2018)
2. Abrial, J.-R.: The B-Book: Assigning Programs to Meanings. Cambridge Press, Cambridge (1996)
3. Abrial, J.-R.: Modelling in Event-B: System and Software Engineering. Cambridge Press, Cambridge (2010)
4. Dijkstra, E.W.: A Discipline of Programming. Prentice-Hall, Englewood Cliffs (1976)
5. Hehner, E.C.R.: A more complete model of communicating processes. Theor. Comput. Sci. **26**, 105–120 (1983)
6. Hehner, E.C.R.: Predicative programming, part 1 and 2. Commun. ACM **27**(2), 134–151 (1984)
7. Hennessy, M.C.: Algebraic Theory of Process. The MIT Press, Cambridge (1988)
8. Hoare, C.A.R., et al.: Laws of programming. Commun. ACM **30**(8), 672–686 (1987)
9. Jones, C.B.: Systematic Software Development Using VDM. Prentice Hall, New York (1986)
10. Plotkin, G.D.: A structural approach to operational semantics. Technical Report, DAIMI-FN-19, Aarhus University, Denmark (1981)
11. Spivey, J.M.: The Z Notation: A Reference Manual. Prentice Hall, New York (1992)
12. Jifeng, H., Seidel, K., McIver, A.: Probabilistic models for the guarded command language. Sci. Comput. Program. **28**(2–3), 171–192 (1997)

Space for Traffic Manoeuvres: An Overview

Ernst-Rüdiger Olderog[✉]

Department of Computing Science, University of Oldenburg, Oldenburg, Germany
olderog@informatik.uni-oldenburg.de

Abstract. Dense traffic on roads is calling for advanced driver assistance systems or even autonomous driving to increase the safety (collision freedom). How can we prove that such systems guarantee safety? Realising that safety on roads is a primarily spatial property, we started an approach to car safety that decomposes spatial from dynamic reasoning; it is based on a dedicated Multi-lane Spatial Logic (MLSL) [1], which abstracts from the continuous car dynamics, and controllers using MLSL formulas. The paper gives an overview of recent results in pursuing this approach.

1 Introduction

The news are full of reports on automation of car driving, ranging from advanced driver assistance systems to self-driving cars. This poses the challenge of proving safety (collision freedom) of traffic manoeuvres performed according to such automated systems. Different types of roads pose different challenges. On motorways all cars drive in the same direction, on country roads opposing traffic can occur, and in urban traffic complex road topologies like crossings have to be considered. Since cars have a dynamic behaviour that interacts with discrete controllers, they represent hybrid, i.e., mixed discrete-continuous systems. Thus safety is a hybrid system verification problem:

(1) car dynamics + car controllers + assumptions $\models$ safety.

Many approaches apply therefore methods of hybrid system verification to prove safety of traffic manoeuvres.

Early examples can be found in the context of the California PATH (Partners for Advanced Transit and Highways) project on automated highway systems. Here cars driving in groups called platoons are considered [2], and the manoeuvres include joining and leaving the platoon, and lane change. Lygeros et al. [3] sketch a safety proof for car platoons taking car dynamics into account, but admitting *safe collisions*, i.e., collisions at a low speed. Jula et al. [4] provide calculations of safe longitudinal distances between cars based on car dynamics. More recent is the work of Platzer et al. [5,6], who represent traffic applications in a differential dynamic logic $d\mathcal{L}$. This logic is well suited for specifying

© Springer Nature Switzerland AG 2018
C. Jones et al. (Eds.): Zhou-Festschrift, LNCS 11180, pp. 211–230, 2018.
https://doi.org/10.1007/978-3-030-01461-2_11

and verifying hybrid systems, and it is supported by the dedicated interactive theorem prover KeYmaera [7].

The problem is how to conquer the complexity of hybrid system verification. Abstraction, design patterns, and separation are concepts that are employed.

Althoff et al. [8] propose a bottom-up strategy, where a given hybrid model is gradually abstracted to Markov chains, for which the set of reachable states is analysed. Controller design patterns are exploited in Damm et al. [9], where a proof rule for collision freedom of two traffic agents based on criticality functions is proposed. This proof rule has been applied to verify a distance controller for cars. However, it is not clear how to extend this approach to deal with arbitrarily many cars on a motorway.

Our key observation was that safety is a *spatial property*: cars behave safely (avoid collisions) if at every moment they occupy disjoint spaces on the road. We first explicated this idea in [1] by introducing an abstract model of multi-lane motorway traffic based on spatial properties of local views of cars. The properties are expressed in a new dedicated *Multi-Lane Spatial Logic* (MLSL). Thus our approach replaces (1) by

(2) spatial logic + abstract car controllers + assumptions $\models$ safety,

thereby hiding the car dynamics. The spatial logic provides a discrete model of the traffic. In [10] we showed how it is linked to the underlying dynamic model.

Thus our approach is in line with work on controller design for hybrid systems that separate the dynamics from the control layer. Raisch et al. [11,12] introduce abstraction and refinement to support a hierarchical design of hybrid control systems. Van Schuppen et al. [13] introduce synthesis of control laws for piecewise-affine hybrid systems based on simplices. Novel is our emphasis on spatial properties at the control layer.

The definition of MLSL was inspired by work in and following up the ProCoS project. ProCoS stands for "Provably Correct Systems", a basic research project funded by the European Commission from 1989 to 1995 [14,15]. In ProCoS the universities of Oxford, Kiel, and Oldenburg, and the Technical University of Denmark at Lyngby collaborated. Its goal was to develop a mathematical basis for the development of embedded, real-time computer systems.

The research in ProCoS was much influenced by the work of two Chinese scientists contributing to the project at Lyngby and Oxford: Zhou Chaochen and He Jifeng. Zhou Chaochen and A.P. Ravn initiated a major conceptual development of ProCoS: the *Duration Calculus* (DC), an interval-based logic for specifying real-time requirements inspired by Moskowski's (discrete) interval temporal logic [16], The first paper on it was published by Zhou Chaochen, C.A.R. Hoare and A.P. Ravn in 1991 [17].

DC formulae are evaluated on intervals of the time domain, which is usually given by the set $\mathbb{R}_{\geq 0}$ of non-negative real numbers (continuous time). Additionally, discrete DC is investigated, where the time domain is given by the set $\mathbb{N}$ of natural numbers. Central to DC is the integral operator to measure the duration of a state and the chop operator (denoted by ;) from interval logic: a DC formula

$F_1; F_2$ holds on an interval $[b, e]$ if there exists a chop point $m \in [b, e]$ such that the formula F_1 holds on the initial subinterval $[b, m]$ and the formula F_2 on the final subinterval $[m, e]$.

The challenge to extend DC to cope also with spatial aspects has first been addressed by A. Schäfer, who developed the *Shape Calculus* (SC) [18,19]. SC formulae are evaluated on n-dimensional polyhedras in $\mathbb{R}^n$ for $n \geq 2$. Typically, one dimension represents time, the others space. SC has an extended chop operator, which takes a vector $\boldsymbol{d} \in \mathbb{R}^n$ as a parameter. Instead of chopping intervals at a chop point, SC chops polyhedra by an $(n - 1)$-dimensional hyperplane that is orthogonal to $\boldsymbol{d}$. Schäfer showed how to reason about the safety of movements of robots in time and space in his calculus [20]. However, the calculations are quite complicated.

Traffic on roads is restricted to two-dimensional movements. Therefore MLSL is a two-dimensional spatial logic for specifying properties of multi-lane traffic. The dimension modelling the direction of the traffic flow is continuous given by the real numbers $\mathbb{R}$, whereas the other dimension modelling the number of lanes is discrete given by a finite subset of the natural numbers $\mathbb{N}$. So we will only specify whether or not a car is occupying (part of) a lane, but not how much of it. However, in the direction of traffic flow we can distinguish real-valued lengths of an occupied space.

MLSL formulae are evaluated on local views, which contain finite two-dimensional parts of the infinite multi-lane road. Central for the practical expressiveness are two chop operators, one in each dimension. An MLSL formula $\phi_1 \frown \phi_2$ expresses that the current view V can be divided into two horizontally adjacent subviews V_1 and V_2 such that ϕ_1 holds in V_1 and ϕ_2 in V_2. An MLSL formula $\frac{\phi_2}{\phi_1}$ expresses that the current view V can be divided into two vertically adjacent subviews V_1 and V_2 where ϕ_1 holds in V_1 and ϕ_2 in V_2.

Our paper is organised as follows. In the subsequent Sect. 2, we recall our abstract model of multi-lane traffic on motorways and define the basic version of MLSL. In Sect. 3, we recall the basic lane change controller for safe lane changes. In Sect. 4, we state the Safety Theorem. In Sect. 5, we describe how formally link the abstract spatial to the underlying dynamic model of cars. In Sect. 6, we review results that have been obtained for (un)decidability and tool support for MLSL. In the final Sect. 7, we briefly discuss the challenges of traffic on country roads and in urban settings, and indicate some future work.

2 Model

In [1], we introduced an abstract model of multi-lane highway traffic. Cars have unique identifiers drawn from an infinite set $\mathbb{I} = \{A, B, \ldots\}$. The road is considered infinite in length with positions represented by real numbers in $\mathbb{R}$ and finite in width with lanes represented by a finite set of natural numbers, $\mathbb{L} = \{0, \ldots, N\}$. On a highway, all traffic proceeds in one direction, with increasing position values, in pictures shown from left to right: see Fig. 1. Assuming an

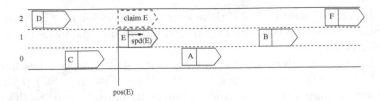

Fig. 1. Multi-lane highway with lanes 0,1,2 and cars $A, \ldots, F$ driving to the right. The rectangular box around each car identifier indicates the size of the car. The extension to the right with the angle represents the braking distance of the car at its current speed. The reservation of a car at its current position is the space comprising its size plus its braking distance. A claim of a car is represented by a space of the same size as a reservation, but surrounded by dashed lines. For example, car E at position $pos(E)$ and with speed $spd(E)$ is preparing for a lane change manoeuvre by claiming space on its neighbouring lane 2.

infinite length of the road frees us from distinguishing the beginning and end of the road.

A *traffic snapshot* describes where at a certain moment cars are positioned on the road and what their current speed is. The latter determines how much space a car reserves or claims because the length of a reservation or claim is taken as the size of the car plus the braking distance of the car. Formally, it is a structure $\mathcal{T} = (pos, spd, res, clm)$, where

- $pos : \mathbb{I} \to \mathbb{R}$ records the car positions (measured at their back),
- $spd : \mathbb{I} \to \mathbb{R}$ records the current speeds,
- $res : \mathbb{I} \to \mathcal{P}(\mathbb{L})$ records the reserved lanes,
- $clm : \mathbb{I} \to \mathcal{P}(\mathbb{L})$ records the claimed lanes.

The evolution of the traffic is modelled by transitions $\mathcal{T} \xrightarrow{\alpha} \mathcal{T}'$ between traffic snapshot, where α is an action of the following type:

$$\mathcal{T} \xrightarrow{t} \mathcal{T}' \quad \text{– time passes and all cars proceed in their current lane,}$$

$$\mathcal{T} \xrightarrow{c(C,n)} \mathcal{T}' \quad \text{– car } C \text{ puts a claim on lane } n,$$

$$\mathcal{T} \xrightarrow{wd\_c(C)} \mathcal{T}' \quad \text{– car } C \text{ withdraws its claim,}$$

$$\mathcal{T} \xrightarrow{r(C)} \mathcal{T}' \quad \text{– car } C \text{ converts its claim into a reservation,}$$

$$\mathcal{T} \xrightarrow{wd\_r(C,n)} \mathcal{T}' \quad \text{– car } C \text{ withdraws all reservations, except for lane } n.$$

Although the road itself is considered as infinite, at each moment only a finite view for each car is relevant: see Fig. 2. Formally, a view is a structure $V = (L, X, E)$, where

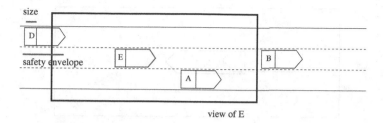

view of E

Fig. 2. The large rectangle shows the view of car E. Thus E cannot see car B.

- L is a subinterval of $\mathbb{L}$,
- X is a finite subinterval of $\mathbb{R}$,
- $E \in \mathbb{I}$ is the identifier of the car under consideration.

2.1 Multi-Lane Spatial Logic

Formulae of the Multi-Lane Spatial Logic MLSL describe the properties of traffic snapshots that we need to safeguard traffic manoeuvres. In its basic form, the syntax of MLSL [1] uses car variables c, d, among them a special variable ego, and is defined by the following set of formulae ϕ:

$$\phi ::= true \mid c = d \mid free \mid re(c) \mid cl(c) \qquad \text{(atoms)}$$

$$\mid \phi_1 \wedge \phi_2 \mid \neg\phi_1 \mid \exists c\colon \phi_1 \qquad \text{(first-order logic)}$$

$$\mid \phi_1 \frown \phi_2 \mid \begin{matrix} \phi_2 \\ \phi_1 \end{matrix} \qquad \text{(spatial chop operators)}$$

The formal semantics of MLSL is given by a satisfaction relation $\models$ between models and formulae. A *model* $\mathcal{M} = (\mathcal{T}, V, \nu)$ comprises a traffic snapshot $\mathcal{T}$, a view V, and valuation ν of the car variables. The definition of $\mathcal{M} \models \phi$ is by induction on the structure of ϕ [1].

Informally, the atoms *free*, $re(c)$, and $cl(c)$ express that in the considered traffic snapshot $\mathcal{T}$ the (space in the) view V is free of any car, that V is *reserved* by the car C denoted by $\nu(c)$, and that it is *claimed* (for a forthcoming lane change) by that car C, respectively. The informal meaning of the two spatial operators is as follows: the horizontal chop $\phi_1 \frown \phi_2$ expresses that the current view V can be divided into two horizontally adjacent subviews V_1 and V_2 such that ϕ_1 holds in V_1 and ϕ_2 in V_2, the vertical chop $\begin{matrix} \phi_2 \\ \phi_1 \end{matrix}$ expresses that the current view V can be divided into two vertically adjacent subviews V_1 and V_2 where ϕ_1 holds in V_1 and ϕ_2 in V_2. We use juxtaposition for the vertical chop to have a correspondence to the visual layout in traffic snapshots.

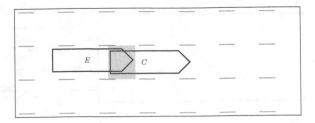

Fig. 3. The shaded area show a collision, i.e., an overlap of the reservations of car E and C.

We highlight the derived operator $\langle\phi\rangle$, pronounced *somewhere* ϕ, that combines the two chop operators and is essential when applying MLSL:

$$\langle\phi\rangle \;\equiv\; true \frown \begin{pmatrix} true \\ \phi \\ true \end{pmatrix} \frown true.$$

Example 1 (Collision check). Consider Fig. 3 of a traffic snapshot. To refer to the shaded area, we use the formula $\langle re(ego) \wedge re(c)\rangle$. Assuming that the valuation ν yields $\nu(ego) = E$ and $\nu(c) = C$, the formula expresses that somewhere there is a space where the reservations of the cars E and C overlap. The *collision check* can now be expressed by existentially quantifying over all cars different from ego: $cc \;\equiv\; \exists c\colon c \neq ego \wedge \langle re(ego) \wedge re(c)\rangle$. Finally, the safety from ego's perspective is expressed by its negation: $\neg cc$.   □

3   Controller

To safeguard lane change manoeuvres, every car will be equipped with a suitable controller. In general, we consider a variant of Timed Automata with data variables, called Automotive Controlling Timed Automata (ACTA). In ACTA guards and invariants are given by MLSL formulae and constraints on clocks and data. The actions of ACTA are those that appear in the transitions on traffic snapshots (see Sect. 2) or updates of clocks and data.

For defining the controller for a car E, we have to be explicit what E knows of other cars. Formally, we employ a *sensor function* describing what a car E can see of the spaces of other cars. In this paper, we assume *perfect knowledge*: E sees the full *safety envelope* of every other car D in its view, i.e., the size of D plus the safety space needed for braking to come to a complete standstill. In Fig. 2, car E sees (part of the safety envelope of) car D under the assumption of perfect knowledge. In reality, each car will have only limited knowledge of the other cars due to restrictions of its sensors. For example, a car E may see the size of other cars in its neighbourhood. Then car E cannot see car D in the view shown in Fig. 2.

Controller LCP: Lane Change under Perfect Knowledge. The controller LCP [1] of each car, referred to by the car variable ego, uses the following protocol cycle with four states $q_0, \ldots, q_3$ when performing a successful lane change: see Fig. 4.

- In the initial state q_0, car ego drives on its current lane, stored in the variable n, such that *no collision* occurs, i.e., the collision check fails (cf. Example 1). This is expressed by $\neg cc \equiv \neg \exists c: c \neq$ ego $\wedge \langle re(\text{ego}) \wedge re(c) \rangle$ stating that there is no other car c such that somewhere the reservations of ego and c overlap. At any moment, car ego may *claim* a new lane, say to its left, by proceeding to state q_1 with the action $c(\text{ego}, n + 1)$.
- In state q_1, the controller of car ego checks for a *potential collision*. This is expressed by $pc \equiv \exists c : c \neq$ ego$\wedge \langle cl(\text{ego}) \wedge (re(c) \vee cl(c)) \rangle$ stating that there is another car c such that somewhere the claim of ego overlaps with a reservation or claim of c. If pc holds, car ego withdraws its claim by performing the action wd_c(ego) and returning to the initial state q_0. If $\neg pc$ holds, car ego proceeds to state q_2.
- In state q_2, the controller of car ego continues to check $\neg pc$ up to a time-out *to*. If another car claims the same lane, pc holds and car ego withdraws its claim by performing the action wd_c(ego) and returning to the initial state q_0. If by the time-out $\neg pc$ still holds, car ego *reserves* the new lane by proceeding to state q_3 with the action r(ego).
- In state q_3, car ego changes lanes by gradually moving to the new lane. We assume that this lane change is completed within an upper time bound t_{lc}. Then car ego *withdraws* the reservation of the old lane by proceeding to state q_0 with the action wd_r(ego, l), where l records the new lane $n + 1$.

This protocol is implemented by the ACTA shown in Fig. 4. It uses a clock variable x and data variables n, l for storing lane numbers. The states q_0, q_2, q_3 have the invariants $\neg cc$, $\neg pc \wedge x \leq to$, $x \leq t_{lc}$, respectively. Transitions between states q and q' have the form

$$q \xrightarrow{g/a;r} q'$$

for a guard g, an action a, and a clock reset r.

4   Safety

A traffic snapshot is *safe* if it satisfies the property

$$Safe \equiv \forall c, d : c \neq d \Rightarrow \neg \langle re(c) \wedge re(d) \rangle.$$

We can prove that the lane-change controller LCP guarantees safety under the following *assumptions*:

A1. There is an initial safe traffic snapshot $\mathcal{T}_0$.
A2. Every car E has a distance controller DC keeping the property

$$\neg cc \equiv \neg \exists c: c \neq \text{ego} \wedge \langle re(\text{ego}) \wedge re(c) \rangle$$

invariant under time transitions, i.e., while E is driving on its current lane without changing lanes.

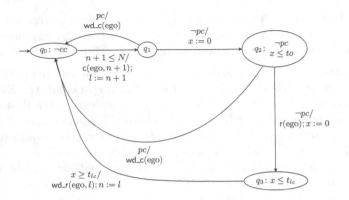

Fig. 4. The lane change controller LPC.

A3. Every car E is equipped with the controller LCP.

Theorem 1 (Safety of DC and LCP). *Under the assumptions A1–A3, every traffic snapshot $\mathcal{TS}$ that is reachable from $\mathcal{T}_0$ by transitions allowed by the controllers DC and LPC is safe.*

Proof. The proof proceeds by induction on the number of transitions needed to reach $\mathcal{T}$ from $\mathcal{T}_0$ and can be found in [1, 10]. □

5 Linking

In Sects. 2 and 3 we have introduced an abstract spatial model for reasoning about safety of traffic manoeuvres. It hides the underlying car dynamics by leaving the lengths of reservations and claims of cars uninterpreted. These lengths depend on the speeds and resulting braking distances of the cars.

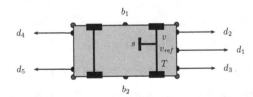

Fig. 5. The sensors and actuators assumed for each car.

In [10] we linked the spatial and dynamic model of traffic. Whereas the spatial model uses MLSL formulae built up from atoms like

$$free, re(c), cl(c),$$

the dynamic model is built up from differential equations for the car dynamics as well as sensors and actuators assumed for each car as shown in Fig. 5 from [10]. We assume that each car is equipped with the following observers:

- v gives its own velocity,
- d_1 gives the distance to the car ahead in the same lane,
- d_2 (d_3) give the distance to the car ahead in the left (right) neighboring lane,
- d_4 (d_5) give the distance to the car behind in the left (right) neighboring lane, and
- b_1 (b_2) tell whether a car on the lane next to the left (right) one is "blinking", indicating a desired lane change to the left (right) neighboring lane.

Using Fig. 6, where a car E follows a car C, we outline the dynamic model from [10]. Differential equations describe the motion of car E:

$$\dot{d}_1(t) = v_C(t) - v_E(t)$$
$$\dot{v}_E(t) = -a(d_1(t), v_C(t)) v_E(t)^2 + u(t),$$

where $u(t) \in [\underline{u}, \overline{u}]$ and a is an auxiliary function. The safety distance d_s of car E with initial velocity v_E^0 can be calculated from these equations.

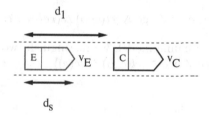

Fig. 6. Cars E and C with their velocities v_E and v_C, the distance d_1 between them, and the safety distance (extension of the safety envelope) d_s of E.

5.1 Linking: Distance Controller DC

DC keeps the property "no collision"

$$\neg cc \equiv \neg \exists c \colon c \neq \text{ego} \wedge \langle re(\text{ego}) \wedge re(c) \rangle$$

invariant under time transitions, i.e., when the car moves in its current lane and does not initiate or perform any lane change. Note that "no collision" is a symmetric property, looking forward and backward from car E at cars C as shown in Fig. 7.

We replace this symmetric property by the property "no collision forward":

$$\neg ccf \equiv \neg \exists c \colon c \neq \text{ego} \wedge \langle re(\text{ego}) \wedge re(c) \rangle \wedge \langle c \text{ ahead ego} \rangle$$

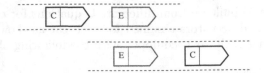

Fig. 7. Car E looking forward and backward for a car C on its lane.

The idea is that if each car is looking forward to prevent collisions then the symmetric property "no collision" is satisfied. The *linking predicate* is now

$$\neg ccf \Leftarrow d_s < d_1$$

stating that whenever the safety distance d_s is below the distance to the front car, the spatial property ccf is satisfied.

5.2   Linking: Lane-Change Controller LPC

The only safety critical transition of the controller LPC is the one from state q_2 to state q_3 that turns a claim into a reservation. This transition is guarded by the spatial formula "no potential collision":

$$\neg pc \equiv \neg \exists c : c \neq \text{ego} \wedge \langle cl(\text{ego}) \wedge (re(c) \vee cl(c)) \rangle .$$

For linking it with the dynamic model, we distinguish two cases:
Case 1 : $\phi_{re} \equiv \neg \exists c : c \neq \text{ego} \wedge \langle cl(\text{ego}) \wedge re(c) \rangle$

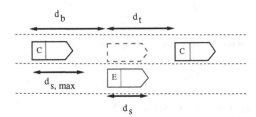

Fig. 8. Potential collision check of car E w.r.t. other reservations.

The formula ϕ_{re} states that no (other) car c on ego's target lane has a reservation overlapping with ego's claim. The car c may be (i) ahead of ego (or aligned with ego) or (ii) behind ego. In subcase (i), the concrete controller looks forward using the observables d_s giving the safety distance needed for car ego at its current speed and d_t (with t either 2 or 3) measuring the distance to the next car c in front of ego on the *target* lane of its lane change maneuver. The concrete controller checks the inequality $d_s < d_t$. In subcase (ii), the concrete controller looks *backward* using the observables d_b (with b either 4 or 5) measuring the distance to the next car behind ego on the target lane and $d_{s,max}$, the maximal braking distance of any car, i.e., an *overapproximation* of the actual braking distance of that car. The concrete controller checks the inequality $d_{s,max} < d_b$. The subcases are summarised in Fig. 8. The *linking predicate* is here $\phi_{re} \Leftarrow d_s < d_t \wedge d_{s,max} < d_b$.

Case 2 : $\phi_{cl} \equiv \neg \exists c : c \neq$ ego $\wedge \langle cl(\text{ego}) \wedge cl(c) \rangle$

The formula ϕ_{cl} states that no other car c has a claim on ego's target lane overlapping with ego's claim. Such a car c may only be in a lane *next* to ego's target lane. In this case, the concrete controller checks with its sensor b_t (with t either 1 or 2) on the side of the target lane for a turn signal of some car c on the lane next to the target lane. The formula ϕ_{cl} is satisfied if $\neg b_t$ holds. This case is summarised in Fig. 9. The *linking predicate* is here $\phi_{cl} \Leftarrow \neg b_t$.

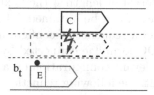

Fig. 9. Potential collision check of car E w.r.t. other claims: car E and C put claims on the same target lane.

6 Tool Support

When the foundations of an approach are laid, the search for tool support starts. We first report about negative results, dealing with undecidability.

6.1 Satisfiability Problem

The *Satisfiability Problem* for MLSL is defined as follows.

Given: an MLSL formula ϕ.

Question: $\exists \mathcal{M} = (\mathcal{T}, V, \nu) : \mathcal{M} \models \phi$?

Thus we look for a model $\mathcal{M}$ consisting of a traffic snapshot $\mathcal{T}$, a view V and a valuation ν that satisfies the formula ϕ. Two undecidability results have been established.

The first undecidability result is inspired by the undecidability proof for the satisfiability problem of the Duration Calculus (DC) by Zhou, Hansen and Sestoft [21,22], where the authors show that the Halting Problem of two-counter machines can be reduced to the satisfiability problem of Duration Calculus. The key idea is that in a *time interval* of fixed length 4 the current configuration of a given two-counter machine consisting of the control state and the arbitrarily large values of the two counters can be encoded by DC formulae. The first part of length 1 encodes the control state, the second part of length 1 the value of the first counter, the third part of length 1 a separator symbol, and the forth part of length 1 the second counter.

The encoding exploits that in DC with a continuous time domain arbitrarily many value changes of an observable (time-dependent state variables) can occur within a time interval of fixed length 1. Thus the arbitrarily large value of a counter can be represented within such a time interval. Also, it is convenient that in DC observables can range over arbitrary finite domains, here the set of control states plus some extra separator symbols. Further DC formulae specify how for each given time interval of length 4 the next time interval of length 4 encoding the next configuration can be obtained. The computation of the two-counter machine consisting of a sequence of configurations is then encoded by a corresponding sequence of DC formulae connected by the chop operator, where each formula specifies the relevant configuration on a time interval of length 4.

Inspired by this DC result, the following reduction has been shown in [23, 24]:

Halting Problem Problem for two-counter machines
$\leq$ Satisfiability Problem for MLSL with length measurement ℓ.

Here the symbol $\leq$ denotes *reducibility*. The idea is that in a *spatial interval* of fixed length 5 the current configuration of a given two-counter machine consisting can be encoded by an MLSL formulae with length measurement. Instead of DC observables, MLSL has only its three atoms $free, re(c)$ and $cl(c)$ for encoding the control states and the values of the counters. Since in traffic snapshots each car c can have only one reserved or claimed space in each lane, existential quantification is used. For example, the sequence of spatial length 1

$$(\exists c : cl(c) \frown \exists c : re(c) \frown free \frown \exists c : re(c) \frown \exists c : cl(c)) \land \ell = 1$$

with two existential reservations separated by a free space and framed by an initial and final existential claim encodes the second control state. The formula without the two embracing existential claims encodes the value 2 of one of the counters. A configuration of a given two-counter machine is then encoded by an MLSL formula with length measurement as follows. The first part of length 1 encodes the control state, the second part of length 1 the value of the first counter, the third part of length 1 an existential claim as separator, the forth part of length 1 the second counter, and the fifth part of length 1 an existential claim as final marker. The encoding exploits that reservations of cars can be arbitrarily short. Further MLSL formulae specify how for each given spatial interval of length 5 the next spatial interval of length 5 encoding the next configuration can be obtained.

In [25], a second undecidability result has been established for MLSL. The proof shows the reduction

$$\text{Empty Intersection Problem for context-free languages}$$
$$\leq \text{ Satisfiability Problem for MLSL.}$$

The idea is that an MLSL formula describes that each of the given two context-free grammars G_D and G_U have one derivation producing that same word of terminal symbols. The different terminal and nonterminal symbols of the grammars are encoded by sequences of reservations of different cars. Adjacent symbols are separated by free space. A derivation in grammar G_D is growing downwards from the top lane, using one lane for each (intermediate) sentential form, and a derivation in grammar G_U is growing upwards from the bottom lane, also using one lane for each (intermediate) sentential form. The encoding exploits that the width of the road can initially be chosen arbitrarily large. MLSL formulae express how a derivation step in one of the two grammars proceeds, thereby relating the reservations and free spaces of two adjacent lanes. These MLSL formulae are finally combined into one MLSL formula that is satisfied if and only if the context-free grammars G_D and G_U can produce the same terminal word.

As indicated above, the undecidability results for DC and MLSL exploit some artefacts of the models. In DC the time-dependent observables can change their values arbitrarily often within a given finite time interval. In MLSL cars can be arbitrarily small or roads may have arbitrarily many lanes. These assumptions enable the reductions to given undecidable problems. However, in the real world these assumptions are not met. What can be shown under more realistic assumptions? For MLSL, this is only partially explored. In the following we report on positive results in our search for tool support.

6.2   Search for Tool Support: Positive Results

One approach due to S. Linker is based on EMLSL, an extension of MLSL with modalities, that allows for an abstract formalisation of controllers and formal interactive proofs either manual in a formal proof system or mechanised inside Isabelle/HOL: see Sect. 6.3.

A second approach deals with checking MLSL formulae on specific given traffic snapshots. This would be needed when evaluating a guard or an invariant in a controller for the current traffic snapshot. Here two translations have been pursued. One translation by C. Bischopink in his BSc thesis (2016) is from MLSL into Quantified differential Dynamic Logic (QdL) developed by A. Platzer [26]. Another translation by M. Fränzle, M.R. Hansen and H. Ody [27] is from a variant of MLSL with so-called scopes into Quantified Linear Integer-Real Arithmetic (QLIRA): see Sect. 6.4.

A third approach connects our work on MLSL and controllers based on it with the model checker UPPAAL for timed automata. In [28], we consider a hazard warning protocol that combines spatial and timed properties. The verification of the timing conditions for a chain of cars communicating with each other requires an induction where the inductive step involving only the controllers of two cars has been checked by translation into and use of UPPAAL. In [29], liveness properties of an extended lane change controller maintaining MLSL invariants are checked with UPPAAL.

6.3   EMLSL with Modalities

In [24], S. Linker developed an extended version of MLSL, called EMLSL, that contains the following modalities to be able to reason about transitions inside the logic:

$\Box_{c(d)}$ - after all claims of car d,

$\Box_{r(d)}$ - after all reservations of car d,

$\Box_{wd\_c(d)}$ - after all withdrawals of claims of car d,

$\Box_{wd\_r(d)}$ - after all withdrawals of reservations of car d,

$\Box_\tau$ - after all *time* transitions,

G   - globally, i.e. after all sequences of transitions.

Example 2 (Formal Safety Specification). Using EMLSL, Linker [24] expresses the safety requirements for a car e and the properties of the distance controller and the lane change controller as follows:

Local safety of a car e : $safe(e) \equiv \forall c : c \neq e \wedge \neg \langle re(c) \wedge re(e) \rangle$

Global safety: $Safe \equiv \forall e : \mathbf{G}\ safe(e)$

Distance Controller: $DC \equiv \mathbf{G}\ \forall c, d : c \neq d \rightarrow$
$$(\neg \langle re(c) \wedge re(d) \rangle \rightarrow$$
$$\Box_\tau \neg \langle re(c) \wedge re(d) \rangle)$$

Potential collision check: $pc(c, d) \equiv c \neq d \wedge \langle cl(d) \wedge (re(c) \vee cl(c)) \rangle$

Lane Change controller: $LC \equiv \mathbf{G}\ \forall d : (\exists c : pc(c, d) \rightarrow \Box_{r(d)} \bot)$

The formula DC expresses that for different cars c and d when their reservations are disjoint they stay so under time transitions. The formula LC expresses that for all cars d whenever there is a potential collision with another car c then d does not perform any reservation action. Based on these specifications, Linker conducts formal safety proofs in two different ways. The first approach uses a system of *labelled natural deduction* for EMLSL introduced in [24]. Natural deduction allows for proofs from assumptions that can be eliminated later. For each logical operator the system contains an introduction and an elimination rule as known from first-order logic [30]. The *labels* refer to information about the semantics of EMLSL formulae that is available in the proof system. These are the labels ts for traffic snapshot and v for view. A labelled formula is then of the form $ts, v : \phi$, where ϕ is an EMLSL formula. Using this proof system for EMLSL, Linker [24] proved manually the following deduction:

$$\{ts, v : \mathrm{DC},\ ts, v : \mathrm{LC},\ ts, v : \forall e : safe(e)\}$$
$$\vdash\ ts, v : \forall e : \mathbf{G}\ safe(e).$$

The second approach uses a formalisation of the semantics of EMLSL in Isabelle/HOL to conduct a fully mechanised proof of an analogous safety result [31].

6.4 MLSL with Scopes

In [27], M. Fränzle, M.R. Hansen and H. Ody develop the idea that the satisfiability of MLSL becomes decidable if inside MLSL formulae car quantifiers $\exists c$ and the atom *free* refer only to *finite set* of cars. To this end, the authors introduce the set MLSLS of MLSL formulae (prefixed) with scopes. The scopes are motivated by sensors allowing only for a limited knowledge of other cars (cf. Sect. 3). The changes in the syntax and semantics of MLSLS are as follows:

- Syntax: a scoped formula is of the form $cs : \phi$ for a finite set $cs \subseteq CVar$.
- Semantics: models $M = (CS, \mathcal{T}, V, \nu)$ contain now a finite set $CS \subseteq \mathbb{I}$ of car identifiers. The inductive definition of the satisfaction relation $\models$ has the following new core cases:

$$M \models cs : \phi \ \text{ iff }\ (\{\nu(c) \mid c \in cs\}, \mathcal{T}, V, \nu) \models \phi,$$
$$M \models \exists c : \phi \ \text{ iff }\ (CS, \mathcal{T}, V, \nu \oplus \{c \mapsto C\}) \models \phi \text{ for some } C \in CS,$$
$$M \models free \ \text{ iff }\ \text{no car } C \in CS \text{ is in one-lane view } V.$$

An MLSLS formula ϕ_0 is *well-scoped* iff every subformula $\exists c : \phi$ and every atom *free* occurs inside a scoped formula $cs : \phi'$. Thus for checking the satisfiability of well-scoped MLSLS formulas only models M with finitely many cars need to be considered.

M. Fränzle, M.R. Hansen and H. Ody show in [27] that this can be exploited for a decidability result. The idea is to establish a reduction to the satisfiability problem of Quantified Linear Integer-Real Arithmetic (QLIRA), which is decidable:

$$
\begin{aligned}
&\text{Satisfiability Problem for well-scoped MLSLS} \\
\leq\ &\text{Satisfiability Problem for QLIRA.}
\end{aligned}
$$

The reduction uses the set $\mathbb{N}$ of natural numbers for encoding car identifiers and lanes and the set $\mathbb{R}$ of real numbers for encoding positions and spacing.

7   Conclusion

So far our presentation concentrated on motorways. There analysis is simplified by the fact that all cars drive in one direction. Other types of roads have also been investigated.

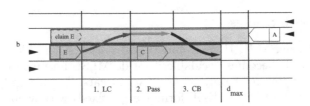

Fig. 10. Country roads: overtaking manoeuvre of car E in the presence of opposing traffic represented by car A.

In [32], we studied overtaking manoeuvres on country roads: see Fig. 10. This manoeuvre comprises lane change (LC), passing the car ahead (Pass), and changing back (CB). The challenge is opposing traffic. Thus a car E overtaking another car C has to check for enough space on the target lane (despite of opposing traffic, here A, for which an extra space d_{max} is added to absorb the movement of A while E is overtaking) and for enough space on the original lane (to reenter in front of C). The latter point is safeguarded in [32] by a suitable communication att (for $attention$) of E that asks C to help E when reentering the original lane in front of C: see Fig. 11. In particular, C will deny car D to perform a lane change in front of C.

To this end, each car has an additional *helper controller HC*, as shown in Fig. 12. for car C in the role of ego. With the transition from q_0 to q_1 car E behind C informs C that it has the intention of overtaking C. The transition from q_1 to the urgent state q_2 takes a request from car D that indicates with a

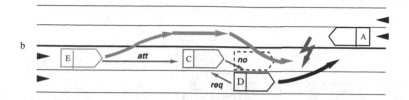

Fig. 11. Via communications car C helps car E to reenter in front of C.

claim the desire to change its lane and move in front of C. This request is denied immediately by answering "no" to C. With the transition from q_1 to q_0, the helper controller of C returns to its initial state when the car E has completed its overtaking manoeuvre and is thus in front of E.

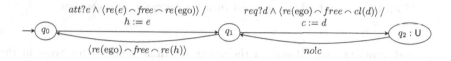

Fig. 12. The helper controller HC inside car C.

In [33], M.Schwammberger and M. Hilscher study the safety of car manoeuvres at crossings in urban traffic. There disjointness of curved spaces needs to be guaranteed. In Fig. 13, car E has the shaded curved space as its view. Along this view (extended) MLSL formulae are used to express spatial properties.

In all cases, adapted versions of the spatial logic MLSL served to establish the safety of traffic manoeuvres. For future work we leave the following topics:

- *Imperfect knowledge.* If cars do not know the extension of reservations of other cars, explicit communication between them is needed. For motorways this has been discussed in [1]. For country roads, S. Lampe studied this setting in his BSc thesis (2017).
- *Dense traffic.* For simplicity the extension of a reservation of a car includes the full braking distance needed to come to a complete standstill. This is safe but unrealistic in dense traffic. We can reduce the extension of reservations by taking the speed of the previous car into account.
- *Automatisation.* Clearly, more research on automatisation and tool support is desirable. First steps towards synthesis of controllers for lane change manoeuvres are reported in [34].

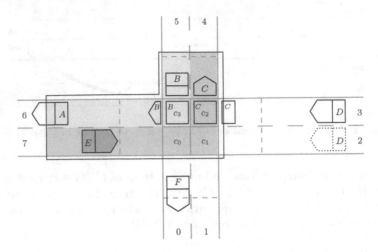

Fig. 13. Urban traffic: a planned turn left by car E at a crossing.

Acknowledgements. My interest in the safety of traffic manoeuvres arose in the Project H3 (Cooperating Traffic Agents) of the collaborative research center AVACS (Automatic Verification and Analysis of Complex Systems, 2004–2015). In particular, I thank Werner Damm, Andre Platzer, and Jan-David Quesel for inspiring discussions.

The following colleagues and students helped to shape the results on the spatial approach to traffic safety, many of them reported in this paper: Anders P. Ravn, Rafael Wisniewsky, Gregor v. Bochmann, Martin Fränzle, Michael R. Hansen, Sven Linker, Martin Hilscher, Heinrich Ody, Maike Schwammberger, Christopher Bischopink, Lasse Hammer, Christian Harken, and Sven Lampe. Many thanks to all of them!

We also thank the anonymous reviewers for their helpful comments that improved the presentation.

References

1. Hilscher, M., Linker, S., Olderog, E.-R., Ravn, A.P.: An abstract model for proving safety of multi-lane traffic manoeuvres. In: Qin, S., Qiu, Z. (eds.) ICFEM 2011. LNCS, vol. 6991, pp. 404–419. Springer, Heidelberg (2011). https://doi.org/10.1007/978-3-642-24559-6_28
2. Varaija, P.: Smart cars on smart roads: problems of control. IEEE Trans. Autom. Control **AC–38**, 195–207 (1993)
3. Lygeros, J., Godbole, D.N., Sastry, S.S.: Verified hybrid controllers for automated vehicles. IEEE Trans. Autom. Control **43**, 522–539 (1998)
4. Jula, H., Kosmatopoulos, E.B., Ioannou, P.A.: Collision avoidance analysis for lane changing and merging. Technical report UCB-ITS-PRR-99-13, California Partners for Advanced Transit and Highways (PATH), University of California at Berkeley (1999)
5. Arechiga, N., Loos, S.M., Platzer, A., Krogh, B.H.: Using theorem provers to guarantee closed-loop system properties. In: American Control Conference (ACC) 2012, pp. 3573–3580. IEEE (2012)

6. Loos, S.M., Platzer, A., Nistor, L.: Adaptive cruise control: hybrid, distributed, and now formally verified. In: Butler, M., Schulte, W. (eds.) FM 2011. LNCS, vol. 6664, pp. 42–56. Springer, Heidelberg (2011). https://doi.org/10.1007/978-3-642-21437-0_6

7. Platzer, A.: Logical Analysis of Hybrid Systems: Proving Theorems for Complex Dynamics. Spinger, Berlin (2010)

8. Althoff, M., Stursberg, O., Buss, M.: Safety assessment of autonomous cars using verification techniques. In: American Control Conference (ACC) 2007, pp. 4154–4159. IEEE (2007)

9. Damm, W., Hungar, H., Olderog, E.R.: Verification of cooperating traffic agents. Int. J. Control **79**, 395–421 (2006)

10. Olderog, E.R., Ravn, A.P., Wisniewski, R.: Linking discrete and continuous models, applied to traffic manoeuvres. In: Hinchey, Mike G., Bowen, Jonathan P., Olderog, Ernst-Rüdiger (eds.) Provably Correct Systems. NASA Monographs in Systems and Software Engineering, pp. 95–120. Springer, Berlin (2017). https://doi.org/10.1007/978-3-319-48628-4

11. Moor, T., Raisch, J., O'Young, S.: Discrete supervisory control of hybrid systems based on l-complete approximations. Discret. Event Dyn. Syst. **12**, 83–107 (2002)

12. Moor, T., Raisch, J., Davoren, J.: Admissiblity criteria for a hierarchical design of hybrid systems. In: Proceedings of the IFAD Conference on Analysis and Design of Hybrid Systems, pp. 389–394. St. Malo (2003)

13. Habets, L.C.G.J.M., Collins, P., van Schuppen, J.: Reachability and control synthesis for piecewise-affine hybrid systems on simplices. IEEE Trans. Autom. Control **51**, 938–948 (2006)

14. He, J., et al.: Provably correct systems. In: Langmaack, H., de Roever, W.-P., Vytopil, J. (eds.) FTRTFT 1994. LNCS, vol. 863, pp. 288–335. Springer, Heidelberg (1994). https://doi.org/10.1007/3-540-58468-4_171

15. Hinchey, M.G., Bowen, J.P., Olderog, E.R.: Provably Correct Systems. NASA Monographs in System and Software Engineering, 328 p. Springer, Berlin (2017). ISBN 978-3-319-48627-7

16. Moszkowski, B.: A temporal logic for multilevel reasoning about hardware. Computer **18**, 10–19 (1985)

17. Chaochen, Z., Hoare, C.A.R., Ravn, A.P.: A calculus of durations. Inf. Process. Lett. **40**, 269–276 (1991)

18. Schäfer, A.: A calculus for shapes in time and space. In: Liu, Z., Araki, K. (eds.) ICTAC 2004. LNCS, vol. 3407, pp. 463–477. Springer, Heidelberg (2005). https://doi.org/10.1007/978-3-540-31862-0_33

19. Schäfer, A.: Axiomatisation and decidability of multi-dimensional duration calculus. Inf. Comput. **205**, 25–64 (2007)

20. Schäfer, A.: Specification and verification of mobile real-time systems. Ph.D thesis, Department of Computing, University of Oldenburg (2006)

21. Chaochen, Z., Hansen, M.R., Sestoft, P.: Decidability and undecidability results for duration calculus. In: Enjalbert, P., Finkel, A., Wagner, K.W. (eds.) STACS 1993. LNCS, vol. 665, pp. 58–68. Springer, Heidelberg (1993). https://doi.org/10.1007/3-540-56503-5_8

22. Chaochen, Z., Hansen, M.R.: Duration calculus: a formal approach to real-time systems. Monographs in Theoretical Computer Science. An EATCS Series. Springer, Berlin (2004)

23. Linker, S., Hilscher, M.: Proof theory of a multi-lane spatial logic. Log. Methods Comput. Sci. **11** (2015)

24. Linker, S.: Proofs for traffic safety: combining diagrams and logics. Ph.D thesis, Department of Computing, University of Oldenburg (2015)
25. Ody, H.: Undecidability results for multi-lane spatial logic. In: Leucker, M., Rueda, C., Valencia, F.D. (eds.) ICTAC 2015. LNCS, vol. 9399, pp. 404–421. Springer, Cham (2015). https://doi.org/10.1007/978-3-319-25150-9_24
26. Platzer, A.: Quantified differential dynamic logic for distributed hybrid systems. In: Dawar, A., Veith, H. (eds.) CSL 2010. LNCS, vol. 6247, pp. 469–483. Springer, Heidelberg (2010). https://doi.org/10.1007/978-3-642-15205-4_36
27. Fränzle, M., Hansen, M.R., Ody, H.: No need knowing numerous neighbours. In: Meyer, R., Platzer, A., Wehrheim, H. (eds.) Correct System Design. LNCS, vol. 9360, pp. 152–171. Springer, Cham (2015). https://doi.org/10.1007/978-3-319-23506-6_11
28. Olderog, E.-R., Schwammberger, M.: Formalising a hazard warning communication protocol with timed automata. In: Aceto, L., Bacci, G., Bacci, G., Ingólfsdóttir, A., Legay, A., Mardare, R. (eds.) Models, Algorithms, Logics and Tools. LNCS, vol. 10460, pp. 640–660. Springer, Cham (2017). https://doi.org/10.1007/978-3-319-63121-9_32
29. Schwammberger, M.: Introducing liveness into multi-lane spatial logic lane controllers using uppaal. In: Gleirscher, M., Kugele, S., Linker, S., (eds.) Proceedings of the Safe Control of Autonomous Vehicles (SCAV). EPTCS (2018), to appear
30. van Dalen, D.: Logic and Structure. Universitext, 3rd edn. Springer, Berlin (1994)
31. Linker, S.: Spatial reasoning about motorway traffic safety with Isabelle/HOL. In: Polikarpova, N., Schneider, S. (eds.) IFM 2017. LNCS, vol. 10510, pp. 34–49. Springer, Cham (2017). https://doi.org/10.1007/978-3-319-66845-1_3
32. Hilscher, M., Linker, S., Olderog, E.-R.: Proving safety of traffic manoeuvres on country roads. In: Liu, Z., Woodcock, J., Zhu, H. (eds.) Theories of Programming and Formal Methods. LNCS, vol. 8051, pp. 196–212. Springer, Heidelberg (2013). https://doi.org/10.1007/978-3-642-39698-4_12
33. Hilscher, M., Schwammberger, M.: An abstract model for proving safety of autonomous Urban traffic. In: Sampaio, A., Wang, F. (eds.) ICTAC 2016. LNCS, vol. 9965, pp. 274–292. Springer, Cham (2016). https://doi.org/10.1007/978-3-319-46750-4_16
34. Bochmann, G.V., Hilscher, M., Linker, S., Olderog, E.R.: Synthesizing and verifying controllers for multi-lane traffic maneuvers. Form. Asp. Comput. 29, 583–600 (2017)
35. Larsen, K.G., Mikučionis, M., Taankvist, J.H.: Safe and optimal adaptive cruise control. In: Meyer, R., Platzer, A., Wehrheim, H. (eds.) Correct System Design. LNCS, vol. 9360, pp. 260–277. Springer, Cham (2015). https://doi.org/10.1007/978-3-319-23506-6_17
36. Xu, B., Li, Q.: A spatial logic for modeling and verification of collision-free control of vehicles. In: Wang, H., Mokhtari, M., (eds.) 21st International Conference on Engineering of Complex Computer Systems (ICECCS), pp. 33–42. IEEE Computer Society (2016)

Cloud Robotics: A Distributed Computing View

Wang Huaimin[1], Ding Bo[1(✉)], and Jie Xu[2]

[1] College of Computer, National University of Defense Technology, Hunan
410073, China
{hmwang,dingbo}@nudt.edu.cn
[2] School of Computing, University of Leeds, Leeds LS29JT, UK
J.Xu@leeds.ac.uk

Abstract. As an interdiscipline of distributed computing and robots, cloud robotics concerns augmenting robot capabilities by connecting them to the powerful backend cloud computing infrastructure. It is a field of great potential, and most recent discussions on this topic are from the point of view of robotics. In this paper, we discuss this field mainly from the aspect of distributed and cloud computing, i.e., "what distributed computing technologies can contribute to cloud robotics?" and "what challenges does cloud robotics bring to distributed computing?" This paper also presents our early experience towards a cloud robotic software infrastructure which is based on the newly-emerged edge computing model and supports the direct deployment of existing ROS (Robot Operating System) packages.

Keywords: Distributed computing · Cloud robotics · Collective intelligence
Quality of service

1 Introduction

"Connecting" is the eternal theme of distributed computing. In the past half-century, we have witnessed the continuous evolution of devices to be connected, from a few terminals on the ARPANET to numerous ubiquitous computing devices on the Internet. The driven forces behind this amazing evolution were two-fold. Firstly, "the whole is greater than the sum of the parts", thus connections inside the cyberspace are always strongly encouraged. This is also the primary source of strength of distributed computing. Secondly, connections among computation nodes also imply the connections among their human users. Thus, crowd intelligence [1] in the human society can be exploited on an unprecedented scale with distributed computing. It is beyond all doubt that these two forces, i.e., connecting entities in the cyberspace and connecting the human intelligence, will continue to drive the prosperity of distributed computing.

However, the above-mentioned two forces will not be the only ones at work in the future. Today, more and more computing devices are able to interact with the world directly by physical sensors and actuators instead of only reside in the cyberspace.

C. Jones et al. (Eds.): Zhou-Festschrift, LNCS 11180, pp. 231–245, 2018.
https://doi.org/10.1007/978-3-030-01461-2_12

Along with this trend, distributed computing is starting a new journey of connecting the entities in the physical space. Cloud robotics [2], a recently-emerged cross discipline of robotics and cloud computing, is an effort towards this goal with far-reaching significance.

The word "cloud robotics" was first coined by the roboticist in 2010 [3]. In a cloud robotic system, robots, which perform complex tasks in the physical space, are seamlessly connected to the cloud, which acts as a back-end support center in the cyber space. The entities in the cyber and physical space achieve complementary advantages with the help of the network. In the field of robotics, cloud robotics has been regarded as "a key to the next generation robots" [2] and interests have grown dramatically in recent years. For example, "Robots that teach each other", being realized on cloud robotics, was ranked as a breakthrough technology of the year 2016 by the MIT Technology Review[1]; A major concern of the US NRI (National Robotic Initiative) 2.0 published in 2017 is how robots can learn to perform more effectively and efficiently using large pools of information from the cloud[2].

Up to now, discussions on cloud robotics are mostly conducted from the point of view of robotics. However, we can foresee that the "cloud in the cyber space + robots in the physical space" architecture is also a paradigm which has a far-reaching impact on the development of distributed computing. It is a key to enable the next-generation distributed system which can not only connect the cyber-space entities (as well as its users) but also connect the entities in the physical world. In this paper, we discuss cloud robotics from this aspect, focusing on two sides of a coin: "What distributed computing technologies can contribute to the development of cloud robotics?" and "what challenges does cloud robotics bring to distributed computing research?"

The remainder of this paper is organized as follows. In Sect. 2, we will focus on the driven forces of the emergence of cloud robotics, mainly from the aspect of computing techniques. Section 3 focuses on the roles of cloud in this novel computing paradigm. Section 4 discusses the challenges to the traditional distributed computing technology brought by cloud robotics. Section 5 presents our early experience in this field.

2   From Backend Computer to Cloud

Roboticists have long been plagued by the limited capability of onboard computers. Take SLAM (Simultaneous Localization and Mapping), a problem being regarded as a "holy grail" in the field of robotics which provides the means to make a robot truly Autonomous [4]. It aims at simultaneously drawing a surrounding map and locating a mobile robot itself. Although related algorithms have been improved largely in the past three decades, the huge memory and CPU footprint still limits its usage in large-scale scenarios. On the common embedded computing boards without a GPU accelerator, the

---

[1] 10 Breakthrough Technologies, https://www.technologyreview.com/lists/technologies/2016/

[2] National Robotics Initiative 2.0: Ubiquitous Collaborative Robots (NRI-2.0), https://www.nsf.gov/pubs/2017/nsf17518/nsf17518.htm

3D dense SLAM algorithm can only achieve a performance of 5.5 fps at most even with a very low-resolution visual data input (256 pixels on each dimension) [5].

A straightforward way to address this challenge is connecting the robot with high-performance back-end computer(s). It is common in traditional robotic research. As early as the 1960s, attempts have been made to connect robots with time-shared computers [6]. Although they have some similarities to cloud robotic systems, there exist essential differences. A "robot + backend computer" system is usually designed for a dedicated task with a tightly-coupled structure and closed boundary. However, the following recent achievements in distributed computing make things different:

- *Computing as utilities.* With the development of distributed computing, people can get massive computing capabilities by loosely connecting a lot of computers together instead of building a dedicated and expensive monolith. Moreover, with the cloud technology, computing capabilities can be accessed like other on-demand utilities such as water and electricity. A recent record of this kind of practice is made in June 2017: On a dynamically-formed, short-lived virtual machine cluster which has 580,000 cores based on the Google Compute Engine, 300 CPU-years of computation is completed in several hours[3].
- *Big data as services.* According to IDC, approximately 80 billion devices will be connected and the amount of data created worldwide annually will hit 180 zetta-bytes by 2025. These big datasets contain knowledge missing in traditional small-scale datasets, which are most likely to contribute to robot's intelligence. Moreover, mining the potential of such large-scale data requires powerful infrastructure and well-designed software. The development of cloud computing makes it possible to store, analyze, and access them in a service-oriented style conveniently.
- *Network as ubiquitous facility.* Another significant progress in the past decades is the development and popularity of network infrastructure, from high-speed global backbones to various "last-mile" access methods, such as Wi-Fi, satellite and the upcoming 5G communication. It makes it possible for the robots to seamlessly access the cyber-space entities.

These three aspects in distributed computing jointly contribute to the emergence of cloud robotics: "Computing as utilities" enables robots to obtain computation support in a loosely-coupled and on-demand style, "Big data as services" enables robots to break their native knowledge limitations by mining the potential of big data, and "Network as ubiquitous infrastructure" enables the former two actions can be done anytime anywhere. They also differentiate cloud robotic systems with previous "robot + backend computer" systems, which only focus on computation support and have a fixed structure with a closed boundary.

---

[3] 220,000 cores and counting. https://cloudplatform.googleblog.com/2017/04/220000-cores-and-counting-MIT-math-professor-breaks-record-for-largest-ever-Compute-Engine-job.html

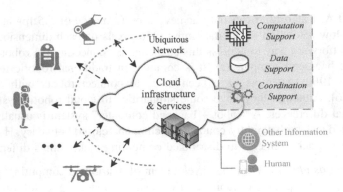

Fig. 1. Architecture of cloud robotic systems

3   Cloud Roles

As shown in Fig. 1, a cloud robotic system is an open and loosely-coupled distributed system involving the robots which can directly interact with the physical space and the cloud computing infrastructure in the cyber space which provides computation, data and coordination support to the former. This section focuses on the roles of the cloud in cloud robotics and discusses these three aspects of support in depth. A set of cases are chosen from existing cloud robotic practices to illustrate the driven forces to introduce cloud and related distributed computing techniques into robotics.

3.1   Computation Support

To achieve autonomy in complex settings, many robot algorithms are computationally intensive. Most of them are even inherently parallelized, such as visual data processing, high-dimensional motion planning, and machine learning by neural networks. In the past, because of the limitation of available resources, robotic engineers have to adopt compromised solutions or to introduce expensive, dedicatedly-designed hardware. The emergence of cloud robotics points out another way, that is, part of the computation can be offloaded to the cloud on necessary. The aforementioned SLAM problem is a typical example of computation offloading and also a case which has been intensively studied by the cloud robotic community.

–   (Case1: Cloud-supported SLAM) Robotic vision-based SLAM involves heavy and continuously-iterated computation, such as raw sensor data processing, feature extraction and matching, loop closure detection, etc. This process also exhibits a high degree of parallelism and are an excellent source for GPU accelerators and cluster computing. In a seminal work presented in [7], the performance of FastSLAM, a classic SLAM algorithm, is proved to be increased by orders of magnitude after being migrated to a Hadoop cluster and connecting the robot with this cluster.

3.2 Data Support

As an autonomous entity acts in the real world, robots need a large volume of data, in particular, the knowledge hidden in the data, to support their appropriate decision and action. Traditionally, they can only rely on the very little prebuilt-in data as well as its prebuilt-in knowledge acquiring algorithms with limited capabilities. With the cloud, robots can access a huge amount of data being not possible to be maintained by its onboard computer. And a large computational infrastructure is also the foundation to the successful processing, analysis and knowledge mining of various data at runtime. The following two cases are both related to robotic grasping, a task aims at enabling a robot arm to grasp a specific object. It is a seemingly simple but actually quite complex action which has been studied for several decades [8].

- (Case2: Grasping with big data-based services) In the traditional robotic grasping research, the planning of a grasp heavily relies on the knowledge of the target object. Accurate object recognition is the premise. Today, there are already a set of cloud services on the Internet which can provide object recognition function. Based on big data from the Internet, it can easily achieve the accuracy that a robot cannot achieve while only relying on its local data. In [9], an example which utilize an early cloud recognition engine, Google goggles, to facilitate robot grasping is presented.
- (Case3: Learning from robot's experience) People can grasp an object even without knowing its name. They just try and then learn from their experience. Google's hand-eye coordination experiment [10] is a mimetic of this data-driven method: By collecting the gripper and camera data from over 800,000 "trial and error" attempts and train a large convolutional neural network in the backend, robots successfully learn how to grasp a wide range of different objects, including novel objects not seen during training.

The above two cases illustrate two kinds of cloud data that can contribute to robots: (1) Datasets existed on the Internet and human world, which are collected by human crowdsourcing (e.g., image datasets with tags), recorded from real-life (e.g., human driving data) or gathered by other entities (e.g., the data from a smart traffic system). By accessing these data or the cloud services based on these data (e.g., image or voice recognition service), robots can learn from human intelligence or other information systems. (2) Datasets accumulated by the robot itself. The dataset in Case 3 is a typical example. By introducing the cloud computing infrastructure, it is possible to collect, store and process such data on an amazing scale. By leveraging machine learning and other data mining techniques, the robot's intelligence can be lifted to a new level.

3.3 Coordination Support

In a cloud robotic system, the cloud infrastructure is usually supposed to provide support for multiple robots instead of a single one. Therefore, the cloud can not only augment the individual capabilities but also facilitate the coordination among these robots. In concrete, the coordination support from the cloud can be divided into two layers: knowledge sharing and behavior coordination.

Knowledge sharing is the basis of robot coordination. Contrary to human, robots can instantaneously transmit the data they get over the network. It makes knowledge sharing much more easy to be realized, especially while a common repository, i.e., the cloud, exists in the backend. Each robot can contribute its data incrementally to the cloud and access the accumulated data when necessary. In this manner, robots are no longer insulated individuals but a collective whose knowledge can grow over time continuously. The following case illustrated this idea.

- (Case4: Million object challenge) The million object challenge[4] aims at collecting a corpus of robotic manipulation experiences for one million real-world objects. It is realized by knowledge sharing among the robots all over the world through the cloud robotic paradigm. As indicated in its webpage, "If we had all 300 research Baxters (a robot type) working, we could reach our goal of one million objects in just eleven days."
- Furthermore, the cloud can easily form a global view by aggregating data from a large number of robots and get knowledge on the global scale. Based on this global view and knowledge, it can act as an efficient coordinator for multi-robot behavior as shown in the following case. This is similar to many collective coordination actions in the human society, which is much more efficient while there exists a powerful backend command/support center.
- (Case5: Cloud-based robot task control) RoboEarth, an early project in cloud robotics, aims at building a World Wide Web for robots. As part of this project, a centralized task control system for multi-robot operations is presented in [11]. In this system, the task-required knowledge, such as environment knowledge, can be collected on the global scale, being most complete and up-to-date. And then, based on acquired information, the task planning layer allows multiple robots to cooperation by spreading duties.

4 Challenges to Distributed Computing

In the field of distributed computing, cloud robotics is not the first attempt to integrate cloud computing with frontend devices. A typical early attempt in this trend is the mobile cloud computing [5], a computing paradigm mainly concerns offloading computation of mobile devices (e.g., smartphones) to the cloud to save the processing capability, storage resources and battery lifetime. Another ongoing practice is the cloud of things [6], in which the cloud is similarly introduced to break the resource limitation of IoT (Internet of Things) devices. The cloud can also support the running of the whole IoT system, performing complex tasks such as large-scale data analysis.

Cloud robotics subsumes a portion of research issues of these predecessors in distributed computing. However, in contrast with traditional computing devices, robots

---

[4] Million object challenge. http://h2r.cs.brown.edu/million-object-challenge/

possess two unique features, which opens up a set of new challenges unique to cloud robotics (Fig. 2): (1) Deep cyber-physical integration. Robots are able to percept the physical world and, more importantly, manipulate it directly. Thus, QoS (Quality of Service), such as real-time assurance which is not a major concern in traditional cloud computing, becomes a key factor. (2) Autonomy. Robots exhibit autonomous or even human-like behavior as a whole. It implies heavy computation, a great demand for data and powerful machine learning algorithms for each individual. The coordination on the collective level has to be considered as well. These issues are barely touched in existing "cloud + terminal" research.

4.1 QoS-Awarness

Since robots directly manipulate the physical world, various constraints in the physical world will be mapped into robotic software in the form of Quality of Service, such as request response time and software reliability. For example, if an object recognition engine does not return a result before a time deadline, it just causes poor human user experience in mobile cloud computing. In contrast, it may lead to a catastrophic traffic accident on an auto-pilot vehicle if an obstacle is not recognized appropriately in time. However, a cloud robotic system is an open system. While we adding the remote cloud to the backend of robots, the introduction of uncertainty (e.g., unpredictable network latency) is inevitable. This situation gets worse while many services on the Internet and even the Internet itself are designed based on the "best-effort" model. To address this challenge, the following questions should be studied.

Differentiated QoS levels. Not all robotic tasks have strict QoS requirements. Some of them only need relaxed QoS, and in many cases even "a result is better than no result". Therefore, in a cloud robotic system, it is unnecessary to guarantee QoS at any time as strictly as robot's native software, which is also nearly impossible in practice. Instead, the platform should be able to provide flexible QoS guarantee on different levels and a concrete task can select from them with the tradeoff between capability augmentation and QoS. For instance, a hard real-time controller may have to run on the robot's onboard computer, but tasks with soft real-time requirement such as machine learning can chose to run on the cloud.

QoS-friendly cloud models. A prominent advantage of cloud computing is the low marginal management cost by concentrating and intensifying the resources (Fig. 3.a). However, it also means broad network access with a high degree of unpredictability and unforeseeable resource competition with other clients on the cloud. In addition, with a remote cloud being not fully under control, availability and privacy may have to be sacrificed. All these aspects have serious effects on the QoS assurance. Therefore, the traditional cloud model needs enhancement to be more QoS-friendly for robots.

In the newly-emerged edge computing paradigm (Fig. 3.b), on-demand services are provided by small-scale "edge" clouds instead of a centralized cloud being thousands of miles away. Since the resources and the network link to clients are easier to be controlled, edge clouds can provide highly-responsive services, support scalability via edge analytics and enforce privacy policies [12]. This kind of cloud can be placed in UAV operating centers or on robot command vehicles, and the powerful backbone

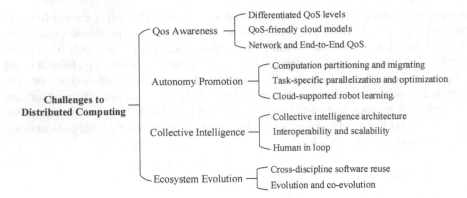

Fig. 2. Challenges to Distributed Computing

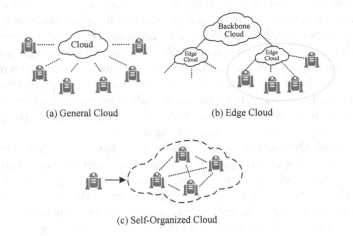

(a) General Cloud   (b) Edge Cloud

(c) Self-Organized Cloud

Fig. 3. Different cloud models in cloud robotics

cloud in the large-scale datacenter intervenes only when it is really necessary. Another potential variant of traditional cloud model is the self-organized cloud (Fig. 3.c). It consolidates idle resources of multiple robots themselves by virtualization and other cloud techniques. Since there is no need for continuous connection to a real cloud, it is useful under certain circumstances.

Network and End-to-End QoS. Appropriate network QoS, such as message priority and latency budget, is critical to the operation of cloud robotic systems. For instance, in a multiple UAV system, control commands issued from the backend should be delivered in a high priority while other data such as non-essential video captured by the UAV's camera can be delayed or even dropped if the network is overly congested. There already exist some studies on the management of packet loss, link delay, jitter and other network QoS properties in traditional distributed applications. They should be adapted and enhanced to fulfill the more stringent QoS requirement of robot systems. Furthermore, in order to gain end-to-end QoS and avoid unwanted situations such as priority inversion, the specified QoS properties should be propagated and inherited among each link in the "robot-network-cloud" chain. Only in this way, the system-level and end-to-end QoS property can be assured.

4.2 Autonomy Promotion

A robot is an intelligent machine that performs complex tasks in the physical world without explicit and continuous human control. As regarding each individual robot, the introduction of the cloud is supposed to promote such kind of autonomy. A similar concept named "computation offloading" [13], which concerns statically or dynamically migrating compute-intensive tasks from front-end devices with poor resources to the cloud, has been thoroughly studied in mobile cloud computing in the past decade. However, traditional research did not take the characteristics of robot tasks, such as QoS and computation parallelization, into account. And what is s more, the promotion of autonomy not only means heavy computation but also the great demand for data and knowledge. Therefore, while subsuming a portion of research issues of its predecessor, the autonomy promotion opens up a set of unique challenges to cloud robotics.

Computation partitioning and migrating. For a specific task, which part should be performed on the cloud need to be well thought out in a cloud robotic system. Existing works in partitioning mainly concern how to trade off between benefits and costs, achieving the goal of improving human user experience or saving local resources such as the battery life. However, for a robotic task, the impact on QoS should be taken into account as well, such as real-time property degradation and the risk of losing connection with the cloud. In addition, apart from the preconfigured partitioning model (i.e., computing-intensive codes are encapsulated as cloud services in advance and robots invoke them at runtime), there are already some initial attempts towards adaptive and on-demand offloading such as [14] and [15]. In this model, the cloud provides an environment that allows the robot to dynamically manage and run its compute-intensive code. Its realization needs a unified "cloud-robot" software architecture and the infrastructure which allows the flexible computation migration between robots and the cloud.

Task-specific parallelization and optimization. The pursuit of robot autonomy (e.g., promotion of perception precision and optimization of decision) is nearly endless. It means that the "ceiling" of computation requirement is much higher than that of traditional frontend devices such as smartphones. For example, robots are being expected to operate in ever-larger environments. However, the computation in SLAM algorithms based on EKF (Extended Kalman Filter) increases in quadratic time in the scale of the map. To cope with the amazing computation complexity, simply migrating robotic algorithms to the cloud server is far from adequate. Aggressive modifications are necessary to take advantage of multiple CPUs, rich memory, GPU accelerators and other cloud resources. Algorithms with the potential to exploit the above-mentioned features should be given priority in practice. Besides, to accommodate the distributed computing environment, existing algorithms may have to be enhanced to cope with time-varying network latency, limited bandwidth and QoS degradation.

Cloud-supported robot learning. A revolution driven by machine learning, especially deep learning, is taking place in the field of robotics. Deep learning has reached great success in complicated perception tasks (e.g., object recognition) highly related to robot autonomy. Some subfields, such as deep reinforcement learning [10], also exhibits great potential in robot control problems such as navigation and grasping. Since the training and prediction process is extremely compute-intensive and can be naturally parallelized, introducing the cloud into robot learning is a practicable choice. Take object recognition as an example. The state-of-the-art deep neural network algorithm [3] can only achieve a very poor performance (≤ 1 Hz) on a common desktop CPU. In contrast, with the powerful GPU-based parallel computing acceleration on the server, its performance can easily meet the real-time control requirements of many mobile robots. Another reason making the cloud indispensable in robot learning is the data support as we have discussed in Sect. 3.2, since deep learning is also extremely data-intensive.

4.3 Collective Intelligence

Collective intelligence is another challenge brought by robot autonomy. As a concept stems from the social science, collective intelligence emerges from the collaboration, cooperation, and competition of a group of individuals[5]. Recently, the development of distributed computing, such as the prosperity of the Internet and cloud computing, has promoted human social collective intelligence to a new level by connecting people on an unprecedented scale. As robots are also autonomous individuals and they can naturally coordinate through means in the cyber space, the cloud also has great potential to promote the emergence of robot collective intelligence. As illustrated in Sect. 3.3, there are already some initial attempts towards enabling robotic knowledge sharing and behavior coordination. However, a lot of challenges remains.

Collective intelligence architecture. The two major architecture styles having been thoroughly discussed in distributed computing are centralized (hierarchical) and peer-to-peer. However, both of them are not suitable for cloud-supported collective intelligence: The former one has to enforce stringent control from cloud to autonomous robots and the peer-to-peer one neglects the great potential of the backend cloud. An ideal architecture may be a mixture of these two ones, in which the cloud acts as an orchestrator instead of a controller. The role of the cloud can be analogous to that of a government in a market economy. Although this idea sounds very attractive, it is of great challenge in realization, especially in substantiating this style to be computable.

Interoperability and scalability. In classical cloud computing, the cloud only acts as a service provider that responds to requests passively. However, in a cloud robotic system, the cloud has to proactively send command or update information to the robots. Thus, firstly, the traditional "clients-to-cloud" interaction model is not enough and a well-defined "cloud-to-clients" model should be introduced. Secondly, the interoperation on the semantic level of both robotic data and robot behavior should be considered, especially while different robots are following different technical systems

---

[5] Wikipedia: Collective Intelligence. https://en.wikipedia.org/wiki/Collective_intelligence

today. Thirdly, for small-scale collective, the intelligence can be engineered, usually by introducing the cloud as a powerful backend with a global view and a vast amount of knowledge. However, for large-scale collectives, it is difficult to engineering everything. We may have to learn from complex systems and introduce related techniques such as mechanism design, behavior emergence and conflict resolution among multi-scale goals. The cloud provides an ideal base for substantiating these techniques.

Human in loop. Robotic tasks and robots themselves are highly associated with human. In cloud-supported collective intelligence, the role of human cannot be ignored. Basically, it can be divided into the following three categories: (1) human as an administrator of a robotic collective, (2) human as a call center, who is responsible for provide support when the robot's request is beyond the cloud capability, and (3) human as robot's partners, for example, as the recipients of robotic services or equal entities who can contribute to collective intelligence equally. For each kind of role, there exist a group of open issues have to be addressed. For example, human computation such as Amazon Mechanical Turk can provide support when the robot's request is beyond the cloud capability. However, the costs of human intervention with the cost of robot failure should be cautiously balanced [2].

4.4 Ecosystem Evolution

Another challenge to distributed computing society, not only on the technology level but also on the methodology level, is to lay the foundation of cloud robotic software ecosystem. A valuable lesson learned from existing practices is that complex distributed computing systems, like cloud robotic systems discussed in this paper, should not be built entirely from scratch and its construction is an ever-lasting growing procedure.

Cross-discipline software reuse. On the one hand, software reuse on the infrastructure level should be promoted. In traditional distributed systems, middleware and framework can significantly promote software reuse by encapsulating solutions of common problems. Similarly, there are many common problems in cloud robotics, which can be encapsulated into infrastructure and significantly simplify the development of cloud robotic system. On the other hand, the established development method in the robotic community, such as the broad adoption of ROS (Robot Operating System) [16] and the existing open-source software accumulation based on it, should be encouraged in building the cloud robotic software system. These two aspects both need the joint effort of the fields of distributed computing and robotics.

Evolution and co-evolution. A cloud robotic system should be able to adapt and evolve at runtime. For example, a collective should be able to learn from its experience and its capability can grow along with environmental and task changes. Furthermore, from the point of view of distributed computing, robots can be regarded as the tentacles of the cyber-space entities (such as cloud services and existing information systems) to the physical world. While the cyber-space entities evolve, which are very common today, a set of theory and technical means should be introduced to support the co-evolution of the cloud robotic systems.

5   Our Early Experience

Based on the observations on future directions, we started our research and practices. In this section, the overall architecture of micROS-Cloud, a cloud robotic software infrastructure towards the edge cloud model in Fig2, is presented. Some of the initial achievements towards its realization are also introduced.

5.1   MicROS-Cloud Architecture

As we have mentioned, micROS-cloud is expected to run on the "edge" cloud which is in the proximity of a group of robots. It is supposed to be connected to the robots directly and provide support to the robots seamlessly. Its underlying implementation is based on a modified version of ROS, a widely-adopted software infrastructure in the robotic community without cloud robotic supports. As shown in Figure 4, it is made up of the following parts:

- *Interoperability protocol.* It is responsible for the interoperation between robots and cloud, which can be chosen from WebSocket, DDS (Data Distribution Service for Real-time Systems) [17], and the ROS original protocol. All of them allows the "cloud to clients" reversed interaction.
- *Service container.* It provides PaaS (Platform as a Service) environment for cloud services. There are two kinds of service containers: Proprietary Service Framework and Cloudroid. The former supports the cloud services design dedicatedly to run on micROS-cloud, and the latter allows existing ROS packages being deployed as cloud services, whose details will be presented in the next subsection.
- *Knowledge base.* It stores knowledge highly related to the robotic mission. The knowledge can be stored in the backend database explicitly or in trained neural networks (such as CNNs) implicitly.
- *Management portal.* It enables the human operator to manage the deployed cloud services as well as the knowledge data.
- *Cloud phase transition.* It is the kernel component to enable the interaction between the edge cloud and the existing cloud services on the Internet. Its implementation is highly task-specific, and an example will be shown in the next subsection.

5.2   Initial Results

With the architecture presented in Fig.3, we have carried out a set of initial practices. All of them are open sourced in public for further investigation by other researchers in this field[6].

MicROS-drt. As discussed in Sect. 4.1, the dissemination of data with QoS assurance is an essential issue for distributed robotic systems. MicROS-drt [18] is an

---

[6] The code of micROS-drt can be accessed https://github.com/cyberdb/micROS-drt, the code of Cloudroid can be accessed at https://github.com/cyberdb/Cloudroid, and the code of object recognition with the support of the public cloud can be accessed at https://github.com/liyiying/cloudrobot-semantic-map

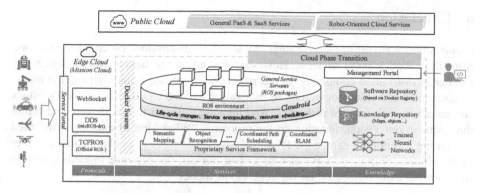

Fig. 4. MicROS-cloud software infrastructure architecture

infrastructure to achieve this goal. It elaborately adapting and encapsulating a mature data distribution standard, DDS, into ROS, the widely-adopted robotic software infrastructure. Evaluation results in terms of scalability, latency jitter and transport priority, as well as the experiment on real robots, have been validated the advantages of DDS over the original ROS protocols.

Cloudroid. Cloudroid [15] is a QoS-aware container for cloud services, which supports the direct deployment of existing ROS packages onto the cloud, transparently transforming them into cloud services which can be accessed in an on-demand style. Four fundamental mechanisms are deliberately designed to support the transparent transformation from the ROS package model to the general cloud service model, including (1) self-contained VM encapsulation, (2) cloud bridging, (3) on-demand servant instantiation and (4) service stub automatic generation. Besides, the QoS mechanisms built in the client-side stub and the resource scheduling/isolation mechanisms on the cloud side can do their best to maintain the desirable QoS property cooperatively. A set of experiments based on ROS packages being widely used in real-life robot practices show that robot's capability can be transparently and significantly enhanced with the cloud robotic architecture and the Cloudroid infrastructure, and specific QoS objectives can be guaranteed in this process. In some tasks, the introduction of cloud shows orders of magnitude performance promotion.

Semantic mapping service. This cloud service illustrates the feasibility of the cooperation of the edge cloud and the public cloud [19]. The cloud has great potential in supporting robotic semantic mapping because of its rich computing resources. However, how to utilize the vast knowledge on the Internet is still an open problem. In this work, we design a set of mechanisms to enable the edge cloud to seek help from the public cloud, such as CloudSight and Goolge Cloud Vision API, while it encounters an object that it cannot recognize in semantic mapping. In this way, we can minimize the recognition latency of objects which can be predicted while not sacrificing the ability to recognize strange and unexpected objects.

6 Conclusion

Cloud robotics is still in its early stage. Most recent discussions on cloud robotics are from the robotics point of view. However, this emerging field is also a significant frontier of distributed computing. In this paper, we discussed it mainly from the aspect of distributed and cloud computing. Its motivation and the cloud roles in cloud robotics are described with a set of real cases. And then we outlined the challenges and future directions in our vision, focusing on the problems "What kind of existing distributed computing technology can be used?" And "what challenges does cloud robotics bring to distributed computing?". We also described our early experience towards a robotic software infrastructure based on the edge cloud model.

Acknowledgements. This work is partially supported by the National Natural Science Foundation of China (No. 61751208), the Advanced Research Program (No. 41412050202) and the special program for the applied basic research of the National University of Defense Technology under Grant No.ZDYYJCYJ20140601

References

1. Li, W., et al.: Crowd intelligence in AI 2.0 era. Front. Inf. Technol. Electron. Eng. **18**(1), 15–43 (2017)
2. Kehoe, B., Patil, S., Abbeel, P., Goldberg, K.: A survey of research on cloud robotics and automation. IEEE Trans. Autom. Sci. Eng. **12**(2), 398–409 (2015)
3. Kuffner, J.J.: Cloud-enabled robots. In: Proceedings of IEEE-RAS International Conference on Humanoid Robotics (2010)
4. Durrant-Whyte, H., Bailey, T.: Simultaneous localization and mapping: part I. Robot. Autom. Mag. **13**(2), 99–110 (2006)
5. Nardi, L., et al.: Introducing SLAMBench, a performance and accuracy benchmarking methodology for SLAM. In: Proceedings of IEEE International Conference on Robotics and Automation (2015)
6. McCarthy, J., Earnest, L.D., Reddy, D.R., Vicens, P.J.: A computer with hands, eyes, and ears. In: Proceedings of Joint Computer Conference (1968)
7. Arumugam, R., et al.: DAvinCi: a cloud computing framework for service robots. In: Proceedings of IEEE International Conference on Robotics and Automation (2010)
8. Sahbani, A., El-Khoury, S., Bidaud, P.: An overview of 3D object grasp synthesis algorithms. Robot. Auton. Syst. **60**(3), 326–336 (2012)
9. Kehoe, B., Matsukawa, A., Candido, S., Kuffner, J., Goldberg, K.: Cloud-based robot grasping with the google object recognition engine. In: Proceedings of IEEE International Conference on Robotics and Automation (2013)
10. Levine, S., Pastor, P., Krizhevsky, A., Quillen, D.: Learning hand-eye coordination for robotic grasping with deep learning and large-scale data collection. In: Proceedings of International Symposium on Experimental Robotics (2016)
11. Janssen, R., van de Molengraft, R., Bruyninckx, H., Steinbuch, M.: Cloud based centralized task control for human domain multi-robot operations. Intell. Serv. Robot. **9**(1), 63–77 (2016)
12. Satyanarayanan, M.: The emergence of edge computing. Computer **50**(1), 30–39 (2017)

13. Dinh, H.T., Lee, C., Niyato, D., Wang, P.: A survey of mobile cloud computing: architecture, applications, and approaches. Wirel. Commun. Mob. Comput. **13**(18), 1587–1611 (2013)
14. Mohanarajah, G., Hunziker, D., D'Andrea, R., Waibel, M.: Rapyuta: a cloud robotics platform. IEEE Trans. Autom. Sci. Eng. **12**(2), 481–493 (2015)
15. Hu, B., Wang, H., Zhang, P., Ding, B., Che, H.: Cloudroid: a cloud framework for transparent and QoS-aware robotic computation outsourcing. In: Proceedings of IEEE 10th International Conference on Cloud Computing (2017)
16. Quigley, M., et al.: ROS: an open-source robot operating system. In: Proceedings of ICRA Workshop on Open Source Software (2009)
17. Pardo-Castellote, G.: OMG data-distribution service: architectural overview. In: Proceedings of Distributed Computing Systems Workshops (2003)
18. Ding, B., Wang, H., Fan, Z., Zhang, P., Liu, H.: MicROS-drt: supporting real-time and scalable data distribution in distributed robotic systems. Robot. Biomim. **3**(1), 1–8 (2016)
19. Yiying, L., Huaimin, W., Bo, D., Wei, Z.: RoboCloud: augmenting robotic visions for open environment modeling using Internet knowledge. Sci. China Inf. Sci. **61**(5), 050102 (2018)

Analyzing Interrupt Handlers via Interprocedural Summaries

Xueguang Wu[2], Liqian Chen[2(✉)], and Ji Wang[1,2]

[1] State Key Laboratory of High Performance Computing, Changsha, China
wj@nudt.edu.cn
[2] School of Computer, National University of Defense Technology, Changsha, China
{xueguangwu,lqchen}@nudt.edu.cn

Abstract. Interrupts are a commonly used facility to guarantee real-time response in embedded systems, and thus are frequently encountered in embedded software. Modeling interrupt preemption as function calls, is a natural choice for analyzing or verifying programs involving interrupts. Therefore, interprocedural analysis of interrupt handlers is highly desired when analyzing programs with interrupts. In this paper, we present two interprocedural analysis approaches specifically for analyzing interrupt handlers. One is based on tabulation of procedure summaries, while the other is based on procedure summaries that are built by partitioning inputs. These two approaches fit for interrupt handlers with different features. Finally, we show preliminary experimental results obtained by our prototype implementation.

Keywords: Interprocedural analysis · Interrupts
Abstract interpretation

1 Introduction

Interrupts are a commonly used facility to guarantee real-time response of high-priority events in embedded systems, and thus are frequently encountered in embedded software. In a program consisting of tasks and interrupts, during the running of a task, an interrupt handler (also known as interrupt service routine or ISR) is invoked once an interrupt is triggered. The task is preempted and resumes only when the interrupt handler has terminated. Such kind of programs are often called interrupt-driven programs (IDPs). In IDPs, interrupts may cause unexpected interleaving executions and even unexpected erroneous behaviors, of which programmers may be unaware. Interrupt related bugs are difficult to detect using testing techniques, due to the fact that the triggering of an interrupt depends largely on the underlying hardware as well as environment and it may occur at any time. Therefore, it is highly desired to leverage the analysis and verification techniques to ensure the correctness of programs in the presence of interrupts.

© Springer Nature Switzerland AG 2018
C. Jones et al. (Eds.): Zhou-Festschrift, LNCS 11180, pp. 246–262, 2018.
https://doi.org/10.1007/978-3-030-01461-2_13

In general, when an interrupt is triggered, the task (or the handler of a preempted lower-priority interrupt) will not resume until the handler of that (higher-priority) interrupt has terminated. In other words, the task and interrupt handlers in an IDP can be viewed as sharing a same stack. It means that, in IDPs, interrupt preemption can be modelled as a function call. Hence, one predominant approach to analyze IDPs is to first sequentialize IDPs into sequential programs and then leverage the existing techniques for sequential programs to analyze the sequentialized programs [29–31]. However, since an interrupt may be triggered at any time, function calls to the interrupt handler could be inserted to the original program after each atomic instruction. Hence, after modelling interrupt preemption as functions calls, the resulting programs may involve a large amount of function calls to interrupt handlers. To effectively analyze such programs, interprocedural analysis techniques are of great desire. However, completely context-sensitive approaches (e.g., those implemented based on syntactic or semantic inlining techniques) may be too costly, while completely context-insensitive methods may be too imprecise.

In this paper, we first discuss the features of interrupt handlers in practice. Then we propose two interprocedural analyses that are designed specifically to deal with interrupt handlers with different features. One approach is based on tabulated procedure summaries. The other approach is based on the procedure summaries that are built by partitioning inputs. Finally, we show preliminary experimental results on a set of benchmark and industry programs.

The rest of this paper is organized as follows. Section 2 discusses the features of the real-world IDPs in embedded systems. Section 3 presents the approach based on tabulation of procedure summaries. In Sect. 4, we show the approach based on procedure summaries that are built by partitioning inputs. Section 5 presents our implementation together with preliminary experimental results. Section 6 discusses some related work. Finally, conclusions as well as suggestions for future work are given in Sect. 7.

2   Features of Interrupt Handlers

In this section, we discuss the features of interrupt handlers in IDPs. First of all, interrupt handlers usually do not involve calls to recursive functions, for the consideration of guaranteeing real time response. Hence, for sequentialized IDPs, one can always inline all the calls to the invoked ISRs to derive a simple context sensitive analysis. However, the sequentialized IDPs often involve a large amount of calls to ISRs after sequentialization [29, 30]. Thus, we need to consider more interprocedural analysis methods to improve the efficiency, especially for large-scale IDPs.

Looking to the IDPs in practice, we may simply classify interrupt handlers into two kinds by their scale, i.e., small ISRs and large ISRs. The large ISRs often contain complicate event processing routine inside, e.g., involving a complicate process of collecting and processing the data received by sensors or hardware buses. The small ISRs often contain a very simple event processing routine, e.g., setting an interrupt-happening flag or increasing a counter. Sometimes, it is required to keep ISRs small because there exists strict real time constraints. If an ISR is too complicated, it is very hard to guarantee the real-time constraints of the whole system. In practice, for a low-priority interrupt which does not respond to very urgent event, to shorten the ISR, developers often play the following trick: set a flag variable in the ISR to indicate that the interrupt has already been fired, and move the complex event processing routine into tasks. Then during the running of tasks, tasks will check regularly the interrupt-happening flag and perform the complex event processing routine when needed. Some small ISRs may also include very simple event processing routine. For example, ISRs used in the serial communication interface receive and send one byte each time.

Take practical IDPs from industry as examples. The 1553-bus [1] and the CAN-bus [2] interrupts are widely used in aerospace industry. The embedded systems (or subsystems) involving 1553-bus interrupt often have strict real time constraints. Hence, the interrupt handlers of 1553-bus interrupts are often very simple, usually only setting an interrupt-happening flag, while letting the tasks deal with most of the event processing routines. On the other hand, the embedded systems (or subsystems) involving CAN-bus interrupt are often not so strict over the real time constraints. Hence, the interrupt handlers of CAN-bus interrupts often perform the event processing routine inside the ISRs, while the tasks in such a system are usually simple. Large and small ISRs are also encountered in many other industry control systems. The widely used TI 2833x series digital signal processors (DSP) also support these kinds of interrupts.

Considering the different features of these two kinds of interrupt handlers, we propose to use different inter-procedural analysis methods to analyze them. For large ISRs, we propose to use the analysis based on tabulated procedure summaries, which will be introduced in Sect. 3. For small ISRs, we propose to use the analysis utilizing procedure summaries via partitioning inputs, which will be introduced in Sect. 4.

3   Tabulation of Procedure Summaries

The main idea of tabulating procedure summaries is to store the input contexts and the corresponding output results that have been encountered for a procedure in a tabular manner. During the analysis, when encountering a new function calling, we check first whether the input context of this calling already exists in the tabulated procedure summaries. If it exists, we could simply reuse the corresponding stored output result in the tabulated summaries, with no need to re-analyze the function body. Hence, based on the tabulated procedure summaries, we can avoid re-analyzing some function calls to improve the analysis efficiency.

The concrete semantics of a function calling can be viewed as a mapping from a calling context to an output context, i.e., $\tau[\![f]\!] \overset{\text{def}}{=} C \to C$, where $C \subseteq \wp(\Sigma)$ wherein Σ represents a set of environments (taking into account both the local and global variables). The abstract semantics of a function calling can be defined as a mapping from an abstract context to another abstract context, i.e., $\tau[\![f]\!]^{\sharp} \stackrel{\text{def}}{=} D^{\sharp} \rightarrow D^{\sharp}$, where $D^{\sharp}$ represents a set of abstract contexts represented by abstract elements in an abstract domain. During the analysis of a program, we store for each function the new encountered pairs of inputs and outputs. Then when we encounter a new function calling, we first determine whether we need to analyze the function body, by comparing the current input calling context with the previous stored input calling contexts in the tabulated summary. Different scenarios are shown in Fig. 1.

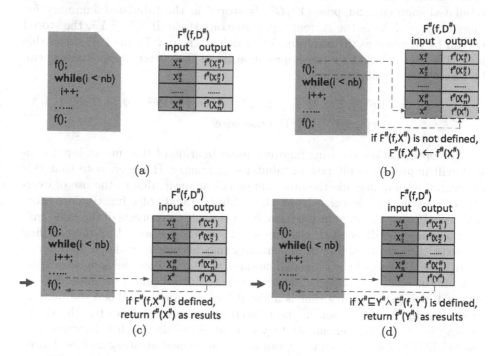

Fig. 1. Interprocedural analysis based on tabulated procedure summaries

The interprocedural analysis based on tabulated procedure summaries can be formalized as follows:

$$\tau[\![f]\!]^{\sharp}(X^{\sharp}) \stackrel{\text{def}}{=} \begin{cases} F^{\sharp}(f, X^{\sharp}) & \text{if } F^{\sharp}(f, X^{\sharp}) \downarrow \\ \tau[\![body(f)]\!]^{\sharp}(X^{\sharp}) & \text{otherwise} \end{cases} \tag{1}$$

where $F^{\sharp}$ is a partial mapping: $\mathcal{F} \times D^{\sharp} \rightarrow D^{\sharp}$, and $f \in \mathcal{F}$, $F^{\sharp}(f, X^{\sharp})$ returns the corresponding output result $O^{\sharp}$ under the given input abstract context $X^{\sharp}$, if $(X^{\sharp}, O^{\sharp})$ is stored in the tabulated summary for f. We use $F^{\sharp}(f, X^{\sharp}) \downarrow$ to denote that $F^{\sharp}(f, X^{\sharp})$ is defined in the tabulated summary (otherwise, denoted as $F^{\sharp}(f, X^{\sharp}) \uparrow$). We call such a function $F^{\sharp}$ a *tabulation function*. $\tau[\![body(f)]\!]^{\sharp}(X^{\sharp})$ analyzes the function body of f given the input $X^{\sharp}$, stores the result in the tabulated summary, and then returns the output result. At the beginning, the tabulation function $F^\sharp$ is empty. A new entry will be added to the tabulated summary for f when the encountered input context has never been met, as shown in Fig. 1(b). This process can be formalized as $F^\sharp(f, X^\sharp) \leftarrow \tau[\![body(f)]\!]^\sharp(X^\sharp)$. If the input calling context exists in the tabulated summary (i.e., having been met before), the output stored in the tabulated summary can be directly returned as the analysis result, as show in Fig. 1(c).

Since the abstract transfer function is monotone, it is safe to use an over-approximation of the current input context to check with the entries of the tabulated summary. Suppose $(Y^\sharp, O^\sharp)$ is stored in the tabulated summary for function f, and $X^\sharp$ is the current input abstract state. If $X^\sharp \sqsubseteq^\sharp Y^\sharp$, the stored $O^\sharp$ can be returned as the result for $X^\sharp$, which is a sound. Figure 1(d) shows this idea. The idea of using an over-approximation of the current input context can be formalized as follows:

$$\tau[\![f]\!]^\sharp(X^\sharp) \stackrel{\text{def}}{=} \begin{cases} F^\sharp(f, Y^\sharp) & \text{if } X^\sharp \sqsubseteq Y^\sharp \wedge F(f, Y^\sharp) \downarrow \wedge F(f, X^\sharp) \uparrow \\ \tau[\![body(f)]\!]^\sharp(X^\sharp) & \text{otherwise} \end{cases} \quad (2)$$

The optimization via using an over-approximation of the current input context will improve the hit rate in tabulated summary. However, note that this optimization may degrade the precision of the analysis, due to the use of over-approximation. On the other hand, the calling contexts of a function are often different. During the fixpoint iteration, even the calling contexts of the same calling point may be different. If the tabulated summary stores all of these calling contexts, the size of the tabulated summary may become quite large. In order to control the growing of the tabulated summary, we may consider some strategies to limit the size of tabulated summary, such as introducing a threshold for the size of tabulated summary that is allowed for one function. When the number of the entries for a function in the tabulated summary reaches the threshold, we may use some replacement strategy to control the size, such as least recently used (LRU) replacement strategy, random replacement strategy and least used on average replacement strategy, etc. The replacement strategy is quite similar to the Cache replacement strategy. The simplest replacement strategy would be using a $\top^\sharp$ as the input context to analyze a function when the threshold is met. Due to the fact that all the input contexts are smaller than $\top^\sharp$ in partial order, the analysis result is always sound.

Example 1. The IDP shown in Fig. 2 consists of one task ($main()$ function), one interrupt ($isr()$ function), and two shared variables x and y. The $main()$ function is sequentialized by invoking $isr()$ function after each atomic statement (we assume that the program syntax allows atomic parallel assignment). We use $brandom()$ function to denote non-deterministic branch condition. For the program in Fig. 2, we use interprocedural analysis based on tabulated procedure summaries, on top of the box abstract domain. The results of tabulated analysis are as follows:

```
int x, y;
void main(){                              void isr(){
    (x, y) := ([0, 90], [0, 9]);              if(x < 100)
    if(brandom())  { isr(); //① }                 x := 0;
    (x, y) := (10, 0);                        else
    if(brandom())  { isr(); //② }                 x := x + 10;
    (x, y) := ([99, 110], [5, 10]);           if(y < 10)
    if(brandom())  { isr(); //③ }                 y := 10;
}                                         }
```

Fig. 2. An example of a sequentialized IDP

$$F^\sharp = \begin{cases} (isr, \{x \in [0, 90], y \in [0, 9]\}) & \mapsto \{x = 0, y = 10\} \\ (isr, \{x = 10, y = 0\}) & \mapsto \{x = 0, y = 10\} \\ (isr, \{x \in [99, 110], y \in [5, 10]\}) & \mapsto \{x \in [0, 120], y = 10\} \end{cases}$$

Note that the calling contexts of the three different locations are all different. If we use the tabulation function defined in (1), the analysis efficiency will not be improved by the tabulated summary. The analysis results are the same as the results given by the context sensitive analysis.

However, if we use the tabulation function defined in (2), for the function $isr()$, the tabulated analysis get the following tabulated summary at ③:

$$F^\sharp = \begin{cases} (isr, \{x \in [0, 90], y \in [0, 9]\}) & \mapsto \{x = 0, y = 10\} \\ (isr, \{x \in [99, 110], y \in [5, 10]\}) & \mapsto \{x \in [0, 120], y = 10\} \end{cases}$$

The first input calling context for function $isr()$ is $X_1 = \{x \in [0, 90], y \in [0, 9]\}$. The second input calling context for function $isr()$ is $X_2 = \{x = 10, y = 0\}$, which satisfies $X_2 \sqsubseteq X_1$. And thus the analysis will directly reuse the analysis results of the first function calling (at ①) as the result for the second function calling (at ②), i.e., $\{x = 0, y = 10\}$. The analysis based on the tabulated summary improves the analysis efficiency by avoiding re-analyzing function $isr()$ at ②.

Note that the analysis based on tabulated procedural summaries defined via (1) will not cause precision loss compared with context sensitive interprocedural analysis, since it always uses exactly the input calling context to compare with those stored in the tabulated summaries. On the other hand, when the new encountered input calling contexts are often different (when using (1)) with or not under-approximations (when using (2)) of those stored in the tabulated summaries, the analysis based on the tabulated procedural summaries may not improve the analysis efficiency and even degrade the efficiency due to extra tabulation costs.

4   Procedure Summary Based on Partitioning Inputs

As we mentioned before, the tabulated procedure summary may not improve the analysis efficiency under some situations. To this end, we propose another approach for constructing procedure summaries, by pre-partitioning the inputs. The main idea to first analyze the input-output relation of the function body using abstract domains, without considering any input contexts. However, since the precise input-output relation of the function body may be very complicated and hard to compute, we pre-partition the inputs of the function according to the disjunctive information associated with the function body. Then for each partition of the inputs, we analyze the input-output relation of the function body using abstract domains, taking into account the constraints associated with that partition (i.e., as precondition). After that, we get the input-output relations for each input partition, which compose together the procedure summary for the function. When encountering a function calling, our analysis directly makes use of the pre-analysis results stored in the summary to compute the output, according to the relations between the current input context and the pre-partitioned inputs.

How to get the pre-partitioned input context is the key point to this approach, which directly affects the precision of the analysis results. Since different input contexts will drive the function under analysis to take different execution paths, we need to consider the path conditions. Enumerating all the path conditions to pre-partition the input context will make procedure summary more precise. However, this will also make the procedure summary grow exponentially. Our main idea is to choose a small set of branch conditions to partition the inputs, e.g., to choose those branch conditions that appear earlier in the program traces during execution. We use variables with subscript 0 to denote the values of those input shared variables at the beginning of the function body, such as x_0, y_0, z_0, etc. And we use symbolic execution to compute the values of variables in those considered branch conditions, such that those branch conditions can be all represented in terms of symbolic variables denoting the initial values of shared variables (i.e., in terms of x_0, y_0, z_0, etc.). We use $\mathbb{P}$ to denote the finite set of predicates (over symbolic variables denoting initial values of shared variables) drawn from the considered branch conditions.

In this paper, we use binary decision tree (BDT) [5] to encode the procedure summary based on partitioning inputs. BDT is a kind of directed acyclic graph. In this paper, each branch node in BDT denotes a predicate in $\mathbb{P}$. Each branch node has two outcoming edges, which represent whether the predicate is true or false. Each path from the root to a leaf defines a partition over the input. The combination of the evaluation values of the predicates along the path, which we call a path condition, describes the restriction of the partition. We use $\mathcal{PC}$ to denote the set of path conditions derived from a binary decision tree. Each leaf node stores the input-output relations (in terms of abstract values in an abstract domain) of the function when the input satisfies the partition restriction defined by the path condition from the root to this leaf node. We denote the binary decision tree in parenthesized form

$$[\![p_1 : [\![p_2 : (a_1), (a_2)]\!], [\![p_2 : (a_3), (a_4)]\!]]\!]$$

where p_1, p_2 are predicates in $\mathbb{P}$, and $a_j(1 \leq j \leq 4)$ is an abstract value in an abstract domain (that is used to encode the input-output relations of a function). It means that if p_1 and p_2 are true then a_1 holds, if p_1 is true and p_2 is false then a_2 holds, if p_1 is false and p_2 is true then a_3 holds, otherwise, a_4 holds.

We use $leaf : \mathcal{PC} \to D^\sharp$ to represent the process of analyzing the function body and getting the input-output relation denoted by an abstract value in $D^\sharp$, under the partition restriction described by a path condition $pc \in \mathcal{PC}$. The meaning of $leaf$ can be formalized as follows:

$$leaf(pc) \overset{\text{def}}{=} \tau[\![pc \wedge body(f)]\!]^\sharp(\top^\sharp)$$

Based on the constructed BDT, during the analysis, if encountering a function calling, the analysis will combine those involved results stored in BDT and get the output results. In more details, we first find out which paths in the BDT are feasible for the current input context of function f, by checking whether the intersection of the current input context and the path condition is not empty. Then, for each feasible path, we make use of the input-output relation stored in the leaf of that path and the current input context, to compute the output results. Lastly, we use the join operator in the abstract domain to compute the over-approximation of the output results of all feasible paths. This process can be formalized as follows:

$$\tau[\![f]\!]^\sharp(X^\sharp) \overset{\text{def}}{=} \bigsqcup{}^\sharp \{leaf(pc) \sqcap^\sharp X_0^\sharp \sqcap^\sharp pc \mid pc \in \mathcal{PC}, X_0^\sharp \sqcap^\sharp pc \neq \bot^\sharp\}$$

where $X_0^\sharp$ denotes the abstract value of $X^\sharp$ by renaming all variables in $X^\sharp$ into those with the subscript 0.

Figure 3 depicts an example of interprocedural analysis based on procedure summaries by partitioning inputs. Figure 3(a) shows the BDT summary for function f, where only two predicates in branch conditions are considered. In Fig. 3(b), there are two calls to function f, for each of which only one path is feasible. For the first calling, the stored $f^\sharp(b_1 \wedge b_2)$ in the BDT summary is returned. For the second calling, the stored $f^\sharp(\neg b_1 \wedge \neg b_2)$ in the BDT summary is returned. Note that the situation shown in Fig. 3(b) is only a special case. In general, several paths in BDT may be feasible for a given input context. In such case, we need to compute an over-approximation of all results given by those feasible paths.

Example 2. For the sequentialized IDP in Fig. 4, if we directly inline all the function calls and use the box abstract domain to analyze the program, we will get the following results: { ① $\mapsto \{x = 0, y = 10\}$, ② $\mapsto \{x = 190, y = 10\}$, ③ $\mapsto$ $\{x = [0, 120], y = 10\}$ }.

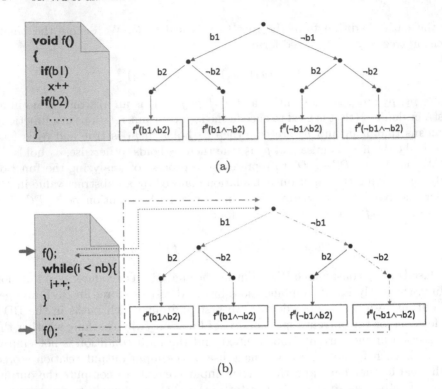

Fig. 3. Inter-procedural analysis based on the BDT procedure summary

As shown in Fig. 5, to compute for $isr()$ the procedure summaries via partitioning inputs, we first get a set of predicates $\{x_0 < 100, y_0 < 10\}$ (we remind that the variables v_0 with subscript 0 denote the initial values of variables v at the entry of the function). Using this predicate set to partition the inputs, we get 4 partitions. Then we analyze the interrupt handler $isr()$ for each partition. The resulting BDT summary on top of the box abstract domain is shown in Fig. 5(a). During the analysis of the main function, for the callings to function $isr()$, we make use of the BDT summary. The input calling context at ① is $\{x = -1, y = 0\}$, which implies the only feasible path condition $x_0 < 100 \wedge y_0 < 10$. Then we directly return as the analysis result at ① the abstract value stored in the corresponding leaf, i.e., $\{x = 0, y = 10\}$. The analysis for the function calling at ② is similar, which results in $\{x \in [110, +\infty], y = 10\}$. For the function calling at ③, all the four paths shown in Fig. 5(a) are feasible. Hence, the output result is the join of the abstract values stored at the four leaves, and we get $\{x \in [0, +\infty], y \in [10, +\infty]\}$. Compared with the results given by analysis inlining all function calls, we get less precise results at ② and ③.

Figure 5(b) shows the BDT summary on top of the octagon abstract domain, where x_0 (x) and y_0 (y) represent the values of variables at the entry (exit) of the function. The analysis based on the BDT summary will give the following results:

$\{ \ \textcircled{1} \mapsto \{x = 0, y = 10\}, \textcircled{2} \mapsto \{x = 190, y = 10\}, \textcircled{3} \mapsto \{x = [0, 120], y = 10\} \ \}$, which is as precise as that given by the analysis inlining all function calls.

```
int x, y;
void main(){                            void isr(){
    (x, y) := (−1, 0);                      if(x < 100)
    if(brandom())  { isr(); //①}            x := 0;
    (x, y) := (180, [5, 9]);            else
    if(brandom())  { isr(); //②}            x := x + 10;
    (x, y) := ([99, 110], [5, 10]);         if(y < 10)
    if(brandom())  { isr(); //③}            y := 10;
}                                       }
```

Fig. 4. Another example of sequentialzed IDP

In practice, some results stored in the BDT summary may never be used in any calling contexts. Therefore, if we compute all the input-output relations for all partitions, we may perform some extra computation which will not benefit the analysis. Hence, we could construct the BDT summary on-the-fly. In other words, we could compute input-output relations for a partition only when the current calling context implies the feasibility of this partition, and then store the results in the BDT summary. Through this optimization, we can relieve some unnecessary computation of the BDT summary. Note that, due to the abstraction involved in the BDT summary, analysis based on the BDT summary may cause imprecise analysis results, compared with the analysis based on the tabulated summary or the analysis inlining all function calls.

5   Implementation and Experiments

We have implemented a prototype tool for analyzing sequentialized IDPs [30], which use Fixpoint [9] as its fix-point iteration engine, Apron [10] as its abstract domain and CIL [17] as its front-end. Our tool supports both context-insensitive analysis [9] and context-sensitive analysis (by inlining). By default, we inline all function calls by utilizing the CIL supported inline tool, and then perform numerical static analysis over the resulting program after inlining. In this paper, we have implemented further the two interprocedural analysis methods respectively described in Sects. 3 and 4. During the experiments, we assume that all function callings to normal functions except interrupt handlers have already been inlined.

Our experiments were conducted on a selection of benchmarks and real-world programs. Some test cases come from open source web sites for embedded systems, e.g., Nxt_gs, UART, iRobot3 and HBM. Some test cases come from embedded control software in industry, e.g., Ping_pong, ADC_Ctl, Dev_Ctl, as well as those programs with "DSP_" prefix.

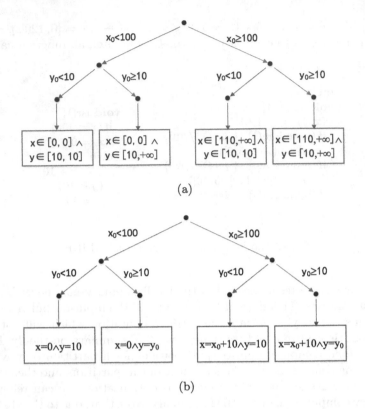

Fig. 5. The BDT procedure summary on top of abstract domains

Experimental results for different interprocedural analyses. We first utilize the box abstract domain to evaluate different interprocedural analysis methods. The results are shown in Table 1. "Ctx" and "in-Ctx" represent context sensitive and insensitive analysis respectively, "Tabul." represents the analysis based on tabulated procedure summary, "#Warns" represents the number of warnings.

From the analysis results in Table 1, we can see that context sensitive analysis is more precise than context insensitive analysis. On the other hand, the time consumption of the analysis based on tabulated procedure summary is in most cases between that of the context sensitive and insensitive analysis. Note that during the experiments, we use the tabulated procedure summary defined via (1). Hence, the precision of the analysis based on tabulated procedure summary is the same as the context sensitive analysis. Moreover, we find that the analysis time of context insensitive analysis for some industry applications is much less than context sensitive analysis, e.g., the case of ADC_Ctl. And for some other industry applications, the time of context insensitive analysis is between the context sensitive analysis and the tabulated analysis, e.g., the case of Dev_Ctl. We find that there is a large infinite loop in the main task of ADC_Ctl and all the event process routines are implemented in that infinite loop, while Dev_Ctl

Table 1. Experimental results for different inter-procedural analyses

Program			Analysis of Ctx		Analysis of in-Ctx		Analysis of Tabul.	
Name	#Vars	LOC	Time (s)	#Warns	Time (s)	#Warns	Time (s)	#Warns
Nxt_gs	27	552	0.040	2	0.034	5	0.035	2
UART	47	1215	0.128	0	0.123	9	0.228	0
iRobot3	55	793	0.069	2	0.056	2	0.070	2
HBM	36	1312	0.112	4	0.102	4	0.083	4
Ping_pong	21	842	0.054	0	0.104	11	0.098	0
ADC_Ctl	334	404 K	343.5	70	3.72	104	184.7	70
Dev_Ctl	1352	534 K	5325	538	549	663	183.6	538

does not have such feature. During analyzing ADC_Ctl, context insensitive analysis will accelerate the fix-point iteration process, which will greatly reduce the iteration time of analyzing the large infinite loop.

Experimental results for analysis based on tabulated procedure summary. In order to evaluate the analysis based on the tabulated procedure summary, we analyze all the industry applications. Table 2 shows the analysis results, where "Mem" represents the memory consumption, "#Hit" represents the hit rate of tabulated summary, i.e., the number of hits to the number of all function callings. Note that we use the tabulated procedure summary defined via (1), and thus the warning numbers are the same as that of the context sensitive analysis.

Table 2. Experiments for analysis based on tabulated procedure summary

Program			Analysis of Ctx		Analysis of Tabul.			#Warns
Name	#Vars	LOC	Time (s)	Mem (GB)	Time (s)	#Hit	Mem (GB)	
ADC_Ctl	334	404 K	343.5	1.63	184.7	864/11474	1.54	70
Dev_Ctl	1352	534 K	5325	3.37	183.6	858/1141	3.12	538
DSP_Ctl1	1240	58 K	206.9	1.47	219.0	14/9309	1.44	155
DSP_Ctl2	640	98 K	299.1	1.53	275.0	568/7708	1.43	150
DSP_Ctl3	1074	142 K	1823.6	2.51	1523.1	1819/11349	2.11	439
DSP_Ctl4	978	82 K	1068.3	1.02	962.5	1543/9490	1.05	203

From Table 2, we find that the analysis time is negatively correlated with the hit rate to the tabulated summary. E.g., the hit rate of the Dev_Ctl is almost upper to 75%, while the analysis time of using tabulated procedure summary is only 3% of that of the context sensitive analysis. On the other hand, we find that when the hit rate is quite low, tabulated analysis may be slower than context sensitive analysis, e.g., the case of DSP_Ctl1. This is due to the fact that the tabulated analysis needs to maintain the tabulated summary and search the calling context in the tabulated summary, which will introduce extra time costs.

Note that the number of calling contexts in #Hit is the number of function callings during the iterations, not the function calling number appearing in program syntax. Moreover, we find that the memory consumption for the analysis based on the tabulated summary is not more than the context sensitive analysis method. This is due to the fact that for context sensitive analysis method, we need to store all the analysis results at each program point of the program after inlining, while for tabulated analysis, if the analysis context is hit in the tabulated summary, we do not need to store the intermediate analysis results, but only store the analysis results at the exit point of function.

Experimental results for analysis using the BDT procedure summary. The results are shown in Table 3, where BDT-oct and BDT-box represent respectively analyses using the octagon and the box abstract domain. The time of the analysis based on the BDT summary consists of two parts: the time to build the BDT summary and the static analysis time. The results in #Time show the total time (and the time of building the BDT summary). For large programs, we only chose several branch conditions in functions as the predicates to partition the inputs.

Table 3. Experimental results for analysis based on the BDT summary

Program			Analysis of Ctx		Analysis of BDT-box		Analysis of BDT-oct	
Name	#Vars	LOC	Time (s)	#Warns	Time (s)	#Warns	Time (s)	#Warns
Nxt_gs	27	552	0.040	2	0.004(0.016)	5	0.022(0.035)	5
UART	47	1215	0.128	0	0.139(0.003)	9	0.192(0.005)	9
iRobot3	55	793	0.069	2	0.035(0.009)	2	0.270(0.152)	2
HBM	36	1312	0.112	4	0.098(0.006)	4	0.103(0.008)	3
Ping_pong	21	842	0.054	0	0.056(0.018)	10	0.155(0.085)	10
ADC_Ctl	334	404 K	343.5	70	184(5.5)	88	262(29.8)	83
Dev_Ctl	1352	534 K	5325	538	216(4.8)	640	282.7(30.9)	531

We find that when using the box abstract domain that cannot represent the relationship between variables, the precision of the analysis based on the BDT summary is almost the same as the context-insensitive analysis results. On the other hand, when using the octagon abstract domain, the precision of the analysis based on the BDT summary may be even better than that of context sensitive analysis method, e.g., the case of Dev_Ctl. Moreover, in most cases, especially for small IDPs, the time of the analysis based on the BDT summary may be more than that of the context sensitive analysis. This is due to the fact that we need to analyze the function for each partition and also need to compute an over-approximation of the results when the current input calling context implies the feasibility of many paths in BDT.

6   Related Work

Analysis of interrupt-driven programs. There exist a variety of techniques targeting at analyzing and verifying IDPs, including program transformation

[11,14,31], abstract interpretation [16,18,23,25,29,30], model checking [4,13,26, 31], symbolic execution [27,28], etc. We now briefly review some of those that are closely related to our techniques.

Kidd et al. [11] propose a sequentialization method for priority preemptive scheduling systems, wherein the main idea is to use a single stack for all tasks and to model preemptions by function calls. Inspired by this work, our previous works [29–31] first sequentialize IDPs into sequential programs, and then leverage existing analysis and verification techniques to analyze the sequentialized programs, including techniques of numeric abstract interpretation and bounded model checking. Monniaux [16] proposes a numerical static analysis method for a concurrent USB driver, which dynamically invokes interrupts for each access to the shared memory in tasks. Ouadjaout et al. [18] present a static analysis by abstract interpretation to verify functional properties of device drivers in the TinyOS operating system. They perform a modular analysis to analyze every interrupt independently and then aggregate their results to over-approximate the effect of preemption, which avoids reanalyzing interrupts in every context.

Recently, Liang et al. [13] propose a new symbolic partial-order encoding that can capture more precisely the interleaving semantics of nested interrupts than native threads, via SAT/SMT formula. Based on this new encoding, they develop a tool i-CBMC, as an extension of CBMC, to support verification of IDPs. Sung et al. [25] present an iterative abstract interpretation framework for verifying IDPs, which first analyzes each interrupt handler in isolation and then propagates the results to other interrupt handlers. The iterative process continues until results on all interrupt handlers stabilize.

Interprocedural analysis. Interprocedural analysis of sequential programs has received much attention in the literature [3,6,22,24]. In general, many of the existing approaches can be classified as one of the two predominant approaches: the summary-based (or functional) approach and the call-strings (or k-CFA) approach [15,24].

For concurrent programs with recursive procedures, the context-sensitive and synchronization-sensitive interprocedural analysis problem is known to be undecidable [21], even for programs with finite-domain variables. Qadeer et al. [19] propose the first notion of procedure summaries for multithreaded programs, i.e., summaries of transactions within a procedure. The summary of a procedure then comprises the summaries of all transactions within the procedure. They also provide a method to compute transactional summaries in the presence of multiple threads. To sidestep the undecidability issue, bounding the number of context switches is a good choice often adopted [12,20], which essentially allows reducing the concurrent program to a sequential one. However, the technique of bounding number of context switches is not sound, but very useful for bug finding, because many bugs can be found after a few context switches.

Recently, Jeannet [8] generalizes the relational interprocedural analysis of sequential programs to the concurrent case. They propose a general interprocedural analysis method that combines stack and data abstractions, for concurrent programs, even in the presence of unbounded recursion and infinite-state variables like integers. Based on this method, an interprocedural analyzer ConcurInterproc [7] is developed for concurrent programs.

7 Conclusion and Future Work

We have presented two interprocedural analysis approaches for analyzing interrupt handlers in IDPs. One is based on tabulation of procedure summaries, which stores the input contexts together with the corresponding output results that have been encountered for a procedure in a tabular manner and is more like context-sensitive interprocedural analysis. The other is based on procedure summaries that are built by partitioning inputs and can be encoded via binary decision tree. The two approaches fit for different features of the interrupt handlers. The preliminary experimental results show that both approaches are promising for certain interrupt handlers.

For future work, we will consider designing more interprocedural analyses that fit for analyzing interrupt handlers and conducting more experiments on large realistic IDPs.

Acknowledgments. We thank Antoine Miné for his helpful discussions on this work. This work is supported by the National Key R&D Program of China (No. 2017YFB1001802), and the NSFC Program (Nos. 61872445, 61532007).

References

1. https://en.wikipedia.org/wiki/MIL-STD-1553
2. https://en.wikipedia.org/wiki/CAN_bus
3. Bourdoncle, F.: Interprocedural abstract interpretation of block structured languages with nested procedures, aliasing and recursivity. In: Deransart, P., Maluszyński, J. (eds.) PLILP 1990. LNCS, vol. 456, pp. 307–323. Springer, Heidelberg (1990). https://doi.org/10.1007/BFb0024192
4. Brylow, D., Damgaard, N., Palsberg, J.: Static checking of interrupt-driven software. In: ICSE 2001, pp. 47–56. IEEE (2001)
5. Chen, J., Cousot, P.: A binary decision tree abstract domain functor. In: Blazy, S., Jensen, T. (eds.) SAS 2015. LNCS, vol. 9291, pp. 36–53. Springer, Heidelberg (2015). https://doi.org/10.1007/978-3-662-48288-9_3
6. Cousot, P., Cousot, R.: Static determination of dynamic properties of recursive procedures. In: IFIP Conference on Formal Description of Programming Concepts, pp. 237–277. North-Holland (1977)
7. Jeannet, B.: The ConcurInterproc Analyzer. http://pop-art.inrialpes.fr/interproc/concurinterprocweb.cgi
8. Jeannet, B.: Relational interprocedural verification of concurrent programs. Softw. Syst. Model. **12**(2), 285–306 (2013)
9. Jeannet, B.: The fixpoint solver. http://pop-art.inrialpes.fr/~bjeannet/bjeannet-forge/fixpoint/
10. Jeannet, B., Miné, A.: APRON: a library of numerical abstract domains for static analysis. In: Bouajjani, A., Maler, O. (eds.) CAV 2009. LNCS, vol. 5643, pp. 661–667. Springer, Heidelberg (2009). https://doi.org/10.1007/978-3-642-02658-4_52

11. Kidd, N., Jagannathan, S., Vitek, J.: One stack to run them all - reducing concurrent analysis to sequential analysis under priority scheduling. In: van de Pol, J., Weber, M. (eds.) SPIN 2010. LNCS, vol. 6349, pp. 245–261. Springer, Heidelberg (2010). https://doi.org/10.1007/978-3-642-16164-3_18
12. Lal, A., Touili, T., Kidd, N., Reps, T.W.: Interprocedural analysis of concurrent programs under a context bound. In: Ramakrishnan, C.R., Rehof, J. (eds.) TACAS 2008. LNCS, vol. 4963, pp. 282–298. Springer, Heidelberg (2008). https://doi.org/10.1007/978-3-540-78800-3_20
13. Liang, L., Melham, T., Kroening, D., Schrammel, P., Tautschnig, M.: Effective verification for low-level software with competing interrupts. ACM Trans. Embed. Comput. Syst. 17(2), 36:1–36:26 (2017)
14. Liu, H., Jiang, Y., Zhang, H., Gu, M., Sun, J.: Taming interrupts for verifying industrial multifunction vehicle bus controllers. In: Fitzgerald, J., Heitmeyer, C., Gnesi, S., Philippou, A. (eds.) FM 2016. LNCS, vol. 9995, pp. 764–771. Springer, Cham (2016). https://doi.org/10.1007/978-3-319-48989-6_48
15. Mangal, R., Naik, M., Yang, H.: A Correspondence between two approaches to interprocedural analysis in the presence of join. In: Shao, Z. (ed.) ESOP 2014. LNCS, vol. 8410, pp. 513–533. Springer, Heidelberg (2014). https://doi.org/10.1007/978-3-642-54833-8_27
16. Monniaux, D.: Verification of device drivers and intelligent controllers: a case study. In: EMSOFT 2007, pp. 30–36. ACM (2007)
17. Necula, G.C., McPeak, S., Rahul, S.P., Weimer, W.: CIL: intermediate language and tools for analysis and transformation of C programs. In: Horspool, R.N. (ed.) CC 2002. LNCS, vol. 2304, pp. 213–228. Springer, Heidelberg (2002). https://doi.org/10.1007/3-540-45937-5_16
18. Ouadjaout, A., Miné, A., Lasla, N., Badache, N.: Static analysis by abstract interpretation of functional properties of device drivers in TinyOS. J. Syst. Softw. 120, 114–132 (2016)
19. Qadeer, S., Rajamani, S.K., Rehof, J.: Summarizing procedures in concurrent programs. In: POPL 2004, pp. 245–255. ACM (2004)
20. Qadeer, S., Rehof, J.: Context-bounded model checking of concurrent software. In: Halbwachs, N., Zuck, L.D. (eds.) TACAS 2005. LNCS, vol. 3440, pp. 93–107. Springer, Heidelberg (2005). https://doi.org/10.1007/978-3-540-31980-1_7
21. Ramalingam, G.: Context-sensitive synchronization-sensitive analysis is undecidable. ACM Trans. Program. Lang. Syst. 22(2), 416–430 (2000)
22. Reps, T.W., Horwitz, S., Sagiv, S.: Precise interprocedural dataflow analysis via graph reachability. In: POPL 1995, pp. 49–61. ACM Press (1995)
23. Schwarz, M.D., Seidl, H., Vojdani, V., Lammich, P., Müller-Olm, M.: Static analysis of interrupt-driven programs synchronized via the priority ceiling protocol. In: POPL 2011, pp. 93–104. ACM (2011)
24. Sharir, M., Pnueli, A.: Two approaches to interprocedural data flow analysis. In: Program Flow Analysis: Theory and Applications, Chapter 7, pp. 189–233. Prentice-Hall (1981)
25. Sung, C., Kusano, M., Wang, C.: Modular verification of interrupt-driven software. In: ASE 2017, pp. 206–216. IEEE Computer Society (2017)
26. Vörtler, T., Höckner, B., Hofstedt, P., Klotz, T.: Formal verification of software for the Contiki operating system considering interrupts. In: DDECS 2015, pp. 295–298. IEEE Computer Society (2015)
27. Wang, Y., Shi, J., Wang, L., Zhao, J., Li, X.: Detecting data races in interrupt-driven programs based on static analysis and dynamic simulation. In: Internetware 2015, pp. 199–202. ACM (2015)

28. Wang, Y, Wang, L., Yu, T., Zhao, J., Li, X.: Automatic detection and validation of race conditions in interrupt-driven embedded software. In: ISSTA 2017, pp. 113–124. ACM (2017)
29. Wu, X., Chen, L., Miné, A., Dong, W., Wang, J.: Numerical static analysis of interrupt-driven programs via sequentialization. In: EMSOFT 2015, pp. 55–64. IEEE Press (2015)
30. Wu, X., Chen, L., Miné, A., Dong, W., Wang, J.: Static analysis of runtime errors in interrupt-driven programs via sequentialization. ACM Trans. Embed. Comput. Syst. **15**(4), 70 (2016)
31. Wu, X., Wen, Y., Chen, L., Dong, W., Wang, J.: Data race detection for interrupt-driven programs via bounded model checking. In: SERE 2013 (Companion), pp. 204–210. IEEE (2013)

Author Index